GRAMMAR
FOR THE WELL-TRAINED MIND

KEY TO
YELLOW WORKBOOK

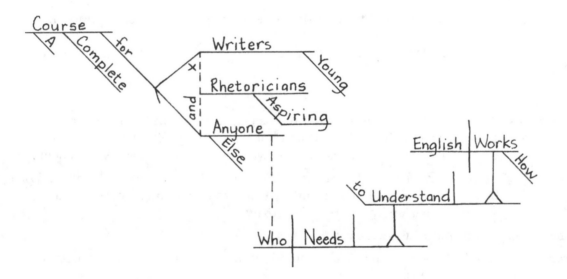

By Susan Wise Bauer
with Jessica Otto and Audrey Anderson,
Diagrams by Patty Rebne

Layout and Design by Shannon Zadrozny

WELL-
TRAINED
MIND
PRESS

Visit welltrainedmind.com for additional information regarding Figures in Motion.

1 2 3 4 5 6 7 8 9 10 B&B 30 29 28 27 26 25 24 23 22
GYK-1022

Names: Bauer, Susan Wise, author. | Otto, Jessica, author. | Anderson, Audrey, 1986- author. | Rebne, Patty, illustrator. | Zadrozny, Shannon, designer. | Bauer, Susan Wise. Grammar for the well-trained mind. Yellow workbook.

Title: Grammar for the well-trained mind. Key to Yellow workbook / by Susan Wise Bauer, with Jessica Otto and Audrey Anderson ; diagrams by Patty Rebne ; layout and design by Shannon Zadrozny.

Other titles: Key to Yellow workbook

Description: Charles City, Virginia : Well-Trained Mind Press, [2022] | For instructors of grades 5 and above.

Identifiers: ISBN: 978-1-945841-36-1 (paperback) | 978-1-945841-62-0 (ebook) | 978-1-945841-37-8 (ebook for Kindle)

Subjects: LCSH: English language--Grammar--Study and teaching (Middle school) | English language-- Grammar--Study and teaching (Secondary) | English language--Rhetoric--Study and teaching (Middle school) | English language--Rhetoric--Study and teaching (Secondary)

Classification: LCC: LB1631 .B395 2022 | DDC: 428.00712--dc23

For a list of corrections, please visit **www.welltrainedmind.com/corrections**.

Table of Contents

Introduction to Nouns and Adjectives

— LESSON 1 —

Introduction to Nouns
Concrete and Abstract Nouns

Exercise 1A: Abstract and Concrete Nouns

Decide whether the underlined nouns are abstract or concrete. Above each noun, write *A* for abstract or *C* for concrete. If you have difficulty, ask yourself: Can this noun be touched, seen, or experienced with another one of the senses? If so, it is a concrete noun. If not, it is abstract.

A loose <u>tooth</u> will not rest until it's pulled out. (African proverb)
<small>C</small>

Two <u>wrongs</u> don't make a <u>right</u>. (English)
<small>A</small>   <small>A</small>

Make <u>haste</u> with <u>leisure</u>. (German)
<small>A</small>   <small>A</small>

Draw not your <u>bow</u> 'til your <u>arrow</u> is fixed. (Russian)
<small>C</small>   <small>C</small>

He who digs too deep for a <u>fish</u> may come out with a <u>snake</u>. (African)
<small>C</small>   <small>C</small>

Shared <u>joy</u> is a double joy; shared <u>sorrow</u> is half a sorrow. (Swedish)
<small>A</small>   <small>A</small>

It's better to light a <u>candle</u> than curse the <u>darkness</u>. (Chinese)
<small>C</small>   <small>C</small>

Evil enters like a <u>needle</u> and spreads like an oak <u>tree</u>. (Ethiopian)
<small>C</small>   <small>C</small>

Turn your face to the <u>sun</u> and the <u>shadows</u> will fall behind you. (New Zealander)
<small>C</small>   <small>C</small>

Exercise 1B: Using Concrete and Abstract Nouns

Identify each noun as concrete or abstract. Write a sentence that includes the given noun and at least one noun of the opposite type (so, if the given noun is a concrete noun, you must use it and also include an abstract noun of your choice).

    Underline the additional noun in your sentence and label it as *C* for concrete or *A* for abstract. (It's fine to use more than one extra noun, but you only need to label one.)

    The first is done for you.

Note to Instructor: Sample sentences are provided, but student answers will vary.

	C or A?	Your Sentence
happiness	A	She laughed with happiness during the <u>movie</u>. ^(C)
mug	C	I felt <u>sadness</u> ^(A) when I saw that my favorite mug was missing.
boots	C	The boots were a gift from his grandfather, so wearing them gave him a feeling of <u>joy</u>. ^(A)
delight	A	What a delight to see our <u>friends</u> again! ^(C)
exhaustion	A	The <u>athletes</u> ^(C) experienced exhaustion after the first big game.
oats	C	The horses showed great <u>excitement</u> ^(A) about the oats we gave them.

— **LESSON 2** —

Introduction to Adjectives
Descriptive Adjectives, Abstract Nouns
Formation of Abstract Nouns from Descriptive Adjectives

Exercise 2A: Descriptive Adjectives, Concrete Nouns, and Abstract Nouns

Decide whether the underlined words are concrete nouns, abstract nouns, or descriptive adjectives. Above each, write *DA* for descriptive adjective, *CN* for concrete noun, or *AN* for abstract noun.

The sentences below were taken from *The Boxcar Children*, by Gertrude Chandler Warner. Some have been slightly adapted.

Not a soul passed them on the <u>country</u>^{DA} <u>road</u>^{CN}. All the <u>houses</u>^{CN} they saw were <u>dark</u>^{DA} and <u>still</u>^{DA}.

Benny tumbled into the <u>bed</u>^{CN} with a great <u>sigh</u>^{CN} of <u>satisfaction</u>^{AN}.

Each of them quickly scraped together a <u>fragrant</u>^{DA} <u>pile</u>^{CN} for a <u>pillow</u>^{CN}, and once more lay down to sleep with hardly a thought of <u>fear</u>^{AN}.

Jess saw an <u>old</u>^{DA} freight or box <u>car</u>^{CN}. Her first thought was one of fear; her second, <u>hope</u>^{AN} of shelter.

It stood on <u>rusty</u>^{DA} <u>broken</u>^{DA} nails which were nearly covered with dead <u>leaves</u>^{CN}. Then the <u>thunder</u>^{CN} cracked overhead.

It seemed to the children that the <u>sky</u>^{CN} would split, so sharp were the <u>cracks</u>^{CN} of thunder. But not a <u>drop</u>^{CN} of <u>rain</u>^{CN} reached them in their <u>roomy</u>^{DA} retreat.

Exercise 2B: Descriptive Adjectives and Abstract Nouns

For each sentence, identify the underlined word as *DA* for descriptive adjective or *AN* for abstract noun. Then change the underlined word to the other form (adjective to noun or noun to adjective) and rewrite the sentence with the new form. You may rearrange, add, or subtract words as necessary to make a sensible sentence. Your new sentence doesn't have to match the original exactly in meaning, but it should be close.

The first is done for you.

The house had a <u>charm</u> **[AN]** that appealed to me.

The charming house appealed to me.

Bertie's favorite book is one filled with <u>silly</u> **[DA]** stories.

stories of silliness

The puppy was easy to train because of her <u>intelligence</u> **[AN]**.

intelligent puppy

The <u>loudness</u> **[AN]** of the drums drowned out the singers' voices.

loud drums

Chloé wrote a story filled with <u>danger</u> **[AN]** and excitement!

dangerous story

Alex is a <u>graceful</u> **[DA]** performer on the stage.

performer of gracefulness

Exercise 2C: Color Names

Underline all the color words in the following sentences. Then write *A* for adjective or *N* for noun above each underlined color word.

These sentences are taken from Ruth Plumly Thompson's *Grampa in Oz*. Some have been slightly adapted.

King Fumbo of Ragbad shook in his carpet slippers. He had removed his <u>red</u> **[A]** shoes, so he could not very well shake in them.

He turned a sickly <u>green</u> **[N]** and began to tremble violently.

Then, muttering apologies, the old soldier seized a curtain cord and tied Fumbo to a <u>red</u> **[A]** pillar.

The country of the west, which was settled by the Munchkins, was marked in <u>blue</u> **[N]**; the northern Gilliken country in <u>purple</u> **[N]**.

But soon these villages became farther and farther apart, and the country more wild and unsettled, and just as the sun slipped down behind the treetops they came to the edge of a deep <u>blue</u> **[A]** forest.

Beneath slithered the road and not until the last length of <u>yellow</u>[N] had flashed by did Dorothy and Percy Vere let go.

Urtha, wearied by her strange adventures, had fallen fast asleep in the middle of counting the stars, and lay in a fragrant heap, her lovely <u>violet</u>[A] eyes closed tight.

As he straightened up, the long, <u>green</u>[A] bottle of patent medicine caught his eye.

And the loyal little Winkies have built him a splendid tin castle in the center of their pleasant <u>yellow</u>[A] country.

— LESSON 3 —

Common and Proper Nouns
Capitalization and Punctuation of Proper Nouns

Exercise 3A: Capitalizing Proper Nouns

Write a proper noun for each of the following common nouns. Don't forget to capitalize all of the important words of the proper noun. If the proper noun requires quotation marks, include them.

   You may either write your answers below or use a computer. If you are handwriting your answers, underline any proper noun that should be italicized.

> **Note to Instructor:** Sample answers are given below; answers will vary. The proper nouns for *book* and *movie* should either be italicized or underlined to indicate italics; the proper noun for *song* should be in quotation marks.

Common Noun	Proper Noun
book	*Wonder*
song	"Country Roads"
movie	*Little Women*
store	Barnes and Noble
state	Virginia
team	Chicago Bulls

Exercise 3B: Proper Names and Titles

On your own paper, rewrite the following sentences properly. Capitalize and punctuate all names and titles correctly.

> **Note to Instructor:** The original sentences are provided first. The corrected sentences follow.
> If the student is using a computer, underlined titles should be italicized.

sesame street is the longest-running television show of all time.
the orient express is a train made famous by the author agatha christie.

in 1893, two sisters, patty and mildred hill, wrote the song happy birthday to you.
shel silverstein created many humorous poems, including where the sidewalk ends.
lucy maude montgomery was the author of the popular novel entitled anne of green gables.

Sesame Street is the longest-running television show of all time.
The Orient Express is a train made famous by the author Agatha Christie.
In 1893, two sisters, Patty and Mildred Hill, wrote the song "Happy Birthday to You."
Shel Silverstein created many humorous poems, including "Where the Sidewalk Ends."
Lucy Maud Montgomery was the author of the popular novel entitled Anne of Green Gables.

Exercise 3C: Proofreading for Proper Nouns

In the following sentences, indicate which proper nouns should be capitalized by underlining the first letter of the noun three times. This is the proper proofreader's mark for "capitalize." The first word in the first sentence is done for you.

harriet tubman was born in maryland between 1820 and 1825.

her original name was araminta harriet ross, but she later changed it to harriet.

she was born a slave, but she escaped in 1849 through the secret network called the underground railroad.

during her lifetime, tubman used the underground railroad to lead more than 300 slaves to freedom.

she was given the nickname "moses" because of her brave actions which led many to safety.

— LESSON 4 —
Proper Adjectives
Compound Adjectives (Adjective-Noun Combinations)

Exercise 4A: Forming Proper Adjectives from Proper Nouns

Form adjectives from the following proper nouns. (Some will change form and others will not.) Write each adjective into the correct blank below. If you are not familiar with the proper nouns, you may look them up online on Encyclopaedia Britannica, Wikipedia, or some other source (this will help you complete the sentences as well). This exercise might challenge your general knowledge! (But you can always ask your instructor for help.)

| Italy | Iraq | Buddha | Alaska | Mars |
| Hippocrates | Japan | Greece | Antarctica | Maccabeus |

The National Cherry Blossom Festival is an annual event in Washington, D.C., showcasing the gift

of Japanese cherry trees to our country and celebrating the friendship between our nations.

One of my favorite dishes is avgolemono soup, a traditional _Greek_ food.

Hanukkah celebrates the second-century victory of Jewish people over their enemies during the
 Maccabean Revolt.

The Safafeer market in Baghdad is a famous place to buy beautiful copper pieces made by
 Iraqi artisans.

Taking an _Alaskan_ cruise is a popular way to see glaciers and amazing wildlife such as
humpback whales, sea otters, and bald eagles.

James took a class to learn true _Italian_ cooking, such as pasta e fagioli.

Tibet has hundreds of monasteries dedicated to the study of the _Buddhist_ religion.

Scientists must determine how humans can survive the _Martian_ climate in order for
astronauts to attempt life on that planet.

Because of the continent's location, the _Antarctic_ summer begins in October.

Doctors must take the _Hippocratic_ oath and promise to protect their patients.

Exercise 4B: Capitalization of Proper Adjectives

In the following sentences, correct each lowercase letter that should be capitalized by underlining
it three times.

Then, underline each proper adjective. Finally, circle each proper adjective that has not
changed its form from the proper noun.

the seven wonders of the world include the brazilian statue known as christ the redeemer.

in 2017, alex honnold became the first person to reach the el capitan summit without the use of
any ropes or safety equipment. his incredible feat was filmed and turned into a documentary,
which later won an oscar award.

hungarian designer erno rubik invented the rubik's cube in 1975. more than 300 million of the
toys have now been sold. the fastest solving time was set by chinese speedcuber yusheng du, who
finished the puzzle in 3.47 seconds.

jane goodall is a british scientist who has dedicated her life to the study of chimpanzees. she
is most famous for her studies of chimp behavior in a tanzanian game reserve, which is now
known as gombe stream national park. in 2002, she was given a united nations award for her
contributions to science.

the world record for high diving was set by dana kunze in 1983, when he dove from a height of 173 feet. Later, swiss diver oliver favre attempted to break the record but injured his back in the process.

Exercise 4C: Hyphenating Attributive Compound Adjectives

Hyphens prevent misunderstanding! Explain to your instructor the differences between each pair of phrases. The first is done for you. If you're confused, ask your instructor for help.

> **Note to Instructor:** These are intended to be fun, not frustrating. Use the suggestions below to help the student, and give answers if the student is stumped. There may be other ways to interpret these beyond the suggestions provided!

friendly-looking dog
friendly looking dog
> *(both a dog who looks friendly and a friendly dog whose purpose is to look around)*

sweet-smelling flower
sweet smelling flower
> *(both a flower that smells sweet and a sweet flower that smells things)*

cold-blooded animal
cold blooded animal
> *(both an animal whose blood temperature matches its environment and a cold animal who has a circulatory system)*

off-campus housing
off campus housing
> *(both housing that is not located on the campus and housing that is located on the campus but is not quite right)*

green-eyed monster
green eyed monster
> *(both a monster that has green eyes and a green monster that has eyes)*

Introduction to Personal Pronouns and Verbs

— LESSON 5 —

Noun Gender
Introduction to Personal Pronouns

Exercise 5A: Introduction to Noun Gender

How well do you know your animals? Fill in the blanks with the correct name (and don't worry too much if you don't know the answers . . . this is mostly for fun).

Animal	Male	Female	Baby	Group of Animals
duck	drake	duck	duckling	flock
ant	drone	queen	antling OR antlet	army, colony, nest, OR swarm
hawk	tiercel	hen	eyas	cast
pig	boar/barrow	sow/gilt	piglet	herd, drift OR drove
zebra	stallion	mare	colt, foal	dazzle OR zeal of zebras
tiger	tiger	tigress	cub, whelp	streak OR ambush
whale	bull	cow	calf	pod, herd OR school
goose	gander	goose	gosling	gaggle OR wedge

Exercise 5B: Nouns and Pronouns

Write the correct pronoun above the underlined word(s). The first is done for you.

Marie Curie was awarded the Nobel Prize for important discoveries in the field of radiation. <u>Curie</u> ^She discovered the radioactive elements plutonium and radium.

French scientist Louis Pasteur created pasteurization, a process which prevents bacteria from growing in liquids such as milk and wine and allows them to last longer before spoiling. <u>Pasteur</u> ^He also developed a vaccine for the deadly disease of rabies.

Bacteriologist Alexander Fleming discovered that mold, growing on a slide in his laboratory,

                                  He

kept bacteria from reproducing. <u>Alexander Fleming</u> studied the effects of mold on bacteria, and

    He

<u>Alexander Fleming</u> used the results of his work to invent penicillin, a life-saving medicine.

In 2019, the first known images of a black hole were taken. The algorithms used to capture the

image of the black hole were developed by researcher Katie Bouman and her team. The image

      she

<u>Katie Bouman</u> helped to obtain will allow scientists to learn more about the mysterious black hole

                         it

and the function of <u>the black hole</u> in space. In an interview after the image was revealed, Katie

                           we

remarked, "The one <u>Katie and her team</u> showed a picture of is 55 million light years away!"

In 1895, Wilhelm Roentgen was working in his lab and observed crystals growing on a table near

                    He   they

a cathode ray tube. <u>Roentgen</u> discovered that the rays could not pass through bone, but <u>the rays</u>

                 He

could go through tissue. <u>Roentgen</u> began to study the rays, which led to the invention of the

modern-day X-ray.

Exercise 5C: Substituting Pronouns

The following passage is from E. Nesbit's *The Enchanted Castle*. This version sounds very
awkward because the pronouns *I*, *you*, *he*, *she*, *it*, *we*, and *they* have all been replaced by nouns.

    Choose the nouns that can be replaced by pronouns, cross them (and any accompanying
words such as "the") out, and write the appropriate pronouns above them.

    You may also need to cross out and replace some verbs or helping verbs if necessary to
maintain agreement.

> **Note to Instructor**: The original text (very slightly adapted) is below, followed by the version
> provided to the student. Show the original to the student so she can compare her work to it. The
> two may not match perfectly, but if the student has done a reasonable job replacing nouns with
> pronouns to make a more readable passage, accept her work.

ORIGINAL

    The incident of the invisible Princess had surprised, and the sudden decision to be a
detective had brought its own anxieties… Only now a new feeling had come to Gerald as he
walked through the gardens; by day those gardens were like dreams, by night like visions. He
could not see his feet as he walked, but he saw the movement of the dewy grass-blades that his
feet dispersed. And Gerald had that extraordinary feeling so difficult to describe, and yet so real
and so unforgettable: the feeling that he was in another world, that had covered up and hidden
the old world as a carpet covers the floor. The floor was there all right, underneath, but what
Gerald walked on was the carpet that covered it, and the carpet was drenched in magic, as the
turf was drenched in dew.

    The feeling was very wonderful; perhaps you will feel it someday. There are still some places
in the world where it can be felt, but they grow fewer every year…

    Something enormously long and darkly grey came crawling towards Gerald slowly, heavily…
As the thing writhed past Gerald, he reached out his hand and touched the side of its gigantic tail.
It was of stone.

STUDENT WORKBOOK VERSION

The incident of the invisible Princess had surprised, and the sudden decision to be a detective had brought its own anxieties… Only now a new feeling had come to Gerald as Gerald walked through the gardens; by day those gardens were like dreams, by night like visions. Gerald could not see his feet as Gerald walked, but Gerald saw the movement of the dewy grass-blades that his feet dispersed. And Gerald had that extraordinary feeling so difficult to describe, and yet so real and so unforgettable: the feeling that Gerald was in another world, that had covered up and hidden the old world as a carpet covers the floor. The floor was there all right, underneath, but what Gerald walked on was the carpet that covered the floor, and the carpet was drenched in magic, as the turf was drenched in dew.

The feeling was very wonderful; perhaps the reader will feel the feeling someday. There are still some places in the world where the feeling can be felt, but the places grow fewer every year…

Something enormously long and darkly grey came crawling towards Gerald slowly, heavily… As the thing writhed past Gerald, Gerald reached out his hand and touched the side of its gigantic tail. The thing was of stone.

Exercise 5D: Pronouns and Antecedents

Circle the personal pronouns in the following sentences, and draw an arrow from each pronoun to its antecedent. If the noun and pronoun are masculine, write *m* in the margin. If they are feminine, write *f*; if neuter, write *n*. Look carefully. Some sentences may have more than one personal pronoun, and some personal pronouns may share an antecedent! In addition, some antecedents may not actually appear in the sentences provided.

These sentences are from *The Story of Doctor Dolittle*, by Hugh Lofting. Some have been slightly adapted.

But soon the animals began to get worried. And one evening when the Doctor was asleep before the kitchen-fire, they began talking in whispers.   n

So it was agreed that the monkey, Chee-Chee, was to do the cooking and mending; the dog was to sweep the floors; the duck was to dust and make the beds; the owl, Too-Too, was to keep the accounts, and the pig was to do the gardening. They made   n
Polynesia, the parrot, housekeeper and laundress, because she was the oldest.   f

Then the animals made a vegetable and flower stall outside the garden-gate and sold radishes and roses to the people that passed by along the road. But still they didn't   n
seem to make enough money to pay all the bills—and still the Doctor wouldn't worry.

Then the crocodile and the monkey and the parrot were very glad and began to sing, because they were going back to Africa, their real home.   n

And one day when an old lady with rheumatism came to see the Doctor, (she) sat on the hedgehog who was sleeping on the sofa and never came to see (him) anymore, but drove every Saturday all the way to Oxenthorpe, another town ten miles off, to see a different doctor.

f, m

So, as time went on, the Doctor got more and more animals; and the people who came to see (him) got less and less. Till at last (he) had no one left.

m, m

"(I) can never be quite sure of my age," said Polynesia. "(It) is either a hundred and eighty-three or a hundred and eighty-two."

f, n

— LESSON 6 —

Review Definitions

**Introduction to Verbs
Action Verbs, State-of-Being Verbs
Parts of Speech**

Exercise 6A: Identifying Action Verbs

Underline the verbs in the following passage. Mark them as *A* for action verbs or *B* for being verbs. This passage has been slightly adapted from *The Wonders of the Jungle: Book One*, by Prince Sarath Gosh.

Here <u>come</u> all the animals! The buffaloes, the blue deer, the red deer, the wild pigs, the hyenas, the wolves, the red dogs, and many others. <u>Watch</u> and <u>see</u> how each kind of animal <u>comes</u>. The moon <u>shines</u> clear above the trees, and we <u>see</u> a long way up the stream.

<u>See</u> the buffaloes! They <u>come</u> a little above the elephants. But they do not <u>come</u> one behind another in a line, like the elephants. They <u>come</u> three or four together.

The buffaloes <u>drink</u> three or four at a time because they <u>are</u> like a body of soldiers, one row behind another. Sometimes twenty or thirty rows <u>make</u> up a herd. We <u>see</u> only the first row drinking now, but soon we <u>see</u> the others behind.

And why do the buffaloes <u>come</u> like a body of soldiers? Because they <u>fear</u> their enemy—the tiger! Once upon a time the buffaloes <u>scattered</u> about, and the tiger <u>ate</u> many of them, one at a time. Then those that <u>escaped</u> from the tiger <u>joined</u> together like a body of soldiers, so that they could <u>beat</u> off the tiger. But now <u>watch</u> the first row drinking. They <u>are</u> all bull buffaloes, the Papas of the herd; you can <u>tell</u> that by their huge horns, a yard long on each side of the head. You see how the buffaloes stand side by side, so that their horns almost touch one another. That is the way the buffaloes march to the stream from their feeding place—horn to horn. Why? Because no prowling tiger passes those horns.

Watch the first row as it finishes; the whole row wheels around to the side like soldiers. Then those march to the back of the herd, and stand there in a row.

Meanwhile the second row in the front steps to the water. These also are bull buffaloes. When they finish, they also wheel, march to the back of the herd, and there stand behind the first row. In this way four or five rows of bulls drink, one after the other, and go to the back of the herd.

Next come about a dozen rows of cow buffaloes and their calves, or children. You see again, like the elephants, the Mammas and children among the buffaloes are also in the middle, safe from all harm.

Then at the end there are four or five rows of bull buffaloes again. They guard the Mammas and the children from enemies in the back.

Exercise 6B: Choosing Verbs

Provide both an appropriate action and state-of-being verb for each of the following nouns or pronouns. The first is done for you.

> **Note to Instructor:** The student's answers should be exactly the same as those listed in the state-of-being column. The verbs in the action column are samples; answers may vary.

	State-of-Being	Action
The computer	is (or was)	crashed
Some students	are/were	studied
We	are/were	read
He	is (or was)	spoke
The clouds	are/were	gathered
An insect	is (or was)	buzzed
Cells	are/were	multiply
The door	is (or was)	closed
Tomato plants	are/were	grew
Owls	are/were	flew

Exercise 6C: Strong Action Verbs

Good writers use descriptive and vivid verbs!

In the following sentences, replace the underlined state-of-being and action verbs, which are bland and general, with more vigorous and colorful action verbs. The first is done for you.

You may use a thesaurus if necessary.

Camille Flammarion, the author of *Astronomy for Amateurs*, from which these sentences were taken, used much more interesting verbs! Your instructor will show you her original sentences when you're finished.

Note to Instructor: Accept any appropriate verbs, but ask the student to compare her answers with the original sentences below.

The crimson disk of the Sun has _gone_ beneath the ocean.
The crimson disk of the Sun has _plunged_ beneath the ocean.

These exquisite double stars _go_ in gracious and splendid couples around one another, as in some majestic valse, marrying their multi-colored fires in the midst of the starry firmament.

Everywhere we find the Sun; everywhere we _see_ his work, extending from the infinitely great to the infinitely little.

We embark upon a ray of light, and _move_ rapidly to the portals of our Universe.

The fable of the dragon _eating_ the Sun or Moon during the eclipses is universal.

Our Sun, that _is_ so calm and majestic, is in reality the seat of fierce conflagrations.

The molecules _light_ and burn like true stars with a brilliancy that is often magnificent.

There is an immense variety in the brilliancy of the shooting stars, from the weak telescopic sparks that _go_ like a flash of lightning, to the incandescent *bolides* or *fire-balls* that _glow_ in the atmosphere.

The globe of fire _changes_, and splits up into luminous fragments, scattered in all directions.

Here, we constantly _get_ a pure and dazzling white light from our burning luminary. Its ray, indeed, _has_ the potentiality of every conceivable color, but picture the fantastic illumination of the worlds that _are_ round these multiple and colored suns as they shed floods of blue and roseate, red, or orange light around them!

The glacial zones are where the Sun _is_ constantly above or below the horizon for several days.

ORIGINAL VERSION

The crimson disk of the Sun has <u>gone</u> beneath the ocean.
The crimson disk of the Sun has <u>plunged</u> beneath the ocean.

These exquisite double stars <u>revolve</u> in gracious and splendid couples around one another, as in some majestic waltz, marrying their multi-colored fires in the midst of the starry firmament.

Everywhere we find the Sun; everywhere we <u>recognize</u> his work, extending from the infinitely great to the infinitely little.

We embark upon a ray of light, and <u>glide</u> rapidly to the portals of our Universe.

The fable of the dragon <u>devouring</u> the Sun or Moon during the eclipses is universal.

Our Sun, that <u>appears</u> so calm and majestic, is in reality the seat of fierce conflagrations.

The molecules <u>incandesce</u> and burn like true stars with a brilliancy that is often magnificent.

There is an immense variety in the brilliancy of the shooting stars, from the weak telescopic sparks that <u>vanish</u> like a flash of lightning, to the incandescent *bolides* or *fire-balls* that <u>explode</u> in the atmosphere.

The globe of fire <u>bursts</u>, and splits up into luminous fragments, scattered in all directions.

Here, we constantly <u>receive</u> a pure and dazzling white light from our burning luminary. Its ray, indeed, <u>contains</u> the potentiality of every conceivable color, but picture the fantastic illumination of the worlds that <u>gravitate</u> round these multiple and colored suns as they shed floods of blue and roseate, red, or orange light around them!

The glacial zones are where the Sun <u>remains</u> constantly above or below the horizon for several days.

— LESSON 7 —

Helping Verbs

Exercise 7A: Action and Helping Verbs

Underline the action verbs in both columns of sentences once. The sentences in the second column each contain at least one helping verb. Underline these helping verbs twice. These sentences are adapted from "Our Dog Rolf" by Frau Paula Moekel in *Muenchner Nachrichten*.

COLUMN 1	COLUMN 2
Rolf <u>recognized</u> letters and numerals.	He <u>was</u> <u>wagging</u> his tail with delight!
Rolf <u>understood</u> me.	Rolf <u>can</u> <u>recognize</u> any money.
He <u>reads</u> his own name easily.	He <u>would</u> <u>rap</u> "yes" or "no."
He <u>remembers</u> names and numbers over quite a period of time.	The numbers <u>were</u> <u>written</u> down.
Rolf <u>used</u> the same paw for decimals and units.	At the close of his tests, Rolf <u>was</u> <u>rewarded</u> with a cake.
One public appearance <u>brought</u> him praise from a large circle of acquaintances.	Rolf <u>has</u> <u>made</u> frequent public appearances.

Exercise 7B: Providing Missing Helping Verbs

Fill in each blank with a helping verb. Sometimes, more than one helping verb might be appropriate.

This excerpt is adapted from *The House on the Borderland*, by William Hope Hodgson.

Note to Instructor: Accept any answers that make sense. Hodgson's original sentences are below.

Right away in the west of Ireland lies a tiny hamlet called Kraighten. It _is_ situated, alone, at the base of a low hill. Far around there spreads a waste of bleak and totally inhospitable country; where, here and there at great intervals, one _may/might/could_ come upon the ruins of some long desolate cottage—unthatched and stark. The whole land is bare and unpeopled, the very earth scarcely covering the rock that lies beneath it, and with which the country abounds, in places rising out of the soil in wave-shaped ridges.

Yet, in spite of its desolation, my friend Tonnison and I _had_ elected to spend our vacation there. He _had_ stumbled on the place by mere chance the year previously, during the course of a long walking tour, and discovered the possibilities for the angler in a small and unnamed river that runs past the outskirts of the little village.

It was early one warm evening when my friend and I arrived in Kraighten. We _had_ reached Ardrahan the previous night, sleeping there in rooms hired at the village post office, and leaving in good time on the following morning, clinging insecurely to one of the typical jaunting cars.

It _had_ taken us all day to accomplish our journey over some of the roughest tracks imaginable, with the result that we were thoroughly tired and somewhat bad tempered. However, the tent had to be erected and our goods stowed away before we _could_ think of food or rest. And so we set to work, with the aid of our driver, and soon had the tent up upon a small patch of ground just outside the little village, and quite near to the river.

Then, having stored all our belongings, we dismissed the driver, as he had to make his way back as speedily as possible, and told him to come across to us at the end of a fortnight. We _had_ brought sufficient provisions to last us for that space of time, and water we _could/might_ get from the stream. Fuel we _did_ not need, as we _had_ included a small oil-stove among our outfit, and the weather was fine and warm.

Tonnison _had_ got the stove lit now and was busy cutting slices of bacon into the frying pan; so I took the kettle and walked down to the river for water. On the way, I had to pass close to a little group of the village people, who eyed me curiously, but not in any unfriendly manner, though none of them ventured a word.

— LESSON 8 —

First, Second, and Third Person
Capitalizing the Pronoun *I*

Exercise 8A: Capitalization and Punctuation Practice

Correct the following sentences. Mark through any incorrect small letters and write the correct capitals above them. Insert quotation marks if needed. Use underlining to indicate any italics.

> **Note to Instructor:** The correct sentences are below.

In September of 1622, the ship named <u>Nuestra Señora de Atocha</u> set sail from Havana, Cuba as a part of a large fleet of ships headed to Spain. The <u>Atocha</u> bore so much gold, silver, copper, and jewels that workers had labored for two months simply to load all of the wealth. The cargo included valuables from Peru, Mexico, Colombia, Venezuela, and Panama, and the ship was heavily armed with more than 18 bronze cannons. It was manned by a crew of more than 200 sailors and slaves. It was only a short distance into the journey when a hurricane overcame the fleet, sinking seven vessels and scattering the wreckage across the ocean floor, just off the coast of the islands now known as the Florida Keys.

King Philip IV sent another group of ships to recover the lost treasure, but after many years, only half of the contents of one vessel, the <u>Santa Margarita</u>, were brought to the surface, and all efforts to rescue the items were eventually abandoned.

The <u>Atocha</u> lay undisturbed on the ocean floor until 1969, when treasure hunter Mel Fisher began his quest for the missing ship. He and his crew searched the depths, only locating tiny pieces of the massive treasure over a span of several years. Then one day in 1985, Fisher's son sent his father a message, declaring, "We have found the main pile!"

Fisher's discovery included emeralds, gold, silver, coins, cannons, and jewelry estimated at a value of $400 million. Some items from both the <u>Atocha</u> and the <u>Santa Margarita</u> are now housed at the Mel Fisher Maritime Museum in Key West, Florida, where the public can view them.

Exercise 8B: Person, Number, and Gender

Label each personal pronoun in the following selection with its person (*1*, *2*, or *3*) and number (*S* or *PL*). For third-person-singular pronouns only, indicate gender (*M*, *F*, or *N*). The first is done for you.

The selection below is adapted from Agatha Christie's *Poirot Investigates*.

> **Note to Instructor:** We have only addressed subject personal pronouns so far, but this passage contains personal pronouns that act as objects and possessives as well. The student may or may not mark these additional personal pronouns; the key below indicates these in parentheses. Answers NOT in parentheses are subject pronouns, which the student should be sure to mark.

As usual, Poirot was right. After a short interval, the American film star was ushered in, and
1PL   (1PL)
we rose to our feet.

  3SF

    Mary Marvell was undoubtedly one of the most popular actresses on the screen. She had only

                         (3SF)   (3PL)

lately arrived in England in company with her husband, Gregory B. Rolf, also a film actor. Their

                                                     (3PL)

marriage had taken place about a year ago in the States and this was their first visit to England.

3PL

They had been given a great reception. Every one was prepared to go mad over Mary Marvell... All

                               (1S)   1S   (3PL)

these details passed rapidly through my mind as I joined with Poirot in greeting our fair client.

    Miss Marvell was small and slender, very fair and girlish-looking, with the wide innocent

blue eyes of a child.

                             (3SF)   3SF

    Poirot drew forward a chair for her, and she commenced talking at once.

    2S   1S   (1S)

    "You will probably think me very foolish, Monsieur Poirot, but Lord Cronshaw was telling me

                           2S   (3SM)   1S   1S

last night how wonderfully you cleared up the mystery of his nephew's death, and I felt that I just

      (2S)   1S   3SN   (1S)

must have your advice. I dare say it's only a silly hoax—Gregory says so—but it's just worrying me

to death."

3SF

    She paused for breath. Poirot beamed encouragement.

                   2S   1S

    "Proceed, Madame. You comprehend, I am still in the dark."

                                  (3S)

    "It's these letters." Miss Marvell unclasped her handbag, and drew out three envelopes which

3SF

she handed to Poirot.

Introduction to the Sentence

— LESSON 9 —
The Sentence
Parts of Speech and Parts of Sentences
Subjects and Predicates

Exercise 9A: Parts of Speech vs. Parts of the Sentence

Label each underlined word with the correct part of speech AND the correct part of the sentence.

part of speech   _noun_   _verb_

The <u>water</u> <u>is</u> cold.

part of the sentence   _subject_   _predicate_

part of speech   _pronoun_   _verb_

<u>We</u> <u>roasted</u> marshmallows.

part of the sentence   _subject_   _predicate_

part of speech   _noun_   _verb_

The <u>goat</u> <u>munched</u> our reservation.

part of the sentence   _subject_   _predicate_

part of speech   _pronoun_   _verb_

<u>He</u> <u>laughed</u> at us.

part of the sentence   _subject_   _predicate_

Exercise 9B: Parts of Speech: Nouns, Adjectives, Pronouns, and Verbs

Label each underlined word with the correct part of speech. Use *N* for noun, *A* for adjective, *P* for pronoun, and *V* for verb.

These sentences are from *The Mysterious Stranger*, by Mark Twain.

<u>We</u> passed out through the <u>parlor</u>, and there <u>was</u> Marget at the spinnet teaching Marie
Lueger. So one of the deserting <u>pupils</u> was back; and an <u>influential</u> one, too; the others would
follow. <u>Marget</u> <u>jumped</u> up and <u>ran</u> and thanked <u>us</u> again, with <u>tears</u> in her eyes—this was the

18

third time—for saving her and her uncle from being turned into the street, and we told her again
we hadn't done it; but that was her way, she never could be grateful enough for anything a person
did for her; so we let her have her say. And as we passed through the garden, there was Wilhelm
Meidling sitting there waiting, for it was getting toward the edge of the evening, and he would
be asking Marget to take a walk along the river with him when she was done with the lesson. He
was a young lawyer, and succeeding fairly well and working his way along, little by little. He was
very fond of Marget, and she of him. He had not deserted along with the others, but had stood
his ground all through. His faithfulness was not lost on Marget and her uncle. He hadn't so very
much talent, but he was handsome and good.

Exercise 9C: Parts of the Sentence: Subjects and Predicates

In each of the following sentences, underline the subject once and the predicate twice. Find the
subject by asking, "Who or what is this sentence about?" Find the predicate by saying, "Subject
what?"

Orcas are large dolphins.

They hunt in groups.

These giant animals are carnivores.

Sometimes, they are called "killer whales."

Orcas are extremely intelligent and social animals.

Each pod uses its own language of sounds for communication.

These mammals can be found in all oceans of the world.

— LESSON 10 —

Subjects and Predicates
Diagramming Subjects and Predicates
Sentence Capitalization and Punctuation
Sentence Fragments

Exercise 10A: Sentences and Fragments

If a group of words expresses a complete thought, write *S* for sentence in the blank. If not, write *F*
for fragment.

since the beach is crowded	F
let's go get ice cream	S
it is fine to leave our bicycles here	S

she likes mint chocolate chip ice cream best   _____S_____

that snow cone looks refreshing   _____S_____

the empty sunscreen bottle   _____F_____

if we need more   _____F_____

Exercise 10B: Proofreading for Capitalization and Punctuation

Add the correct capitalization and punctuation to the following sentences. In this exercise you will use proofreader's marks. Indicate letters which should be capitalized by underlining three times. Indicate ending punctuation by using the proofreader's mark for inserting a period: ⊙ Indicate words which should be italicized by underlining them and writing *ital* in the margin.

on august 25, 1916, president woodrow wilson signed a law creating national parks in the united states⊙

the first park to open was yellowstone national park⊙

today, there are 58 national parks in america⊙

alaska and california have the most parks of any state⊙

the most popular park is the great smoky mountain area, which stretches across parts of north carolina and tennessee⊙

arizona is home to one of the most famous parks, the grand canyon⊙

yellowstone contains one of the most popular tourist sites in any park, a geyser known as old faithful⊙

grand teton national park in wyoming is home to diverse and fascinating wildlife, such as black bears, grizzly bears, elk, moose, and bald eagles⊙

photographer ansel adams brought attention to the beauty of the parks with his stunning images⊙

his book, parmelian prints of the high sierras, brought attention to the need to preserve   *ital*
these incredible areas of land⊙

> **Note to Instructor:** "Parmelian" refers to a genus containing types of lichens. The student may need to be told the definition and that the word is used as an adjective in the title of the book.

Exercise 10C: Diagramming

Find the subjects and predicates in the following sentences. Diagram each subject and predicate on your own paper. You should capitalize on the diagram any words that are capitalized in the sentence, but do not put punctuation marks on the diagram. If a proper name is the subject, all parts of the proper name go onto the subject line of the diagram.

The first one is done for you.

A light rain fell in the morning.

| rain | fell |

Frogs croaked loudly in the lake.

| Frogs | croaked |

Yellow flowers bloomed on the path.

| flowers | bloomed |

Baby birds ate worms in their nest.

| birds | ate |

Horses grazed happily.

| Horses | grazed |

Maram picked vegetables from the garden.

| Maram | picked |

I mowed the grass.

| I | mowed |

Mom drank coffee on the porch.

| Mom | drank |

— LESSON 11 —

Types of Sentences

Exercise 11A: Types of Sentences: Statements, Exclamations, Commands, and Questions

Identify the following sentences as *S* for statement, *E* for exclamation, *C* for command, or *Q* for question. Add the appropriate punctuation to the end of each sentence.

	Sentence Type
Do you know how to play an instrument?	Q
I learned a new piece on the piano.	S
Practice piano every day.	C
Please learn this new song by next week.	C
What a lovely sound this piano makes!	E
Could I practice in the morning?	Q

I can't wait for my recital!   <u>E</u>

My brother plays the violin.   <u>S</u>

Are my grandparents coming to the recital?   <u>Q</u>

Cover the piano to protect it from dust.   <u>C</u>

Exercise 11B: Proofreading for Capitalization and Punctuation

Proofread the following sentences. If a lowercase letter should be capitalized, draw three lines underneath it. Add any missing punctuation by writing it into the sentence.

<u>w</u>hat a perfect day for a hike!

<u>p</u>lease refill the water bottles.

<u>h</u>ave you seen my backpack?

<u>p</u>ack some extra snacks.

<u>w</u>hat trail should we take?

<u>d</u>on't forget the bug spray.

<u>t</u>he hike to the waterfall is amazing!

Exercise 11C: Diagramming Subjects and Predicates

On your own paper, diagram the subjects and predicates of the following sentences. Remember that the understood subject of a command is "you," and that the predicate may come before the subject in a question.

Are you tired?

you | Are

Read this book before Friday.

(you) | Read

Close the oven.

(you) | Close

Maureen walked here.

Maureen | walked

The dog loved his new toy.

dog | loved

Thunder boomed loudly!

Thunder | boomed

Did the movie begin?

movie | Did begin

The water is cold!

water | is

— LESSON 12 —

Subjects and Predicates
Helping Verbs
Simple and Complete Subjects and Predicates

Exercise 12A: Complete Subjects and Complete Predicates

Match the complete subjects and complete predicates by drawing lines between them.

Note to Instructor: Our solutions are listed below, but accept any reasonable answers.

In the forest, a lion	captured the mouse with his paw.
A tiny mouse	was in pain and roared loudly.
The surprised and angry lion	ran to the lion and ate through the rope, freeing him.
The frightened mouse	accidentally ran across the lion's nose.
Intrigued by the mouse's offer, the lion	became caught in a hunter's trap tied with rope.
Several days later, the lion	lay sleeping under a tree.
Stuck in the trap, the lion	heard the lion's cry.
From across the forest, the mouse	let the mouse go.
Quickly, the mouse	begged for her freedom and promised to help the lion in return.

Exercise 12B: Simple and Complete Subjects and Predicates

In the following sentences, underline the simple subject once and the simple predicate twice. Then, draw a vertical line between the complete subject and the complete predicate.

The first is done for you.

These sentences are adapted from J. M. Barrie's *Peter and Wendy*.

<u>Hook</u>|<u>stood</u> shuddering, one foot in the air.

The astounded <u>brothers</u>|<u>were dragged</u> away to hack and hew and carry.

The little <u>house</u>|<u>looked</u> so cosy and safe in the darkness.

Peter|was a superb swordsman and parried with dazzling rapidity.

"In two minutes, the ship|will be blown to pieces!"

A million golden arrows|were pointing it out to the children.

Of all delectable islands, Neverland|is the smallest and most compact.

Neverland|is always more or less an island, with astonishing splashes of color here
and there.

Exercise 12C: Diagramming Simple Subjects and Simple Predicates

On your own paper, diagram the simple subjects and simple predicates from Exercise 12B.

Hook stood shuddering, one foot in the air.

Hook | stood

The little house looked so cozy and
safe in the darkness.

house | looked

"In two minutes, the ship will be
blown to pieces!"

ship | will be blown

Of all delectable islands, Neverland is the
smallest and most compact.

Neverland | is

The astounded brothers were dragged
away to hack and hew and carry.

brothers | were dragged

Peter was a superb swordsman and
parried with dazzling rapidity.

Peter | was

A million golden arrows were pointing it
out to the children.

arrows | were pointing

Neverland is always more or less an
island, with astonishing splashes of
color here and there.

Neverland | is

— REVIEW 1 —

Weeks 1-3

Topics

Concrete/Abstract Nouns
Descriptive Adjectives
Common/Proper Nouns
Capitalization of Proper Nouns and First Words in Sentences
Noun Gender
Pronouns and Antecedents
Action Verbs/State-of-Being Verbs
Helping Verbs
Subjects and Predicates
Complete Sentences
Types of Sentences

Review 1A: Types of Nouns

Fill in the blanks with the correct description of each noun. The first is done for you.

	Concrete / Abstract	Common / Proper	Gender (M, F, N)
Maya Angelou	C	P	F
cookie	C	C	N
Puerto Rico	C	P	N
calendar	C	C	N
queen	C	C	F
excitement	A	C	N
nephew	C	C	M
bell	C	C	N
Smithsonian Magazine	C	P	N
surprise	A	C	N
Andes Mountains	C	P	N

Review 1B: Types of Verbs

Underline the complete verbs in the following sentences. Identify any helping verbs as *HV*. Identify the main verb as *AV* for action verb or *BV* for state-of-being verb.

        AV
The northern lights <u>occur</u> in the skies near the earth's poles.

  HV   AV
They <u>can appear</u> as bright green, red, violet, or blue lights.

      AV
The lights <u>dance</u> in the sky.

  HV   AV
They <u>may shine</u> as rippling bands or a steady light.

In some countries, such as Greenland, people <u>can</u> <u>see</u> the lights almost every night.
<small>HV AV</small>

The southern lights <u>transform</u> skies in Antarctica and New Zealand.
<small>AV</small>

The lights <u>form</u> from gases such as oxygen and nitrogen.
<small>AV</small>

These gases <u>collide</u> with electrically-charged protons and electrons.
<small>AV</small>

That collision <u>causes</u> the lights.
<small>AV</small>

Review 1C: Subjects and Predicates

Draw one line under the simple subject and two lines under the simple predicate in the following sentences. Remember that the predicate may be a verb phrase with more than one verb in it. If the subject is an understood "you" in a command, write "(you)" in the left margin and underline it once to indicate that it is the simple subject.

<u>Bridges</u> <u>permit</u> travel over waterways and canyons.

The first <u>bridges</u> <u>were built</u> in Greece for chariots.

Early <u>bridges</u> in China <u>were made</u> from stone.

Roman <u>architects</u> <u>used</u> cement for very strong bridges.

Suspension or hanging <u>bridges</u> <u>were constructed</u> in South America.

Today's <u>bridges</u> <u>are formed</u> from steel and concrete.

<u>Arches</u> <u>make</u> a bridge stronger.

The <u>arches</u> <u>distribute</u> the weight more evenly.

<u>You</u> <u>can create</u> your own bridge from a log or beam.

(You) <u>Make</u> it a strong and sturdy bridge!

Review 1D: Parts of Speech

Identify the underlined words as *N* for noun, *P* for pronoun, *A* for adjective, *AV* for action verb, *HV* for helping verb, or *BV* for state-of-being verb.

The following passage is from Louisa May Alcott's *Jo's Boys*.

"If anyone had told <u>me</u> what wonderful changes were to take place here in <u>ten</u> years,
<small>P   A</small>
<u>I</u> wouldn't have believed it," <u>said</u> Mrs Jo to Mrs Meg, as <u>they</u> <u>sat</u> on the piazza at Plumfield one
<small>P   AV   P   AV</small>
<u>summer</u> day, looking about them with <u>faces</u> full of <u>pride</u> and <u>pleasure</u>...
<small>A   N   N   N</small>

Jo <u>put</u> her hand on her sister's, and both sat silent for a <u>little</u> while, surveying the <u>pleasant</u>
<small>AV   A   A</small>
scene before them with mingled <u>sad</u> and <u>happy</u> thoughts.
<small>A   A</small>

It certainly did look as if magic had been at work, for quiet Plumfield was transformed into a busy little world. The house seemed more hospitable than ever, refreshed now with new paint, added wings, well-kept lawn and garden, and a prosperous air it had not worn when riotous boys swarmed everywhere and it was rather difficult for the Bhaers to make both ends meet. On the hill, where kites used to be flown, stood the fine college which Mr Laurence's munificent legacy had built. Busy students were going to and fro along the paths once trodden by childish feet, and many young men and women were enjoying all the advantages that wealth, wisdom, and benevolence could give them.

Just inside the gates of Plumfield a pretty brown cottage, very like the Dovecote, nestled among the trees, and on the green slope westward Laurie's white-pillared mansion glittered in the sunshine; for when the rapid growth of the city shut in the old house, spoilt Meg's nest, and dared to put a soap-factory under Mr Laurence's indignant nose, our friends emigrated to Plumfield, and the great changes began.

Review 1E: Capitalization and Punctuation

Use proofreading marks to indicate correct capitalization and punctuation in the following sentences. Be careful: Some of these may have more than one sentence, so ending punctuation will need to be inserted to split sentences correctly!

small letter that should be capitalized: = beneath the letter.

italics: single underline

insert period: ⊙

insert exclamation point: ↑

insert question mark: ⸮

insert quotation marks: ❝❞

insert comma: ⌃

charles lindbergh completed the first solo flight across the atlantic ocean in his plane, the spirit of st. louis⊙

robert louis stevenson wrote many children's poems, including ❝bed in summer,❞ which describes how hard it is to sleep when it is still light outside⊙

the u.s.s. arizona was sunk at pearl harbor on december 7, 1941⊙

did you know that mario is the most famous nintendo character of all time⸮

gifted violinist itzhak perlman became famous at age 13, when he appeared on the ed sullivan show⊙

kitagawa utamaro was a master of the japanese art of woodblock printing⊙

in 2019 at a meet held in monaco, sifan hassan ran a mile in 4 minutes and 12.33 seconds, setting a new world record for women⊙

the national anthem of great britain is entitled "god save the queen," the queen herself does not sing it when it is played in her presence.

the book goodnight moon appeared on reader's digest's list of the greatest children's books of all time.

Review 1F: Types of Sentences

Identify the following sentences as *S* for statement, *C* for command, *E* for exclamation, or *Q* for question. If the sentence is incomplete, write *I*.

These sentences are adapted from "The Fir Tree," by Hans Christian Andersen.

	Sentence Type
The sun shone, and the soft air fluttered its leaves.	S
Fell to the earth with a crash.	I
Look what is sticking to the ugly old fir tree.	C
"Do you know where those trees were taken?"	Q
The young fir tree wished very much to know.	S
What would become of them?	Q
This is beautiful!	E
Rejoice in your youth.	C
How do I know this is so?	Q
"Will the trees of the forest come to see me?"	Q
Who came and peeped among the branches.	I
Christmas time drew near.	S
Many trees were cut down.	S

Verb Tenses

— LESSON 13 —

Nouns, Pronouns, and Verbs

Sentences

Simple Present, Simple Past, and Simple Future Tenses

Exercise 13A: Simple Tenses

	Simple Past	Simple Present	Simple Future
I	shopped	shop	will shop
You	laughed	laugh	will laugh
She	called	calls	will call
We	liked	like	will like
They	skipped	skip	will skip

Exercise 13B: Using Consistent Tense

When you write, you should use consistent tense—if you begin a sentence in one tense, you should continue to use that same tense for any other verbs in the same sentence. The following sentences use two verb tenses. Cross out the second verb and rewrite it so that the tense of the second verb matches the tense of the first one.

The first sentence is done for you.

For a bit of fun, see if you can guess which movie each of these sentences is referring to!

Hagrid <u>delivered</u> a letter to Harry that ~~contains~~ his invitation to Hogwarts. *(contained)*
(Harry Potter and the Sorcerer's Stone)

Luke <u>discovers</u> that Darth Vader ~~was~~ his father. *(is)*
(Star Wars: The Empire Strikes Back)

Buzz Lightyear and Woody <u>became</u> good friends, but they ~~begin~~ as enemies. *(began)*
(Toy Story 1)

Carl <u>will ride</u> his hot-air balloon to Paradise Falls, and his explorer pal Russell ~~helped~~ him along the adventurous route. *(will help)*
(Up)

Charlie <u>won</u> the golden ticket and ~~chooses~~ ^{chose} his grandfather as his guest for the fantastical tour.
(Charlie and the Chocolate Factory)

Dorothy <u>will find</u> her way home, and she ~~was reunited~~ ^{will reunite} with Aunt Em and Uncle Henry.
(The Wizard of Oz)

Nemo <u>becomes</u> lost at sea, and his father, Marlin, ~~needed~~ ^{needs} Dory's help to find his son.
(Finding Nemo)

Exercise 13C: Forming the Simple Past Tense

Using the rules for forming the simple past, put each one of the verbs in parentheses into the simple past. Write the simple past form in the blank. Be sure to spell the past forms of regular verbs correctly, and to use the correct forms of irregular verbs.

These sentences are taken from "Shippeitaro," translated by Valfrid Hedman.

Note to Instructor: If the student is unfamiliar with irregular verbs, give all necessary help.

Long, long ago, in the good old days when there were (are) still fairies and giants, trolls and dragons, valiant knights and distressed maidens, a brave young warrior went (goes) into the world in search of adventure.

For a while, he paused (pauses) without encountering anything more special, but finally one evening, he found (finds) himself next to a deserted and lonely mountain. No village, no cottage visible, not even a charcoal burner's hut, although they are so often found (find) on the outskirts of the forest. He followed (follows) a weak and well-grassed path, but at last he also lost (loses) sight of it. Twilight approached (approaches) and in vain he struggled (struggles) to find the lost path. With each attempt, he seemed (seems) more and more hopelessly clinging to thorn bushes and long grass that grew densely everywhere. Weak and tired, he fumbled (fumbles) forward in the ever-increasing darkness until he suddenly arrived (arrives) at a small deserted and half-ruined temple. However, it still contained (contains) a sanctuary. There was (is), of course, shelter from cold dew, and so he decided (decides) to spend his night in the temple. He had (has) no food; tangled in his cloak and placing his excellent sword beside him, he fell (falls) to rest and soon fell (falls) into a deep sleep.

At midnight, he woke (wakes) up to a horrible noise. At first he thought (thinks) he dreamed (dreams), but the noise continued (continues), and the whole building echoed (echoes) with the most horrible cries and howls. The young warrior lifted (lifts) gently and looked (looks) out of the hole in the dilapidated wall. He saw (sees) a strange and creepy vision. A group of disgusting cats spun (spin) a wild and horrible dance, and their screams echoed (echo) into a quiet night. From their horrible cries, the young warrior distinguished (distinguish) the following words:

"Tell it not to Shippeitaro!

Listen for his bark!

Tell it not to Shippeitaro!

Keep it close and dark!"

A beautiful full moon __illuminated__ (illuminates) this horrible play with its rays, which the young warrior __watched__ (watches) in amazement and horror. When midnight __was__ (is) over, the ghost cats __disappeared__ (disappear) and everything __was__ (is) quiet again.

— LESSON 14 —

Simple Present, Simple Past, and Simple Future Tenses
Progressive Present, Progressive Past, and Progressive Future Tenses

Exercise 14A: Forming the Simple Past and Simple Future Tenses

Form the simple past and simple future of the following regular verbs.

Past	Present	Future
baked	bake	will bake
closed	close	will close
begged	beg	will beg
challenged	challenge	will challenge
brushed	brush	will brush
added	add	will add
fixed	fix	will fix
ended	end	will end
cried	cry	will cry

Exercise 14B: Progressive Tenses

Circle the ending of each verb. Underline the helping verbs.

is sing(ing)

am rid(ing)

are sew(ing)

have been hik(ing)

will be walk(ing)

am think(ing)

were study(ing)

had been kayak(ing)

Exercise 14C: Forming the Progressive Past, Present, and Future Tenses

Complete the following chart. Be sure to use the spelling rules above.

> **Note to Instructor:** This exercise drills progressive verbs and also prepares the student for the introduction of person in next week's lessons. If the student asks why the helping verbs change, you may either say, "You'll find out next week" or turn to Lesson 18 and do it out of order. (The first method is recommended for students who are doing this course for the first time; person has not yet been covered in order to allow the student to concentrate on the tenses being introduced.)

	Progressive Past	Progressive Present	Progressive Future
I sweep	I was sweeping	I am sweeping	I will be sweeping
I cook	I was cooking	I am cooking	I will be cooking
I take	I was taking	I am taking	I will be taking
I swim	I was swimming	I am swimming	I will be swimming
You count	You were counting	You are counting	You will be counting
You type	You were typing	You are typing	You will be typing
You flip	You were flipping	You are flipping	You will be flipping
You plant	You were planting	You are planting	You will be planting
We wish	We were wishing	We are wishing	We will be wishing
We live	We were living	We are living	We will be living
We hug	We were hugging	We are hugging	We will be hugging
We care	We were caring	We are caring	We will be caring

Exercise 14D: Simple and Progressive Tenses

Fill in the blanks with the correct form of the verb in parentheses.

In 1890, George Washington Carver __was studying__ (progressive past of *study*) art at college when a professor noticed how well Carver sketched (simple past of *sketch*) plants and encouraged (simple past of *encourage*) him to pursue a degree in botany.

Carver was an excellent student and graduated (simple past of *graduate*) as the first African American to receive a Bachelor of Science degree. His reputation as a skilled botanist led him to Tuskegee University, where he worked (simple past of *work*) and researched.

While Carver was examining (progressive past of *examine*) soil chemistry, he discovered that farmers who were growing (progressive past of *grow*) the same crop for many years were depleting (progressive past of *deplete*) the soil.

Carver observed (simple past of *observe*) that nitrogen was added back to the soil when the farmers were planting (progressive past of *plant*) other crops such as peanuts, sweet potatoes, and soybeans.

However, since many farmers were harvesting (progressive past of *harvest*) these plants, there was now a surplus of them, and the growers were becoming (progressive past of *become*) frustrated with what to do with the abundance of crops they could not sell.

Carver decided (simple past of *decide*) to learn what other products could be made from peanuts and sweet potatoes.

After much research, Carver learned (simple past of *learn*) that these plants could be used in over 300 items which ranged (simple past of *range*) from foods to cleaning products to office supplies.

Today, when you are enjoying (progressive present of *enjoy*) a baked sweet potato, or perhaps you are baking (progressive present of *bake*) it into a pie, you can thank Dr. Carver for helping to make this humble vegetable so popular!

— LESSON 15 —

Simple Present, Simple Past, and Simple Future Tenses
Progressive Present, Progressive Past, and Progressive Future Tenses
Perfect Present, Perfect Past, and Perfect Future Tenses

Exercise 15A: Perfect Tenses

Fill in the blanks with the missing forms.

Simple Past	Perfect Past	Perfect Present	Perfect Future
I wondered	I had wondered	I have wondered	I will have wondered
I skipped	I had skipped	I have skipped	I will have skipped

Simple Past	Perfect Past	Perfect Present	Perfect Future
I lied	I had lied	I have lied	I will have lied
I climbed	I had climbed	I have climbed	I will have climbed
We inspected	We had inspected	We have inspected	We will have inspected
We opened	We had opened	We have opened	We will have opened
We clapped	We had clapped	We have clapped	We will have clapped
We debated	We had debated	We have debated	We will have debated
He carved	He had carved	He has carved	He will have carved
He tripped	He had tripped	He has tripped	He will have tripped
He illustrated	He had illustrated	He has illustrated	He will have illustrated
He dined	He had dined	He has dined	He will have dined

Exercise 15B: Identifying Perfect Tenses

Identify the underlined verbs as perfect past, perfect present, or perfect future. The first one is done for you.

perfect present
I have decided to learn karate.

perfect past   perfect past
I had studied martial arts before, and I had enjoyed my classes.

perfect present   perfect present
I have started lessons this week, and my sensei has given me exercises to practice at home, too.

perfect future
By next month, I will have learned enough skills to earn my yellow belt.

perfect present   perfect past
My sensei has taught karate for many years, and she had earned her black belt when she was a teenager.

perfect present   perfect present
Some students from my karate studio have competed and have won trophies in competitions around the area.

perfect future
At the end of the year, I will have practiced enough to compete as well.

Exercise 15C: Perfect, Progressive, and Simple Tenses

Each underlined verb phrase has been labeled as past, present, or future. Add the label *perfect*, *progressive*, or *simple* to each one. The first one has been done for you.

simple   perfect   simple
PAST   PAST   PAST
Khadija finished her breakfast. She had eaten, but she was almost too excited to taste

simple   simple   progressive   progressive

PAST   PRESENT   PRESENT   FUTURE

the food, because she <u>thought</u>, "I <u>know</u> what <u>is happening</u> today: My family <u>will be going</u> to the

state fair!"

                  simple   simple   simple

                  FUTURE   PAST   PRESENT

Khadija's mother declared, "We <u>will need</u> tickets," so Khadija <u>announced</u>, "I <u>volunteer</u> to wait in

           simple   progressive   progressive

           PAST   PAST   PAST

the line!" While she <u>waited</u>, Khadija <u>was enjoying</u> the sounds of music and <u>was savoring</u> the

                                            perfect

                                          PAST

smells of delicious fried treats she would enjoy. Suddenly, the breakfast she <u>had eaten</u> seemed so

                perfect   simple

                PAST   PAST

long ago! After several hours <u>had passed</u>, Khadija and her family <u>began</u> the long walk back to the

      progressive   perfect

        PAST   PAST

van. They <u>were laughing</u> about all the fun they <u>had experienced</u> that day.

   progressive   simple   simple

   FUTURE   PAST   PAST

"We <u>will be doing</u> this again next year!" Khadija <u>exclaimed</u>; and the whole family <u>agreed</u>.

— LESSON 16 —

Simple Present, Simple Past, and Simple Future Tenses
Progressive Present, Progressive Past, and Progressive Future Tenses
Perfect Present, Perfect Past, and Perfect Future Tenses
Irregular Verbs

Exercise 16A: Irregular Verb Forms: Simple Present, Simple Past, and Simple Future

Fill in the chart with the missing verb forms.

Note to Instructor: If this is the student's first time through the course, she has not yet covered number and person of verbs, which affects some irregular forms. If the student uses an incorrect form, simply tell her the correct form. Have her cross out the incorrect answer and write the correct answer in its place.

	Simple Past	**Simple Present**	**Simple Future**
I	began	begin	will begin
You	went	go	will go
She	shrank	shrinks	will shrink
We	chose	choose	will choose

	Simple Past	Simple Present	Simple Future
They	held	hold	will hold
I	made	make	will make
You	shone	shine	will shine
He	paid	pays	will pay
We	rode	ride	will ride
They	taught	teach	will teach
I	took	take	will take
You	swept	sweep	will sweep
It	stank	stinks	will stink
We	bore	bear	will bear
They	woke	wake	will wake
I	won	win	will win
You	became	become	will become
We	broke	break	will break
They	wept	weep	will weep

Exercise 16B: Irregular Verbs: Progressive and Perfect Tenses

Fill in the remaining blanks. The first row is done for you.

Simple Present	Progressive Past	Progressive Present	Progressive Future	Perfect Past	Perfect Present	Perfect Future
begin	was beginning	am beginning	will be beginning	had begun	have begun	will have begun
eat	was eating	am eating	will be eating	had eaten	have eaten	will have eaten
blow	was blowing	am blowing	will be blowing	had blown	have blown	will have blown
choose	was choosing	am choosing	will be choosing	had chosen	have chosen	will have chosen
lend	was lending	am lending	will be lending	had lent	have lent	will have lent

Simple Present	Progressive Past	Progressive Present	Progressive Future	Perfect Past	Perfect Present	Perfect Future
make	was making	am making	will be making	had made	have made	will have made
flow	was flowing	am flowing	will be flowing	had flown	have flown	will have flown
tear	was tearing	am tearing	will be tearing	had torn	have torn	will have torn
spend	was spending	am spending	will be spending	had spent	have spent	will have spent
wake	was waking	am waking	will be waking	had woken	have woken	will have woken
hold	was holding	am holding	will be holding	had held	have held	will have held
fly	was flying	am flying	will be flying	had flown	have flown	will have flown
see	was seeing	am seeing	will be seeing	had seen	have seen	will have seen
bring	was bringing	am bringing	will be bringing	had brought	have brought	will have brought
send	was sending	am sending	will be sending	had sent	have sent	will have sent
sell	was selling	am selling	will be selling	had sold	have sold	will have sold
forget	was forgetting	am forgetting	will be forgetting	had forgotten	have forgotten	will have forgotten
dig	was digging	am digging	will be digging	had dug	have dug	will have dug
get	was getting	am getting	will be getting	had gotten	have gotten	will have gotten

WEEK 5

More About Verbs

— LESSON 17 —

Simple, Progressive, and Perfect Tenses
Subjects and Predicates
Parts of Speech and Parts of Sentences
Verb Phrases

Exercise 17A: Simple, Progressive, and Perfect Tenses

All the bolded verbs are in the past tense. Label each bolded verb as simple (*S*), progressive (*PROG*), or perfect (*PERF*). These sentences are adapted from *The Radio Boys' First Wireless*, by Allen Chapman.

"I **was going** [PROG] to hear what the doctor has to say. I **got** [S] a letter the other day from a cousin of mine out in Michigan, and he **told** [S] me all about a set that he made and **put** [S] up himself and **said** [S] he was just crazy about it. He wanted me to go into it so that he and I might talk together. Of course, though, I guess he **was kidding** [PROG] me about that. Michigan is a long way off, and it takes more than a day to get there on a train."

"My dad **was reading** [PROG] in the papers the other night about a man in New Jersey who **was talking** [PROG] to a friend nearby and told him that he **was going** [PROG] to play a phonograph record for him. A man over in Scotland, over three thousand miles away, **had heard** [PERF] every word he **had said** [PERF] and the phonograph too. A ship two thousand miles out on the Atlantic heard the same record, and so did another ship in a harbor in Central America."

There **was** [PROG] a loud guffaw behind the lads, accompanied by snickers, and the friends turned around to see three boys who were following them.

"What's the joke, Buck?" asked Bob coldly, as he **looked** [S] from one to the other.

"You're the joke," **answered** [S] Buck insolently; "that is, if you believe all that stuff I heard you pulling off just now."

"I **wasn't talking** [PROG] to you," replied Bob, restraining himself with some difficulty.

"Telephoning without wires! You might as well talk of walking without legs."

This argument **seemed**[S] to him so overpowering that he **swelled**[S] out his chest and looked

triumphantly at his two companions, whose faces instantly **took**[S] on the same expression.

"But say, fellows, forget about Buck and listen to this," said Herb. " It's a good one that I **had**[PERF]

heard yesterday. Why is—"

He was interrupted by a shout from Bob.

"Look," he cried, "look at that auto! It's running wild!"

Exercise 17B: Identifying and Diagramming Subjects and Predicates, Identifying Verb Tenses

Underline the subject once and the predicate twice in each sentence. Be sure to include both the main verb and any helping verbs when you underline the predicate. Identify the tense of each verb or verb phrase (*simple past, present,* or *future; progressive past, present,* or *future; perfect past, present,* or *future*) on the line. Then diagram each subject and predicate on your own paper.

These sentences are adapted from Mabel Powers's *Stories the Iroquois Tell Their Children.*

<u>Summer</u> <u><u>is</u></u> the time for work.   <u>simple present</u>

Summer | is

<u>Bees</u> <u><u>store</u></u> their honey.   <u>simple present</u>

Bees | store

<u>Squirrels</u> <u><u>will gather</u></u> their nuts.   <u>simple future</u>

Squirrels | will gather

<u>It</u> <u><u>was</u></u> at the time of the Harvest Moon.   <u>simple past</u>

It | was

A <u>line</u> of fires <u><u>was burning</u></u> around the camp.   <u>progressive past</u>

line | was burning

The <u>wind</u> <u><u>had thrown</u></u> them off the trail.   <u>perfect past</u>

wind | had thrown

The <u>Peacemaker</u> <u><u>listened</u></u> to the grievance of the one and then the other.   <u>simple past</u>

Peacemaker | listened

The <u>two</u> <u>will depart</u> in peace—no longer enemies, but friends.   simple future

$$\underline{two \mid will\ depart}$$

"On my great wings, <u>I</u> <u>will bear</u> him far away from the hunters."   simple future

$$\underline{I \mid will\ bear}$$

A <u>rabbit</u> <u>was running</u> swiftly down the trail.   progressive past

$$\underline{rabbit \mid was\ running}$$

<u>Who</u> <u>will fly</u> the Great Sky Trail?   simple future

$$\underline{Who \mid will\ fly}$$

<u>We</u> <u>have given</u> them soft hearts and kind minds.   perfect present

$$\underline{We \mid have\ given}$$

"A deep <u>sleep</u> <u>will fall</u> on him."   simple future

$$\underline{sleep \mid will\ fall}$$

— LESSON 18 —

Verb Phrases
Person of the Verb
Conjugations

Exercise 18A: Third Person Singular Verbs

In the simple present conjugation, the third person singular verb changes by adding an -s. Read the following rules and examples for adding -s to verbs in order to form the third person singular. Then, rewrite the first person verbs as third person singular verbs. The first of each set is done for you.

Usually, add -s to form the third person singular verb.

First Person Verb		Third Person Singular Verb
I like	he	likes
I speak	she	speaks
I work	it	works

Add -es to verbs ending in -s, -sh, -ch, -x, or -z.

First Person Verb		Third Person Singular Verb
we watch	it	watches
we fix	he	fixes
we fish	she	fishes

If a verb ends in -y after a consonant, change the y to i and add -es.

First Person Verb		Third Person Singular Verb
I cry	it	cries
I fly	he	flies
I worry	she	worries

If a verb ends in -y after a vowel, just add -s.

First Person Verb		Third Person Singular Verb
we say	he	says
we destroy	she	destroys
we journey	it	journeys

If a verb ends in -o after a consonant, form the third person singular by adding -es.

First Person Verb		Third Person Singular Verb
I overdo	she	overdoes
I forgo	it	forgoes
I go	he	goes

Exercise 18B: Simple Present Tenses

Choose the correct form of the simple present verb in parentheses, based on the person. Cross out the incorrect form.

Rishi and Anju (decide/~~decides~~) to build a computer.

Rishi (~~research~~/researches) what parts to buy, while Anju (~~make~~/makes) a list of them.

They (go/~~goes~~) online to order the parts.

Rishi (~~ride~~/rides) his bike to the post office when the siblings (hear/~~hears~~) that their order is ready.

"We should (count/~~counts~~) all the parts to make sure they are all here," (~~say~~/says) Anju.

"While you (check/~~checks~~), I will set up a work table," Rishi (~~reply~~/replies).

Rishi and Anju (spend/~~spends~~) all day on their computer, only stopping when their dad (~~tell~~/tells) them it is time to eat.

At the dinner table, they (talk/~~talks~~) about their project. They (look/~~looks~~) forward to a fun summer working together!

Exercise 18C: Perfect Present Tenses

Write the correct form of the perfect present verb in the blank. These sentences are slightly adapted from Mark Twain's *A Connecticut Yankee in King Arthur's Court*.

How I ___have longed___ [long] for you!

Then I ___have slept___ [sleep] well, sure enough.

I couldn't keep from thinking about it, and contemplating it, just as one does who ___has struck___ [strike] oil.

Chains cease to be needed after the spirit ___has gone___ [go] out of a prisoner.

You ___have seen___ [see] that kind of people who will never let on that they don't know the meaning of a new big word.

The handsome and popular Sir Charolais of Gaul, who ___has won___ [win] every heart by his polished manners and elegant conversation, will pull out to-day for home.

— LESSON 19 —

Person of the Verb
Conjugations
State-of-Being Verbs

Exercise 19A: Forming Progressive Present Tenses

Fill in the blanks with the correct helping verbs.

Regular Verb, Progressive Present

	Singular	Plural
First person	I _am_ finishing	we _are_ finishing
Second person	you _are_ finishing	you _are_ finishing
Third person	he, she, it _is_ finishing	they _are_ finishing

Exercise 19B: Forming Progressive Past and Future Tenses

Fill in the blanks with the correct helping verbs.

Regular Verb, Progressive Present

	Singular	Plural
First person	I _am_ jumping	we _are_ jumping
Second person	you _are_ jumping	you _are_ jumping
Third person	he, she, it _is_ jumping	they _are_ jumping

Regular Verb, Progressive Past

	Singular		Plural
First person	I __was__ jumping		we __were__ jumping
Second person	you __were__ jumping		you __were__ jumping
Third person	he, she, it __was__ jumping		they __were__ jumping

Regular Verb, Progressive Future

	Singular		Plural
First person	I __will be__ jumping		we __will be__ jumping
Second person	you __will be__ jumping		you __will be__ jumping
Third person	he, she, it __will be__ jumping		they __will be__ jumping

— LESSON 20 —

Irregular State-of-Being Verbs

Helping Verbs

Exercise 20A: Simple Tenses of the Verb *Have*

Try to fill in the missing blanks in the chart below, using your own sense of what sounds correct as well as the hints you may have picked up from the conjugations already covered. Be sure to use pencil so that any incorrect answers can be erased and corrected!

Simple Present

	Singular		Plural
First person	I __have__		we __have__
Second person	you __have__		you __have__
Third person	he, she, it __has__		they __have__

Simple Past

	Singular		Plural
First person	I __had__		we __had__
Second person	you __had__		you __had__
Third person	he, she, it __had__		they __had__

Simple Future

	Singular		Plural
First person	I will __have__		we __will have__
Second person	you __will have__		you __will have__
Third person	he, she, it __will have__		they __will have__

Exercise 20B: Simple Tenses of the Verb *Do*

Try to fill in the missing blanks in the chart below, using your own sense of what sounds correct as well as the hints you may have picked up from the conjugations already covered. Be sure to use pencil so that any incorrect answers can be erased and corrected!

Simple Present

	Singular		Plural
First person	I __do__		we __do__
Second person	you __do__		you __do__
Third person	he, she, it __does__		they __do__

Simple Past

	Singular		Plural
First person	I __did__		we __did__
Second person	you __did__		you __did__
Third person	he, she, it __did__		they __did__

Simple Future

	Singular		Plural
First person	I will __do__		we __will do__
Second person	you __will do__		you __will do__
Third person	he, she, it __will do__		they __will do__

WEEK 6

Nouns and Verbs in Sentences

— LESSON 21 —

Person of the Verb
Conjugations
Noun-Verb/Subject-Predicate Agreement

Exercise 21A: Person and Number of Pronouns

Identify the person and number of the underlined pronouns. Cross out the incorrect verb(s) in parentheses. The first one is done for you.

These sentences are adapted from Madeline Yale Wynne's "The Little Room."

	Person	Singular/Plural
<u>She</u> (is/~~are~~) an echo, that's all.	third	singular
"<u>It</u> (is/~~are~~) a pretty story, Pepita."	third	singular
"The house is just as it was built; there have never been any changes, so far as <u>we</u> (~~knows~~/know)."	first	plural
"<u>They</u> (~~makes~~/make) me think of the Maine woman who wanted her epitaph to be: 'She was a hard-working woman.'"	third	plural
<u>I</u> (wonder/~~wonders~~) if the other people in the car can hear us?	first	singular
"Don't, Roger. You have no idea how loud <u>you</u> (~~speaks~~/speak)."	second	singular
<u>You</u> (~~does~~/do) well to remember him.	second	singular
Margaret looked at her husband. He kissed her, "<u>I</u> (~~does~~/do) not like to hear you speak of your mother in connection with it."	first	singular

Exercise 21B: Identifying Subjects and Predicates

Draw two lines underneath each simple predicate and one line underneath each simple subject in the following sentences. If a phrase comes between the subject and the predicate, put parentheses around it to show that it does not affect the subject-predicate agreement.

<u>Sloths</u> often <u>reside</u> in Central and South America.

<u>Trees</u> (in tropical rainforests) <u>create</u> the perfect home for these mammals.

<u>Algae</u> (on the sloths' fur) <u>provides</u> excellent camouflage.

Three-toed <u>sloths</u> usually <u>perch</u> on the branches.

The <u>diet</u> (of a sloth) <u>consists</u> of vegetation like flowers and leaves.

Once a week, <u>sloths</u> slowly <u>descend</u> from their trees.

The <u>meal</u> (in a sloth's stomach) <u>will digest</u> over the course of an entire week.

Exercise 21C: Subject-Verb Agreement

Cross out the incorrect verb in parentheses so that subject and predicate agree in number and person. Be careful of any confusing phrases between the subject and predicate.

The teacher of the science classes (~~choose~~/ chooses) Jasmine and Gabriel to work on the project.

Jasmine and Gabriel (decide/~~decides~~) to demonstrate how oil spills harm animals.

Jasmine, using library books, (~~research~~/ researches) the effect of oil spills on birds.

She and Gabriel (gather/~~gathers~~) supplies so that they can (conduct/~~conducts~~) an experiment.

Gabriel gently drops a bird feather into a pan of water and the students in the class (watch/~~watches~~) the feather repel the moisture.

Next, Jasmine, with a dropper, (~~place~~/ places) oil in the water, and Gabriel, using brushes, (~~coat~~/ coats) the feather in the oil and water mixture.

The students around the table (observe/~~observes~~) that the oil (~~cause~~/ causes) the feather to lose its natural waterproofing, which is what (~~happen~~/ happens) to birds in an oil spill.

— LESSON 22 —

Formation of Plural Nouns
Collective Nouns

Exercise 22A: Collective Nouns

Write the collective noun for each description. Then fill in an appropriate singular verb for each sentence. (Use the simple present tense!) The first is done for you.

Note to Instructor: Allow the student to look up the collective nouns as needed. Sample verbs are provided, but answers will vary.

Description		Collective Noun	Verb	
a group of bees	The	swarm	enters	the hive.
group of fish	The	school	swims	to the surface.
people who determine a verdict	The	jury	makes	a decision.
many ants	The	army	eats	our picnic.
	OR	colony		
several newborn kittens	The	litter	sleeps	in the basket.

group of dancers   This __troupe__   __performs__   the ballet.

many pearls put together in a row   This __string__   __glows__   around her neck.

                                             OR __necklace__

Exercise 22B: Plural Noun Forms

Read each rule and the example out loud. Then rewrite the singular nouns as plural nouns in the spaces provided.

Note to Instructor: Make sure that the student reads the rules and examples out loud, not to herself!

Usually, add -s to a noun to form the plural.

Singular Noun	Plural Noun
cat	cats
trail	trails
paper	papers
ring	rings

Add -es to nouns ending in -s, -sh, -ch, -x, or -z.

Singular Noun	Plural Noun
bus	buses
flash	flashes
lunch	lunches
tax	taxes
waltz	waltzes

If a noun ends in -y after a consonant, change the y to i and add -es.

Singular Noun	Plural Noun
sky	skies
curry	curries
strawberry	strawberries
theory	theories

If a noun ends in -y after a vowel, just add -s.

Singular Noun	Plural Noun
kidney	kidney
chimney	chimneys
decoy	decoys
highway	highways

Some words that end in -f or -fe form their plurals differently. You must change the f or fe to v and add -es.

Singular Noun	Plural Noun
leaf	leaves
afterlife	afterlives
half	halves
midwife	midwives

Words that end in *-ff* form their plurals by simply adding *-s*.

Singular Noun	Plural Noun
spinoff	spinoffs
whiff	whiffs
tariff	tariffs

Some words that end in a single *-f* can form their plurals either way.

Singular Noun	Plural Noun
turf	turfs/turves
scarf	scarfs/scarves

If a noun ends in *-o* after a vowel, just add *-s*.

Singular Noun	Plural Noun
bamboo	bamboos
duo	duos
ratio	ratios
stereo	stereos

If a noun ends in *-o* after a consonant, form the plural by adding *-es*.

Singular Noun	Plural Noun
potato	potatoes
mosquito	mosquitoes
domino	dominoes
buffalo	buffaloes

To form the plural of foreign words ending in *-o*, just add *-s*.

Singular Noun	Plural Noun
avocado	avocados
grotto	grottos
staccato	staccatos
tempo	tempo
palazzo	palazzos

Irregular plurals don't follow any of these rules!

Singular Noun	Irregular Plural Noun
tooth	teeth
louse	lice
trout	trout
axis	axes
baggage	baggage
dozen	dozen/dozens
swine	swine
ellipsis	ellipses

Exercise 22C: Plural Nouns

Complete the following excerpt by filling in the plural form of each noun in parentheses. The following passage is slightly adapted from *The Fatal Eggs*, by Mikhail Bulgakov.

"Undernourishment!"

The scientist was perfectly right. Vlas should have been fed with flour and the (toad) _toads_ with flour (weevil) _weevils_, but the disappearance of the former determined that of the latter likewise, and Persikov tried to shift the twenty surviving (specimen) _specimens_ of tree-(frog) _frogs_ onto a diet of (cockroach) _cockroaches_ ... Consequently, these last remaining specimens also had to be thrown into the rubbish (pit) _pits_ in the Institute yard. (Thing) _Things_ went from bad to worse. When Vlas died the Institute (window) _windows_ froze so hard that there were icy (scroll) _scrolls_ on the inside of the (pane) _panes_. The (rabbit) _rabbits_, (fox) _foxes_, (wolf) _wolves_, and (fish) _fish_ died, as well as every single grass-snake. Persikov brooded silently for days on end, then caught pneumonia, but did not die. When he recovered, he started coming to the Institute twice a week and in the round hall, where for some reason it was always five (degree) _degrees_ below freezing point irrespective of the temperature outside, he delivered a cycle of (lecture) _lectures_ on "The (Reptile) _Reptiles_ of the Torrid Zone" in galoshes, a fur cap with ear-(flap) _flaps_ and a scarf, breathing out white steam, to an audience of eight. The rest of the time he lay under a rug on the divan in Prechistenka, in a room with (book) _books_ piled up to the ceiling, coughing, gazing into the (jaw) _jaws_ of the fiery stove which Maria Stepanovna stoked with gilt (chair) _chairs_, and remembering the Surinam toad. But all (thing) _things_ come to an end. So it was with 'twenty and 'twenty-one, and in 'twenty-two a kind of reverse process began. Firstly, in place of the dear departed Vlas there appeared Pankrat, a young, but most promising zoological caretaker, and the Institute began to be heated again a little. Then in the summer with Pankrat's help Persikov caught fourteen common (toad) _toads_. The (terrarium) _terrariums_ came to life again... In 'twenty-three Persikov gave eight lectures a week, three at the Institute and five at the University, in 'twenty-four thirteen a week, not including the (one) _ones_ at workers' (school) _schools_, and in the spring of 'twenty-five distinguished himself by failing no less than seventy-six (student) _students_, all on (amphibian) _amphibians_. "What, you don't know the difference between amphibians and reptilia?" Persikov asked. "That's quite ridiculous, young man. Amphibia have no (kidney) _kidneys_. None at all. So there. You should be ashamed of yourself."

"Well, kindly retake the exam in the autumn," Persikov said politely and shouted cheerfully to Pankrat: "Send in the next one!" Just as amphibians come to life after a long drought, with the first heavy shower of rain, so Professor Persikov revived in 1926 when a joint Americano-Russian company built fifteen-story apartment (block) _blocks_ in the centre of Moscow, beginning at the corner of Gazetny Lane and Tverskaya, and 300 workers' (cottage) _cottages_ on the (outskirt) _outskirts_, each with eight (apartment) _apartments_, thereby putting an end once and for all to the terrible and ridiculous accommodation shortage which made life such a misery for Muscovites from 1919 to 1925.

You would not have recognised the Institute either. They painted it cream, equipped the amphibian room with a special water supply system, replaced all the plate glass with (mirror) _mirrors_ and donated five new (microscope) _microscopes_ , glass laboratory tables, some 2,000-amp arc lights, reflectors and museum (case) _cases_ .

— LESSON 23 —

Plural Nouns
Descriptive Adjectives
Possessive Adjectives
Contractions

Exercise 23A: Introduction to Possessive Adjectives

Read the following nouns. Choose a person that you know to possess each of the items. Write that person's name, an apostrophe, and an *s* to form a possessive adjective.

Note to Instructor: Even if the person's name ends in *-s*, the student should still add *'s* to form the possessive: "Marcus's football."

Example: Pablo   Pablo's   bicycle
                          [Name]'s   dog
                          [Name]'s   phone
                          [Name]'s   soccer ball
                          [Name]'s   bedroom
                          [Name]'s   bowl

Exercise 23B: Singular and Plural Possessive Adjective Forms

Fill in the chart with the correct forms. The first row is done for you. Both regular and irregular nouns are included.

Noun	Singular Possessive	Plural	Plural Possessive
backpack	backpack's	backpacks	backpacks'
glass	glass's	glasses	glasses'
city	city's	cities	cities'
man	man's	men	men's
tomato	tomato's	tomatoes	tomatoes'
ray	ray's	rays	rays'
ocean	ocean's	oceans	oceans'
gas	gas's	gases	gases'
wife	wife's	wives	wives'
mouse	mouse's	mice	mice's
roof	roof's	roofs	roofs'

Exercise 23C: Common Contractions

Drop the letters in grey print and write the contraction in the blank. The first one is done for you.

Full Form	Common Contraction	Full Form	Common Contraction
I am	I'm	they have	they've
who would	who'd	who has	who's
you had	you'd	it would	it'd
we are	we're	must not	mustn't
could have	could've	when is	when's
it will	it'll	how is	how's
had not	hadn't	why will	why'll
I would	I'd	might not	mightn't

— LESSON 24 —

Possessive Adjectives

Contractions

Compound Nouns

Exercise 24A: Using Possessive Adjectives Correctly

Cross out the incorrect word in parentheses.

(~~Your~~/ You're) missing (your/~~you're~~) keys.

(Their/~~They're~~) new house is the one (~~their~~/they're) building down the street.

(Yours/~~your's~~) is the blue cup next to (hers/~~she's~~).

(~~Its~~/It's) the cafe around the corner. You will see (its/~~it's~~) red awning.

My seat is next to (yours/~~your's~~) and in front of (his/~~he's~~).

(~~Its~~/It's) time for the dog to get (his/~~he's~~) vaccinations.

We wanted to watch (their/~~they're~~) show, but (~~their~~/they're) sold out of tickets.

If (~~your~~/you're) sleepy, I think that (your/~~you're~~) sleeping bag is next to (theirs/~~theres~~).

(Hers/~~She's~~) will be the last car to arrive. (~~Hers~~/She's) running late.

(~~Its~~/It's) a mystery which has never been solved. (Its/~~It's~~) resolution will be a relief!

Exercise 24B: Compound Nouns

Underline each simple subject once and each simple predicate (verb) twice. Circle each
  compound noun.

Many <u>people</u> <u>perished</u> because of the lack of (lifeboats) on the *Titanic*.

My sister-in-law was a taxi driver for twelve years.

Before our trip, we ate breakfast at sunrise

Can you find the train station?

I put my workbook on the bookshelf

We ate our takeout dinner in the dining room

It was the three-year-old's birthday!

The trial of the famous safecracker began today at the courthouse downtown

Exercise 24C: Plurals of Compound Nouns

Write the plural of each singular compound noun in parentheses in the blanks to complete
the sentences.

Every year during our camping trip, all the (grown-up) _grown-ups_ and kids in our family pick
(blackberry) _blackberries_ .

The recipe called for two (handful) _handfuls_ of chocolate chips.

All of my (hairbrush) _hairbrushes_ are missing!

My community's pool has three (diving board) _diving boards_ and two (concession stand)
concession stands .

The group of (passerby) _passersby_ kindly helped with our flat tire.

All of the (five-year-old) _five-year-olds_ were scooping up (bucketful) _bucketfuls_ of sand on
the beach.

Both (father-in-law) _fathers-in-law_ lit the (candlestick) _candlesticks_ that were on the
wedding tables.

The awards were given to the winner and both (runner-up) _runners-up_ .

— REVIEW 2 —
Weeks 4-6

Topics
Simple, Progressive, and Perfect Tenses
Conjugations
Irregular Verbs
Subject/Verb Agreement
Possessives
Compound Nouns
Contractions

Review 2A: Verb Tenses

Write the tense of each underlined verb phrase on the line in the right-hand margin: *simple past, present*, or *future*; *progressive past, present*, or *future*; or *perfect past, present*, or *future*. Watch out for words that interrupt verb phrases but are not helping verbs (such as *not*).

These sentences are adapted from Frances Hodgson Burnett's *A Little Princess*.

	Verb Tense
"Oh, I never had such a dream before." She scarcely <u>dared</u> to stir; but at last she <u>pushed</u> the bedclothes aside, and put her feet on the floor with a rapturous smile.	simple past
	simple past
"I <u>am dreaming</u>—I am getting out of bed," she <u>heard</u> her own voice say;	progressive present
	simple past
"I don't know who it is," she <u>said</u>; "but somebody <u>cares</u> for me a little. I have a friend."	simple past
	simple present
"You must introduce me and I <u>will introduce</u> you," said Sara. "But I knew her the minute I <u>saw</u> her—so perhaps she knew me, too."	simple future
	simple past
"Yes, little Sara, it is. We <u>have reached</u> it at last." And though she was only seven years old, she <u>knew</u> that he felt sad when he said it.	perfect present
	simple past
The fact was, however, that she <u>was dreaming</u> and thinking odd things… about grown-up people and the world they <u>belonged</u> to.	progressive past
	simple past
"She <u>says</u> it has nothing to do with what you look like, or what you have. It has only to do with what you THINK of, and what you <u>DO</u>."	simple present
	simple present
"The streets <u>are shining</u>, and there are fields and fields of lilies, and everybody <u>gathers</u> them."	progressive present
	simple present

He <u>had made</u> wonderful preparations for her birthday. Among other things, he <u>had ordered</u> a new doll in Paris.

perfect past

perfect past

"Miss Minchin knows she <u>will have worked</u> for nothing. It <u>was</u> rather nasty of you, Lavvy, to tell about her having fun in the garret."

perfect future

simple past

"You <u>will go</u> to a nice house where there will be a lot of little girls, and you will play together, and I <u>will send</u> you plenty of books...."

simple future

simple future

"She <u>has locked</u> herself in, and she <u>is</u> not <u>making</u> the least particle of noise."

perfect present

progressive present

And the streets <u>are shining</u>. And people are never tired, however far they <u>walk</u>. They can float anywhere they like.

progressive present

simple present

She only <u>said</u> the kind of thing little girls always <u>say</u> to each other by way of beginning an acquaintance, but there <u>was</u> something friendly about Sara, and people always felt it.

simple past

simple present

simple past

Review 2B: Verb Formations

Fill in the charts with the correct conjugations of the missing verbs. Identify the person of each group of verbs.

PERSON: _Third_

	Past	**Present**	**Future**
SIMPLE	she worried	she worries	she will worry
PROGRESSIVE	she was worrying	she is worrying	she will be worrying
PERFECT	she had worried	she has worried	she will have worried

PERSON: _First_

	Past	**Present**	**Future**
SIMPLE	I whistled	I whistle	I will whistle
PROGRESSIVE	I was whistling	I am whistling	I will be whistling
PERFECT	I had whistled	I have whistled	I will have whistled

PERSON: _Second_

	Past	**Present**	**Future**
SIMPLE	you wondered	you wonder	you will wonder
PROGRESSIVE	you were wondering	you are wondering	you will be wondering
PERFECT	you had wondered	you have wondered	you will have wondered

PERSON: ___Third___

	Past	Present	Future
SIMPLE	they guessed	they guess	they will guess
PROGRESSIVE	they were guessing	they are guessing	they will be guessing
PERFECT	they had guessed	they have guessed	they will have guessed

Review 2C: Person and Subject/Verb Agreement

Cross out the incorrect verb in parentheses.

Do I not (~~destroys~~/destroy) my enemies when I (~~makes~~/make) them my friends?
    —Abraham Lincoln

Remember always that you not only (~~has~~/have) the right to be an individual, you (~~has~~/have) the obligation to be one.
    —Eleanor Roosevelt

Whoever (is/~~are~~) happy will make others happy, too.
    —Anne Frank

She (walks/~~walk~~) in beauty like the night/Of cloudless climes and starry skies.
    —Lord Byron

I (~~likes~~/like) these plants that you (~~calls~~/call) weeds.
    —Lucy Larcom

You (~~has~~/have) brains in your head. You (~~has~~/have) feet in your shoes. You can steer yourself any direction you (~~chooses~~/choose).
    —Dr. Seuss

Forgiveness (is/~~are~~) the attribute of the strong.
    —Mahatma Gandhi

How glorious a greeting the sun (gives/~~give~~) the mountains!
    —John Muir

The sun (looks/~~look~~) down on nothing half so good as a household laughing together over a meal.
    —C. S. Lewis

We (~~was~~/were) scared, but our fear (was/~~were~~) not as great as our courage.
    —Malala Yousafzai

I (~~believes~~/believe) every human has a finite number of heartbeats. I don't intend to waste any of mine.
    — Neil Armstrong

Review 2D: Possessives and Compound Nouns

Complete the chart below, writing the singular possessive, plural, and plural possessive of each singular pronoun or compound noun. The first one has been done for you.

Noun	Possessive	Plural	Plural Possessive
professor	professor's	professors	professors'
chairperson	chairperson's	chairpersons	chairpersons'
he	his	they	theirs
book	book's	books	books'
you	your	you	your
wolf	wolf's	wolves	wolves'
deer	deer's	deer	deer's
I	my	we	our
dragonfly	dragonfly's	dragonflies	dragonflies'
bedroom	bedroom's	bedrooms	bedrooms'
it	its	they	their
class	class's	classes	classes'
she	her	they	their
schoolbus	schoolbus's	schoolbuses	schoolbuses'

Review 2E: Plurals and Possessives

In the following sentences, provide the possessive, the plural, or the plural possessive for each noun in parentheses as indicated. These sentences are from *The Swiss Family Robinson*, by Johann David Wyss.

The forest still extended about a (stone, singular, possessive) _stone's_ throw to our right, and Fritz, who was always on the look-out for (discovery, plural) _discoveries_ observed a remarkable tree, here and there, which he approached to examine; and he soon called me to see this wonderful tree, with (wen, plural) _wens_ growing on the trunk.

In the (captain, singular, possessive) _captain's_ cabin we found some (service, plural) _services_ of silver, pewter (plate, plural) _plates_ and (dish, plural) _dishes_, and a small chest filled with bottles of choice wines. All these we took, as well as a chest of (eatable, plural) _eatables_, intended for the (officer, plural, possessive) _officers'_ table.

I had looked at (Jack, singular, possessive) _Jack's_ site for the bridge, and thought my little architect very happy in his selection; but it was at a great distance from the timber. I recollected the simplicity of the harness the (Laplander, plural) _Laplanders_ used for their reindeer. I tied (cord, plural) _cords_ to the (horn, plural) _horns_ of the cow.

She wanted, also, some wild (fowl, plural, possessive) _fowls'_ (egg, plural) _eggs_ to set under her (hen, plural) _hens_. Francis wished for some (sugarcane, plural) _sugarcane or sugarcanes_.

Then, with the hatchet making an opening at each end, we took (wedge, plural) _wedges_ and (mallet, plural) _mallets_, and the wood being tolerably soft, after four (hour, plural possessive) _hours'_ labour, we succeeded in splitting it completely.

I slept on moss and cotton in Mr. (Willis, singular, possessive) _Willis's_ room, with my two younger (son, plural) _sons_ . Everyone was content, waiting till our (arrangement, plural) _arrangements_ had been completed.

However, I assured her, our new guest would need no attention, as he would provide for himself at the river-side, feeding on small (fish, plural) _fishes_ , (worm, plural) _worms_ , and (insect, plural) _insects_ .

Fritz and I then, with a chisel and small axe, made an opening about three (foot, plural) _feet_ square, below the (bee, plural possessive) _bees'_ entrance.

Review 2F: Contractions

In the following sentences, form contractions from the words in parentheses. These sentences are adapted from *Violets and Other Tales*, by Alice Moore Dunbar-Nelson.

" _I'm_ (I am) so warm and tired," cried Mama Hart plaintively.

" _You'd_ (You had) better come with us, Flo. _You're_ (You are) wasting time."

Still, for all the suffering _I've_ (I have) experienced, _I'd_ (I would) be willing to go through it all again just to go over those five months.

There's (There is) none I place above you.

I _can't_ (cannot) imagine where you get your meddlesome ways from.

"Dinner! _Who's_ (Who has) got time to fool with dinner this evening?"

"Maybe _it'll_ (it will) snow," he muttered.

"Then _won't_ (will not) I have fun! Ugh, but the wind blows!"

"Gracious man, _we've_ (we have) tried."

And _he'll_ (he will) be the victor longer than anyone else.

" _She's_ (She is) a good girl, that Lillian."

"Besides, we must. _It's_ (It is) late, and you _couldn't_ (could not) find your crowd."

"Why, my Louis says _they're_ (they are) putting canvas cloths on the floor."

" _They'll_ (They will) never miss you; _we'll_ (we will) get you a rig."

" _Let's_ (Let us) go on!"

There were tears in her eyes, hot, blinding ones that _wouldn't_ (would not) drop for pride.

I wonder what _he's_ (he is) up to now.

There _isn't_ (is not) much warmth in a bit of a jersey coat.

There _wasn't_ (was not) one of us who imagined we would have only to knock ever so faintly on the portals of fame and they would fly wide for our entrance into the magic realms.

WEEK 7

Compounds and Conjunctions

— LESSON 25 —

Contractions
Compound Nouns
Diagramming Compound Nouns
Compound Adjectives
Diagramming Adjectives
Articles

Exercise 25A: Contractions Review

Write the two words that form each contraction on the blanks to the right. Some contractions have more than one correct answer. The first is done for you.

Contraction	Helping Verb	Other Word
he'll	will	he
wasn't	was	not
I'll	will	I
wouldn't	would	not
you're	are	you
isn't	is	not
who're	are	who
didn't	did	not
you've	have	you

Exercise 25B: Diagramming Adjectives and Compound Nouns

On your own paper, diagram every word of the following sentences.

Sydney's fishtank bubbled.

A tiny music box played.

58

My dishwasher broke.

The mayor-elect spoke.

Exercise 25C: Compound Nouns

Using the list of words below, make as many single-word compound nouns as you can. Many words in this list can be used twice or more.

Column A	Column B	
hair	world	hairstyle
swim	ache	swimsuit
back	style	backbone
tooth	paper	toothache
wall	take	wallpaper
under	bone	underworld
out	suit	outtake

Exercise 25D: Compound Adjectives

Correctly place hyphens in the following phrases.

fifty-two weeks

cold-blooded animal

a five-year winning streak

the three-page well-written paper

a middle-aged person

a strong-willed toddler

the brightly-lit soccer field

Exercise 25E: Diagramming Adjectives, Compound Nouns, and Compound Adjectives

On your own paper, diagram every word in the following sentences. These are adapted from *The Magical Land of Noom*, by Johnny Gruelle.

A pale blueish-green tint slanted.

The homemade Flying Machine disappeared.

The soft-voiced cow was eating.   A steady buzz-buzz grew.

All pretty fairy tales end.

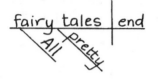

— LESSON 26 —

Compound Subjects
The Conjunction *And*
Compound Predicates
Compound Subject-Predicate Agreement

Exercise 26A: Identifying Subjects, Predicates, and Conjunctions

Underline the subjects once and the predicates twice in each sentence. Circle the conjunctions that join them. The first one is done for you.

These sentences are adapted from Solomon Northup's *Twelve Years a Slave*.

With the return of spring, Anne (and) I conceived the project of taking a farm in the neighborhood.

We reached that city before dark, (and) stopped at a hotel southward from the Museum.

Towards evening, on the first day of the calm, Arthur (and) I were in the bow of the vessel.

The roar of cannon (and) the tolling of bells filled the air.

I bowed my head upon my fettered hands, (and) wept most bitterly.

Pen, ink, (and) paper were furnished.

Exercise 26B: Diagramming Compound Subjects and Predicates

Draw one line under the subject[s] and two lines under the predicate[s] in the following sentences. Circle any conjunctions that connect subjects and/or predicates. When you are finished, diagram the subjects, predicates, and conjunctions ONLY of each sentence on your own paper.

These sentences are adapted from "Maese Perez, the Organist," by Gustavo Adolfo Becquer. Translated by Rollo Ogden.

The confusion (and) clangor lasted a few seconds.

The two women turned (and) disappeared.

I went to the choir (and) opened the door.

The Mother Superior (and) the nuns rushed to the organ-loft.

The organ gave a strange sound (and) was silent.

Light (and) sound were expressed by the organ's hundred voices.

Exercise 26C: Forming Compound Subjects and Verbs

Combine each of these sets of simple sentences into one sentence with a compound subject and/or a compound predicate joined by *and*. Use your own paper.

The ducks waddle in the yard.
The ducks eat insects in the yard.

> The ducks waddle and eat insects in the yard.

The nurse takes my temperature.
The nurse gives me medicine.
The nurse checks my blood pressure.

> The nurse takes my temperature, gives me medicine, and checks my blood pressure.

Matteo toured the exhibit at the museum.
Lucia toured the exhibit at the museum.
Martina toured the exhibit at the museum.

> Matteo, Lucia, and Martina toured the exhibit at the museum.

During the storm, rain fell from the sky.
During the storm, hail fell from the sky.

> During the storm, rain and hail fell from the sky.

The glass blower heated the glass.
The glass blower rolled the glass.
The glass blower shaped the glass.

> The glass blower heated, rolled, and shaped the glass.

Exercise 26D: Subject-Verb Agreement with Compound Subjects

Choose the correct verb in parentheses to agree with the subject. Cross out the incorrect verb.

The veterinarian and her assistant (talk/~~talks~~) calmly to the nervous puppy.

The assistant (~~pet~~/pets) the puppy while the vet carefully (~~give~~/gives) the vaccination.

While the puppy (~~chew~~/chews) on a treat, the vet and her assistant (examine/~~examines~~) him.

After the assistant (~~weigh~~/weighs) the puppy, the vet (~~make~~/makes) notes on the chart.

Before the puppy leaves, the vet and her assistant (inform/~~informs~~) the animal's owner that the puppy is healthy.

The owner and his puppy (walk/~~walks~~) out of the office and (get/~~gets~~) in the car to drive home.

— LESSON 27 —

Coordinating Conjunctions
Complications in Subject-Predicate Agreement

Exercise 27A: Using Conjunctions

Fill the blanks in the sentences below with the appropriate conjunctions. You must use each conjunction (*and, or, nor, for, so, but, yet*) at least once. (There is more than one possible answer for many of the blanks!)

These sentences are adapted from *Among the Meadow People*, by Clara Dillingham Pierson.

> **Note to Instructor:** The answers below are the conjunctions found in the original text, but you should accept any conjunction that makes sense, as long as the student uses each conjunction at least once.

I have been telling the Daisies and the Cardinals that they should grow in such a place, __but__ they wouldn't listen to me.

One may have a comfortable home, kind neighbors, and plenty to eat, __yet__ if he is in the habit of thinking disagreeable thoughts, not even all these good things can make him happy.

During the days when the four beautiful green-blue eggs lay in the nest, Mrs. Robin stayed quite closely at home. She said it was a very good place, __for__ she could keep her eggs warm and still see all that was happening.

The Robin on the fence huddled down into a miserable little bunch, __and__ thought: "They don't care whether I ever have anything to eat. No, they don't!"

When you have lived as long as I have, you will know that neither Grasshoppers __nor__ Tree Frogs can have their way all the time.

That was much pleasanter than having to grow up all alone, as most young Frog-Hoppers do, never seeing their fathers and mothers __or__ knowing whether they ever would.

The more he thought about it the more he squirmed, until suddenly he heard a faint little sound, too faint for larger people to hear, __and__ found a tiny slit in the wall of his chrysalis.

Still it had held him for eight days already and that was as long as any of his family ever hung in the chrysalis, __so__ it was quite time for it to be torn open and left empty.

She loved her babies so that she almost disliked to see them grow up, __yet__ she knew it was right for them to leave the nest.

If they heard their father __or__ their mother flying toward them, they would stretch up their necks and open their mouths.

You can just fancy what a good time the baby Spiders had. There were a hundred and seventy of them, __so__ they had no chance to grow lonely, even when their mother was away.

He thought this, __but__ he didn't say it.

Exercise 27B: Subject-Predicate Agreement: Troublesome Subjects

Circle the correct verb in parentheses so that it agrees with the subject noun or pronoun in number.

Six miles (is / are) the distance of the race.

Three-fourths of the cake (was / were) eaten by the children.

The horses or the donkey (grazes / graze) in the field.

Jerry's cheerleading squad (has / have) won the championship!

This batch of muffins (smell / smells) delicious!

The baseball team (run / runs) laps every day before practice.

Ten pounds of produce (weigh / weighs) too much for this bag.

Five bottles of juice (is / are) divided among the students.

One cup of chocolate chips (need / needs) to go into the batter.

The jury (vote / votes) on the verdict today.

My aunt and uncle (visit/ visits) us each summer, and our whole family (stay /stays) at the beach together.

One-half of the Lego pieces (was /were) dumped across the table.

The rabbit in the bushes (hide/hides) from predators.

The flock of geese (scatter/ scatters) across the field.

The flock of geese (fly /flies) in a formation.

She and her friends (organize/ organizes) a charity auction each year.

Exercise 27C: Fill in the Verb

Choose a verb or verb phrase that makes sense to complete each sentence. Put that verb or verb phrase in the present tense. Be sure the verb or verb phrase agrees in number with its subject!

> **Note to Instructor:** Sample answers are inserted below, but accept any reasonable answer as long as it is in the correct person and number (indicated in parentheses after each sentence).

The boat in the waves __rocks__ wildly during the storm. **(3rd-person singular)**

The plot of vegetables __grows__ during the summer. **(3rd-person singular)**

Sixty dollars __is__ too much for that game. **(3rd-person singular)**

The students' essays about the short story __contain__ interesting thoughts. **(3rd-person plural)**

The chickens in the coop __cluck__ all day long. **(3rd-person plural)**

Those pickles in the jar __taste__ like homemade. **(3rd-person plural)**

A sample of cheeses __is__ the appetizer. **(3rd-person singular)**

The plates or the platter __sits__ on the shelf. **(3rd-person singular)**

Two-thirds of the class __takes__ the test. **(3rd-person singular)**

— LESSON 28 —
Further Complications in Subject-Predicate Agreement

Exercise 28A: Subject-Verb Agreement: More Troublesome Subjects

Find the correct verb (agrees with the subject in number) in parentheses. Cross out the incorrect verb.

The Wind in the Willows (is /are) her favorite book.

Each of the paintings (hang/ hangs) in a different part of the museum.

Highlights (is /are) a magazine for children.

Statistics (is/~~are~~) my favorite class.

Thirty percent of the team (~~practice~~/practices) every weekday.

The popular British dish of fish and chips (~~taste~~/tastes) delicious with malt vinegar.

There (~~is~~/are) three packages in the mailbox.

Every one of the performers (~~take~~/takes) a bow.

Checkers (is/~~are~~) an easy game to learn.

Pliers (belong/~~belongs~~) in this tool box.

Here under the bed (~~is~~/are) the missing library books.

Physics (has/~~have~~) to be taken before you graduate.

Cacti (contain/~~contains~~) water which many animals use.

The Philippines (~~celebrate~~/celebrates) Independence Day on June 12.

Ellipses (mark/~~marks~~) a missing portion of a quote.

Anne of Green Gables (~~take~~/takes) place in Prince Edward Island, Canada.

There (is/~~are~~) a new movie I want to see.

Every one of the women (~~own~~/owns) a small business.

Bangers and mash (~~appear~~/appears) on many menus in Scotland.

Each of the fonts (~~show~~/shows) up differently on the screen.

Exercise 28B: Correct Verb Tense and Number

Complete each of these sentences by writing the correct number and tense of the verb indicated in the blank. The sentences are adapted from Harriet Pyne Grove's *Greycliff Wings*.

There [simple present of *am*] _is_ her letter, Virgie. I forgot to tell you to read it.

Then she laughed. "Please forgive me, Miss West, I did not realize what I [progressive past of *say*] _was saying_ ."

"There [simple present of *am*] _are_ so many places about the campus that would make a fine setting."

A vineyard of well-trained grape-vines [simple past of *am*] _was_ on a slope and stretched for quite a distance.

"I suppose that shed or something down there [simple present of *am*] _is_ for the hydroplane."

The black letters of the name [progressive past of *show*] _were showing_ clearly against a pearl-grey side.

The glasses [simple past of *am*] __were__ all focused upon the little hollow before them, Hilary's face growing brighter as she watched.

Remember to keep your wits about you and feel that the game depends on how well each of you [simple present of *play*] __plays__ .

Early after lunch, a number of girls [simple past of *start*] __started__ off for their ride.

A procession of worn, dusty men [progressive past of *march*] __were marching__ away toward the camp.

Two or three of the girls [progressive present of *rush*] __are rushing__ to help Hilary up.

Neither Lilian or I [simple present of *appear*] __appear__ really small enough for fairies, but in the costumes we look smaller.

Juniors and seniors on the bank [progressive past of *hold*] __were holding__ their breath.

WEEK 8

Introduction to Objects

— LESSON 29 —

Action Verbs
Direct Objects

Exercise 29A: Direct Objects

In the following sentences, underline the subjects once and the predicates twice. Circle each direct object.

Ancient <u>Egyptians</u> <u>were building</u> (pyramids) around 2780 BC.

The <u>workers</u> <u>used</u> (limestone) and (granite) for the structures.

<u>They</u> <u>carved</u> the (stone) with chisels.

<u>Laborers</u> <u>dragged</u> immense, heavy (stones) to the building site with sleds.

After a pharaoh's death, <u>embalmers</u> <u>mummified</u> the pharaoh's (body)

Often, the <u>embalmers</u> <u>would mummify</u> the pharaoh's (pets), too.

<u>Craftspeople</u> <u>placed</u> (furniture) and (treasures) into the pyramid.

The <u>pharaoh</u> and his <u>family</u> <u>would need</u> these (items) in the afterlife.

Egyptian <u>culture</u> <u>valued</u> the (afterlife)

<u>Workers</u> and <u>priests</u> <u>laid</u> the pharaoh's (body) inside the pyramid.

The <u>priests</u> <u>sealed</u> the (tomb)

Sadly, many tomb <u>robbers</u> <u>opened</u> the (pyramids)

<u>They</u> <u>stole</u> (jewels) (gold) and (silver)

In 1923, archaeologist <u>Howard Carter</u> <u>discovered</u> King Tut's (tomb) and <u>found</u> valuable (items)

<u>He</u> and his <u>team</u> <u>recovered</u> many important (artifacts)

Exercise 29B: Diagramming Direct Objects

On your own paper, diagram the subjects, verbs, and direct objects ONLY in the sentences from Exercise 29A.

Ancient Egyptians were building pyramids around 2780 BC.

Egyptians | were building | pyramids

The workers used limestone and granite for the structures.

workers | used | limestone
and granite

They carved the stone with chisels.

They | carved | stone

Laborers dragged immense, heavy stones to the building site with sleds.

Laborers | dragged | stones

After a pharaoh's death, embalmers mummified the pharaoh's body.

embalmers | mummified | body

Often, the embalmers would mummify the pharaoh's pets, too.

embalmers | would mummify | pets

Craftspeople placed furniture and treasures into the pyramid.

Craftspeople | placed | furniture
and treasures

The pharaoh and his family would need these items in the afterlife.

pharaoh
family | and | would need | items

Egyptian culture valued the afterlife.

culture | valued | afterlife

Workers and priests laid the pharaoh's body inside the pyramid.

workers
priests | and | laid | body

The priests sealed the tomb.

priests | sealed | tomb

Sadly, many tomb robbers opened the pyramids.

robbers | opened | pyramids

They stole jewels, gold, and silver.

They | stole | jewels
and gold
silver

In 1923, archaeologist Howard Carter discovered King Tut's tomb and found valuable items.

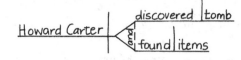

Howard Carter | discovered | tomb
and found | items

He and his team recovered many important artifacts.

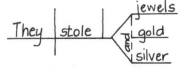

He
team | and | recovered | artifacts

— LESSON 30 —

Direct Objects
Prepositions

Exercise 30A: Identifying Prepositions

In the following sentences (adapted from "The Monkey and the Crocodile," in *Jataka Tales*, retold by Ellen C. Babbitt), find and circle each preposition.

The monkey soon moved away (from) that tree. But the Crocodile found him, far (down) the river, living (in) another tree. (In) the middle (of) the river was an island covered (with) fruit-trees.

Half-way (between) the bank (of) the river and the island, a large rock rose (from) the water. The Monkey could jump (to) the rock, and then (to) the island. The Crocodile watched the Monkey crossing (from) the bank (of) the river (to) the rock, and then (to) the island.

He thought (to) himself, "The Monkey will stay (on) the island all day, and I'll catch him (on) his way home (at) night."

The Monkey had a fine feast, while the Crocodile swam, watching him (during) the day.

Exercise 30B: Word Relationships

The following sentences all contain action verbs. Underline each subject once and each action verb twice. If the sentence has an action verb followed by a direct object, write *DO* above the direct object.

If the sentence contains a preposition, circle the preposition and draw a line to connect the two words that the preposition shows a relationship between. The first two are done for you.

The geese (near) the lake honked noisily.

Savannah likes popcorn (with) butter.

Five tiny caterpillars ate the leaves (of) the milkweed plants.

Jonatan bakes fresh bread every Saturday.

We visited the park (under) the St. Louis Arch.

The scariest scene (of) the movie is happening now!

(After) class, Jayden and Naveah taught the new choreography.

Ali was fishing (from) the new pier.

Is Roma coming (to) the class?

The lime slushy spilled (on) the seat.

The *Mona Lisa* hangs (in) the Louvre.

Did you find your phone yet? (DO)

Exercise 30C: Diagramming Direct Objects

On your own paper, diagram the subjects, predicates, and direct objects ONLY from the sentences above. If a sentence does not have a direct object, do not diagram it.

Savannah likes popcorn with butter.

Savannah | likes | popcorn

Jonatan bakes fresh bread every Saturday.

Jonatan | bakes | bread

After class, Jayden and Naveah taught the new choreography.

Jayden / Naveah | taught | choreography

Five tiny caterpillars ate the leaves of the milkweed plants.

caterpillars | ate | leaves

We visited the park under the St. Louis Arch.

We | visited | park

Did you find your phone yet?

you | Did find | phone

— LESSON 31 —

Definitions Review
Prepositional Phrases
Object of the Preposition

Exercise 31A: Objects of Prepositional Phrases

Fill in the blanks with a noun as the object of the preposition to complete the prepositional phrases.

Note to Instructor: Answers will vary. Suggestions are provided.

The cat's favorite spot is by the ___couch___ .

Under the ___bed___ , Mom found the missing book.

The whole family hiked to the ___waterfall___ .

Matt puts ketchup on his ___eggs___ .

A large bear was spotted near the ___campsite___ .

Will Mia sing during the ___concert___ ?

Exercise 31B: Identifying Prepositional Phrases

Can you find all eleven of the prepositional phrases in the following excerpt, adapted from "The Four Dragons," a traditional Asian folktale?

Underline each complete prepositional phrase. Circle each preposition. Draw a box around each object of a preposition.

The four dragons went happily back. But ten days passed, and not a drop of rain came down. The people suffered more, some eating bark, some grass roots. Seeing all of this, the four dragons felt very sorry, and they knew the Jade Emperor only cared about pleasure, and never took the people to heart. They could only rely upon themselves and could relieve the people of their miseries. But how? Seeing the vast sea, the Long Dragon said that he had an idea.

"What is it? Out with it, quickly!" the other three demanded.

"Look, is there not plenty of water in the sea where we live? We should scoop it and spray it toward the sky. The water will be rain drops and will save the people and their crops," said Long Dragon.

"Good idea!" said the others as they clapped their hands with joy.

Exercise 31C: Remembering Prepositions

Can you remember all forty-six prepositions without looking back at your list? The first letter of each preposition has been given for you.

A	B	D	E	F	I	L
aboard	before	down	except	for	in	like
about	behind	during		from	inside	
above	below				into	
across	beneath					
after	beside					
against	between					
along	beyond					
among	by					
around						
at						

N	**O**	**P**	**S**	**T**	**U**	**W**
near	of	past	since	through	under	with
	off			throughout	underneath	within
	on			to	until	without
	over			toward	up	
					upon	

— LESSON 32 —

Subjects, Predicates, and Direct Objects
Prepositions
Object of the Preposition
Prepositional Phrases

Exercise 32A: Identifying Prepositional Phrases and Parts of Sentences

In the following sentences, circle each prepositional phrase. Once you have identified the prepositional phrases, underline subjects once, underline predicates twice, and label direct objects with *DO*.

Things to watch out for:

1) Words that could be prepositions but are acting as other parts of speech instead. If it doesn't have an object, it's not a preposition!

2) In some of these sentences, subjects and predicates are inverted so that the predicate comes first. Find the verb first, then ask, "Who or what [verb]?" to find the subject. Remember that the subject will not be the object of a preposition!

These sentences are adapted from "The Story of Ali Cogia, Merchant of Bagdad," a traditional Arab folktale. The first is done for you.

Ali Cogia lived (in Bagdad) and owned a shop. *DO*

He planned a journey (to Mecca) *DO*

He took a large vase, placed money in the bottom, filled it with olives, and carried it (to his friend) (for safekeeping) *DO DO DO DO*

(After many months) the friend (in Bagdad) looked (into the vase) and saw the gold. *DO*

He took the gold and hid it. *DO DO*

(After another month) Ali Cogia returned (to Bagdad) and asked (for his vase)

The <u>gold</u> <u>was missing</u> ⟨from the vase⟩

<u>Ali Cogia</u> <u>asked</u> ⟨for the truth⟩

The <u>merchant</u> <u>denied</u> the charge ⟨against him⟩
                  DO

⟨In the end⟩ the <u>truth</u> ⟨of the theft⟩ <u>was discovered</u> ⟨by a wise child's discerning questions⟩

Exercise 32B: Diagramming

On your own paper, diagram all of the uncircled parts of the sentences from Exercise 32A.

                         DO

<u>Ali Cogia</u> <u>lived</u> ⟨in Bagdad⟩ and <u>owned</u> a shop.

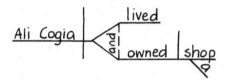

           DO

<u>He</u> <u>planned</u> a journey ⟨to Mecca⟩

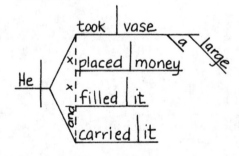

      DO   DO   DO   DO

<u>He</u> <u>took</u> a large vase, <u>placed</u> money ⟨in the bottom⟩ <u>filled</u> it ⟨with olives⟩ and <u>carried</u> it ⟨to his friend⟩ ⟨for safekeeping⟩

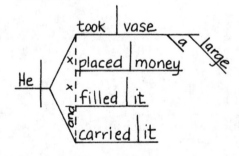

                                       DO

⟨After many months⟩ the <u>friend</u> ⟨in Bagdad⟩ <u>looked</u> ⟨into the vase⟩ and <u>saw</u> the gold.

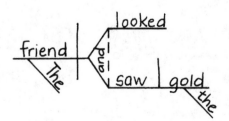

He took the gold and hid it.

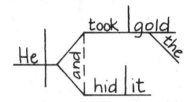

After another month Ali Cogia returned to Bagdad and asked for his vase

Ali Cogia < returned / asked

The gold was missing from the vase

gold | was missing
The

Ali Cogia asked for the truth

Ali Cogia | asked

The merchant denied the charge against him

merchant | denied | charge
The   the

In the end the truth of the theft was discovered by a wise child's discerning questions

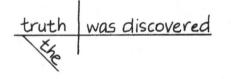

truth | was discovered
the

WEEK 9

Adverbs

— LESSON 33 —

Adverbs That Tell How

Exercise 33A: Identifying Adverbs That Tell *How*

Underline the adverbs telling how in the following sentences, and draw arrows to the verbs that they modify.

Amelia Earhart <u>famously</u> flew across the Atlantic Ocean, the first woman to do so.

She <u>quickly</u> became famous and began writing <u>honestly</u> about her experiences as a pilot.

Earhart <u>bravely</u> piloted from Honolulu to California in 1935, a risky journey.

She and Fred Noonan, an experienced navigator, <u>carefully</u> planned a new challenge: a flight around the world.

News organizations <u>excitedly</u> reported every step of the preparation for the trip.

Earhart had <u>skillfully</u> handled dangerous flying conditions on many occasions.

However, this trip would have many errors which caused the plane to drift <u>significantly</u> off course.

On July 2, 1937, a naval ship in the area received a radio transmission in which Earhart <u>briefly</u> described the plane's problems.

Besides being off course, the plane was <u>rapidly</u> running out of fuel.

<u>Tragically</u>, Earhart and Noonan disappeared that day. They were never found.

People <u>still</u> study how the pair <u>mysteriously</u> vanished. This event is considered an unsolved mystery of the modern era.

Exercise 33B: Forming Adverbs from Adjectives

Turn the following adjectives into adverbs.

Adjective	Adverb	Adjective	Adverb
rapid	rapidly	happy	happily
careful	carefully	generous	generously

Adjective	Adverb	Adjective	Adverb
easy	easily	merry	merrily
safe	safely	warm	warmly
powerful	powerfully		

Exercise 33C: Diagramming Adverbs

Diagram the following sentences on your own paper.

The baby goat leaps energetically.

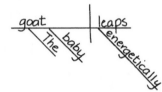

I quickly dropped the hot pan.

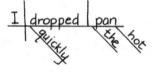

The movie ended abruptly.

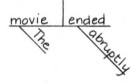

Did you listen intently?

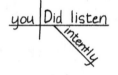

Anna slowly savored the warm cookie.

The chef deftly whisked the ingredients.

— LESSON 34 —

Adverbs That Tell When, Where, and How Often

Exercise 34A: Telling When

Martin dropped his recipe cards for crêpes. Help him get organized by numbering the following sentences from 1 to 6 so he can make the crêpes.

3	Whisk 1 1/2 cups of flour into the wet ingredients.
4	Pour only a few tablespoons of batter into the hot pan, and spread the batter around the pan in a thin layer.
6	Serve warm with either a sweet or savory filling.
1	First, preheat a buttered skillet or crêpe pan.
5	When bubbles start to form on the crêpe, flip it over and cook the other side.
2	While the butter is melting in the pan, beat two eggs with three cups of milk in a separate bowl.

Exercise 34B: Distinguishing Among Different Types of Adverbs

Put each of the following adverbs in the correct category, according to the question each one answers.

badly	safely	seldom	second
away	wearily	usually	soon
constantly	then	far	anywhere

When	**Where**	**How**	**How Often**
then	anywhere	badly	seldom
second	away	safely	usually
soon	far	wearily	constantly

Exercise 34C: Identifying Adverbs of Different Types

Underline the adverbs in the following sentences that tell *when*, *where*, or *how often*. For now, do not underline any prepositional phrases acting as adverbs.

The violinist bowed <u>first</u> and the concert began.

My dad makes homemade pizza <u>weekly</u>.

The team meets <u>downstairs</u>.

Emma's kitten destroyed the chair <u>immediately</u>.

<u>There</u> is a canoe by the dock.

Blizzards happen <u>rarely</u> in this part of the country.

Sylvia arrived <u>early</u> for the show.

Our vacation begins <u>tomorrow</u>.

Please take the trash <u>outside</u>.

<u>Here</u> are your keys.

Exercise 34D: Diagramming Different Types of Adverbs

Diagram the following sentences on your own paper.

The science students cleaned the lab
thoroughly yesterday.

Tonight, the play will end dramatically.

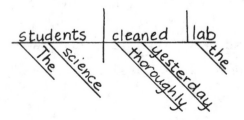

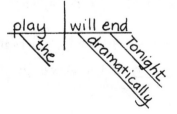

The lioness and her cubs stalked the prey silently.

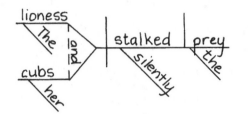

Marieke will run laps later and will eat a snack afterward.

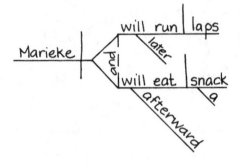

The delighted dog's tail wagged wildly.

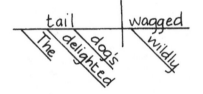

— LESSON 35 —

Adverbs That Tell To What Extent

Exercise 35A: Identifying the Words Modified by Adverbs

Draw an arrow from each underlined adverb to the word it modifies. These sentences are from Jules Verne's *An Antarctic Mystery*.

Desolation Islands is the only suitable name for this group of three hundred isles or islets in the midst of the vast expanse of ocean, which is <u>constantly</u> disturbed by austral storms.

"Cannot we talk <u>very</u> <u>well</u> here?" I observed.

I lived <u>there</u> for several weeks, and I can affirm, on the evidence of my own eyes and my own experience, that the famous English explorer and navigator was <u>happily</u> inspired when he gave the islands that significant name.

"My ship is not intended to carry passengers. I <u>never</u> have taken any, and I <u>never</u> intend to do so."

Captain Len Guy proved himself a true seaman, James West had an eye to everything, the crew seconded them <u>loyally</u>, and Hunt was <u>always</u> foremost when there was work to be done or danger to be incurred.

Hunt stepped back a few paces, shaking his head with the air of a man who did not want so many compliments for a thing so simple, and quietly walked forward to join his shipmates, who were working vigorously under the orders of West.

We had no longer to do with completely frozen vapor, but had to deal with the phenomenon called frost-rime, which often occurs in these high latitudes.

Success seemed very nearly assured, as the captain and the mate had worked out the matter so carefully and skilfully.

In my rambles on the shore, I frequently routed a crowd of amphibians, sending them plunging into the newly released waters.

Besides, when it came to the question of cooking, it mattered very little to him whether it was here or there, so long as his stoves were set up somewhere.

Patterson's note-book says nothing, nor does it relate under what circumstances he himself was carried far away from them.

More than five hundred thousand sheep yield over four hundred thousand dollars' worth of wool yearly.

With these words Captain Len Guy walked quickly away, and the interview ended differently from what I had expected, that is to say in formal, although polite, fashion.

Exercise 35B: Diagramming Different Types of Adverbs

Diagram the following sentences on your own paper.

Read the test instructions very carefully.

You must read the lines much more confidently.

Yesterday, some incredibly fragrant
roses bloomed.

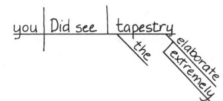

Matteo plays the classical guitar quite
skillfully.

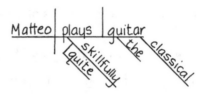

Did you see the extremely elaborate tapestry?

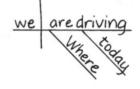

Where are we driving today?

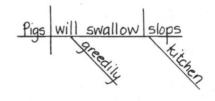

— LESSON 36 —

Adjectives and Adverbs
The Adverb *Not*
Diagramming Contractions
Diagramming Compound Adjectives and Compound Adverbs

Exercise 36A: Practice in Diagramming

On your own paper, diagram every word of the following sentences. They are adapted from *Home Life in All Lands*, by Charles Morris.

The pig finds the truffles and roots them eagerly.

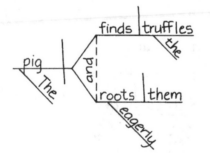

Pigs will swallow kitchen slops greedily.

Pigs actually prefer dry and clean sleep spaces.

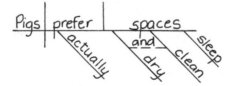

A cat's claws don't touch the ground.

The cat hunts quietly and cautiously.

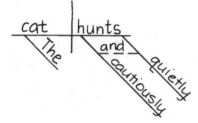

No mouse can pass it safely.

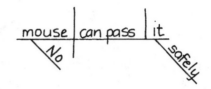

Various cattle breeds differ very much.

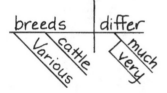

The goose can strike a strong and hard blow.

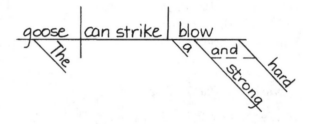

Geese can guard a farm and wake very easily.

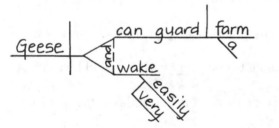

The goose's loud noises can rouse the entire household.

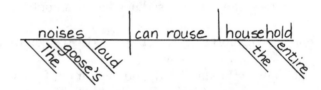

— REVIEW 3 —

Weeks 7-9

Topics

Parts of Speech
Compound Parts of Sentences
Prepositions
Prepositional Phrases
Objects of Prepositions
Subjects and Predicates
Subject-Verb Agreement
Verbs and Direct Objects

Review 3A: Parts of Speech

In the passage below from Henry David Thoreau's *Walden*, identify the underlined words as *N* for noun, *ADJ* for adjective, *ADV* for adverb, *PREP* for preposition, or *CONJ* for conjunction. The first is done for you.

         N   PREP   ADJ   ADJ
The <u>shore</u> is composed <u>of</u> a belt of smooth <u>rounded</u> <u>white</u> stones like paving stones, excepting

CONJ   ADJ   CONJ ADV   ADJ
one <u>or</u> two short <u>sand</u> beaches, <u>and</u> is <u>so</u> steep that in many places a <u>single</u> leap will carry you

PREP   PREP   N   N
<u>into</u> water <u>over</u> your <u>head</u>; and were it not for its remarkable <u>transparency</u>, that would be the last

                N   PREP   ADJ   ADV
to be seen of its <u>bottom</u> till it rose <u>on</u> the <u>opposite</u> side. Some think it is bottomless. It is <u>nowhere</u>

      CONJ   ADJ N   PREP   ADJ
muddy, <u>and</u> a casual observer would say that there were <u>no</u> <u>weeds</u> at all <u>in</u> it; and of <u>noticeable</u>

                            ADV   ADV
plants, except in the little meadows which <u>recently</u> overflowed, which do not <u>properly</u> belong to

          N   ADV   CONJ
it, a closer <u>scrutiny</u> does <u>not</u> detect a flag <u>nor</u> a bulrush, nor even a lily, yellow or white, but only

ADJ ADJ   CONJ
a <u>few</u> <u>small</u> heart-leaves and potamogetons, and perhaps a water-target <u>or</u> two; all which however

    N   ADV   ADJ
a <u>bather</u> might <u>not</u> perceive; and <u>these</u> plants are clean and bright like the element they grow

                       PREP   ADJ
in. The stones extend a rod or two <u>into</u> the water, and then the bottom is <u>pure</u> sand, except in

     ADJ   ADV   N   N
the <u>deepest</u> parts, where there is <u>usually</u> a little <u>sediment</u>, probably from the <u>decay</u> of the leaves

                      ADV ADJ   ADJ   ADV ADJ
which have been wafted on to it <u>so</u> <u>many</u> <u>successive</u> falls, and a <u>bright</u> <u>green</u> weed is brought up

PREP   N
<u>on</u> anchors even in <u>midwinter</u>.

Review 3B: Recognizing Prepositions

Circle the forty-six prepositions from your list in the following bank of words. Try to complete the exercise without looking back at your list of prepositions.

whose   (near)   there   that   (until)

   (with)   (in)   her   (on)   again

(before)   here   (around)   those   (across)

   (up)   (for)   (except)   but   (by)

item   (into)   (like)   yet   and

   (within)   very   nor   (under)   (of)

(behind)   was   (upon)   (from)   going

   (above)   (along)   of   (between)   begin

the   an   (since)   (past)   (to)

   (during)   (aboard)   (at)   this   (without)

(against)   what   if   (beneath)   (toward)

   (among)   (underneath)   (below)   (after)   while

either   an   (beside)   (about)   (beyond)

   my   (inside)   good   (off)

(throughout)   (down)   (through)   (over)   its

Review 3C: Subjects and Predicates

Draw one line under the simple subject and two lines under the simple predicate. Watch out for compound subjects or predicates! Also, remember that in poetry, sometimes the order of words is different than in normal speech—once you have found the verb, ask "who or what" before it to find the subject.

   The following lines are from the poem "The Lady of Shalott" by Alfred, Lord Tennyson.

The yellow-leaved <u>waterlily</u>, the green-sheathed <u>daffodilly</u> <u>tremble</u> in the water chilly.

The sunbeam <u>showers</u> <u>break</u> and <u>quiver</u>.

Four gray <u>walls</u> and four gray <u>towers</u> <u>overlook</u> a space of flowers.

A charmed web <u>she</u> <u>weaves</u> always.

Over the water near, the <u>sheepbell</u> <u>tinkles</u> in her ear.

Sometimes a <u>troop</u> of damsels glad, an <u>abbot</u> on an ambling pad, a curly shepherd <u>lad</u>, or long-hair'd <u>page</u> in crimson clad <u>goes</u> by to tower'd Camelot.

The <u>sun came</u> through the leaves, and <u>flamed</u> upon the brazen greaves of bold Sir Lancelot.

The <u>helmet</u> and the <u>helmet-feather</u> <u>burned</u> like one flame together.

The <u>mirror</u> <u>cracked</u> from side to side.

<u>She</u> <u>chanted</u> loudly, <u>chanted</u> lowly.

<u>She</u> <u>loosed</u> the chain, and down <u>she</u> <u>lay</u>.

Review 3D: Complicated Subject-Verb Agreement

Circle the correct verb form in parentheses.

The cupcake or the cookies (is / (are)) available for dessert.

The squadron ((cheers) / cheer) for the graduating officers.

Because of the intense storm, the herd (is / (are)) split up across the valley.

Three-fourths of the lights (has / (have)) gone out.

She decided that five dollars ((was) / were) too much for the coffee.

Ang and Dara (hands / (hand)) out water to the volunteers.

Where (is / (are)) the scissors?

A basket full of peaches ((sits) / sit) on the kitchen counter.

"Hansel and Gretel" ((tells) / tell) the story of a brother and sister who were lost in the forest.

Two-thirds of the apple ((has) / have) rotted.

Boxes for the delivery truck (sits / (sit)) on the porch.

Review 3E: Objects and Prepositions

Identify the underlined words as *DO* for direct object or *OP* for object of preposition. For each direct object, find and underline twice the action verb that affects it. For each object of a preposition, find and circle the preposition to which it belongs.

These sentences are from *Stella by Starlight*, by Sharon Draper.

Even Dusty was quiet, folded (at) her <u>feet</u>, [OP] but he <u>sniffed</u> the <u>air</u>, [DO] watchful and alert.

None (of) the <u>boys</u> [OP] in the school, not even those <u>taking</u> high school <u>classes</u>, [DO] could beat him (in) a <u>footrace</u>. [OP]

He <u>won</u> two gold <u>medals</u>[DO] in track(at)[OP] the <u>Olympics</u> this summer.

Stella said bye(to)[OP] <u>Tony</u> and <u>grabbed</u> a <u>broom</u>[DO] without being told.

Most every plank of pine wood(inside)[OP] the <u>house</u> was covered(with)[OP] old <u>newspapers</u>.

She <u>found</u> three fresh <u>eggs</u>[DO] and hightailed it back(to)[OP] the <u>warmth</u> of the house.

Maybe it was because she lived(in)such a small <u>speck</u>[OP] (of)a <u>town</u>[OP], and she liked how the newspaper helped her feel like she was part of something bigger.

"I'm the queen(of)the <u>world</u>[OP]!" she shouted(to)the <u>sky</u>[OP].

Mama <u>filled</u> Papa's <u>mug</u>[DO] back up. "It's chilly out there, Jonah," she said, deliberately <u>changing</u> the <u>subject</u>[DO].

WEEK 10

Completing the Sentence

— LESSON 37 —

Direct Objects
Indirect Objects

Exercise 37A: Identifying Direct Objects

Underline the action verbs and circle the direct objects in these sentences. Remember that you can always eliminate prepositional phrases first if that makes the task easier.

The sentences are adapted from R. J. Palacio's *Wonder*.

I like the (sound) of science.

I did not destroy a (Death Star) or (anything.)

At the beginning of every month, I will write a new (precept) on the chalkboard.

By the end of the year, you will have your own (list) of precepts.

Everyone in the world should get a standing (ovation) once in their lives.

Via kissed (Daisy) on the nose.

You would look up and see a billion (stars) in the sky.

Exercise 37B: Identifying Direct Objects and Indirect Objects

Underline the direct and indirect objects in the following sentences. Write *DO* for direct object and *IO* for indirect object. Remember, a sentence can have a *DO* without an *IO*.

Give your <u>sister</u> the <u>game</u>.
IO   DO

Rohan sent <u>Anika</u> a <u>text</u> about the party.
IO   DO

Mom baked <u>us</u> <u>muffins</u> for breakfast today.
IO DO

Is Aidan bringing the <u>book</u> after class?
DO

I sent my <u>grandmother</u> a <u>card</u> yesterday.
IO   DO

Please put the <u>ice cream</u> in the freezer.
IO

Gabrielle read her little <u>sister</u> a <u>story</u> before bedtime.
IO   DO

The director showed the <u>cast</u> a <u>movie</u> after practice.
IO   DO

Exercise 37C: Diagramming Direct Objects and Indirect Objects

On your own paper, diagram the following sentences.

Arianna drew me a lovely picture.

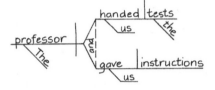

Read me the description.

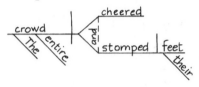

The professor handed us the tests and gave us instructions.

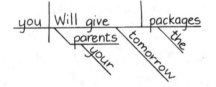

The entire crowd cheered and stomped their feet.

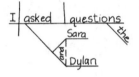

Kaito handed the children juice and snacks.

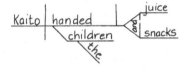

I asked Sara and Dylan the questions.

Will you give your parents the packages tomorrow?

— LESSON 38 —

State-of-Being Verbs

Linking Verbs
Predicate Adjectives

Exercise 38A: Action Verbs and Linking Verbs

In the following sentences, underline the subjects once and the predicates twice. If the predicate is a linking verb, write *LV* above it, circle the predicate adjective, and label it *PA*. If the predicate is an action verb, write *AV* above it, circle the direct object, if any, and label it *DO*. The first is done for you.

These sentences are slightly condensed from Rudyard Kipling's *Just So Stories*.

The Whale ate the starfish and the garfish

   LV   PA   PA
He was (grey) and (woolly)

    AV   DO   DO
They could see stripy (shadows) and blotched (shadows) in the forest.

       LV   PA
"They are too (clever) on the turbid Amazon for poor me!"

                LV PA   PA
The cabin port-holes are (dark) and (green)

            AV   AV   DO
His enemies were hiding in the bushes and would see (him)

                LV PA   PA
The Camel's hump is (black) and (blue)

       LV   PA
"The sun is very (hot) here."

                AV   DO
Can the Leopard change his (spots?)

              LV   PA   PA
The tree trunks were exclusively (speckled) and (sprottled)

                      LV PA   PA
Suleiman-bin-Daoud was (wise) and (strong)

      AV   DO   AV   DO
The Djinn took a (bearing) across the desert, and found the (Camel)

                    AV
His dear families went in a hurry to the banks of the great grey-green, greasy Limpopo River.

Exercise 38B: Diagramming Direct Objects and Predicate Adjectives

On your own paper, diagram ONLY the subjects, predicates, and direct objects or predicate adjectives (along with any conjunctions used to connect compounds) from the sentences in Exercise 38A.

        AV   DO   DO
The Whale ate the (starfish) and the (garfish)

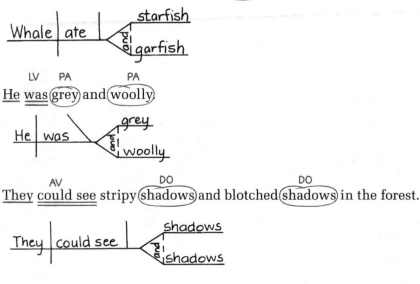

"They are too clever on the turbid Amazon for poor me!"

(LV: are; PA: clever)

Diagram:
```
They | are \ clever
```

The cabin port-holes are dark and green

(LV: are; PA: dark; PA: green)

Diagram:
```
                 dark
port-holes | are \ and
                  green
```

His enemies were hiding in the bushes and would see him

(AV: were hiding; AV: would see; DO: him)

Diagram:
```
         were hiding
enemies < and
         would see | him
```

The Camel's hump is black and blue

(LV: is; PA: black; PA: blue)

Diagram:
```
           black
hump | is \ and
           blue
```

"The sun is very hot here."

(LV: is; PA: hot)

Diagram:
```
sun | is \ hot
```

Can the Leopard change his spots?

(AV: change; DO: spots)

Diagram:
```
Leopard | Can change | spots
```

The tree trunks were exclusively speckled and sprottled

(LV: were; PA: speckled; PA: sprottled)

Diagram:
```
              speckled
trunks | were \ and
               sprottled
```

Suleiman-bin-Daoud was wise and strong

(LV: was; PA: wise; PA: strong)

Diagram:
```
                        wise
Suleiman-bin-Daoud | was \ and
                         strong
```

The <u>Djinn</u> <u>took</u> a (bearing) across the desert, and <u>found</u> the (Camel)

Djinn | took | bearing
       and found | Camel

His dear <u>families</u> <u>went</u> in a hurry to the banks of the great grey-green, greasy Limpopo River.

<u>families</u> | went

— LESSON 39 —

Linking Verbs
Predicate Adjectives
Predicate Nominatives

Exercise 39A: Identifying Predicate Nominatives and Adjectives

In the following sentences, underline the subjects once and the predicates twice. Circle the predicate nominatives or adjectives and label each one *PN* for predicate nominative or *PA* for predicate adjective. Draw a line from the predicate nominative or adjective to the subject that it renames or describes. There may be more than one of each.

<u>Crocodiles</u> <u>are</u> fascinating (animals). *PN*

These <u>animals</u> <u>are</u> (carnivorous) *PA*

<u>They</u> <u>are</u> incredibly fast (swimmers) and (hunters) *PN* *PN*

<u>Australia</u> <u>is</u> (home) to the freshwater crocodile. *PN*

Freshwater <u>crocodiles</u> <u>are</u> quite (bashful) *PA*

The freshwater crocodile's <u>diet</u> <u>is</u> mostly (insects) and (fish) *PN* *PN*

<u>Birds</u>, <u>mammals</u>, and <u>fish</u> <u>are</u> the preferred (food) of a saltwater crocodile. *PN*

Their <u>jaws</u> <u>are</u> (powerful) and (dangerous) *PA* *PA*

Exercise 39B: Writing Predicate Nominatives and Adjectives

Finish each sentence in two ways: with a predicate nominative and with a predicate adjective. If you need to use more than one word in a blank to complete your sentence, circle the word that is the predicate nominative or predicate adjective.

The first is done for you.

Note to Instructor: Sample answers are given. Answers may vary, but the important thing is that the student uses a noun or pronoun for the predicate nominative and an adjective for the predicate adjective.

Sewing is _____ my favorite (hobby) _____. (predicate nominative)

Sewing is _____ enjoyable _____. (predicate adjective)

The Belgian waffles were _____ our (breakfast) _____. (predicate nominative)

The Belgian waffles were _____ delicious _____. (predicate adjective)

The cure is _____ a (medication) _____. (predicate nominative)

The cure is _____ expensive _____. (predicate adjective)

Cucumbers are _____ vegetables _____. (predicate nominative)

Cucumbers are _____ green _____. (predicate adjective)

Many of the books on the shelf are _____ textbooks _____. (predicate nominative)

Many of the books on the shelf are _____ old _____. (predicate adjective)

The little child's hiding place was _____ the (sofa) _____. (predicate nominative)

The little child's hiding place was _____ cozy _____. (predicate adjective)

Exercise 39C: Diagramming Predicate Adjectives and Predicate Nominatives

On your own paper, diagram every word of the following sentences.

The cave exploration was exciting!

Her studio was an old barn.

Bats are mammals.

Tonight's sunset is bright orange and red.

Caron made us bacon and eggs.

Submit the new homework.

The class learned new dance steps.

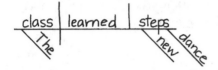

Are you tired?

The washer and the dryer broke.

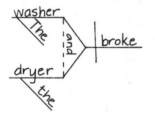

— LESSON 40 —

Predicate Adjectives and Predicate Nominatives
Pronouns as Predicate Nominatives
Object Complements

Exercise 40A: Reviewing Objects and Predicate Adjectives and Nominatives

Identify the underlined words as *DO* for direct object, *IO* for indirect object, *OP* for object of preposition, *PN* for predicate nominative, or *PA* for predicate adjective.

- For each direct object (or direct object/indirect object combination), find and underline twice the action verb that affects it.

- For each object of the preposition, find and circle the preposition to which it belongs.

- For each predicate nominative and predicate adjective, find and draw a box around the linking verb that it follows.

- When you are finished, answer the questions at the end of the selection.

   The following passage is from *Esperanza Rising*, by Pam Muñoz Ryan. It has been condensed and slightly adapted.

   Papa <u>handed</u> <u>Esperanza</u> the <u>knife</u>. This job was usually reserved (for) the eldest <u>son</u> (of) a wealthy <u>rancher</u>, but Esperanza [was] an only <u>child</u> and Papa's <u>pride</u> and <u>glory</u>. She was given the honor.

   The August sun <u>promised</u> a dry <u>afternoon</u> in Aguascalientes, Mexico. Everyone who lived and worked on El Rancho de las Rosas was gathered (at) the <u>edge</u> (of) the <u>field</u>.

   The grapevine clusters [were] <u>heavy</u>. Papa <u>declared</u> <u>them</u> ready. Esperanza's parents stood nearby. Mama [was] <u>tall</u> and <u>elegant</u>, her hair (in) the usual braided <u>wreath</u> that crowned her head, and Papa, barely taller than Mama, his graying mustache twisted up (at) the <u>sides</u>. He <u>swept</u> his <u>hand</u>

toward the grapevines, signaling Esperanza. When she walked (toward) the <u>arbors</u> and glanced
OP

back (at) her <u>parents</u>, they both smiled and nodded, encouraging her forward. When she <u>reached</u>

the <u>vines</u>, she <u>separated</u> the <u>leaves</u> and carefully <u>grasped</u> a thick <u>stem</u>. She put the knife to it, and

with a quick swipe, the heavy cluster of grapes dropped (into) her waiting <u>hand</u>. Esperanza walked

back to Papa and <u>handed</u> <u>him</u> the <u>fruit</u>. Papa <u>kissed</u> <u>it</u> and <u>held</u> <u>it</u> up for all to see.

1. Find the object complement in this passage. Write it in the blank below and cross out the incorrect choices. __Ready__ is an (adjective/~~noun~~) that (describes/~~renames~~) the direct object.

2. Find the compound adjective in this passage. Write it in the blank below and cross out the incorrect choice. __Grapevine__ is in the (attributive/~~predicative~~) position.

Exercise 40B: Parts of the Sentence

Label the following in each sentence: *S* (subject), *LV* (linking verb), *AV* (action verb), *DO* (direct object), *OC-A* (object complement-adjective), *OC-N* (object complement-noun), *IO* (indirect object), or *PN* (predicate nominative).

<pre>
   S   AV   DO   OC-N
The girl named her hamster Peggy.
   S   AV   IO   DO
The girl gave her hamster water.
 S   AV   DO   OC-A
We painted the walls blue.
 S   AV   DO
We painted the walls carefully.
                     S   AV   IO   DO
The hard-working volunteers gave the children a wonderful event.
                     S   AV   DO   OC-A
The hard-working volunteers made the event a reality.
  S   AV   DO   OC-N
They called the painting a masterpiece.
S   AV   DO   OC-N
I considered the salsa spicy.
      S   LV   PA
The judges were strict.
      S   AV   DO   OC-N
The judges named the horse the winner.
      S   AV   IO   DO
The judges gave the horse a blue ribbon.
</pre>

Exercise 40C: Diagramming

On your own paper, diagram the sentences from Exercise 40B.

The girl named her hamster Peggy.   The girl gave her hamster water.

We painted the walls blue.

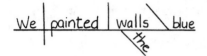

We painted the walls carefully.

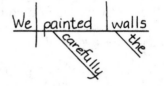

The hard-working volunteers gave the children a wonderful event.

The hard-working volunteers made the event a reality.

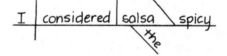

They called the painting a masterpiece.

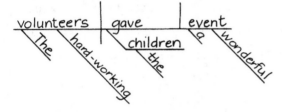

I considered the salsa spicy.

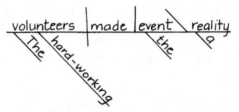

The judges were strict.

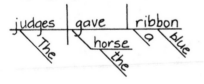

The judges named the horse the winner.

The judges gave the horse a blue ribbon.

WEEK 11

More About Prepositions

— LESSON 41 —

Prepositions and Prepositional Phrases
Adjective Phrases

Exercise 41A: Identifying Adjective Phrases

Underline the adjective phrases in the following sentences. Draw an arrow from each phrase to the word it modifies. The first is done for you.

A fifty-mile span of land was the site of the Panama Canal.

It would shorten a ship's journey and avoid travel around Cape Horn.

Many of the workers on the Canal kept contracting malaria and yellow fever.

These illnesses caused many deaths and caused delays to the construction.

Major Ronald Ross discovered the connection between mosquitoes and these diseases.

The Canal's location on the Isthmus of Panama was an environment with hot, wet weather.

This weather caused an increase in the mosquito population.

The U.S. Army Sanitary Department began work on disease prevention.

The Sanitary Department dug drainage ditches and drained many pools around the Canal area.

The Sanitary Department also built buildings with screens.

The number of deaths decreased rapidly.

Exercise 41B: Diagramming Adjective Phrases/Review

Diagram each sentence from Exercise 41A on your own paper. Follow this procedure, and ask yourself the suggested questions if necessary.

1. Find the subject and predicate and diagram them first.
    What is the verb?
    Who or what [verb]?

2. Ask yourself: Is the verb an action verb? If so, look for a direct object.
    Who or what receives the action of the verb?

    If there is a direct object, check for an indirect object.
    To whom or for whom is the action done?

    Remember that there may be no direct object or no indirect object—but you can't have an indirect object without a direct object. If there is an indirect object, it will always come between the verb and the direct object.

3. Ask yourself: Is the verb a state-of-being verb? If so, look for a predicate nominative or predicate adjective.
    Is there a word after the verb that renames or describes the subject?

4. Find all prepositional phrases. Ask yourself: Whom or what do they describe?

5. Place all other adjectives and adverbs on the diagram. If you have trouble, ask for help.

A fifty-mile span of land was the site of the Panama Canal.

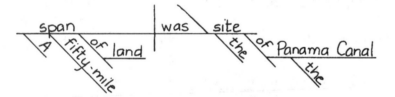

It would shorten a ship's journey and avoid travel around Cape Horn.

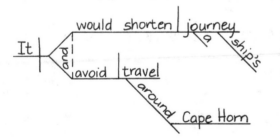

Many of the workers on the Canal kept contracting malaria and yellow fever.

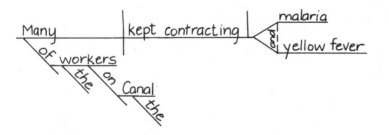

These illnesses caused many deaths and caused delays to the construction.

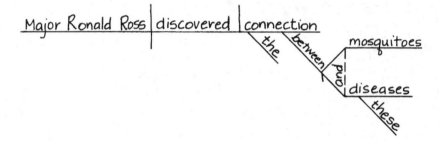

Major Ronald Ross discovered the connection between mosquitoes and these diseases.

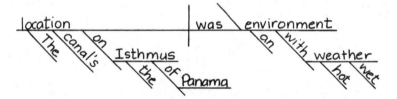

The Canal's location on the Isthmus of Panama was an environment with hot, wet weather.

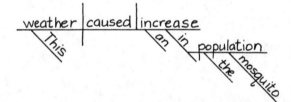

This weather caused an increase in the mosquito population.

The U.S. Army Sanitary Department began work on disease prevention.

The Sanitary Department dug drainage ditches and drained many pools around the Canal area.

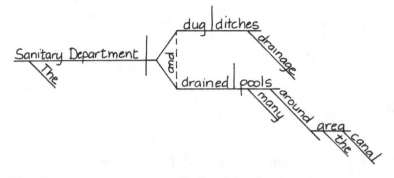

The Sanitary Department also built buildings with screens.

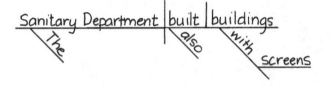

The number of deaths decreased rapidly.

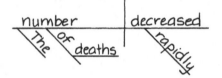

— LESSON 42 —

Adjective Phrases
Adverb Phrases

Exercise 42A: Identifying Adverb Phrases

Underline the adverb phrases in the following sentences and circle the preposition that begins each phrase. Draw an arrow from each phrase to the word it modifies. Be careful not to underline any prepositional phrases that function as adjectives! These sentences are adapted from *What If? Serious Scientific Answers to Absurd Hypothetical Questions*, by Randall Munroe.

The first is done for you.

The common cold is caused (by) various viruses.

(After) a few days, your immune system destroys the virus.

When you fight the virus, you are immune (to) that particular rhinovirus strain.

Earth's most powerful radio signal beams (from) the Arecibo telescope.

This massive dish sits (in) Puerto Rico and can function (like) a radar transmitter.

Signals bounce (off) Mercury and the asteroid belt.

The Curiosity rover is sitting (in) Gale Crater (on) Mars.

Liquid water does not last (on) Mars, because it is too cold and there's too little air.

The power delivered (to) the ground (by) sunlight outweighs the power delivered (to) the ground (by) lightning.

Perpetual nighttime thunderstorms occur (in) Lake Maracaibo.

The Empire State Building is frequently struck (by) lightning.

Exercise 42B: Diagramming Adverb Phrases

On your own paper, diagram the following five sentences from Exercise 42A.

After a few days, your immune system destroys the virus.

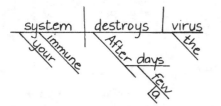

Earth's most powerful radio signal beams from the Arecibo telescope.

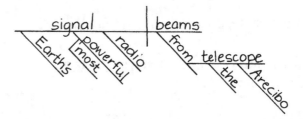

This massive dish sits in Puerto Rico and can function like a radar transmitter.

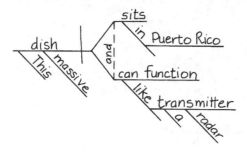

Perpetual nighttime thunderstorms occur in Lake Maracaibo.

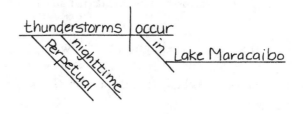

The Empire State Building is frequently struck by lightning.

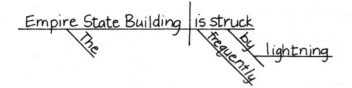

— LESSON 43 —

Definitions Review
Adjective and Adverb Phrases
Misplaced Modifiers

Exercise 43A: Distinguishing Between Adjective and Adverb Phrases

Underline all the prepositional phrases in the following sentences. Write *ADJ* above the adjective phrases and *ADV* above the adverb phrases. These sentences are adapted from Marguerite Henry's *Misty of Chincoteague*.

A wild, ringing neigh shrilled from the hold of the Spanish galleon.
                                                  ADV   ADJ

The wind was dying with the sun.
                     ADV

It was not the cry of an animal in hunger.
                   ADJ   ADJ

The captain's eyes were fixed on his men, but his thoughts raced to the rich land where
                              ADV   ADV
he was bound.

His beady eyes darted to the lookout man in the crow's nest, then to the men on deck.
                     ADV   ADJ   ADV   ADJ

> **Note to Instructor:** "in the crow's nest" is an ADJ phrase, since it tells us "which man." "To the men" refers to where his eyes darted, so it is an ADV phrase.

The stallion neighed to the mares, who were struggling to keep afloat.
                     ADV

The ponies were exhausted and their coats were heavy with water, but they were free!
                                                          ADV

With wild snorts of happiness, they buried their noses in the long grass.
ADV   ADJ   ADV

Then they rolled in the wiry grass and they gave great whinnies of happiness.
                 ADV   ADJ

The sea gave them protection from their fiercest enemies.
                              ADJ

Exercise 43B: Correcting Misplaced Modifiers

Circle the misplaced adjective and adverb phrases in the following sentences. Draw an arrow to show where the phrase should be.

For some of the sentences, the phrase may make sense where it is—but if a phrase doesn't communicate what the author wants it to, it is misplaced. Assume that each sentence contains a phrase that is misplaced (that is, a different meaning was intended), correct as instructed above, and explain to your instructor how the placement changes the meaning.

The first is done for you, with a sample explanation provided.

(Under the surfboard,) the surfer spotted the shark swimming.

> *Under the surfboard* as initially placed indicates that the surfer was positioned under the board itself. In the corrected position, the phrase tells the reader where the shark was located.

The car was going too quickly down the road (with blue stripes)

> As initially placed, *with blue stripes* indicates that the road had blue stripes. As corrected, it demonstrates that the car has blue stripes.

The musician played my favorite song (in a sparkly, sequined hat)

> In the initial placement, the song was wearing *a sparkly, sequined hat*. In the correct location, it is clear that the musician was wearing the hat.

The nurse (in my shoulder) gave me a shot.

> As originally written, the sentence indicates that the nurse is *in my shoulder*. When rewritten, the shot is being placed *in my shoulder*.

(With long whiskers,) Gerald carried the cat.

> *With long whiskers* originally seems to describe Gerald. Once correctly placed, it describes the cat.

(Under the plate) he found one more cookie.

> *Under the plate* as originally placed seems to imply that the subject is *under the plate*. When moved correctly, the sentence shows that the cookie is *under the plate*.

The old, haunted house finally collapsed (on the beach)

> This sentence is not incorrect but could be more clear. *On the beach* needs to follow the noun *house*, in order to clarify the house's location. As originally written, it indicates that the collapse itself was on the beach.

(From the garden) Dad fried zucchini.

> The original sentence seems to indicate that Dad was frying the zucchini while he was in the garden. Once corrected, we can see that the zucchini had been picked *from the garden*.

(In the freezer,) Amelia saw the ice cream.

> As written, *in the freezer* describes where Amelia was located. As corrected, *in the freezer* tells us where the ice cream was located.

The class debated the verdict (in the library)

> The original sentence is confusing, as it demonstrates that the verdict must have occurred *in the library*. There are two potential corrections: *in the library* can go at the start of the sentence or after the noun *class*, to show where the class was located/which class it was.

The zookeeper feeds the lion (in the green jacket.)

> In its original location, *in the green jacket* seems to state that the lion was wearing the green jacket. In the correct location, it's clear that the zookeeper was wearing the green jacket.

The mud covered my shoes (from the yard.)

> As written, *from the yard* states that the shoes came *from the yard*. The corrected version clarifies that the mud came *from the yard*.

— LESSON 44 —

Adjective and Adverb Phrases
Prepositional Phrases Acting as Other Parts of Speech

Exercise 44A: Prepositional Phrases Acting as Other Parts of Speech

In each sentence below, circle any prepositional phrases. Underline the subject of the sentence once and the predicate twice. Then label the prepositional phrases as *ADJ* (adjective phrase), *ADV* (adverb phrase), *S* (subject), *PA* (predicate adjective) or *PN* (predicate nominative).

                    S
(In the wind) is bitterly cold.

                    ADJ   PA
The hotel (down the street) is (under construction)

                    ADV
(You) Now sing (with your loudest voice)

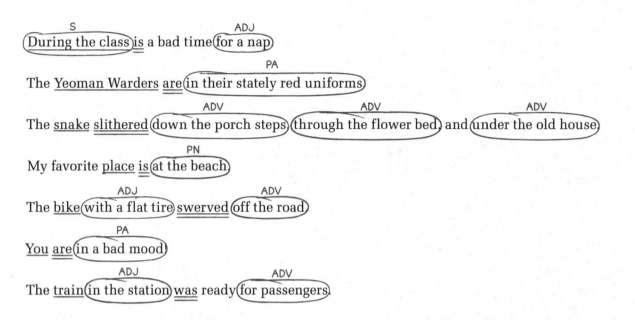

The snake slithered (down the porch steps) (through the flower bed) and (under the old house)

My favorite place is (at the beach)

The bike (with a flat tire) swerved (off the road)

You are (in a bad mood)

The train (in the station) was ready (for passengers)

Exercise 44B: Diagramming

On your own paper, diagram these sentences from Exercise 44A.

In the wind is bitterly cold.

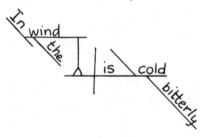

The hotel down the street is under construction.

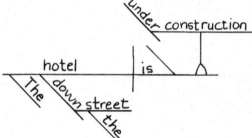

Now sing with your loudest voice.

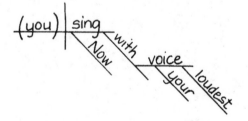

During the class is a bad time for a nap.

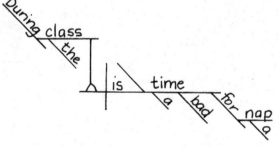

The Yeoman Warders are in their stately red uniforms.

The snake slithered down the porch steps, through the flower bed, and under the house.

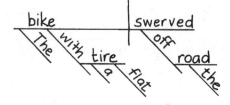

My favorite place is at the beach.

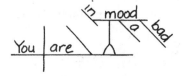

The bike with a flat tire swerved off the road.

You are in a bad mood!

The train in the station was ready for passengers.

WEEK 12

Advanced Verbs

— LESSON 45 —

Linking Verbs
Linking/Action Verbs

Exercise 45A: Distinguishing Between Action Verbs and Linking Verbs

Underline the predicates in the following sentences. Identify each main verb as *AV* for action verb or *LV* for linking verb. If the verb is followed by a direct object (*DO*), predicate adjective (*PA*), or predicate nominative (*PN*), label it.

Remember that a verb with no direct object, predicate adjective, or predicate nominative will most likely be an action verb. Also remember that direct objects, predicate adjectives, and predicate nominatives are never found in prepositional phrases.

The corn <u>grew</u> quickly in the summer.
　　　　AV

The fire <u>grew</u> cold.
　　　LV　PA

The milk <u>tastes</u> spoiled.
　　　　LV　　PA

I <u>tasted</u> the balsamic vinegar.
　AV　　　　　　　DO

The pig <u>seems</u> happy.
　　　LV　　PA

Those actions <u>look</u> suspicious.
　　　　　　LV　　　PA

<u>Are</u> your shoes new?
LV　　　　　PA

The honeysuckle <u>smelled</u> sweet.
　　　　　　　LV　　PA

Terrance <u>smelled</u> the lavender bush.
　　　AV　　　　　DO

Katarzyna <u>became</u> the lead actress.
　　　　LV　　　　PN

The butterflies <u>are migrating</u>.
　　　　　　AV

The fireflies <u>are appearing</u> in the sky.
　　　　　　AV

The desert <u>appeared</u> endless.
　　　　LV

When <u>is</u> the director <u>giving</u> notes to you?
　　　　　　　　AV　DO

Exercise 45B: Distinguishing Among Different Kinds of Nouns

Underline all the nouns in the following sentences. Identify them as *S* for subject, *OP* for object of a preposition, *IO* for indirect object, *DO* for direct object, or *PN* for predicate nominative.

　　S　　　　　　DO
Imani loves horses.

　　　　　　　　　　　PN
They are her favorite animals.

　　S　　　　　　　　OP　　　　　　　DO
Her aunt lives on a ranch and owns two horses.

　　　　　　IO　　　　　　DO
She gives Imani riding lessons.

　　S　　　　　PN
Her aunt is a veterinarian.

　S　　　　　　　　　　DO　　　　　　　　　IO　　　　DO　　　　　　DO
Imani cleans the horses' stalls and feeds the animals apples and carrots.

　　　　　　　　S　　　　　　DO　　　　DO
Eventually, Imani will own a farm and horses.

Exercise 45C: Diagramming Action Verbs and Linking Verbs

Diagram the following sentences.

The old road feels bumpy.

Oviraptors were omnivores.

Oviraptors would eat eggs.

Can you bring me the keys?

The sky grew dark.

Stefan grew sunflowers.

— LESSON 46 —

Conjugations
Irregular Verbs
Principal Parts of Verbs

Exercise 46A: Forming Simple, Perfect, and Progressive Tenses

Fill in the missing blanks in the chart below.

Simple Present

	Singular		Plural
First person	I jump		We __jump__
Second person	You __jump__		You jump
Third person	He, she, it __jumps__		They jump

Simple Past

	Singular		Plural
First person	I __jumped__		We __jumped__
Second person	You __jumped__		You __jumped__
Third person	He, she, it __jumped__		They jumped

Simple Future

	Singular		Plural
First person	I __will jump__		We __will jump__
Second person	You will jump		You __will jump__
Third person	He, she, it __will jump__		They __will jump__

Perfect Present

	Singular		Plural
First person	I __have jumped__		We __have jumped__
Second person	You __have jumped__		You __have jumped__
Third person	He, she, it has jumped		They __have jumped__

Perfect Past

	Singular		Plural
First person	I __had jumped__		We __had jumped__
Second person	You __had jumped__		You had jumped
Third person	He, she, it __had jumped__		They __had jumped__

Perfect Future

	Singular		Plural
First person	I will have jumped		We __will have jumped__
Second person	You __will have jumped__		You __will have jumped__
Third person	He, she, it __will have jumped__		They __will have jumped__

Progressive Present

	Singular	**Plural**
First person	I __am jumping__	We are jumping
Second person	You __are jumping__	You __are jumping__
Third person	He, she, it __is jumping__	They __are jumping__

Progressive Past

	Singular	**Plural**
First person	I __was jumping__	We __were jumping__
Second person	You were jumping	You __were jumping__
Third person	He, she, it __was jumping__	They __were__ jumping

Progressive Future

	Singular	**Plural**
First person	I will be jumping	We __will be jumping__
Second person	You __will be jumping__	You __will be jumping__
Third person	He, she, it __will be jumping__	They __will be jumping__

Exercise 46B: Spanish and English Words

Draw lines to match each English word with its Spanish equivalent. Because English and Spanish have similar backgrounds, you should be able to complete this exercise easily, even if you've never learned any Spanish!

English	**Spanish**
problem	correctamente
action	entrar
anniversary	estudiante
community	acción
student	aparecer
correctly	artista
difficulty	problema
appear	comunidad
enter	dificultad
artist	aniversario

Exercise 46C: Principal Parts of Verbs

Fill in the chart with the missing forms.

	First Principal Part Present	Second Principal Part Past	Third Principal Part Past Participle
I	wait	waited	waited
I	file	filed	filed
I	need	needed	needed
I	cry	cried	cried
I	talk	talked	talked
I	invent	invented	invented
I	worry	worried	worried
I	appear	appeared	appeared
I	shop	shopped	shopped
I	sway	swayed	swayed

Exercise 46D: Distinguishing Between First and Second Principal Parts

Identify each underlined verb as 1 for first principal part or 2 for second principal part. These sentences are from Mary Norton's *The Borrowers*.

Mrs. May <u>lived</u> [2] in two rooms in Kate's parents' house in London; she <u>was</u> [2], I <u>think</u> [1], some kind of relation.

"In fact, you might almost say that he <u>became</u> [2] a borrower himself…"

"You <u>waste</u> [1] hours on those birds," Homily would say.

In the morning, the sun <u>streams</u> [1] in on the toast and marmalade.

She <u>gazed</u> [2] downwards at the upturned face and then she <u>smiled</u> [2] and her eyes <u>slid</u> [2] away into distance.

— **LESSON 47** —

Linking Verbs
Principal Parts
Irregular Verbs

No exercises this lesson.

— LESSON 48 —

Linking Verbs
Principal Parts
Irregular Verbs

Exercise 48A: Principal Parts

Fill in the blanks in the following chart of verbs.

Present	Past	Past Participle
light	lit	lit or lighted
weave	wove or weaved	woven
begin	began	begun
burn	burned or burnt	burnt
foresee	foresaw	foreseen
pay	paid	paid
thrust	thrust	thrust
swell	swelled	swollen or swelled
grind	ground	ground
fling	flung	flung
deal	dealt	dealt
foresake	forsook	forsaken
let	let	let
lose	lost	lost
string	strung	strung
sting	stank	stunk
slink	slunk	slunk
cost	cost	cost
seek	sought	sought
rise	rose	risen
spring	sprang	sprung
slit	slit	slit
shine	shone or shined	shone or shined
spin	spun	spun
rid	rid	rid
mean	meant	meant
lay	laid	laid
speed	sped	sped
wring	wrung	wrung
strive	strove	striven
cut	cut	cut

Present	Past	Past Participle
forecast	forecast	forecast
spend	spent	spent
meet	met	met
drive	drove	driven
bid	bid	bid
lie	lay	lain
understand	understood	understood
throw	threw	thrown
sell	sold	sold
keep	kept	kept
rewind	rewound	rewound

Exercise 48B: Forming Correct Past Participles

Write the correct third principal part (past participle) in each blank. The first principal part is provided for you in parentheses.

The first is done for you.

I had __broken__ (break) the plate.

Her friends have __sent__ (send) her birthday cards.

Mathilde has never __flown__ (fly) by herself.

The fishing rod had nearly __bent__ (bend) in half by the time he had __caught__ (catch) the huge fish!

Have you __chosen__ (choose) which cupcake you would like?

Yesterday, Ben had __driven__ (drive) to the nursery and had __bought__ (buy) two trees for the yard.

Petra had __found__ (find) her phone after I texted her.

Exercise 48C: Forming Correct Past Tenses

Write the correct second principal part (past) in each blank. The first principal part is provided for you in parentheses.

The first is done for you.

Liam __wrote__ (write) a paper about Aaron Burr.

We __swam__ (swim) for an hour yesterday.

Charlotte __brought__ (bring) cucumbers that she __grew__ (grow) in her garden.

I __blew__ (blow) out the candle just before I __heard__ (hear) the first clap of thunder.

Oliver's ankle __felt__ (feel) bruised after he __fell__ (fall) down the steps.

The witness __kept__ (keep) insisting that the defendant was not the person she __saw__ (see).

Tyra __gave__ (give) me the rope and __held__ (hold) onto the end while I climbed down.

Exercise 48D: Proofreading for Irregular Verb Usage

In the passage below, from Jean Craighead George's *My Side of the Mountain*, you will find seven errors in irregular verb usage. Cross out the incorrect forms and write the correct ones above them.

    I looked up to see how much higher I had to go. Then I ~~seed~~ ^{saw} them. There ~~sitted~~ ^{sat} three fussy whitish gray birds. Their wide-open ~~mouths~~ ^{gave} gived them a startled look.

    "Oh, hello," I ~~sayed~~ ^{said}. "You are cute."

When I ~~speaked~~ ^{spoke}, all three blinked at once. All three heads turned and followed my hand as I ~~swinged~~ ^{swung} it up and toward them.

    Something hit my shoulder. I turned my head to see the big female. She had ~~hitted~~ ^{hit} me. She winged out, banked, and started back for another strike.

Exercise 48E: Diagramming

On your own paper, diagram the following four sentences.

Who announced Secretariat the winner of the race?

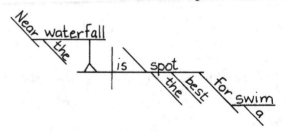

The fog over the lake seems mysterious.

Abuela cooked the chicken and warmed the rice.

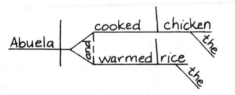

Near the waterfall is the best spot for a swim.

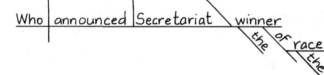

— REVIEW 4 —
Weeks 10-12

Topics:
Direct and Indirect Objects
Linking Verbs
Predicate Adjectives
Predicate Nominatives
Articles
Adjective Phrases
Adverb Phrases
Action vs. Linking Verbs
Irregular Verbs
Principal Parts (Present, Past, Past Participle)

Review 4A: Action vs. Linking Verbs

Identify the underlined verbs as *A* for action or *L* for linking.

A young bottlenose dolphin <u>swam</u> [A] happily in the warm waters of the Florida coastline.

The nets of a crab trap <u>were</u> [L] invisible to her, and she <u>became</u> [L] its victim as she grew tangled in the rope.

She <u>twisted</u> [A] and tried to free herself, but she soon <u>felt</u> [L] exhausted.

A fisherman <u>noticed</u> [A] the moving trap and <u>found</u> [A] the entrapped dolphin.

Rescuers <u>arrived</u> [A] and <u>freed</u> [A] the frightened animal.

They <u>took</u> [A] her to their facility and <u>treated</u> [A] her wounds so that she could <u>become</u> [L] strong again.

The rescuers <u>named</u> [A] her Winter and <u>fitted</u> [A] her with a prosthetic tail to help her swim and play.

Winter <u>grew</u> [L] famous for her incredible recovery and story.

She <u>is</u> [L] an inspiration to many people who come <u>visit</u> [A] her each year at Clearwater Marine Aquarium.

Review 4B: Predicate Adjectives and Predicate Nominatives

Underline the linking verb in each of the following sentences. If the sentence concludes with a predicate nominative or predicate adjective, circle each and write *PA* for predicate adjective or *PN* for predicate nominative above it.

Geodes <u>are</u> beautiful (rocks) [PN]

The inside of a geode <u>is</u> (hollow) [PA]

113

A geode's exterior <u>looks</u> (unremarkable)(PA)

However, the interior <u>appears</u> (sparkling)(PA) and (colorful)(PA)

Minerals such as quartz and pyrite <u>are</u> (common)(PA) in geodes.

The mineral <u>is</u> a (liquid)(PN) and then it crystallizes.

The crystals usually <u>look</u> (blue)(PA) or (purple)(PA)

Geodes <u>are</u> quite (popular)(PA) among rock collectors.

Review 4C: Adjective and Adverb Phrases

In the following excerpt from Joseph Marshall III's *In the Footsteps of Crazy Horse*, identify each underlined prepositional phrase as *ADJ* for adjective phrase or *ADV* for adverb phrase.

Jimmy smiled as he loped <u>across the prairie</u>(ADV). He was riding Little Warrior, a small but sturdy buckskin quarter horse. Grandpa was riding <u>on Dancer</u>(ADV), a muscular bay quarter horse stallion. Grandpa Nyles had a small herd <u>of horses</u>(ADJ).

Their chore was checking Grandpa Nyle's twelve miles <u>of fence</u>(ADJ). They stopped <u>along Horse Creek</u>(ADV), which flowed <u>into the Smoking Earth River</u>(ADV). Grandpa wanted to rest the horses and let them graze. Besides, it was always good to relax <u>in the shade</u>(ADV) <u>of some big, tall cottonwood trees</u>(ADJ). Jimmy took a long stick and poked around <u>in the grasses</u>(ADV) before he sat down. It was a way to scare away snakes. Grandpa had taught him that.

As they sat <u>against the trunk</u>(ADV) <u>of a giant cottonwood tree</u>(ADJ), they listened to the creek gurgling and watched the horses munch <u>on grass</u>(ADV).

Review 4D: Forming Principal Parts

Complete the following excerpt by writing the correct principal part of the verb (first, second, or third) in parentheses. Sentences are adapted from Arthur Conan Doyle's *The Sign of the Four*.

It was a September evening, and not yet seven o'clock, but the day had __been__ (be, 3rd PP) a dreary one, and a dense drizzly fog __lay__ (lie, 2nd PP) low upon the great city. Mud-coloured clouds drooped sadly over the muddy streets. Down the Strand the lamps __were__ (be, 2nd PP) but misty splotches of diffused light which __threw__ (throw, 2nd PP) a feeble circular glimmer upon the slimy pavement. The yellow glare from the shop-windows had __streamed__ (stream, 3rd PP) out into the steamy, vaporous air, and __thrown__ (throw, 3rd PP) a murky, shifting radiance across the crowded thoroughfare. There __was__ (be, 2nd PP) something eerie and ghost-like in the endless procession of faces which flitted across these narrow bars of light,—sad faces and

glad, haggard and merry. I __am__ (be, 1st PP) not subject to impressions, but the dull, heavy

evening, with the strange business upon which we were engaged, combined to make me nervous

and depressed. I had __seen__ (see, 3rd PP) from Miss Morstan's manner that she had __suffered__

(suffer, 3rd PP) from the same feeling. Holmes alone __rises__ (rise, 1st PP) superior to petty

influences. He __held__ (hold, 2nd PP) his open note-book upon his knee, and from time to time he

jotted down figures and memoranda in the light of his pocket-lantern.

Review 4E: Irregular Verbs

Find and correct the SIX errors in irregular verb usage in the following excerpt from *Mr. Popper's Penguins*, by Richard and Florence Atwater. Cross out the incorrect form and write the correct form above it.

The reason Mr. Popper was so absentminded was that he was always dreaming about far-away

countries. He had never ~~good~~ [gone] out of Stillwater. It would have ~~be~~ [been] nice, he often ~~thinked,~~ [thought] if he could

have ~~saw~~ [seen] something of the world.

Whenever he ~~heared~~ [heard] that a Polar movie was in town, he was the first person at the ticket-win-

dow, and often he ~~sitted~~ [sat] through three shows.

Review 4F: Misplaced Modifiers

Circle the misplaced adjective and adverb phrases in the following sentences. Draw an arrow to the place where each phrase should be.

The ring belonged to the man (of silver).

(With red roses) I gave the plants to the customer.

Behind the stadium (of leather) she found a wallet.

Bri showed us pictures of her vacation (after dinner).

He put a piece of toast on the plate (with jam).

The bat ate the fruit (with leathery wings).

Gina made (with noodles) chicken soup for her mom.

The bird ate from the feeder (with red feathers).

Review 4G: Diagramming

Diagram the following sentences.

King's Day is an annual celebration in Amsterdam.

People gather and celebrate the monarch's birthday.

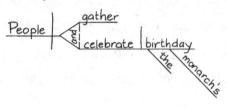

Citizens wear orange in honor of the House of Orange.

Some people in the celebrations dye their hair orange.

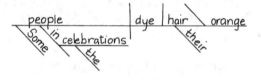

Vendors bake the celebrants a special pastry.

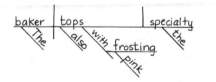

Tompouce is a puff pastry with cream filling.

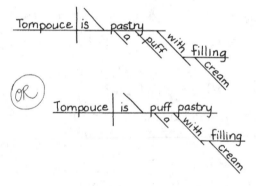

The baker also tops the specialty with pink frosting.

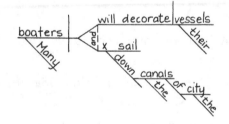

Many boaters will decorate their vessels and sail down the canals of the city.

WEEK 13

Advanced Pronouns

— LESSON 49 —

Personal Pronouns

Antecedents

Possessive Pronouns

Exercise 49A: Personal Pronouns and Antecedents

Circle the personal pronouns in the following sentences, adapted from *Commodore Perry in the Land of the Shogun*, by Rhoda Blumberg. Draw an arrow from each pronoun to the antecedent. In the margin, write the gender (*f, m,* or *n*) and number (*S* or *PL*) of each pronoun.

People panicked, and they carried valuables and furniture in all directions in order to hide from invading barbarians!   nPL

The Emperor Komei was isolated in the royal palace at Kyoto. Although he was worshiped   mS
as a divine descendent of the sun goddess, Amaterasu, he was a powerless puppet.

Commodore Matthew Calbraith Perry was in command of the squadron. He had not come   mS
to invade. He hoped to be a peacemaker.

Perry's mission was to unlock Japan's door. It had been slammed shut against all but a few   nS
Dutch and Chinese traders, the only ones officially allowed in for over 200 years.

Exercise 49B: Identifying Possessive Pronouns

Underline the possessive pronouns in the following sentences from *Shiloh*, by Phyllis Reynolds Naylor. Each possessive pronoun is acting as an adjective. Draw an arrow from the pronoun to the noun it modifies. There may be more than one pronoun in each sentence.

Dara Lynn is dipping bread in her glass of cold tea, and Becky pushes her beans up over the edge of her plate in a rush to get them down.

I don't know anybody who likes him much, but folks around here like to keep to their own business.

Dara Lynn and Becky came up the lane with their packages.

The dog goes as far as the sycamore tree, lies down in the wet grass, head on his paws.

117

Exercise 49C: Using Possessive Pronouns

In the following sentences, write the correct possessive pronoun above the underlined noun(s).

Patrick and Catherine O'Leary lived in Chicago in the 1800s. They never imagined what legend

would start because of the actions of <u>Patrick and Catherine O'Leary's</u> cow. [their]

On the evening of October 8, 1871, an immense fire started in Chicago, and many people claim
that it started when the O'Learys' cow kicked over a lantern in the barn, as Catherine was going

about <u>Catherine's</u> evening chores. [her]

The fire spread quickly, aided by Chicago's famous wind blowing down the streets and the fact

that many of <u>Chicago's</u> buildings were made of wood. [its]

When the fire was finally extinguished, over 300 people had lost <u>the people's</u> lives. [their]

The city had also lost over 17,000 of <u>the city's</u> buildings. [its]

Chicago began to rebuild and soon became known as an architectural wonder. Famous architect

Frank Lloyd Wright built many of <u>Frank Lloyd Wright's</u> famous houses there. [his]

For 25 years, the Sears Tower in Chicago held the record for being the tallest building in
the world. People travelled from all over to get <u>the people's</u> pictures taken on the top floor of
the tower. [their]

Famous baseball player Babe Ruth once said of the baseball stadium, "I'd play for half <u>Babe Ruth's</u>
salary if I could hit in Wrigley Field all the time." [my]

American poet Carl Sandburg wrote a poem about Chicago, in which he answered critics, stating,
"to those who sneer at this <u>Carl Sandburg's</u> city...proud to be Hog Butcher, Tool Maker, Stacker of [his or my]
Wheat, Player with Railroads and Freight Handler to the Nation."

Exercise 49D: Diagramming Possessive Pronouns

On your own paper, diagram every word in the following sentences, slightly adapted from *The Tale of Peter Rabbit*, by Beatrix Potter.

They lived with their Mother in a sand-bank, underneath the root of a very big fir tree.

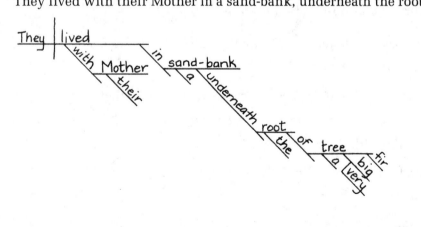

Then old Mrs. Rabbit took a basket and her umbrella.

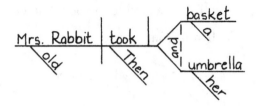

He got caught by the large buttons on his jacket.

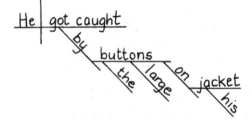

— LESSON 50 —

Pronoun Case

Exercise 50A: Subject and Object Pronouns

Underline all the personal pronouns in the following sentences. Identify them as *S* for subject, *O* for object, or *P* for possessive.

These sentences are from *Life on Surtsey: Iceland's Upstart Island*, by Loree Griffin Burns.

Note to Instructor: *It's* is the shortened form of *it is.*

Iceland sits on the edge of the Arctic Circle, meaning <u>it</u>'s cool. [S] In winter, when the Arctic Circle is tilted away from the sun, Icelanders barely see <u>it</u> [O] during the day. Glaciers, summer days that last twenty hours, and regular volcanic eruptions may sound extreme to <u>you</u> [O] and <u>me</u> [O], but to the average Icelander, <u>it</u> [S] is all pretty humdrum.

As kids, "<u>we</u> [S] stayed outside all the time, when not doing <u>our</u> [P] homework," said Erling Ólaffson, a resident of Iceland.

But on November 14, 1963, an epically unusual event shook the country. A volcano exploded under the sea—<u>she</u> [S] gave birth to an island. When ash and cinder began to spew violently, all Iceland watched <u>them</u> [O]. The materials settled back into the sea, the volcano's base grew wider, and <u>its</u> [P] top grew taller.

Stories of the eruption spread. Erling read <u>them</u> in <u>his</u> local paper. Unlike most people, <u>he</u> could take in the drama from <u>his</u> house. The eruption cloud eventually stretched high enough to be clearly seen in Erling's town of Hafnarfjördur, and <u>his</u> family watched <u>it</u> from <u>their</u> windows.

"<u>I</u> could see smoke over the mountains to the southeast," Erling said. "<u>We</u> saw just a stable smoke column, with no movement. But there was something about <u>it</u>."

Exercise 50B: Using Personal Pronouns Correctly

Choose the correct word(s) in parentheses and cross out the incorrect choice(s). Be sure to choose the grammatically correct choice for writing and not the choice that sounds the best.

My mother and sister and (~~me~~/I) decided to take a trip to Prince Edward Island, Canada.

My sister researched train tickets for (us/~~we~~), and (~~me~~/I) booked a rental car for our stay on the island.

Mom gave (my sister and me/~~my sister and I~~) a bag of our favorite snacks for the trip.

During the train ride, (~~us~~/we) talked about the places on PEI that were most interesting to (us/~~we~~).

Once (~~us~~/we) left the train, Mom navigated the map for my sister while (~~her~~/she) drove the rental car all around the beautiful island.

The trip was magical and gave (us/~~we~~) wonderful memories together.

As Mom, my sister, and (~~me~~/I) journeyed back home, Mom commented that her favorite travel companions of all were (~~us~~/we).

Exercise 50C: Diagramming Personal Pronouns

On your own paper, diagram the following sentences. Personal pronouns are diagrammed exactly like the nouns or adjectives they replace.

I bought her a gift.

Do you see it?

His teammates were we.

It is she.

They showed us the quilts.

He won it!

— LESSON 51 —

Indefinite Pronouns

Exercise 51A: Identifying Indefinite Pronouns

Underline all of the indefinite pronouns in the following sentences. Each sentence may contain more than one pronoun.

These sentences are drawn from *Spooked!: How a Radio Broadcast and The War of the Worlds Sparked the 1938 Invasion of America*, by Gail Jarrow.

<u>No one</u> knew that a group of adults was plotting a different sort of mischief for October 30, 1938.

Men and <u>some</u> of the women would report back to their jobs, if they were lucky enough to have them.

His business in shambles, he decided he had <u>nothing</u> to lose.

<u>Many</u> had lost their houses and farms because they couldn't pay their debt.

<u>One</u> was organized, composed, and practical. <u>Another</u> was wildly creative, intense, and arrogant.

Welles later admitted, "<u>Everybody</u> told me from the moment I was able to hear that I was absolutely marvelous."

<u>Someone</u> in the family switched the radio on and twirled the dial to the evening's entertainment.

Exercise 51B: Subject-Verb Agreement: Indefinite Pronouns

Choose the correct verb in parentheses by crossing out the incorrect verb.

Everything (is/~~are~~) soaked because of the rain!

Most of the tree limbs (~~was~~/were) still intact on that giant oak.

Several of the garden plants (~~seems~~/seem) to be flattened.

Each of the cars (appears/~~appear~~) unscratched.

I saw that something (is/~~are~~) lying near the shed.

Someone from the family (needs/~~need~~) to check it.

On the roof, none of the shingles (~~was~~/were) damaged.

I checked on the chickens, and all of them (~~acts~~/act) like the storm never happened.

(~~Do~~/Does) anyone see the beautiful rainbow?

Exercise 51C: Diagramming Indefinite Pronouns

On your own paper, diagram the following sentences, which are all quotes from the works of William Shakespeare.

Nothing will come of nothing.
(*King Lear*)

We shall part with neither.
(*Comedy of Errors*)

All men make faults.
("Sonnet 35")

Both of you are birds of self-same feather.
(*King Henry the Sixth*, Part III)

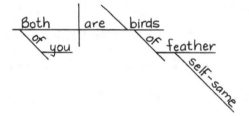

Few are angels. (*King Henry the Eighth*)

— LESSON 52 —

Personal Pronouns
Indefinite Pronouns

Exercise 52A: Subject and Object Pronouns

In the following sentences, cross out the incorrect pronoun.

   These sentences are adapted from *Moon Over Manifest,* by Clare Vanderpool.

The movement of the train rocked (~~I~~/me) like a lullaby.

(I/~~Me~~) closed my eyes to the dusty countryside and imagined the sign (I/me) knew only from stories.

(He/~~Him~~) does his best talking in stories, but in recent weeks, those had become few and far between.

When (I/~~me~~) was younger, (we/~~us~~) spent many a walking hour singing, making up rhymes, playing kick the can.

Uncle Henry won't mind giving (~~they~~/them) away to someone who actually wants to read (~~they~~/them).

The chain of that broken compass was long enough to stretch all the way back into his pocket, with (~~he~~/him) at one end and (~~I~~/me) at the other.

You can count on (~~I~~/me) to be truthful and certifiable in giving the honest-to-goodness scoop each and every week.

"We just figured (~~I~~/you) might like to meet some of the kids before (they/~~them~~) scatter to the four winds for the summer."

"(We/~~Us~~)'ll just head into town, then, as I need to pick up a letter for (~~we~~/us)."

Now, Gideon and (I/~~me~~) had been to many church services.

A proper-looking lady sat quietly in a rocking chair on the porch, not having the life in (~~she~~/her) to rock.

Maybe that was how I found comfort just then, even with (~~he~~/him) so far away.

I didn't know anything about Hattie Mae Harper, except what (she/~~her~~) wrote in her article.

I wondered how many of (~~they~~/them) I was up against.

But mostly (I/~~me~~) could taste the sadness in his voice when (he/~~him~~) told (~~I~~/me) (I/~~me~~) couldn't stay with him for the summer.

Exercise 52B: Possessive and Indefinite Pronouns

In these sentences, taken from *Further Chronicles of Avonlea*, by L. M. Montgomery, cross out the incorrect word in each set of parentheses.

"You should know that perfectly well, Mr. Patterson, better than anyone (does/~~do~~)."

Some (~~pities~~/pity) him.

The sound makes Christopher look up. Something in her face (irritates/~~irritate~~) him.

The little gray house, so close to the purring waves that in storms (~~its~~/their) spray splashed over (its/~~their~~) very doorstep, seemed deserted.

I hoped that spring might work (its/~~their~~) miracle upon her.

Although that scheme is not much good in Avonlea, where everybody (knows/~~know~~) your age.

None of the men in Glenby (~~was~~/were) good enough for her.

Naomi relaxed (her/~~their~~) grip on the girl's arm and sank back exhausted on the pillow.

"You (~~is~~/are) so good at understanding. Very few (~~is~~/are)."

All (~~was~~/were) enjoying themselves hugely.

We went down the road between the growths of young fir that bordered it. I smelled (~~its~~/their) balsam as we passed.

Each of the men (was/~~were~~) mutely imploring (his/~~their~~) neighbor to speak.

Everything (has/~~have~~) gone wrong.

Few of the Lincolns or Carewes (~~marries~~/marry) young, many not at all.

What was it? Was I, too, going mad, or WAS there something out there—(its/~~their~~) cries and moans, (its/~~their~~) longing for human love, yet ever retreating from human footsteps?

Many testimonies followed, each infused with the personality of the giver. Most of them (~~was~~/were) brief and stereotyped.

"If I cannot invite my father to see me married, no one (is/~~are~~) invited."

He said nothing—then or at any other time. From that day no reference to his wife or (her/~~their~~) concerns ever crossed his lips.

Several of her little playmates (~~has~~/have) gone to the harbor.

Exercise 52C: Writing Sentences from Diagrams

Use the diagrams below to reconstruct these sentences from *The Story of the World, Volume 1: Ancient Times*, by Susan Wise Bauer.

Write the original sentence on the blank below each diagram. Pay careful attention to each part of speech! Punctuate each sentence properly.

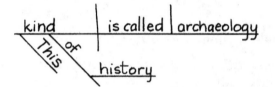

This kind of history is called archaeology.

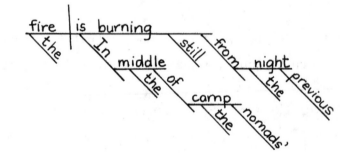

In the middle of the nomads' camp, the fire is still burning from the previous night.

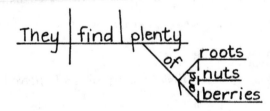

They find plenty of roots, nuts, and berries.

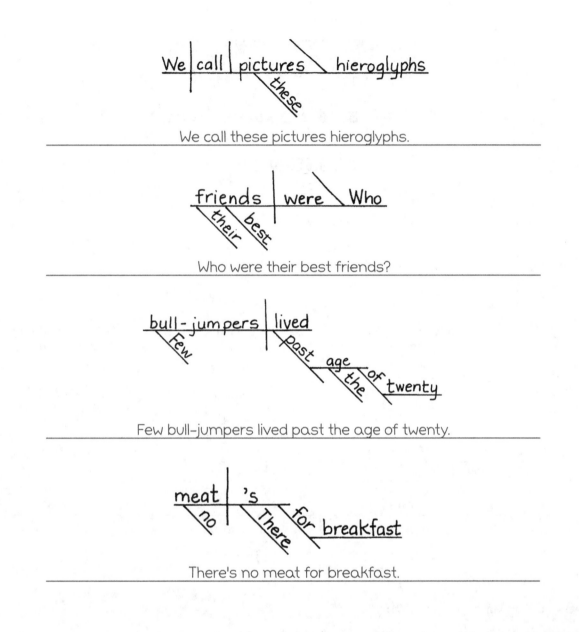

We call these pictures hieroglyphs.

Who were their best friends?

Few bull-jumpers lived past the age of twenty.

There's no meat for breakfast.

WEEK 14

Active and Passive Voice

— LESSON 53 —

Principal Parts
Troublesome Verbs

Exercise 53A: Principal Parts of Verbs

Fill in the chart with the missing forms.

	First Principal Part Present	Second Principal Part Past	Third Principal Part Past Participle
I	decide	decided	decided
I	sip	sipped	sipped
I	sell	sold	sold
I	empty	emptied	emptied
I	beat	beat	beaten
I	grow	grew	grown
I	become	became	become
I	fight	fought	fought

Exercise 53B: Using Correct Verbs

Choose the correct verb in parentheses. Cross out the incorrect verb.

The first thing we needed to do on our camping trip was to (set/~~sit~~) the tent up at our campsite.

Meg (let/~~leaved~~) me start the process. She had (~~lay~~/laid) out the equipment for fishing.

I (~~rose~~/raised) the tent poles and Meg helped me (set/~~sit~~) the sleeping bags inside.

We decided to (~~let~~/leave) the site and explore the lake.

I enjoyed (~~setting~~/sitting) by the water and waiting for the fish to bite.

Once we caught enough for our dinner, we headed back to camp and (set/~~sit~~) the wood in place for the campfire.

After we ate, we enjoyed (lying/~~laying~~) on the grass and naming the constellations we saw twinkling above us.

In the morning, I (~~set~~/sat) by the fire and (set/~~sat~~) the coffeepot over the flames.

Meg (rose/~~raised~~) from her sleeping bag and joined me for breakfast. We would (let/~~leave~~) the sun rise a bit more and then begin our hike.

Exercise 53C: Correct Forms of Troublesome Verbs

Fill in the blanks with the correct form of the indicated verb. The sentences are adapted from Mark Twain's *Autobiography of Mark Twain*.

He said that easier times would come by and by, and that the money could then be
__raised__ no doubt, and that he would enter into it cheerfully and with zeal
and carry it through to the very best of his ability. (raise, simple past)

Mr. Rogers had __let__ Mrs. Clemens and me have our way. (let, past participle)

The best place of all to see the procession was, of course, from this rostrum, so I sauntered upon that rostrum, while as yet it was empty, and __sat__ there. (sit, simple past)

In the summer they __set__ the table in the middle of that shady and breezy floor, and the sumptuous meals—well, it makes me cry to think of them. (set, simple past)

But I had checked myself there; for that way had __lain__ madness. (lay, past participle)

That lady still __lies__ in her bed at the principal hotel in Washington, disabled by the shock. (lie, simple present)

At last we all __rose__ by one blessed impulse and went down to the street door without explanations—in a pile, and no precedence; and so parted. (rise, simple past)

Exercise 53D: Proofreading for Correct Verb Usage

The following excerpts are from *Little House in the Big Woods*, by Laura Ingalls Wilder. Find and correct fifteen errors in verb usage by crossing out the incorrect verbs and writing the correct forms above them. Be careful—some sentences might have more than one!

Then she mixed the pot-liquor with it and ~~sat~~ [set] it away in a pan to cool. When it was cold it would be ~~cutted~~ [cut] in slices.

At night when Laura ~~lie~~ [lay] awake in the trundle bed, she listened and could not ~~heard~~ [hear] anything at all but the sound of the trees whispering together.

A wagon track ~~runned~~ [ran] before the house, but the little girl did not know where it ~~gone~~ [went].

Then they ~~leaved~~ [let] the fire go out, and Pa took all the strips and pieces of meat out of the hollow tree. After that, they ~~leaved~~ [left] it hanging to cool.

One night her father picked her up and carried her to the window so that she might ~~saw~~ [see] the wolves. Two of them ~~sitted~~ [sat] in front of the house.

But she was safe inside the solid log walls. Good old Jack, the brindle bulldog, ~~lied~~ [lay] on guard in front of the door.

Then he ~~lied~~ [laid] away the traps, and he ~~taked~~ [took] his fiddle out of its box and ~~beginned~~ [began] to play.

The garden behind the house had been growing all summer. At night Jack ~~keeped~~ [kept] the deer away.

— LESSON 54 —

Verb Tense
Active and Passive Voice

Exercise 54A: Reviewing Tenses

Write the tense of each underlined verb above it. This excerpt is adapted from *The Story of a Great Schoolmaster*, by H. G. Wells. The first is done for you.

simple past
I knew him personally only during the last eight years of his life; I met him for the first time in

progressive past
1914, when I was proposing to send my sons to his school. But our thoughts and interests drew us

perfect present
very close to one another, I have never missed an opportunity of meeting and talking to him, and

simple past
I was the last person he spoke to before his sudden death. He was sixty-six years of age when he

died. Those last eight years were certainly the richest and most productive of his whole career;

simple present
he grew most in those years; he travelled farthest. I think I saw all the best of him. It is, I think,

perfect present   simple present
no disadvantage that I have known him only in his boldest and most characteristic phase. It saves

perfect past   perfect past
me from confusion between his maturer and his earlier phases. He was a much stratified man. He
had grown steadfastly all his life, he had shaken off many habitual inhibitions and freed himself

from once necessary restraints and limitations. He was, I recall, a rock-climber; he was a mental

simple past
rock-climber also, and though he was very wary of recalcitrance, there were times when his pace

progressive past
became so urgent that even his staff and his own family were tugging, breathless and perplexed,
at the rope.

Exercise 54B: Distinguishing Between Active and Passive Voice

Identify the following sentences as *A* for active or *P* for passive. If you're not sure, ask yourself: Is the subject *doing* the verb, or is the verb *happening* to the subject?

The Great Wall of China was built during the time of the Ming Dynasty.	P
The idea for the wall was imagined by Emperor Qin Shi.	P
The people of China wanted to deter invaders.	A
The Great Wall runs over 5,000 miles of China's mountainous land.	A
The wall was created from stones and dirt.	P
The wall is made of several smaller walls linked together.	P
Much of the wall has been destroyed by the elements over the centuries.	P
During the wall's history, many dynasties repaired the crumbling structure.	A
Guard towers were erected at various points along the way.	P
Many times, merchants used the wall for travel.	A
Soldiers were deployed to protect the travelers.	P

The Three Inner Passes and Three Outer Passes were set along the wall.	P
These passes were heavily fortified.	P
Each year, over 10 million people visit the Great Wall.	A
The wall varies in height from 20 to 23 feet.	A
A car can be driven over the widest portions.	P
Runners can experience this historical site in the annual Great Wall Marathon.	A

Exercise 54C: Forming the Active and Passive Voice

Fill in the chart below, rewriting each sentence so that it appears in both the active and the passive voice. Be sure to keep the tense the same. The first is done for you.

ACTIVE	PASSIVE
A ballet dancer will often progress to pointe shoes after several years of hard work.	Pointe shoes are often progressed to after several years of hard work by a ballet dancer.
Strong glue, cardboard, and fabric form the shoes' tips.	The shoes' tips are formed by strong glue, cardboard, and fabric.
Prima ballerinas may go through a pair of pointe shoes in one performance.	A pair of pointe shoes may be gone through by a prima ballerina in one performance.
A dancer must strengthen her feet and ankles for pointe shoes.	A dancer's feet and ankles must be strengthened for pointe shoes.
Dancers first used pointe shoes in the 1800s.	Pointe shoes were first used in the 1800s.
Ballerinas sew on some portions of the shoes themselves.	Some portions of the shoes are sewn on by the ballerinas themselves.

— LESSON 55 —

Parts of the Sentence
Active and Passive Voice

Note to Instructor: You should adapt the following review to the student's level of knowledge. If the student is clear on the concepts learned so far, and is able to diagram the sentences correctly, you do not need to follow every line of dialogue for every sentence. However, the student should be able not only to diagram the sentences, but to name the parts of the sentence and explain their use.

These sentences are adapted from *Treasury of American Indian Tales,* by Theodore Whitson Ressler.

Many traditional stories were related to him by his friends.

Little Rabbit lived a very happy and carefree life.

His mother and father were standing over him.

Someone or something was moving nearby.

Suddenly, Little Thunderbird felt very much alone.

> **Note to Instructor:** In the dialogues that follow, prompt the student whenever necessary.

Sentence #1

Instructor: Read me the first sentence from your workbook.

Student: Many traditional stories were related to him by his friends.

Instructor: What is the predicate?

Student: Were related.

Instructor: Who or what was related?

Student: Stories.

Instructor: Diagram the subject and the predicate. Does the subject perform the action? (Are the stories relating something?)

Student: No.

Instructor: *Stories* receives the action of the verb. Is *were related* an active or passive verb?

Student: Passive.

Instructor: Repeat after me: In a sentence with a passive verb, the subject receives the action.

Student: In a sentence with a passive verb, the subject receives the action.

Instructor: How many stories were related?

Student: Many.

Instructor: *Many* is an adjective, describing *stories* and answering the question "how many." What questions do adjectives answer?

Student: Which one, what kind, how many, whose.

Instructor: What kind of stories are the many stories?

Student: Traditional.

Instructor: *Many* and *traditional* are both adjectives describing *stories*. Place them on your diagram now.

Instructor: Now we have two phrases ending the sentence. What kind of phrases are these?

Student: Prepositional phrases.

Instructor: We know that prepositional phrases often act as adjectives or adverbs. The first phrase, *to him*, is telling how the stories were related. Where should we put it on the diagram?

Student: Under the verb phrase "were related."

Instructor: The second phrase, *by his friends*, also tells us how the stories were related, so where should it go?

Student: Under the verb phrase "were related."

Instructor: Good. Put those on the diagram, please.

Sentence #2

Instructor: Read the second sentence out loud.

Student: Little Rabbit lived a very happy and carefree life.

Instructor: What are the subject and predicate of the sentence?

Student: Little Rabbit lived.

Instructor: Little Rabbit lived what?

Student: A life.

Instructor: *Life* receives the action of the verb *lived*. What part of the sentence is *life*?

Student: Direct object.

Instructor: When a sentence has a direct object, you can be pretty sure that the subject is performing the action! Repeat after me: In a sentence with an active verb, the subject performs the action.

Student: In a sentence with an active verb, the subject performs the action.

Instructor: Diagram the subject, predicate, and direct object on your own paper. *Life* is the direct object.

> **Note to Instructor:** You may need to remind the student that "Little Rabbit" is a compound noun so both words are kept together on the diagram.

Instructor: What kind of life does Little Rabbit live?

Student: A very happy and carefree life.

Instructor: What kind of words are *happy* and *carefree*?

Student: Adjectives.

Instructor: Add both adjectives to the diagram along with the coordinating conjunction that connects them.

Instructor: What word does very describe?

Student: It describes happy.

Instructor: What type of word modifies an adjective?

Student: An adverb.

Instructor: What adverb question does *very* answer?

Student: To what extent.

Instructor: Add *very* to your diagram now.

Instructor: What part of speech is *a*?

Student: Article.

Instructor: The articles are *a*, *an*, and *the*. Diagram *a* beneath the word it modifies.

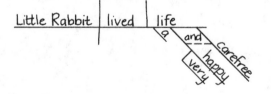

Sentence #3

Instructor: Read the third sentence out loud.

Student: His mother and father were standing over him.

Instructor: What are the two subjects in this sentence?

Student: Mother and father.

Instructor: What is the predicate?

Student: Were standing.

Instructor: Go ahead and diagram the compound subjects and the predicate on your paper now. What coordinating conjunction links the subjects?

Student: And.

Instructor: Put the coordinating conjunction on your diagram as well.

Instructor: What kind of pronoun is *His*?

Student: A possessive pronoun.

Instructor: What are possessive pronouns also known as?

Student: Possessive adjectives.

Instructor: What question does *his* answer?

Student: Whose.

Instructor: Is *his* acting as a possessive pronoun or a possessive adjective here?

Student: A possessive adjective.

Instructor: Go ahead and place it on your diagram.

Instructor: What phrase tells you where his mother and father were standing?

Student: Over him.

Instructor: What kind of phrase is this?

Student: A prepositional phrase.

Instructor: Since the phrase modifies the verb phrase *were standing*, does it act as an adjective or adverb?

Student: An adverb.

Instructor: What is the preposition?

Student: Over.

Instructor: What is the object of the preposition?

Student: Him.

Instructor: Place that prepositional phrase on your diagram.

Sentence #4

Instructor: Read the fourth sentence out loud.

Student: Someone or something was moving nearby.

Instructor: What are the two subjects in this sentence?

Student: Someone, something.

Instructor: What coordinating conjunction connects them?

Student: Or.

Instructor: What part of speech is *Someone*? What part of speech is *something*? (Hint: You learned about these words in Lesson 51).

Student: Indefinite pronouns.

Instructor: What are indefinite pronouns?

Student: Indefinite pronouns are pronouns without antecedents.

Instructor: What is the predicate?

Student: Was moving.

Instructor: Go ahead and diagram the subjects, the coordinating conjunction, and the predicate on your paper.

Instructor: Where was the *Someone or something* moving?

Student: Nearby.

Instructor: What part of speech answers the question where?

Student: Adverb.

Instructor: *Nearby* is an adverb that tells where. Diagram it beneath the verb phrase.

Sentence #5

Instructor: Read the final sentence out loud.

Student: Suddenly, Little Thunderbird felt very much alone.

Instructor: What is the subject of this sentence?

Student: Little Thunderbird.

Instructor: What is the predicate?

Student: Felt.

Instructor: Diagram those words.

Instructor: What kind of verb is *felt*?

Student: Linking verb.

> **Note to Instructor:** If the student cannot identify *felt* as a linking verb, ask "Did Little Thunderbird reach out and feel something?" Then point out that there is no direct object, just a word that refers back to Little Thunderbird. Try not to use the term *predicate adjective* so that you can complete the dialogue below.

Instructor: What word follows the linking verb?

Student: Alone.

Instructor: Is this a predicate adjective or predicate nominative?

Student: Predicate adjective.

Instructor: It describes Little Thunderbird; it doesn't rename him. Add *alone* to your diagram. There are two words that describe the predicate adjective alone. How alone does he feel?

Student: Very much.

Instructor: What do we call a word that describes an adjective?

Student: Adverb.

Instructor: What adverb question does *much* answer?

Student: To what extent.

Instructor: Add *much* to your diagram. What adverb question does *very* answer?

Student: To what extent.

Instructor: Yes. It is saying how much he feels alone. Diagram it under *much*.

Instructor: Now we have one word left: *Suddenly*. What question does *suddenly* answer? What does it tell us?

Student: It tells us when.

Instructor: What kind of word answers the question when?

Student: An adverb.

Instructor: Good. Put that on your diagram now.

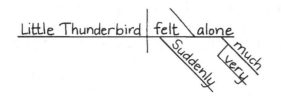

— **LESSON 56** —

Active and Passive Voice

Transitive and Intransitive Verbs

Exercise 56A: Transitive and Intransitive Verbs

Underline each verb serving as a predicate in the following sentences. Write *T* above each transitive verb and *IT* above each intransitive verb. Circle the direct object of each transitive verb. If the transitive verb is passive, draw an arrow from the verb back to the subject to show that the subject receives the action of the verb.

These sentences are adapted from *Biology and Its Makers*, by William A. Locy.

Aristotle <u>founded</u> his (Natural History) only on observation of the structure, physiology, and development of animals.

Soon after the period of Aristotle the center of scientific investigation <u>transferred</u> to Alexandria.

Here mathematics and geography <u>flourished</u>, but natural history <u>was</u> little <u>cultivated</u>.

Note to Instructor: You may have to remind the student that passive verbs are transitive, because the subject is receiving the action of the verb.

Ptolemy <u>had erected</u> a great (museum) and <u>founded</u> a large public (library) in Alexandria.

Aristotle <u>founded</u> his (system) of classification on a plan of organization.

Pliny <u>replaced</u> (it) by a highly artificial one, with a foundation of the incidental circumstance of the abodes of animals— in air, water, or on the earth.

The establishment of Harvey's view <u>replaced</u> Galen's (view) on the movement of the blood.

In 1597, Harvey <u>graduated</u> with an arts degree.

IT
The ancients <u>spoke</u> of spirits and humors in the body.

T
His discovery <u>created</u> modern (physiology)

T
For the first time ever in print, his book <u>demonstrated</u> the (movement) of blood in the body in a circuit.

T
The heartbeat <u>supplied</u> the propelling (force.)

IT
The notochord <u>occurred</u> in all vertebrate animals.

IT
Pasteur <u>might have remained</u> in this field of investigation.

T
Pasteur <u>won</u> his first scientific (recognition) at the age of twenty-five, in chemistry and molecular physics.

T
He <u>applied</u> his (discoveries) to the cure and prevention of diseases.

T
More than thirty "Pasteur institutes," with aims similar to the parent institution, <u>have been established</u> in different parts of the ciapvilized world.

Exercise 56B: Active and Passive Verbs

In the blanks below, rewrite each sentence with an active verb so that the verb is passive. Rewrite each sentence with a passive verb so that the verb is active. You may need to add or rearrange words or phrases to make the sentences grammatical!

These sentences are slightly adapted from *Hanukkah for Kids*, by Leanne Annett.

Jewish families often eat sufganiyah, a jelly donut, during Hanukkah.

Sufganiyah, a jelly donut, is often eaten by Jewish families during Hanukkah.

Many sufganiyot [the plural form] are coated in soft, powdered icing sugar.

Bakers coat many sufganiyot in soft, powdered icing sugar.

Children may be given money and presents from their friends and relatives.

Friends and relatives may give children money and presents.

Often small chocolate coins are given as presents to the children as well.

Often people give small chocolate coins as presents to the children as well.

The Hanukkah Menorah symbolizes the ancient temple and its Menorah.

The ancient temple and its Menorah are symbolized by the Hanukkah Menorah.

One candle on the Menorah is lit each day.

Someone lights one candle on the Menorah each day.

Many people call Hanukkah "the Festival of Lights."

Hanukkah is called "the Festival of Lights" by many people.

Exercise 56C: Diagramming

On your own paper, diagram every word in the following sentences. They are slightly adapted from *Chile: A Primary Source Cultural Guide,* by Jason Porterfield and Corona Brezina.

The Andes Mountains form a wall on the eastern side of Chile.

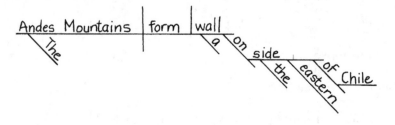

Chile's short rivers are unnavigable and full of rapids and cascades.

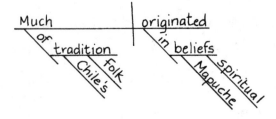

Much of Chile's folk tradition originated in Mapuche spiritual beliefs.

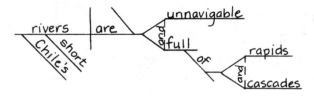

People placed dark stone and earth on hillsides and created geoglyphs.

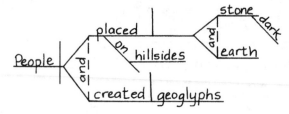

Specialized Pronouns

— LESSON 57 —

Parts of Speech
Parts of the Sentence
Intensive and Reflexive Pronouns

Exercise 57A: Identifying Intensive and Reflexive Pronouns

Underline the intensive and reflexive pronouns in the following sentences. Above each pronoun, write *I* for intensive or *R* for reflexive. If the pronoun is reflexive, also mark it as *DO* (direct object), *IO* (indirect object), or *OP* (object of the preposition). The first is done for you.

R IO
She gave <u>herself</u> the gift of a trip for her birthday.

I
The class presented their project to the author <u>himself</u>.

I
Did you write that song <u>yourself</u>?

R OP
Isaias wants to ride in the backseat by <u>himself</u>.

R OP
The lab's roof collapsed on <u>itself</u>.

R IO
Mom bought <u>herself</u> a new car.

I
The actors <u>themselves</u> had no idea that the microphones were out.

R OP
We reserved the beach chairs for <u>ourselves</u>.

I
I <u>myself</u> have not finished the homework.

I
Please take out the trash <u>yourself</u>.

R DO
The elephants protected <u>themselves</u> from predators by circling around each other.

Exercise 57B: Using Intensive and Reflexive Pronouns Correctly

Each of the following sentences contains errors in the usage of intensive and reflexive pronouns. Cross out the incorrect word and write the correction above it.

her
I gave the tour to Luis and ~~herself~~.

him
Did you drop Teresa and ~~hisself~~ off at the airport?

137

I ate the whole bag of chips ~~myselves~~! ^{myself}

Ashleigh and Tina moved the couch ~~theirselves~~. ^{themselves}

The penguin ~~hisself~~ guarded the egg. ^{himself}

Irena asked Antonio and ~~herself~~ where they had found the book. ^{her}

Exercise 57C: Diagramming Intensive and Reflexive Pronouns

On your own paper, diagram every word in the following sentences.

The valedictorian walked herself to the podium with great confidence.

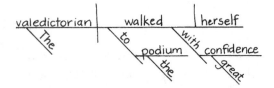

I found the clue itself on an old piece of paper.

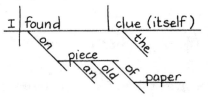

After their slideshow, I approved the plan myself.

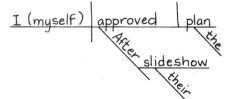

The queen drove herself to her country estate.

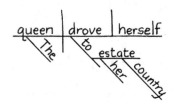

— LESSON 58 —

Demonstrative Pronouns
Demonstrative Adjectives

Exercise 58A: Demonstrative Pronouns and Demonstrative Adjectives

In the sentences below, label every occurrence of *this*, *that*, *these*, and *those* as either *DP* (demonstrative pronoun) or *DA* (demonstrative adjective). Draw an arrow from each demonstrative adjective to the noun it modifies. Label each demonstrative pronoun as *S* (subject), *DO* (direct object), *IO* (indirect object), or *OP* (object of the preposition).

These sentences are taken from *The War That Saved my Life*, by Kimberly Brubaker Bradley.

^{DA}
This story I'm telling starts out four years ago, at the beginning of the summer of 1939.

^{DA}
In the morning, though, those first words stuck in my head until I couldn't stand it anymore.

^{DP OP}
But I wouldn't lie about this.

It was just the two of us that morning, Mam gone I don't know where.
DA

"Pretty soon you'll be going to school anyhow," I said, astonished I hadn't fully realized
DP DO
this before.

It seemed impossible, but all these men had come from one ship.
DA

DP S
"These are the ornaments Becky and I put on our trees together."

I'd become a fighter, that summer.
DA

DP S
That's what happened, though not the way I thought it would.

At one point Miss Smith said, "Ada, would you hand me three of those apples?"
DA

DP S
She threatened to board over my window if I went downstairs again. That was always her
threat to me.

DP DO
The instant I said that, everything changed.

Her eyes narrowed. "I don't know what you're up to, girl. I don't know where you got all
DA
these words."

We were riding again, but this time we took a path Maggie chose, through the woods, down
DA
to the beach.

Exercise 58B: Demonstrative Pronouns

In the blank beneath each sentence, write a possible description of the thing or person that the underlined demonstrative pronoun stands for. Make sure to choose the correct number. (And use your imagination.)

Note to Instructor: The answers below are just examples—accept any description that fits the sentence and is the correct number!

This smells horrible!
The jug of spoiled milk smells horrible!

Mom was delighted by those!
Mom was delighted by the gorgeous hydrangeas!

That seems like it would be scary.
The giant rollercoaster seems like it would be scary.

These are ripe.
The juicy, delicious peaches are ripe.

Exercise 58C: Diagramming

On your own paper, diagram every word in the following three sentences.

Before the storm, the mayor herself will describe this new evacuation plan for the city.

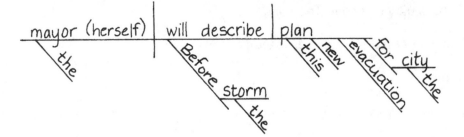

Where should I put these books and those supplies?   Some of that is on her mind.

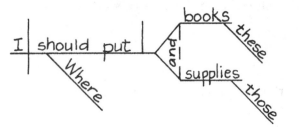   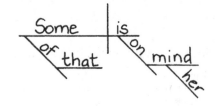

— **LESSON 59** —

Demonstrative Pronouns

Demonstrative Adjectives

Interrogative Pronouns

Interrogative Adjectives

Exercise 59A: Identifying Demonstrative and Interrogative Pronouns

Underline all of the demonstrative and interrogative pronouns in the sentences. There may be more than one in each sentence.

These sentences are taken from *Alice's Adventures in Wonderland*, by Lewis Carroll.

"The March Hare will be much the most interesting, and perhaps as <u>this</u> is May it won't be raving mad—at least not so mad as it was in March." As she said <u>this</u>, she looked up, and there was the Cat again, sitting on a branch of a tree.

"I'm sure <u>those</u> are not the right words," said poor Alice, and her eyes filled with tears again as she went on.

"Beautiful Soup! <u>Who</u> cares for fish, game, or any other dish? <u>Who</u> would not give all else for two pennyworth only of beautiful Soup?"

"Why, <u>what</u> are *your* shoes done with?" said the Gryphon. "I mean, <u>what</u> makes them so shiny?"

"And now <u>which</u> is <u>which</u>?" she said to herself, and nibbled a little of the right-hand bit to try the effect.

First came ten soldiers carrying clubs; <u>these</u> were all shaped like the three gardeners, oblong and flat, with their hands and feet at the corners: next the ten courtiers; <u>these</u> were ornamented all over with diamonds, and walked two and two, as the soldiers did.

"I haven't the least idea <u>what</u> you're talking about," said Alice.

"<u>Who</u> is to give the prizes?" quite a chorus of voices asked.

Exercise 59B: Using Interrogative and Demonstrative Pronouns Correctly

Choose the correct word in parentheses. Cross out the incorrect word.

(~~Whose~~/ Who's) coming to the beach with us today?

(Whose /~~Who's~~) towel is missing?

(~~Who~~/ Whom) did you ask to meet us there?

With (~~who~~/ whom) are you sharing a raft?

(~~This~~/ These) are your fins, and (this /~~these~~) is your snorkel.

(~~That~~/ Those) are mine.

(~~Whose~~/ Who's) going in the water first?

(Who /~~Whom~~) wants to build a sandcastle?

(~~This~~/ These) are strong waves!

(~~Who~~/ What) should we eat first?

(~~Who~~/ Whom) did you ask to swim?

(This /~~These~~) was a wonderful day together!

Exercise 59C: Diagramming Interrogative and Demonstrative Pronouns

On your own paper, diagram the following sentences.

Which is the right book for Algebra?

I must sweep that porch and those steps.

Whose is that beautiful garden?

Who made this?

She said that?

She | said | that

What is your name?

What | is \ name
       \your

We laughed about this and that.

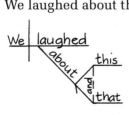

— LESSON 60 —

Pronoun Review

Sentences Beginning with Adverbs

Exercise 60A: Singular/Plural Indefinite Pronouns

Cross out the incorrect verb in each sentence.

All of the competitors (was/were) at the field.
Most of the storm (has/have) passed.
None of the casserole (is/are) eaten.
Some of her game pieces (has/have) broken.
(Is/Are) any of the bananas ripe?
Some of the kittens (is/are) sleeping.
Most of the yard (was/were) overgrown with weeds.
I spoke to the detective, but all of the files (has/have) burned in the terrible fire.

Exercise 60B: Interrogatives and Demonstratives

In each of the following sentences, underline the interrogatives and demonstratives. If they are
acting as adjectives, draw a line from each to the noun it modifies. If they are acting as other parts
of the sentence, label them (S for subject, DO for direct object, IO for indirect object, or OP for
object of the preposition).

These sentences are from *Memoirs of Aaron Burr*, by Aaron Burr and Matthew L. Davis.

Our mutual friend, Stewart, with <u>whom</u> I spent part of the evening, informed me you were still
in Elizabethtown.

Perhaps you will think me a weak, presumptuous being; but permit me, dear sir, to assure you,
<u>this</u> does not proceed from a whim of the moment.

Many of these letters, thus written, are now in existence.

I felt myself interested in the welfare of the province whose constitution you are now framing.

The armies were separated by a range of hills, at that time covered with wood, called the Heights of Gowannus.

What expeditions are on hand?

I have withdrawn abruptly. I would conceal that which I had not confidence to communicate.

What then will be your substitute?

Exercise 60C: Diagramming Practice

On your own paper, diagram every word of the following sentences, also taken from *Memoirs of Aaron Burr*.

What storms and tempests should I have avoided?   There is no better man.

Tryon ran and in his haste left all of his cattle and plunder behind him.

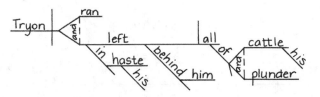

He spent much of his leisure time in the State Department.

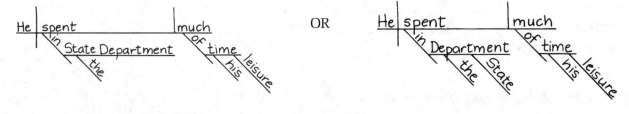

> **Note to Instructor:** *State Department* could be treated as an adjective modifying a noun or as a compound *noun*. Both ways are acceptable answers.

— REVIEW 5 —
Weeks 13-15

Topics
Pronouns and Antecedents
Possessive Pronouns
Subject and Object Pronouns
Indefinite Pronouns (and Subject-Verb Agreement)
Troublesome Verbs
Active and Passive Voice
Conjugating Passive Voice
Intensive and Reflexive Pronouns
Demonstrative and Interrogative Pronouns

Review 5A: Types of Pronouns

Put each pronoun in the word bank in the correct category of pronoun.

myself	its		who	what
our		I		us
them	these		themselves	him
some		she		most
they	this		their	himself
that		all		which

Personal Subject	I	she	they
Personal Object	us	them	him
Personal Possessive	its	our	their
Indefinite	some	most	all
Demonstrative	these	this	that
Interrogative	who	what	which
Intensive/Reflexive	myself	themselves	himself

Review 5B: Using Correct Pronouns

Cross out the incorrect pronoun in parentheses.

The person riding the horse was (she/~~her~~).

Kiley, Abigail, Noah, and (I/~~me~~) carried the boxes into the warehouse.

The campers brought (their/~~they're~~) art projects to Vivaan and (~~I~~/me).

(~~Whose~~/Who's) signing up to bring snacks?

(Who/~~Whom~~) locked (~~hisself~~/himself) out?

Did those students raise the money all by (~~theirselves~~/themselves)?

144

(~~Who~~/Whom) are you riding with?

Treena and (I/~~myself~~) will pick up coffee for the group.

The last passengers on the plane were Jake and (he/~~him~~).

(There/~~their~~) is a new movie theater by (~~there~~/their) house, so (~~their~~/they're) going to see (their/~~they're~~) newest release tomorrow.

Review 5C: Pronouns and Antecedents

Circle the twenty-eight personal pronouns (subject, object, and possessive) in the following excerpts from *The Tale of Despereaux*, by Kate DiCamillo. Draw arrows to each pronoun's antecedent.

"Where are my babies?" said the exhausted mother when the ordeal was through. "Show to me my babies."

The father mouse held the one small mouse up high. "There is only this one," he said.

"Mon Dieu, just the one mouse baby?" asked the mother.

"Just the one. Will you name him?"

"All of that work for nothing," said the mother. She sighed. "Such a disappointment." She was a French mouse who had arrived at the castle long ago in the luggage of a visiting French diplomat. "Disappointment" was one of her favorite words. She used it often.

The mouse mother held a handkerchief to her nose and then waved it in front of her face. She sniffed. "I will name him. Yes. I will name this mouse Despereaux, for all the sadness, for the many despairs in this place. Now, where is my mirror?"

Her husband handed her a small shard of mirror. The mouse mother looked at her reflection and gasped aloud. "Toulèse," she said to one of her sons, "get for me my makeup bag. My eyes are a fright."

Review 5D: Agreement with Indefinite Pronouns

Choose the correct word in parentheses to agree with the indefinite pronouns. Cross out the incorrect word.

We wanted to stop for coffee, but nothing (seems/~~seem~~) to be open.

Did you see that some of the towels (~~is~~/are) still wet?

Pauline said that all of the pot pie (tastes/~~taste~~) burnt.

All of the branches (~~was~~/were) covered with ice.

A few of the students (~~sits~~/sit) outside for lunch.

It was so dark that each of the stars (was/~~were~~) very bright.

Any of those tools (~~works~~/work) for this project.

Everyone (laughs/~~laugh~~) at the comedian's new special.

Several pages (~~is~~/are) ripped.

(~~Does~~/Do) all of the chairs have cushions?

(Does/~~Do~~) all of the deck need painting?

Review 5E: Distinguishing Between Active and Passive Voice

Identify each underlined verb as *A* for active voice or *P* for passive voice. These sentences were taken from *Dirt*, by Bill Buford.

Ten pages <u>were dedicated</u> to making a sauce from an egg.   P

The peppers <u>are roasted</u>; then the tomatoes, but, according to the particularly
French insistence of needing to remove the skin first.   P

Our host, the farmer, never <u>used</u> pesticides, not for any ideological reason
necessarily, but because pesticides were expensive.   A

I <u>had come</u> to Lyon to learn how to cook French food.   A

George <u>joined</u> him, approaching on tiptoes. The boys then <u>talked</u> to the sheep.   A,A

Around a white platter, floppy circles of "tube food" <u>were being arranged</u>.   P

The practice is said to produce a more animated jumble of flavors than if
everything <u>had been plopped</u> in at the same time.   P

We were lucky when we <u>got</u> a loaf hot from the oven, <u>carried</u> it home, and <u>ate</u>
it with salty butter.   A,A,A

It was the bread, Bob's bread, that <u>was talked</u> about.   P

Review 5F: Troublesome Verbs

Choose the correct verb form in parentheses. Cross out the incorrect forms.

Dulce lives outside the small town of Antigua, Guatemala, where her family (raises/~~rises~~)
coffee plants at their *finca*.

Every year, her parents (let/~~leave~~) her attend the festivities known as Semana Santa during the
week that leads up to the Easter holiday.

Local artists plan out elaborate constructions called *alfombras*, which are intricate carpets of
colored sawdust and fresh flowers (lying/~~laying~~) along each city block.

Often, artists will (lie/lay) local items such as coffee beans, fruits, or leaves from tropical plants on their *alfombras*.

On Good Friday, Dulce (sits/sets) on the bus riding into Parque Central, located in the heart of Antigua, where she will meet up with other girls from her church.

Together, they will walk to the street where they will (sit/set) up their *alfombra*. They will have only a few hours to create their masterpiece.

By the time the artisans have (risen/raised) from their posts on Good Friday evening, every street in Antigua will wear a brilliantly-colored carpet.

Nearly one million people have (let/left) their homes to line the sidewalks of the tiny town and watch as giant statues of saints are carried through the streets.

Local parishioners, dressed in long, dark robes, (rise/raise) the heavy statues to their shoulders and walk slowly down the avenues.

Dulce and her friends will (rise/raise) to their feet as the last statue passes and then begin the long walk to the bus stop.

As they (let/leave) the city behind, the sun will be (rising/raising) already.

Dulce waves goodbye to her friends, and she quietly opens the creaking gate that leads into her courtyard. Her mother is (lying/laying) fresh tortillas on a plate and pouring hot coffee for Dulce.

WEEK 16

Imposters

— LESSON 61 —

Progressive Tenses
Principal Parts
Past Participles as Adjectives
Present Participles as Adjectives

Exercise 61A: Identifying Past Participles Used as Adjectives

Underline the past participles used as adjectives in the following sentences, taken from the classic short story "Tobermory," by the British short story writer Saki (given name: Hector Hugh Munro). In the story, which takes place at a house party, the guest Cornelius Appin teaches the cat Tobermory to talk—and the cat immediately begins to tell all of the secrets of the other guests!

Draw a line to the noun or pronoun that each past participle modifies.

In a minute Sir Wilfrid was back in the room, his face white beneath its tan and his eyes dilated with excitement.

His agitation was unmistakably genuine, and his hearers started forward in a thrill of awakened interest.

A Babel-like chorus of startled exclamation arose, amid which the scientist sat mutely enjoying the first fruit of his stupendous discovery.

In the midst of the clamour Tobermory entered the room and made his way with velvet tread and studied unconcern across to the group seated round the tea-table.

A shiver of suppressed excitement went through the listeners, and Lady Blemley might be excused for pouring out the saucerful of milk rather unsteadily.

With the disappearance of his too brilliant pupil Cornelius Appin found himself beset by a hurricane of bitter upbraiding, anxious inquiry, and frightened entreaty.

Exercise 61B: Identifying Present Participles Used as Adjectives

Underline the present participles used as adjectives in the following sentences, taken from *Time Cat: The Remarkable Journeys of Jason and Gareth,* by Lloyd Alexander. Jason has just discovered that his black cat, Gareth, can travel in time—and they're back in ancient Egypt, about to get into some serious trouble.

Draw a line to each word modified.

I was wondering if you thought there might be a special occasion <u>coming</u> up soon?

In the distance, Jason heard the sound of flutes and drums <u>approaching</u>.

Some carried sacred rattles; others held staves topped by <u>glittering</u> golden statues of cats.

<u>Chanting</u> voices filled the air with the "Hymn to the Great Cat."

There were several scribes, Jason saw, all <u>carrying</u> bundles of papyrus scrolls or clay tablets.

"Naturally," said the Chief Scribe, <u>smiling</u> blandly.

Before Jason could turn and race from the hall, the Chief Scribe scooped the <u>bristling,</u> <u>spitting</u> Gareth from his arms.

Exercise 61C: Diagramming Present and Past Participles Used as Adjectives

On your own paper, diagram the following sentences (adapted from *The Wild Cat Book,* by Fiona and Mel Sunquist).

A running cheetah covers 23 feet with each stride.   Cheetahs have enlarged lungs.

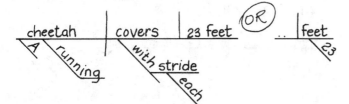

Hunting cheetahs prefer night hours.   A sleeping cheetah has retracted claws.

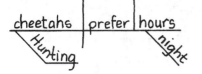

— LESSON 62 —

Parts of Speech and Parts of Sentences
Present Participles as Nouns (Gerunds)

Exercise 62A: Identifying Gerunds

In the following sentences, loosely adapted from *The First Emperor: China's Terracotta Army*, by Jane Portal, underline each subject once and each predicate twice. Write *DO* above any direct objects of the predicate, *IO* above any indirect objects of the predicate, *OP* above any objects of prepositions, and *PN* above any predicate nominatives. Then, circle each gerund.

(Building) walls and (digging) ditches were required of Shang Yang's subjects.

The emperor went even further in (asserting) his central position in the cosmos.

His first task was (constructing) a tomb for his eternal dwelling.

(Producing) thousands of life-sized clay figures was an extraordinary task.

Techniques included (coiling) and (rolling) of clay, and the use of molds.

After (drying) at room temperature, the figures were put into a kiln for (firing).

The craftsmen practiced (painting) the clothes of the figures.

Exercise 62B: Diagramming Verb Forms

On your own paper, diagram every word in the following sentences.

Digging peasants unearthed clay fragments.

Archaeologists have been locating 600 pits of terracotta figurines.

Choice specimens of clay warriors have been unearthed.

The unearthed warriors were facsimiles of the surrounding court.

720,000 workers were laboring on this project.   Shang Yang began conquering.

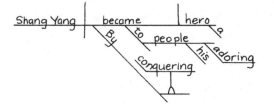

By conquering, Shang Yang became a hero to his adoring people.

— LESSON 63 —

Gerunds
Present and Past Participles as Adjectives
Infinitives
Infinitives as Nouns

Exercise 63A: Identifying Gerunds and Infinitives

Underline the gerunds and infinitives in the following quotes about the nature of life. Identify the imposters as *G* for gerund or *I* for infinitive. Then, identify each gerund or infinitive as a subject (*S*), predicate nominative (*PN*), direct object (*DO*), or object of a preposition (*OP*).

When I went to school, they asked me what I wanted to be when I grew up.
   —John Lennon

If life were predictable it would cease to be life, and be without flavor.
   —Eleanor Roosevelt

The secret of success is to do the common thing uncommonly well.
   —John D. Rockefeller Jr.

Try not to become a man of success. Rather become a man of value.
   —Albert Einstein

If you want to achieve excellence, you can get there today. As of this second, quit doing less-than-excellent work.
   —Thomas J. Watson

The greatest glory in living lies not in never falling, but in rising every time we fall.
   —Nelson Mandela

                                                                                 I DO

If you genuinely want something, don't wait for it—teach yourself <u>to be</u> impatient.
   —Gurbaksh Chahal

> **Note to Instructor:** The understood subject of the imperative verb *teach* is [you]. The direct object of *teach* is *to be*, and *yourself* is the indirect object.

                                              G OP   I PN

The only way out of the labyrinth of <u>suffering</u> is <u>to forgive</u>.
   —John Green
       I DO   I DO

I want <u>to live</u> and <u>feel</u> all the shades, tones and variations of mental and physical experience possible in my life.
   —Sylvia Plath

> **Note to Instructor:** The second verb form, *feel*, is an infinitive with an understood *to*: I want to live and [to] feel.

                                   I PN   I PN

The most important thing is <u>to enjoy</u> your life—<u>to be</u> happy—it's all that matters.
   —Audrey Hepburn
     I DO

I love <u>to see</u> a young girl go out and grab the world by the lapels.
   —Maya Angelou
         I DO

He wants <u>to be</u> nothing except what he is.
   —Herman Hesse
 I S   I PN

<u>To say</u> goodbye is <u>to die</u> a little.
   —Raymond Chandler

Exercise 63B: Diagramming Gerunds and Infinitives

On your own paper, diagram the following sentences.

I want to live and feel.

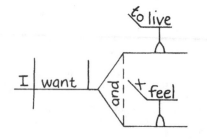

The secret of success is to do.

The greatest glory in living lies in rising.

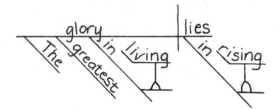

Teach yourself to be.

The only way out of the labyrinth of suffering is to forgive.

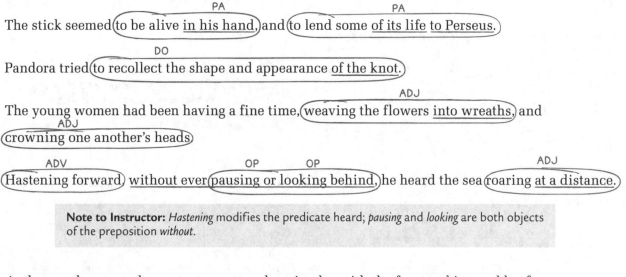

— LESSON 64 —

Gerunds

Present and Past Participles

Infinitives

Gerund, Participle, and Infinitive Phrases

Exercise 64A: Identifying Phrases that Serve as Parts of the Sentence

In the following sentences, begin by underlining each prepositional phrase. Then, circle each group of words that contains a gerund, infinitive, or past participle. Each one serves as a part of the sentence. (Those circled phrases might include some of your prepositional phrases!) Label each circled phrase. Your options are: *ADJ* (adjective), *ADV* (adverb), *S* (subject), *IO* (indirect object), *DO* (direct object), *OC* (object complement), *OP* (object of the preposition), *PN* (predicate nominative), or *PA* (predicate adjective).

These sentences are taken from *A Wonder Book for Girls and Boys,* a retelling of classic Greek myths by the nineteenth-century American novelist Nathaniel Hawthorne.

                                        PA   PA
The stick seemed (to be alive in his hand,) and (to lend some of its life to Perseus.)

                            DO
Pandora tried (to recollect the shape and appearance of the knot.)

                                                                    ADJ
The young women had been having a fine time, (weaving the flowers into wreaths,) and
    ADJ
(crowning one another's heads)

    ADV   OP   OP   ADJ
(Hastening forward) without ever (pausing or looking behind,) he heard the sea (roaring at a distance.)

> **Note to Instructor:** *Hastening* modifies the predicate heard; *pausing* and *looking* are both objects of the preposition *without.*

An honest, hearty welcome to a guest works miracles with the fare, and is capable of
    OP
(turning the coarsest food to nectar and ambrosia.)

He was exceedingly light and active <u>in his figure</u>, <u>like a person</u>(much accustomed <u>to</u>) [ADJ]
(gymnastic exercise.)

(To end the dispute) [S] was old Dame Scarecrow's aim, so she took the eye <u>out of her forehead</u>, and held it forth <u>in her hand</u>.
[ADV]
(Thanking his stars <u>for the lucky accident</u>(of finding the old fellow asleep,) [OP] Hercules stole <u>on tiptoe</u> <u>towards him</u>, and caught him <u>by the arm and leg</u>.

His wife Baucis and himself had dwelt <u>in the cottage</u> <u>from their youth,</u>(earning their bread) [ADJ]
(by honest labor) always poor(but still contented) [ADJ]

Exercise 64B: Diagramming

On your own paper, diagram all of the sentences from Exercise 64A.

For the seventh sentence, only diagram:

"To end the dispute was old Dame Scarecrow's aim."

The stick seemed to be alive in his hand, and to lend some of its life to Perseus.

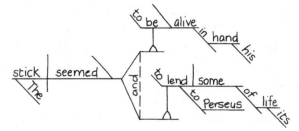

Note to Instructor: The infinitives *to be* and *to lend* both serve as predicate adjectives, following the linking verb *seemed* and describing *stick*. The adjective *alive* follows *to be* and serves as another predicate adjective, while the indefinite pronoun *some* follows *to lend* and serves as a direct object.

Pandora tried to recollect the shape and appearance of the knot.

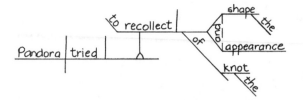

Note to Instructor: The prepositional phrase *of the knot* is adjectival and describes both shape and appearance.

The young women had been having a fine time, weaving the flowers into wreaths, and crowning one another's heads.

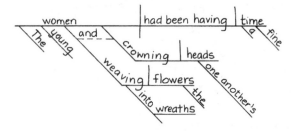

Note to Instructor: The compound possessive adjective *one another's* serves as a single modifier.

Hastening forward, without ever pausing or looking behind, he heard the sea roaring at a distance.

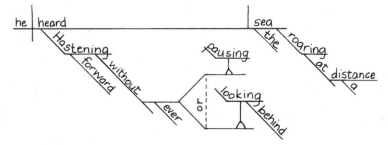

An honest, hearty welcome to a guest works miracles with the fare, and is capable of turning the coarsest food to nectar and ambrosia.

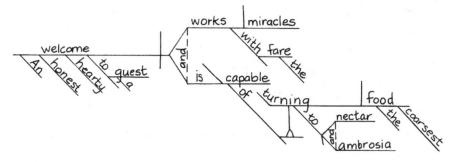

He was exceedingly light and active in his figure, like a person much accustomed to gymnastic exercise.

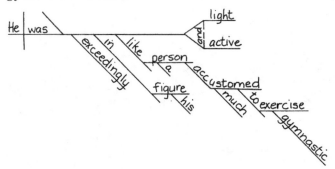

Note to Instructor: The adverb *exceedingly*, the prepositional adverb phrase *in his figure*, and the prepositional adverb phrase *like a person much accustomed to gymnastic exercise* all modify both *light* and *active*, so they come after the predicate adjective slanted line but before the division of the predicate adjective spaces into two.

To end the dispute was old Dame Scarecrow's aim.

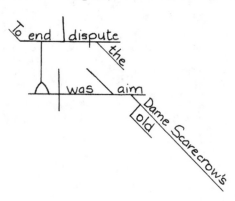

Note to Instructor: If the student asks, this is an odd occurrence of *old* acting as an adverb instead of an adjective—because it is modifying the possessive proper adjective *Dame Scarecrow's*.

Thanking his stars for the lucky accident of finding the old fellow asleep, Hercules stole on tiptoe towards him, and caught him by the arm and leg.

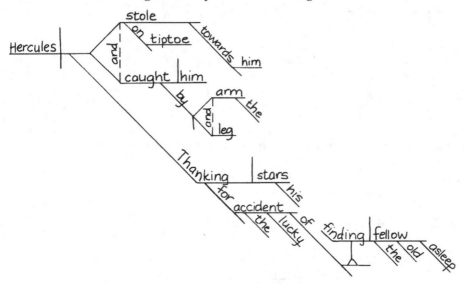

His wife Baucis and himself had dwelt in the cottage from their youth, earning their bread by honest labor, always poor, but still contented.

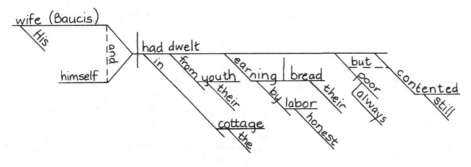

Comparatives and Superlatives, Subordinating Conjunctions

— LESSON 65 —

Adjectives
Comparative and Superlative Adjectives

Exercise 65A: Identifying Positive, Comparative, and Superlative Adjectives

Identify the underlined adjective forms as *P* for positive, *C* for comparative, or *S* for superlative.

These speeches are all taken from the Elizabethan (1592) play *The Tragical History of Doctor Faustus*, by the English playwright Christopher Marlowe. Marlowe was born the same year as William Shakespeare, and many critics think that his use of language is as good as (or better than) Shakespeare's—but while Shakespeare lived to be 52 and wrote over 35 plays, Christopher Marlowe wrote only six plays before he was murdered at the age of 29, after an argument with three other men.

My <u>most excellent</u> lord, I am ready to accomplish your request in all things.
     ^S

Nothing so <u>sweet</u> as magic is to him,
     ^P
Which he prefers before his <u>chiefest</u> bliss.
     ^S

Yea, <u>stranger</u> engines for the brunt of war,
     ^C
Than was the <u>fiery</u> keel at Antwerp's bridge,
     ^P
I'll make my servile spirits to invent.

When all is done, divinity is <u>best</u>.
     ^S

But, leaving off this, let me have a wife,
The <u>fairest</u> maid in Germany.
     ^S

Then up to Naples, <u>rich</u> Campania,
     ^P
Whose buildings <u>fair</u> and <u>gorgeous</u> to the eye,
     ^P   ^P
The streets straight forth, and paved with <u>finest</u> brick
     ^S

'Twas made for man, therefore is man <u>more excellent</u>.
     ^C

When Faustus had with pleasure taken the view
Of rarest things, and royal courts of kings,
      ^S
He stayed his course, and so returned home,

Then read no more; thou hast attained that end:
A greater subject fitteth Faustus' wit.
  ^C

Brighter art thou than flaming Jupiter
^C
When he appeared to hapless Semele;
More lovely than the monarch of the sky
   ^C

Break heart, drop blood, and mingle it with tears,
Tears falling from repentant heaviness
          ^P
Of thy most vile and loathsome filthiness.
     ^S   ^S

> **Note to Instructor:** The adverb *most* modifies both *vile* and *loathsome*: thy most vile and [most] loathsome filthiness.

Exercise 65B: Forming Comparative and Superlative Adjectives

Fill in the blank with the correct form of the adjective in parentheses. These sentences are from another dramatic version of the Dr. Faustus legend: *Faust*, by the German poet Johann Wolfgang von Goethe, translated into English by Bayard Taylor.

Go, find yourself a __more obedient__ slave!   (comparative of *obedient*)

Behind me, field and meadow sleeping,
I leave in deep, prophetic night,
Within whose dread and holy keeping
The __better__ soul awakes to light.   (comparative of *good*)

Why, just such talk as this, for me,
Is that which has the __most attractive__ features!   (superlative of *attractive*)

But still the time may reach us, good my friend.
When peace we crave and __more luxurious__ diet.   (comparative of *luxurious*)

A __most fastidious__ person you appear.   (superlative of *fastidious*)

See, the entrancing
Whirl of their dancing!
All in the air are
__Freer__ and __fairer__.   (comparatives of *free* and *fair*)

Full well you know what here is wanting;
The crowd for __strongest__ drink is panting.   (superlative of *strong*)

The ___fairest___ stars from Heaven he requireth,   (superlative of *fair*)
From Earth the ___highest___ raptures and the ___best___.   (superlatives of *high* and *good*)

Bid the new career
Commence,
With ___clearer___ sense,   (comparative of *clear*)
And the new songs of cheer
Be sung thereto!

No fount of ___newer___ strength is in my brain: (comparative of *new*)
I am no hair's-breadth more in height,
Nor ___nearer___, to the Infinite.   (comparative of *near*)

Mephisto, seest thou there,
Alone and far, a girl ___most pale___ and ___fair___?   (superlatives of *pale* and *fair*)

> **Note to Instructor:** It is not incorrect for the student to write *most pale* and *most fair* or *palest* and *fairest*, but show him the original version and point out that the second *most* can also be understood. (Including it or not is determined by the rhythm of the poetic dialogue, not grammatical correctness!)

And rival storms abroad are surging
A chain of ___deepest___ action forging   (superlative of *deep*)
From sea to land, from land to sea.
Round all, in wrathful energy.

I would I had a ___more cheerful___ strain!   (comparative of *cheerful*)

Exercise 65C: Diagramming Comparative and Superlative Adjectives

On your own paper, diagram the following sentences, from two modern versions of the Faust legend.

> From Stephen Vincent Benét, "The Devil and Daniel Webster," a short story first published in 1936:

Lesser men will be made President and you will be passed over.

After supper he sent the family off to bed, for he had most particular business with Mr. Webster.

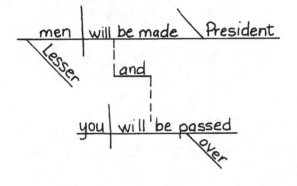

From Dorothy Sayers, "The Devil to Pay," a play first produced in 1939:

That is a most unjust accusation.

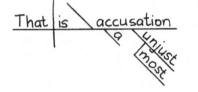

Tomorrow, we shall be richer and more powerful.

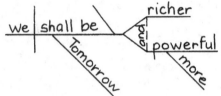

Try to look a little more respectable.

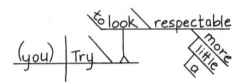

— LESSON 66 —

Adverbs
Comparative and Superlative Adverbs
Coordinating Conjunctions
Subordinating Conjunctions

Exercise 66A: Diagramming Comparatives

Diagram the first two sentences on the frames provided. Diagram the remaining sentences on
your own paper.

These are all adapted from a series of novels by the twentieth-century author Walter Farley. He
first wrote the story of a fiery horse called the Black Stallion who was shipwrecked with a young
boy named Alec Ramsay on a deserted island, and then afterwards wrote many more books about
the Black Stallion, Alec, and all of the Black Stallion's descendants.

The Black Stallion
One sailor was more courageous than the rest.

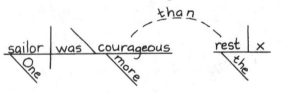

The Black Stallion Revolts
It was larger than the *Drake*.

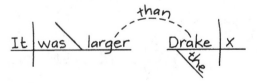

The Island Stallion
It was a long narrow room with a ceiling no higher than the tunnel.

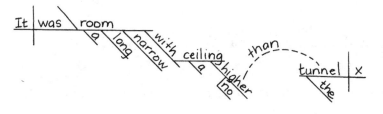

The Black Stallion Revolts
It was more barren than any other part of the island.

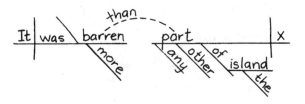

The Black Stallion's Filly
The early afternoon was more balmy than hot.

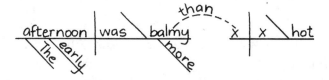

> **Note to Instructor:** The comparative adjective *more balmy* here connects to an understood pronoun: [it] [was] hot.

Exercise 66B: Identifying Positive, Comparative, and Superlative Adverbs

Identify the underlined adverb forms as *P* for positive, *C* for comparative, or *S* for superlative.

These sentences are taken from the novel *Twice Shy*, by Dick Francis. Francis wrote dozens of novels about horse racing in England, and is considered one of the great suspense novelists of the twentieth century.

It appeared that what I'd told them so far did indeed interest them <u>intensely</u>.
P

The office was <u>more accurately</u> a sitting room with armchairs, television, bookshelves and pinewood paneling.
C

It took me a good hour to look everything up, and I thought that if I ever did begin to do it all <u>seriously</u> I would make myself a whole host of <u>more easily</u> accessible tables than those available in the record books.

Before we had finished eating, the telephone rang and <u>most unexpectedly</u> it was Ted Pitts calling from Switzerland.

The police had <u>more moderately</u>[C] pointed out that if it was Angelo who woke first he might complete the job of murdering me: and Angelo was now in his unwaking sleep along the hallway, guarded by a constable night and day.

He looked from me to Jonathan, glancing at him <u>briefly</u>[P] at first and then looking <u>longer</u>[C], <u>more carefully</u>[C], seeing what he didn't believe.

I thrust him again aside and opened the door, and found myself in a short passage which led into a large bedroom which was equipped <u>most noticeably</u>[S] with another vast window looking out to the golf course.

An enveloping wave of weakness washed through me, and I found myself sagging <u>fairly</u>[P] <u>comprehensively</u>[P] against the cupboard and then half lying on the floor.

> **Note to Instructor:** The positive adverb *fairly* modifies the positive adverb *comprehensively*, which itself modifies the present participle *sagging*.

Cassie slept <u>more peacefully</u>[C] than before, the cast becoming less of a problem as she grew used to it.

I was beginning to feel <u>most dreadfully</u>[S] ill, with clamminess creeping over my skin and breaking into a sweat on my forehead.

He shoved the four planks into place between the cellar door and the refrigerator, <u>casually</u>[P] remarking that during the night he'd sawn the wood to fit.

The psychopathic young man had at length erupted as a full-blown coarsened thug, no <u>longer</u>[C] as Jonathan had described him, <u>occasionally</u>[P] high on the drug of recklessness, but <u>more plainly</u>[C], <u>comprehensively</u>[C], violent.

> **Note to Instructor:** The comparative adverb *comprehensively* shares the modifier *more* from the previous comparative adverb *more plainly*: but more plainly, [more] comprehensively, violent. Both adverbs modify the adjective *violent*.

Exercise 66C: Forming Comparative and Superlative Adverbs

Fill in the blank with the correct form of the adverb in parentheses.

These sentences are taken from the novel *To the Hilt*, by Dick Francis.

There was a full net of hay in the stall also, and a head collar for tying up a horse <u>more comfortably</u> than with a bridle. [comfortably]

Then, as daylight <u>more positively</u> arrived, I saddled and bridled him in the shelter. [positively]

> **Note to Instructor:** Both *positively* and *more positively* are acceptable.

"He usually paints nice-looking golf scenes, all sunshine with people enjoying themselves. Sells them to America <u>faster</u> than he can paint them, don't you, Al?" [fast]

"Well," I said, "when you gave me the Hilt to hide all those years ago, the first thing I thought about was metal detectors, because those things find gold almost __more easily__ than any other metal." [easily]

"Make him tell you. Hit him __harder__." [hard]

The bothy faced west, which often gave me long mornings of near-perfect painting light, followed by warm afternoon glows that I'd at first subconsciously translated into mellowing glazes and then, when I found out those pictures sold __most quickly__, into a commercial technique. [quickly]

> **Note to Instructor:** The student should be able to deduce from context that the painter is talking about multiple pictures, and so the ones that sold quickly sell "most" quickly of all of the pictures. If the student uses "more quickly," accept the answer, but point out that "most quickly" is more accurate.

Ivan gave it back to me again __later__, and I have brought it here today. [late]

— LESSON 67 —

Irregular Comparative and Superlative Adjectives and Adverbs

Exercise 67A: Best and Worst Games

Put the following games in the columns according to your opinion. (There are no correct answers—it all depends on you.)

> **Note to Instructor:** Accept any answers!

Monopoly	The Game of Life	Scrabble
Sorry	Candy Land	Battleship

good: _____   **bad:** _____

better: _____   **worse:** _____

best: _____   **worst:** _____

Exercise 67B: Using Comparatives and Superlatives Correctly

Choose the correct form in parentheses. Cross out the incorrect form.

These sentences are from the classic nineteenth-century horse novel *Black Beauty*, by Anna Sewell.

They often hurt themselves, often spoil (~~well~~/good) horses, and tear up the fields, and all for a hare or a fox, or a stag, that they could get (more easily/~~easier~~) some other way.

I always get on (well/~~good~~) with horses, and if I could help some of them to a fair start I should feel as if I was doing some (~~well~~/good).

When he brushed my head he went as (~~careful~~/carefully) over my eyes as if they were his own, and never stirred up any ill-temper.

Though he has not had much experience in driving, he has a (light/~~lightly~~) firm hand and a (quick/~~quickly~~) eye, and he is very (careful/~~carefully~~).

But this man went on laughing and talking, while at every step the stone became (more firmly/~~firmer~~) wedged between my shoe and the frog of my foot.

He stroked my face (~~kind~~/kindly).

Joe is the (best/~~most good~~) of grooms.

This often disordered my health, and made me sometimes (~~heavily~~/heavy) and (~~dully~~/dull), but (more often/~~oftener~~) restless and feverish.

I was sorry for Ginger, but of course I knew very little then, and I thought (most likely/~~likeliest~~) she made the worst of it.

> **Note to Instructor:** The superlative *likeliest* is an adjective form: "the likeliest outcome."

The man, (~~fierce~~/fiercely) pulling at the head of the fore horse, swore and lashed (most brutally/~~brutallest~~).

He had kept his promise so (~~good~~/well) that York thought he might be (~~safer~~/safely) trusted to fill his place while he was away, and he was so clever and honest that no one else seemed so (~~good~~/well) fitted for it.

If you would take it off I am sure he would do (better/~~more good~~)—do try it.

The place is (more/~~most~~) than ten miles away from here, out in the country.

No one (more thoroughly/~~most thoroughly~~) understood his business than he did, and when he was all right there could not be a (~~faithfuller~~/more faithful) or (~~valuabler~~/more valuable) man.

We call them dumb animals, and so they are, for they cannot tell us how they feel, but they do not suffer (less/~~more little~~) because they have no words.

I love horses, and it riles me to see them (~~bad~~/badly) used; it is a (bad/~~badly~~) plan to aggravate an animal till he uses his heels; the (first/~~firstly~~) time is not always the (last/~~lastly~~).

There were also open spaces of fine short grass, with ant-hills and mole-turns everywhere; the (~~baddest~~/worst) place I ever knew for a headlong gallop.

I never was cleaned so (~~light~~/lightly) and (~~quick~~/quickly) as by that little old man.

A woman was standing at her garden gate, shading her eyes with her hand, and looking (~~eager~~/eagerly) up the road.

I needed no whip, no spur, for I was as (eager/~~eagerly~~) as my rider.

As we neared the corner I heard a horse and two wheels coming (~~rapid~~/rapidly) down the hill toward us.

Then he took a piece of iron the shape of my foot, and clapped it on, and drove some nails through the shoe quite into my hoof, so that the shoe was (firmly/~~firm~~) on. My feet felt very (~~stiffly~~/stiff) and (~~heavily~~/heavy), but in time I got used to it.

I know a (great/~~greatly~~) deal, and I can tell you there is not a (~~best~~/better) place for a horse all round the country than this. John is the (best/~~better~~) groom that ever was.

Exercise 67C: Using Correct Adverbs and Adjectives

Choose the correct word in parentheses. Cross out the incorrect word.

The two-year-old racehorse is growing (~~good~~/ well). He's getting more muscular by the day.

The two-year-old racehorse is growing (good/~~well~~). He doesn't bite his groom any more!

The racehorse ran so (~~good~~/ well)! He was much faster than the other horses in the race.

The broodmare remains (bad/~~badly~~); she tries to kick anyone who goes into her stall.

The broodmare remains (~~bad~~/badly); she hates her stall and wants to run around the pasture!

In the race, the steeplechasers did not run (~~slow~~/ slowly); they were (good/~~well~~) at getting over fences!

The newborn foal doesn't feel (~~good~~/ well) today. He had his shots this morning!

The vet looks (bad/~~badly~~) to the foal; he's carrying a syringe!

The vet looks (~~bad~~/badly). He's not wearing his glasses, and he can't see the markings on the syringe!

— LESSON 68 —

Coordinating and Subordinating Conjunctions
Correlative Conjunctions

Exercise 68A: Coordinating and Subordinating Correlative Conjunctions

In each of the following sentences, circle the correlative conjunctions. Underline the words or groups of words that the conjunctions connect. In the blank, write *C* for coordinating or *S* for subordinating.

These sentences have been slightly adapted from the 1909 collection *Persian Literature, Comprising THE SHÁH NÁMEH, THE RUBÁIYÁT, THE DIVAN, and THE GULISTAN, Volume 1.*

(Though) my life may be short, (yet) I may prove my love.   C

The country they inhabited was overrun with herds of wild boars, which destroyed (not only) the produce of their fields, (but also) the fruit and flowers in their orchards and gardens.   C

(Not only) has he despised my orders, (but) he has cruelly occasioned the untimely death of both.   C

His apprenticeship was spent in Arabic Bagdad, sitting at the feet of noted scholars, and taking in knowledge (not only) of his own Persian Sufism, (but also) of the science and learning of the Abbasid Caliphs.   C

(If) the truth must be told, (then) your life approaches its end.   C

His treasury was captured, and the soldiers of his army (either) killed (or) made prisoners of war.   C

My weapon must now be (either) dagger (or) I must draw my sword.   S

O king, thou art the willow-tree, all barren,
With (neither) fruit, (nor) flower.   C

He could (neither) sleep (nor) could he take food.   S

The register, including (both) old (and) young, was accordingly prepared.   C

(Although) your consideration for my happiness has passed away, I (still) wish
to please you.   C

And (though) destruction spoke in every word,
Enough to terrify the stoutest heart,
(Still) he adhered to what he first resolved.   C

(Though) often wonderfully ornate, (still) his style is more sober than that of Háfiz.   S

Exercise 68B: Subject-Verb Agreement

Cross out the incorrect verb in each set of parentheses.

The first king of both the Medes and the Persians (was / ~~were~~) a warrior chief
named Madius.

Neither the Persian troops nor the Median commander (was / ~~were~~) afraid of fighting
the Scythians.

Legend says that both Nebuchadnezzar's palace and his great garden (~~was~~ / were) built
in honor of his Persian wife.

Both Cyrus and the Persian army (~~is~~ / are) remembered for conquering the Medes.

Either camels or an elephant (was / ~~were~~) used to fight against the Lydians.

Not only cavalry but also a siege engine (~~was~~ / were) part of the conquest of Lydia.

Not only terror but also reward (~~was~~ / were) Cyrus's strategies for retaining the loyalty
of his people.

Either the Persians or Carthage (~~were~~ / was) poised to become Rome's greatest enemy.

Exercise 68C: Diagramming

On your own paper, diagram every word of the following sentences, adapted from *The History of
the Ancient World*, by Susan Wise Bauer.

The villain in the story is probably neither Cambyses nor Darius.

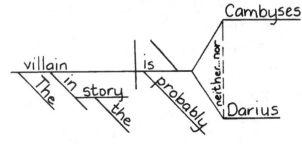

Themistocles died either from illness or from a dose of poison.

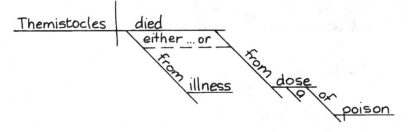

In 424, both Darius II's father and his half-brother died.

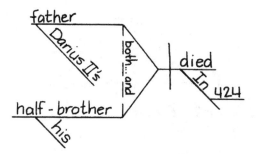

The patricians were gaining not only land but also money.

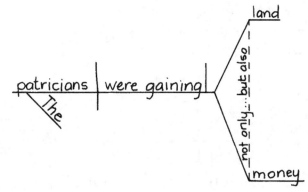

Neither Alexander's fury nor his charm could persuade his men.

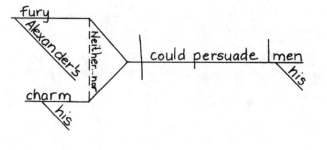

WEEK 18

Clauses

— LESSON 69 —

Phrases
Sentences
Introduction to Clauses

In the phrases and clauses below, the subjects are underlined once and the verbs twice for your reference.

Along with the tomato and garlic	***phrase***	*no subject or verb*
<u>Vinegar</u> <u><u>adds</u></u> a little acid	***clause***	*subject and verb*
While <u>potatoes</u> <u><u>are roasting</u></u>	***clause***	*subject and verb*
<u><u>Make</u></u> the two sauces	***clause***	*verb with understood [you] subject*
<u><u>Are salting</u></u> and <u><u>peppering</u></u> generously	***phrase***	*two verbs, no subject*
The <u>sauce</u> <u><u>should</u></u> not <u><u>be</u></u>	***clause***	*subject and verb*
Two warm and delicious sauces	***phrase***	*subject, no verb*

(Although) tapas bars are popular in Spain	D
Patatas bravas are crispy potatoes eaten with a sauce	I
(Whether) or not you choose to fry the potatoes on the stove	D
(Since) this is a traditional Spanish dish	D
Sprinkle lightly with salt	I

Note to Instructor: although the final clause does not have a stated subject, it is an imperative with an understood subject [you] that can stand on its own..

Exercise 69A: Distinguishing Between Phrases and Clauses

Identify the following groups of words as *phrases* or *clauses*. The clauses may be independent or dependent, but you only need to identify them as *clauses*. In each clause, underline the subject once and the verb twice.

Small, lightly breaded, and fried fritters	phrase
If <u>you</u> <u><u>have</u></u> eggs, potatoes, and onions	clause
Creamy, smooth, and very delicious	phrase
(You) <u><u>Roll</u></u> the dough into logs	clause
If fried until golden brown	phrase
Cleaned <u>squid</u> <u><u>are</u></u> best for this recipe	clause
Plenty of garlic, pepper, and paprika	phrase

Certainly <u>they</u> <u>will ask</u> for the recipe	clause
Tomato-based sauces with a little bit of spice	phrase
Grilled <u>octopus</u> <u>is served</u> with olive oil	clause
Chopped and mixed with the rest of the stuffing	phrase
(You) <u>Coat</u> them in egg and breadcrumbs	clause
Unless <u>you</u> <u>are</u> not very hungry	clause

Exercise 69B: Distinguishing Between Independent and Dependent Clauses

Identify the following clauses as independent (*IND*) or dependent (*DEP*).

These clauses are adapted from José Andrés, *Tapas: A Taste of Spain in America*.

I arrived on these shores twelve years ago	IND
Who thought he knew it all	DEP
Peoples that shaped Spanish cooking	DEP
People will like your cooking	IND
Since I arrived in the United States	DEP
Spanish food is more available than ever	IND
Although the conquistadors mistook them for truffles	DEP
Tapas are a way of living and eating	IND
While they are chatting with their friends	DEP
Press each olive	IND
Until the pit pops out	DEP

Exercise 69C: Turning Dependent Clauses into Complete Sentences

Choose three of the dependent clauses below and attach independent clauses to them to form complete thoughts. Write your three new sentences on your own paper. (The dependent clause can go before or after the independent clause.)

Note to Instructor: The original sentences from José Andrés's *Tapas: A Taste of Spain in America* are found below. Accept any reasonable answers!

Since the Phoenicians first planted olive trees on the Iberian peninsula, olive oil has been the king of Spanish cooking.

You'll know your sofrito is ready when the tomato has broken down and deepened in color.

And even though we don't use firewood in today's kitchens, controlling the heat is still the most important task of anyone aspiring to cook classic paella.

After the cheeses have dried on wood shelves for twenty days and aged in the caves for four months, penicillin spores spread through the cheeses' natural holes, and the resulting blue mold is spectacular.

Cook, shaking the pan in a circular motion every minute or so, until the potatoes are slightly browned.

Take care with the salt because the clams add their own saltiness to the rice.

— LESSON 70 —
Adjective Clauses
Relative Pronouns

Intro 70: Introduction to Adjective Clauses

The following sentences are taken from *Star Trek, The Official Guide to Our Universe: The True Science Behind the Starship Voyages*, written by Andrew Fazekas and published by National Geographic.

Complete each sentence by filling in the blank with the appropriate letter from the clauses below. (This is for fun, so just do your best—you might need to know something about the Star Trek universe to get them all right!)

The game makes the crew vulnerable to a plot by Ktarian Etana Jol, __C__ .

A. which ended up in the Delta Quadrant

The *U. S. S. Enterprise* arrives at Deep Space Station K-7 after being called to protect a shipment bound for Sherman's Planet, __D__ .

B. whom humans respected for their early development of warp drive technology

Most of the action takes place within the Milky Way galaxy's Alpha Quadrant—except for *Voyager*, __A__ .

C. who planted the game on Will Riker in hopes of using mind control to take over the *Enterprise*-D

Amid tension, a trader arrives bearing tribbles: a fuzzy creature __E__ .

D. whose control the Federation and the Klingons are disputing

Vulcans are an ancient humanoid species __B__ .

E. that Uhura delightedly adopts as a pet

Exercise 70A: Identifying Adjective Clauses and Relative Pronouns

Underline the adjective clauses in the following sentences, and circle the relative pronouns. Draw an arrow from each relative pronoun to its antecedent.

These sentences are taken (and occasionally, very slightly condensed) from *The Hitchhiker's Guide to the Galaxy*, by Douglas Adams.

In moments of great stress, every life form (that) exists gives out a tiny subliminal signal.

Near them on the floor lay several rather ugly men (who) had been hit about the head with some heavy design awards.

The speech patterns you actually hear decode the brainwave matrix (which) has been fed into your mind by your Babel fish.

The Dentrassis are an unruly tribe of gourmands, a wild but pleasant bunch (whom) the Vogons had recently taken to employing as catering staff on their long-haul fleets.

As the others started after him he was brought up short by a Kill-O-Zap energy bolt (that) cracked through the wall in front of him and fried a small section of adjacent wall.

He didn't notice anything but the caterpillar bulldozers crawling over the rubble (that) had been his home.

Orbiting this at a distance of roughly ninety-eight million miles is an utterly insignificant little blue-green planet (whose) life forms are amazingly primitive.

The only place they registered at all was on a small black device called a Sub-Etha Sens-O-Matic (which) winked away quietly to itself.

Ford beckoned to Prosser, (who) sadly, awkwardly, sat down in the mud.

Exercise 70B: Choosing the Correct Relative Pronoun

In each sentence, cross out the incorrect relative pronoun. Above the correct pronoun, write *S* for subject, *OP* for object of the preposition, or *DO* for direct object to show how the relative pronoun is used within the dependent clause.

These sentences are slightly adapted from *The First Men in the Moon*, by H. G. Wells.

He knitted his brows like one (who/~~whom~~) encounters a problem.
                                                      S

These beings with big heads, on (~~who~~/whom) the intellectual labours fall, form a sort
                                       OP
of aristocracy in this strange society.

I was a little sorry for the baker, (who/~~whom~~) was a very decent man indeed.
                                           S

He told me of a work-shed he had, and of three assistants (~~who~~/whom) he had trained.
                                                               DO

Gibbs, (who/~~whom~~) had previously seen to this responsibility, had suddenly attempted to shift it
          S
to the man who had been a gardener.

A man (who/~~whom~~) leaves the world when days of this sort are about is a fool!
         S

They are a strange race with (~~who~~/whom) we must inevitably struggle for mastery.
                                    OP

Those (who/~~whom~~) have only seen the starry sky from the earth cannot imagine its appear-
         S
ance when the vague half-luminous veil of our air has been withdrawn.

Exercise 70C: Diagramming Adjective Clauses

On your own paper, diagram every word of the following sentences, slightly adapted from *The Essential Novels: Star Wars Legends 10-Book Bundle*, published by Random House in 2012.

She had interrogated a droid who had crawled out of the destruction.

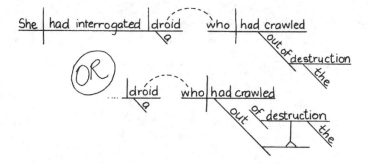

Note to Instructor: The adjective clause *who had crawled out of the destruction* is straightforward, but *out of* can be diagrammed either as a compound preposition, or as the preposition *out* with the prepositional phrase *of the destruction* acting as the object of the preposition.

The admiral was one for whom decisiveness had always been a career hallmark.

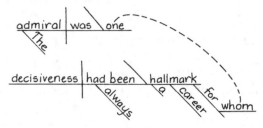

Cronal finally understood the terrible flaw that would bring the Order of the Sith to its ultimate destruction.

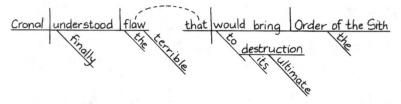

It would roll over Shadowspawn's base like a line of thunderheads whose clouds were toxic smoke, whose rain was fire.

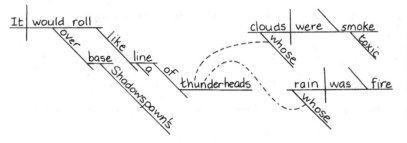

Note to Instructor: In this sentence, *like* acts as a preposition. The two adjective clauses describe *thunderheads*, which have both clouds and rain.

— LESSON 71 —

Adjective Clauses

Relative Adverbs

Adjective Clauses with Understood Relatives

Exercise 71A: Relative Adverbs and Pronouns

In the following sentences, underline each adjective clause. Circle each relative word and label it as *RP* for relative pronoun or *RA* for relative adverb. Draw an arrow from each relative word back to its antecedent in the independent clause.

These sentences are taken from four works of fiction by the British-born writer Jhumpa Lahiri.

They walked past the mathematics building, (where) Mr. Sen taught his classes.
(*Interpreter of Maladies*)

It was centuries ago, (when) the Bay of Bengal's current was stronger.
(*The Lowland*)

Here was an explanation (why) her mother had gone. [RA]
(*The Lowland*)

My parents often hosted friends (who) came from New Jersey or New Hampshire for the weekend, [RP]
to eat elaborate dinners and talk late into the evening about Indian politics.
(*Unaccustomed Earth*)

There were times (when) it had been so cold. [RA]
(*The Namesake*)

Just before Christmas she would go to Calcutta, (where) her parents had returned after a lifetime in [RA]
Massachusetts and (where) in January, she would marry Navin. [RA]
(*Unaccustomed Earth*)

That meant that her bucket, quilts, and the bundle of reeds (which) served as her broom all had to [RP]
be braced under one arm.
(*Interpreter of Maladies*)

She shook the quilts once again underneath the letter boxes (where) she lived, then once again at [RA]
the mouth of the alley, causing the crows (who) were feeding on vegetable peels to scatter in [RP]
several directions.
(*Interpreter of Maladies*)

And yet they had met; after all her adventures, it was he (whom) she had married. [RP]
(*The Namesake*)

For the greater number of her twenty-nine years, Bibi Halldar suffered from an ailment (that) [RP]
baffled family, friends, priests, palmists, spinsters, gem therapists, prophets, and fools.
(*Interpreter of Maladies*)

The following weekend, (when) he visited her again, the phone rang as they were having dinner. [RA]
(*The Lowland*)

You didn't have to tell me why you did it.
(*Interpreter of Maladies*)

> **Note to Instructor:** This is a trick final sentence; the clause *why you did it* is a noun clause, acting
> as the object of the infinitive *to tell*.

Exercise 71B: Missing Relative Words

Draw a caret in front of each adjective clause and insert the missing relative pronoun. (For the
purposes of this exercise, *which* and *that* and *whom* may be used interchangeably.)

   The original sentences are slightly condensed from the comical spooky story "The Canterville
Ghost," by Oscar Wilde.

The only thing that consoled him was the fact ^that he had not brought his head with him.

He had been christened Washington by his parents, in a moment of patriotism ^which / that he never
ceased to regret.

whom / that

This was the housekeeper∧Mrs. Otis, at Lady Canterville's earnest request, had consented to keep in her former position.

which / that

It was his most remarkable impersonation, one∧the Cantervilles had every reason to remember.

that / which

I have come from a modern country, where we have everything∧money can buy.

that / which

He had been very wicked, but he was really sorry for all∧he had done.

which / that

Washington was following with a lighted candle∧he had caught up from the table.

whom / that

He thought of the Dowager Duchess∧he had frightened into a fit as she stood before the glass in her lace and diamonds.

Exercise 71C: Diagramming

On your own paper, diagram the following sentences from your first two exercises.

> **Note to Instructor:** Remember to give all necessary help!

There were times when it had been so cold.

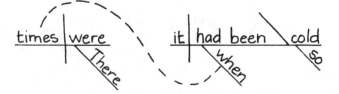

You didn't have to tell me!

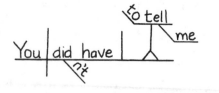

> **Note to Instructor:** The entire infinitive phrase *to tell me* is the direct object of the verb *did have*, which here functions as an action verb with the meaning of *be obliged, be forced*. The pronoun *me* is the indirect object of the infinitive.

It was centuries ago, when the Bay of Bengal's current was stronger.

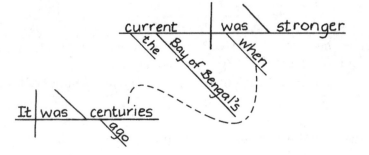

He had been very wicked, but he was really sorry for all he had done.

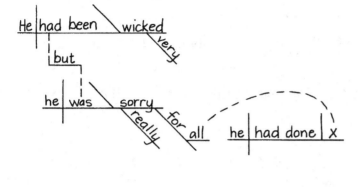

> **Note to Instructor:** The understood relative pronoun *that* acts as the direct object of the verb *had done* and refers back to the pronoun *all*.

— LESSON 72 —

Adverb Clauses

Exercise 72A: Adverb Clauses

In the following sentences, underline each adverb clause. Circle the subordinating word at the beginning of each clause and label it *ADV* for adverb or *SC* for subordinating conjunction. Draw an arrow from the subordinating word back to the verb, adverb, or adjective that the clause modifies.

These sentences are taken from a memoir written by Matthew Henson, who accompanied the explorer Robert Peary on seven different voyages to the Arctic in order to reach the North Pole. Henson was one of the only African-American Arctic explorers in the early years of the twentieth century. He's credited with the co-discovery of the North Pole, along with Robert Peary, in 1909.

My mother died (when) I was seven years old.

February 19, 1909: It was six a.m. when I routed out the boys for breakfast.

> **Note to Instructor:** This is a trick sentence! The clause *when I routed out the boys for breakfast* modifies the time *six a.m.* and is an adjective clause introduced by a relative adverb.

I am writing (while) the tea is brewing.

We were able to make better time (because) we had his trail to follow.

(When) the expedition returned, there were two who went back who had not come north with us.

He had scarcely set foot on the opposite floe (when) the floe on which he had been previously isolated swung off, and rapidly disappeared.

I knew little fear, (though) I did think of the ghosts of other parties, flitting in spectral form over the ice-clad wastes.

Neither Borup nor Marvin had caught up, but we felt that (unless) something had happened to them, they would surely catch up in a few more days.

ADV

(While) we were at work making a pathway, the dogs would curl up and lie down with their noses in their tails.

SC

Our letters, (although) they bore no more recent a date than that of March 23, 1909, were eagerly read.

ADV

It was cold and dark (when) we left camp number one on the morning of March 2, at half past six o'clock.

Exercise 72B: Descriptive Clauses

In the following sentences, underline each dependent clause. Above each, write *ADVC* for adverb clause or *ADJC* for adjective clause. Circle each subordinating word and label it as *ADV* for adverb, *RP* for relative pronoun, or *SC* for subordinating conjunction. Draw an arrow from the subordinating word back (or forward) to the word in the independent clause that the dependent clause modifies.

These sentences are taken from the memoir *Touching My Father's Soul: A Sherpa's Journey to the Top of Everest*, by Jamling T. Norgay. Norgay's father, Tenzing Norgay, made the first ascent of Everest with the New Zealand climber Edmund Hillary. After standing on top of Everest, the two men always refused to say which one of them first set foot on the summit.

Jamling Norgay climbed Everest in 1996, following in his father's footsteps.

ADV   ADVC

(When) I became an adult, and after my father's death, my desire to climb Everest only intensified.

> **Note to Instructor:** It is also fine if the student includes *and after my father's death* in the underlined clause. Technically, *and after my father's death* is a prepositional adverbial phrase that also modifies *intensified*, but it is reasonable to assume that it belongs with the dependent clause.

RP   ADJC

I returned to Darjeeling with troubled thoughts, (which) began to invade my dreams.

RP   ADJC

We presented Rimpoche with kata blessing scarves, in (which) I enclosed some rupee notes.

Rimpoche may have been aware of the deaths on the mountain—the more than 150

RP   ADJC   RP   ADJC

(who) have died attempting to climb it, or about one for every five (who) have reached the summit.

ADV   ADJC

Before 1951, (when) Nepal opened to the outside world for the first time, Everest expeditions

RP   ADJC

were staged out of Darjeeling, a town (that) was created in the mid-1800s by the British raj as a hill station.

> **Note to Instructor:** The adverb *when* is a relative adverb introducing an adjective clause, returning back to 1951 (a time).

First ascents <u>are generally recognized as successful only</u> (when) the climbers return alive.

> **Note to Instructor:** The adverb *only* modifies the verb *are recognized* in the main clause.

(She bowed her head slightly in gratitude and said that (although) the entire afternoon had been
quite windy, it was fortunate (that) the wind had stopped.

> **Note to Instructor:** The entire clause *that although the entire afternoon had been quite windy, it was*
> *fortunate that the wind had stopped* is a noun clause, serving as the object of the verb *said*. The two
> adverb clauses are contained within that noun clause.

Jangbu helped Chen back to camp, (where) most climbers were still asleep, and returned him to
his tent.

> **Note to Instructor:** The relative adverb *where* refers back to the place *camp*.

The Tibetans topped up the lamps with their own melted butter, (which) they had brought in
vacuum flasks.

(When) they departed the South Col for the South Summit on May 26, carrying summit flags, my
father was resigned to the possibility (that) they could reach the top.

Then, (just as) I was becoming used to the disappointment, the summit nearly surprised me.

> **Note to Instructor:** It is also acceptable for the student to simply identify the subordinating
> conjunction *as*, rather than the compound conjunction *just as*.

Exercise 72C: Diagramming

On your own paper, diagram every word of the following sentences from the first two exercises.

We were able to make better time because we had his trail to follow.

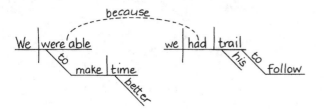

When the expedition returned, there were two who went back who had not come to the north with us.

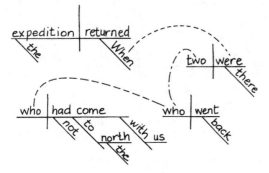

We presented Rimpoche with kata blessing scarves, in which I enclosed some rupee notes.

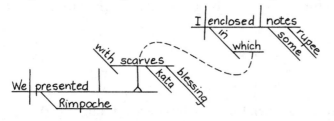

> **Note to Instructor:** You may need to point out that Rimpoche cannot be a direct object because he is not being presented. The prepositional phrase *with kata blessing scarves* acts as the direct object, with Rimpoche (receiving the scarves) as the indirect object.

When they departed the South Col for the South Summit on May 26, carrying summit flags, my father was resigned to the possibility that they could reach the top.

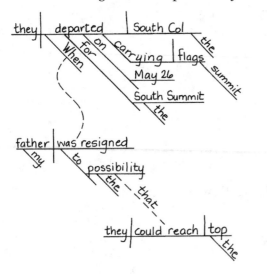

— REVIEW 6 —
Weeks 16-18

Topics

Personal Pronouns: Subject, Object, Possessive, Reflexive
Verb Voice (Active and Passive)
Verb Tense
Adjectives
Gerunds and Participles
Phrases
Clauses (Independent and Dependent)

Review 6A: Pronouns

In the following sentences, taken from *Good Germs, Bad Germs: Health and Survival in a Bacterial World,* by Jessica Snyder Sachs, circle each pronoun. Label each as *S* (subject form of the personal pronoun), *O* (object form of the personal pronoun), *P* (possessive form of the personal pronoun), *R* (reflexive), *INT* (intensive), *I* (indefinite), *INTER* (interrogative), *D* (demonstrative), or *RP* (relative pronoun).

The Eubacteria make themselves known by their production of the more odiferous hydrogen sulfide—familiar the world over for its rotten-egg smell.

"In severe sepsis, while you don't see the major organ damage associated with septic shock, you have cells leaking fluids, bile mixing with blood, oxygen and water mixed together in the lungs," he explains. "It may be that when these barriers begin to fail at the cellular level, it's not long before the organs themselves give out."

> **Note to Instructor:** In the phrase *these barriers*, the demonstrative *these* is an adjective, not a pronoun.

Drug-resistant microbes made up 50 percent or more of the intestinal bacteria in more than one-third of his healthy volunteers—none of whom had taken antibiotics in more than six months.

Something was destroying Ricky's organs, but exactly what or where it lurked in his body remained maddeningly unclear.

> **Note to Instructor:** The relative pronoun *what* refers back to the indefinite pronoun *something*. If the student does not realize this, explain that the *something* was *exactly what*, but the doctors just couldn't define *what* the *something* is! So *something* and *what* refer to the same unknown reality.

For oral antibiotics, (which) get absorbed through the intestinal tract, the challenge is the opposite: to keep the drugs inactive until after (they) get absorbed.

Even after decades of being lectured about antibiotic abuse, too many doctors still think of antibiotics as benign and use (them) with a "(what) can (it) hurt?" attitude.

> **Note to Instructor:** The pronoun *it* is the subject. The interrogative pronoun *what* is the object of the predicate *can hurt*.

Vancomycin-resistant enterococcus made (its) U.S. hospital debut in 1988. Within five years (it) was showing up in nearly one in ten hospital patients, and the majority of (those) (who) spent several days or more on vancomycin. Fortunately, VRE caused no harm in and of (itself) so long as (it) stayed put in a patient's intestines.

The first of (these) is *Streptococcus sanguis*, a bacterium unsurpassed in (its) ability to cling to the smooth enamel face of small incisors.

(All) (that) was required was a little human trickery.

Review 6B: Using Comparative and Superlative Adjectives Correctly

Choose the correct form in parentheses. Cross out the incorrect form.

These sentences are taken from *The Story of Germ Life*, by H. W. Conn.

Bacteria are decidedly the (~~most small~~/smallest) living organisms which our microscopes have revealed.

Their numbers are (~~most great~~/greatest) near the surface of the ground, and decrease in the (~~more up~~/upper) strata of air.

This explanation will enable us (more clearly/~~clearer~~) to understand the relation of different bacteria to disease.

The (most interesting/~~interestingest~~) facts connected with the subject of bacteriology concern the powers and influence in Nature possessed by the bacteria.

A (~~importanter~~/more important) factor of soil fertility is its nitrogen content, without which it is completely barren.

The (~~more large~~/larger) doses of the past, intended to drive out the disease, have been everywhere replaced by (~~more small~~/smaller) doses designed to stimulate the lagging body powers.

From the very (~~most early~~/earliest) period, ever since man began to keep domestic cattle, he has been familiar with dairying.

Creameries which make the (~~most high~~/highest) priced and the (most uniform/~~uniformest~~) quality of butter are those in which the (~~most great~~/greatest) care is taken in the barns and dairies to insure cleanliness and in the handling of the milk and cream.

The butter maker has learned by long experience that ripened cream churns (more rapidly/~~rapider~~) than sweet cream, and that he obtains a (~~more large~~/larger) yield of butter therefrom.

After the (most thorough/~~thoroughest~~) washing which the milk pail receives from
the kitchen, there will always be left many bacteria clinging in the cracks of the tin or
in the wood, ready to begin to grow as soon as the milk once more fills the pail.

The cheese maker finds in the ripening of his cheese the (most difficult/~~difficultest~~)
part of his manufacture.

The art of preparing flax is a process of getting rid of the worthless wood fibres and preserving
the valuable, (~~more long~~/longer), (~~more tough~~/tougher), and (more valuable/~~valuablest~~) fibres,
which are then made into linen.

Review 6C: Verbs

Underline the main verb (along with any helping verbs) in every clause below (both independent
and dependent).

In the space above each verb, write the tense (*SIMP PAST, PRES, FUT; PROG PAST, PRES, FUT;
PERF PAST, PRES, FUT*) and voice (*ACT* for active or *PASS* for passive). For state-of-being verbs,
write *SB* instead of labeling voice.

If the verb is an action verb, also note whether it is transitive (*TR*) or intransitive (*INTR*).

The first is done for you.

These sentences are taken from the Victorian novel *The Tenant of Wildfell Hall*, by Anne Brontë.

SIMP FUT ACT INTR   SIMP FUT SB
Perhaps he <u>will stay</u> among his friends till Christmas; and then, next spring, he <u>will be</u> off again.

SIMP PRES SB
Oh, it <u>is</u> cruel to leave me so long alone!

PERF PRES PASS TR   SIMP PRES ACT TR
I <u>have been accustomed</u> to make him <u>swallow</u> a little wine or weak spirits-and-water, by way of
SIMP PAST SB
medicine, when he <u>was</u> sick.

SIMP FUT ACT TR   SIMP FUT ACT TR
I know you <u>will have</u> a fellow-feeling for the old lady, and <u>will wish</u> to know the last of her history.

PERF PAST ACT TR   PROG PAST ACT TR
The servant <u>had</u> just <u>brought</u> in the tea-tray; and Rose <u>was producing</u> the sugar-basin and tea-caddy
from the cupboard in the black oak side-board.

SIMP PAST ACT INTR
I <u>glanced</u> round the church.

SIMP PRES ACT TR   SIMP FUT ACT TR
Mrs. Markham, I <u>beg</u> you <u>will</u> not <u>say</u> such things.

SIMP FUT PASS TR
We <u>shall be constrained</u> to regard ourselves as unwelcome intruders.

SIMP FUT SB
Well, I <u>shall be</u> neither careless nor weak.

PERF PRES ACT TR
I <u>have had</u> several letters from Arthur already.

SIMP PRES PASS TR   SIMP FUT PASS TR   SIMP PRES PASS TR
Of him to whom less <u>is given</u>, less <u>will be required</u>, but our utmost exertions <u>are required</u> of us all.

PROG PAST ACT INTR   PROG PAST ACT INTR
All who <u>were</u> not <u>attending</u> to their prayer-books <u>were attending</u> to the strange lady.

SIMP PAST PASS TR   PERF PAST ACT TR
I was annoyed at the continual injustice she had done me from the very dawn of our acquaintance.

> **Note to Instructor:** The object of the verb *had done* is *injustice*. The pronoun *me* is the indirect object: She had done me injustice.

Review 6D: Identifying Dependent Clauses

Underline each dependent clause in the following sentences. Circle the subordinating word. Label each clause as either adjective (*ADJ*) or adverb clause (*ADV*), and draw a line from each subordinating word to the word it modifies.

These sentences are taken from *The Annotated African American Folktales*, edited by Henry Louis Gates Jr. and Maria Tatar (Liveright, 2017).

From the Xhosa tale "The Story of Demane and Demazana"

ADJ
Once upon a time there lived a brother and sister, who were twins and orphans. They decided to

ADV
run away from their relatives because they had been treated so badly.

ADJ
Not much later, Demane, who had found nothing that day but a swarm of bees, returned.

ADV
Zim went out to get some water, and while he was gone Demane took his sister out of the sack and put the bees in it.

ADJ
Demane and Demazana took all of Zim's possessions, which were great in number, and soon they became wealthy people.

From the Congolese tale "The Story of the Four Fools"

ADJ
One day a wizard met a boy who was sitting by the roadside, upset and weeping bitter tears.

The captain of the vessel summoned a storm and sent rain down on the glass boat,

ADJ
which shattered. But the carpenter mended it, and the hunter fired away at the rain

ADV
until it stopped.

ADJ
The carpenter then staked his claim, for he had twice mended the ship in which they were sailing.

From "The Maiden, the Frog, and the Chief's Son," a story with uncertain origins

ADJ   ADV
One day the wife he disliked fell ill, and it was not long before she died.

> **Note to Instructor:** The adjective clause *he disliked* has an understood *that* as the subordinating word.

She would take those scrapings and throw them into a pit (where) there were frogs.
                                                                                    ADJ

> **Note to Instructor:** This is an adjective clause modifying a place and introduced by a
> subordinating adverb.

Things went on like that, day after day, (until) it was time for the Festival.
                                                            ADV

(When) she reached the pit, she threw bits of food into it.
   ADV

Review 6E: Present and Past Participles

Underline each present participle and past participle in the following sentences. Some are serving
as nouns; others, as adjectives. Label adjective forms as *ADJ* and draw a line to the word modified.
Label noun forms as *N* and write the part of the sentence that the noun is serving as.

These sentences are taken from *Origin Story: A Big History of Everything,* by David Christian.

We arrive in this universe through no choice of our own, at a time and place not of our choosing.
                                                                                            N
                                                                                  object of preposition

In 1992, the remains of an ancestor (referred to as Mungo 1) discovered by archaeologists in 1968
                                          ADJ   ADJ
were finally returned to the local Aboriginal community.

Like many people, I struggled to link the isolated fields I studied.
                                            ADJ

We can see the links connecting the various scholarly landscapes, so we can think more deeply
                          ADJ
about broad themes such as the nature of complexity, the nature of life, even the nature of our
own species!

I like to imagine a group of people sitting around a fire as the sun was setting forty thousand
                                       ADJ
years ago.

In my imagined twilight conversations around the fire, there are girls and boys, older men
      ADJ
and women, and parents and grandparents, some wrapped in animal furs and cradling babies.
                                                 ADJ   ADJ

Children are chasing one another at the edge of the lake while adults are finishing a meal of
mussels, freshly caught fish and yabbies, and wallaby steak.
                   ADJ

Told over many nights and days, their stories describe the big paradigm ideas of the Lake
ADJ
Mungo people.

The problem is that in a globally connected world, there are so many local origin stories
                                    ADJ
competing for people's trust and attention that they get in one another's way.
ADJ

Sharing also allows us to test the details of our maps against millions of other maps.
N
subject

Review 6F: Diagramming

On your own paper, diagram every word of the following sentences from *Miracle in Lake Placid: The Greatest Hockey Story Ever Told*, by John Gilbert.

The U.S. players hit the ice, absorbing the crowd's added enthusiasm, and immediately went to work.

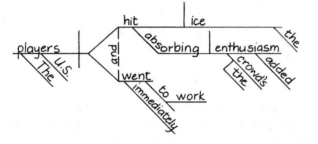

Note to Instructor: Although *to work* can be an infinitive in some contexts, here it is a prepositional phrase, with the noun *work* as the object of the preposition *to* (notice the tail on the *to* line!).

The clock was ticking down when David Christian choreographed the goal that stunned the Russians and changed the course of the game.

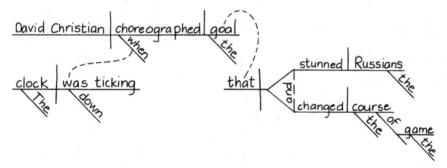

The pass was headed for David Christian at the right point, but as it slid, Eruzione picked it off as he skated left to right to the slot; then he shot, low and to the left.

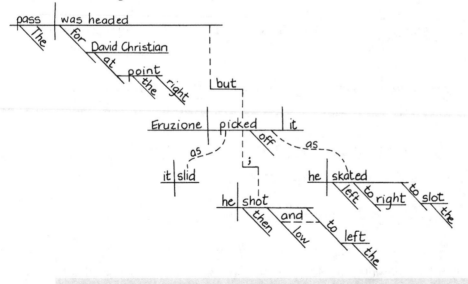

Note to Instructor: I have diagrammed *off* as an adverb modifying *picked* but the verb *picked off* could also be diagrammed on the same line as a single idiomatic expression. In the same way, *left to right* could be diagrammed as a single idiomatic adverb. Notice that although *low* and *to the left* are different grammatical constructions, they function as a pair, so that *and* is correctly diagrammed on a dotted line between them.

Setting up and scoring goals is the flashy part of hockey, but in the last 10 minutes of the biggest hockey game in U.S. history, the ability to think under intense defensive pressure was more important than any highlight-video scoring play.

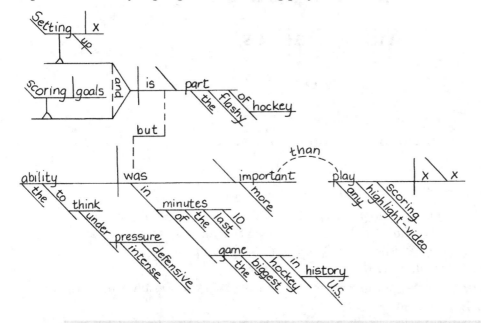

> **Note to Instructor:** The noun *goals* is understood as the object of the first principal part *setting*. I have diagrammed *10* as an adjective modifying *minutes*, but *10 minutes* could also be diagrammed as a single compound noun. The comparison contains understood words: "was more important than any highlight-video scoring play [was] [important]."

More Clauses

— LESSON 73 —

Adjective and Adverb Clauses
Introduction to Noun Clauses

Exercise 73A: Identifying Clauses

In the following sentences, circle each dependent clause. Label each as *N* for noun, *ADJ* for adjective, or *ADV* for adverb. Also indicate the part of speech that each noun clause plays: subject (*S*), direct object (*DO*), predicate nominative (*PN*), or object of the preposition (*OP*). Draw a line from each adjective and adverb clause to the word it modifies.

Some of these clauses may have another clause within them! Do your best to find both, and ask your instructor for help if needed.

These sentences are slightly adapted from Nathaniel Hawthorne's *Tanglewood Tales*. The first is done for you.

N (DO)

Mother, I do believe it has started!

N (DO)

Jason knew that it would be impossible to withstand this blood-thirsty battalion with his single arm.

ADV

While they were crossing the pasture ground, the brazen bulls came towards Jason, lowing,
ADJ   ADV
nodding their heads, and thrusting forth their snouts, which, as other cattle do, they loved to have rubbed and caressed by a friendly hand.

> **Note to Instructor:** The adverb clause *as other cattle do* modifies the verb of the larger adjective clause *which...hand*, which modifies the noun *snouts*.

ADV

But poor King Aegeus, day after day, infirm as he was had clambered to the summit of a
ADJ
cliff that overhung the sea and there sat watching for Prince Theseus, homeward bound.
N (DO)   ADJ
He concluded that his dear son, whom he loved so much, and felt so proud of, had been eaten by the Minotaur.

                                N (S)
(That he trembles and cannot speak) shows his guilt.

                                                                            ADJ
In the center of it there should be a noble palace, (in which Cadmus might dwell, and be their king,
                                                                      ADJ
with a throne, a crown, a sceptre, a purple robe, and everything else (that a king ought to have)

                                          N (DO)
All at once, Cadmus fancied (he saw something glisten very brightly, first at one spot, then at
another, and then at a hundred and a thousand spots together.)

They brought along with them a great many beautiful shells; and sitting down on the moist
                        ADJ
sand, (where the surf wave broke over them) they busied themselves in making a necklace,
            ADJ
(which they hung round Proserpina's neck)

                                                    N (DO)   N (DO)
The good Chiron taught his pupils (how to play upon the harp) and (how to cure diseases)
                    N (DO)
and (how to use the sword and shield)

                                        N (PN)
The truth was (that the Giant touched Mother Earth every five minutes)

Exercise 73B: Creating Noun Clauses

On your own paper, create five sentences by adding a noun clause into each of the blanks below.

   If you have trouble coming up with a dependent clause, try starting out with one of the following subordinating words: *that, how, why, what/whatever, who/whoever* (these are always subjects within the dependent clause), *whom/whomever* (these are always objects within the dependent clause), *where, whether.* (This is not an exhaustive list of the possibilities—just a jumping-off place for you.)

I never knew _____.

_____ was the weirdest thing I ever saw.

Just don't forget _____.

A ridiculously exciting part of the movie was _____

_____.

Note to Instructor: Answers will vary; the sentences below are examples of possible clauses. If the student has trouble with this exercise, show her the sentences below and ask her to model her answers on them. Check the answers carefully to make sure that each noun clause has a subject and verb.

I never knew [what makes gunpowder explode before].
I never knew [that the Battle of Tassafaronga was fought at night].

[Whatever was floating through the air and glowing green] was the weirdest thing I ever saw.
[How the large frog caught and ate the little fish] was the weirdest thing I ever saw.

Just don't forget [why you decided to climb up on the roof in the first place].
Just don't forget [whether or not the tickets need to be printed out instead of downloaded].

A ridiculously exciting part of the movie was [when the trained monkey set off the nuclear device].
A ridiculously exciting part of the movie was [how the fighter pilot landed his jet on the damaged runway covered with burning debris].

Exercise 73C: Diagramming

On your own paper, diagram every word of the following sentences (slightly adapted from *Twice-Told Tales*, by Nathaniel Hawthorne).

One would have thought that the dark old man was chief ruler there.

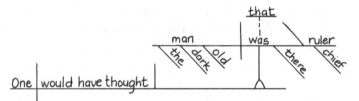

Whatever secret hope had agitated him was quickly dispelled by Dorothy's next speech.

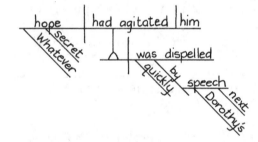

The secret of this phenomenon was that hatred had become the enjoyment of the wretch's soul.

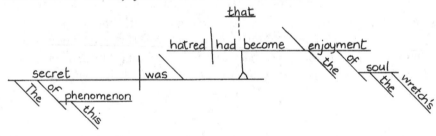

He hardly knew whether he lived or only dreamed of living.

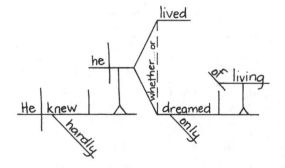

Note to Instructor: The construction *whether...or* serves as a compound conjunction, so it is diagrammed in the same way that "both...and" or *neither...nor* would be diagrammed.

— LESSON 74 —

Clauses Beginning With Prepositions

Exercise 74A: Adjective Clauses Beginning with Prepositions

In the following sentences, circle each adjective clause. Draw a line from the subordinating word back to the word the clause modifies. If the clause begins with a preposition, underline that preposition and label its object with *OP*.

These sentences are taken from the classic young adult novel *Dream of Fair Horses*, by Patricia Leitch.

The woman, (whom we now knew as Mrs. Ramsay) was holding the pony while the girl saddled up.

> **Note to Instructor:** The clause *while the girl saddled up* is an adverb clause modifying *was holding*, not an adjective clause.

The wooden fencing (that surrounded the park) was damaged.

Perdita was packed in next to a Shetland (to whom she took an instant hatred) so that all the
splendour and emotion of the ceremony rolled over me unnoticed.
(OP over whom)

Birds (that had been stones) shuffled and sang; two roe deer, bat-eared and alert, walked warily
into the open; Perdita tugged at her reins wanting to graze.

I would bring her feed, (which Mr. Ramsay had mixed for her the night before) and she would wait
at her trough, glistening-eyed and anxious until I tipped the bucket of oats, bran and chop out
into her trough.

Since there was hardly any space (in which we could exercise) I concentrated on walking and
(OP)
trotting, only asking her for an accuracy (that was well within her scope)

At the celebration, one of Fran's songs was about the autumn people (who were afraid to start
on the winter journey.)

As we swung past the judges Perdita was moving with a grace and assurance (that no amount of
grooming or schooling could have created.)

> **Note to Instructor:** The introductory clause *As we swung past the judges* is an adverb clause modifying *was moving*.

I woke with a shock, starting abruptly into full awareness, trying to escape from

something from which there was no escaping. *OP*

On Saturday mornings we hacked the hunters to the meets where the Ramsays would be waiting for us and on Saturday evenings we sweated over weary, muddied horses and filthy tack.

> **Note to Instructor:** Since *meets* are a location, the clause is introduced by the relative adverb *where* but is still an adjective clause.

I knew the way *that* he could take a simple ordinary situation and turn and twist it until he made you see that the one thing *that* you wanted was the one thing *that* you couldn't possibly have.

> **Note to Instructor:** The adjective clause modifying *way* has an understood *that* introducing it. It also contains four additional clauses: the adverb clause *until he made you see...* modifying *turn and twist*, the noun clause *that the one thing...* acting as the direct object of the infinitive *[to] see*, the adjective clause with understood *[that] you wanted* modifying the first *thing*, and the adjective clause with understood *[that] you couldn't possibly have* modifying the second *thing*.
>
> It isn't necessary for the student to insert the understood *thats* as long as she is aware that they exist.

Una has found a teacher whom she loves who never even shouts at her who accepts Una's spelling and arithmetic and appreciates Una's talent for keeping cupboards tidy and feeding school dinners to the infants.

Exercise 74B: Correct Use of *Who* and *Whom*

Choose the correct pronoun within the parentheses; cross out the incorrect pronoun.

These sentences are slightly condensed from *Original Sin*, a murder mystery set in a publishing office, by P. D. James.

To the left was a curved desk and a switchboard manned by a grey-haired, gentle-faced man (who / ~~whom~~) greeted her with a smile before checking her name on a list.

It was she, Mandy, (who / ~~whom~~) should have been nervous.

They were fond of each other; he was, he knew, the one person at Innocent House in (~~who~~ / whom) she felt she could occasionally confide; but neither was demonstrative.

"Fortunately the printer (who / ~~whom~~) received them was intelligent and thought some of the changes odd, so he telephoned to check."

But at least he would have someone with (~~who~~ / whom) he could share the distresses of the day, a day which now seemed inordinate in length.

"No one was interested in (~~who~~ / whom) he married."

Not for nothing were there those five shelves of crime paperbacks in her bedroom, Agatha Christie, Dorothy L. Sayers, Margery Allingham, Ngaio Marsh, Josephine Tey and the few modern writers (~~who~~ / whom) Joan considered fit to join those Golden Age practitioners in fictional murder.

(Who/~~Whom~~) knew that better than (he/~~him~~)?

But the worst, Maggie confided, were the conceited, usually those whose books sold the least well, but (who/~~whom~~) demanded first-class fares, five-star hotels, a limousine and a senior member of staff to escort them, and (who/~~whom~~) wrote furious letters of complaint if their signings didn't attract a queue round the block.

"They're particular (~~who~~/whom) they get, I suppose."

> **Note to Instructor:** The answer shown is the correct one. Once the student has identified *whom* as the proper choice (the direct object of the verb *get*), you may want to point out that James actually used *who* because this line of dialogue is spoken by an uneducated character using informal diction.

"And (who/~~whom~~) is actually in charge now?"

Exercise 74C: Formal and Informal Diction

On your own paper, rewrite the bolded clauses (which are all written informally) in formal English, placing the preposition before its object. Then read each sentence out loud, substituting the formal clause for the informal clause.

The original sentences are all written formally! They are taken from the novel *The Marrow of Tradition*, by Charles W. Chesnutt.

> **Note to Instructor:** The original sentences are in italics below.

Through the side door leading from the hall into the office, he saw the bell-boy **whom he had spoken to**, seated on the bench provided for the servants.

*Through the side door leading from the hall into the office, he saw the bell-boy **to whom he had spoken**, seated on the bench provided for the servants.*

The fine old house **which they lived in** was hers.

*The fine old house **in which they lived** was hers.*

The major had also invited Lee Ellis, his young city editor, **whom he had a great liking for apart from his business value,** and who was a frequent visitor at the house. These, with the family itself, which consisted of the major, his wife, and his half-sister, Clara Pemberton, a young woman of about eighteen, made up the eight persons **whom covers were laid for**.

*The major had also invited Lee Ellis, his young city editor, **for whom he had a great liking apart from his business value**, and who was a frequent visitor at the house. These, with the family itself, which consisted of the major, his wife, and his half-sister, Clara Pemberton, a young woman of about eighteen, made up the eight persons **for whom covers were laid**.*

An anxious half hour passed, **which the child lay quiet during**, except for its labored breathing.

*An anxious half hour passed, **during which the child lay quiet**, except for its labored breathing.*

He really thought him too much of a gentleman for the town, in view of the restrictions **which he must inevitably be hampered with**.

*He really thought him too much of a gentleman for the town, in view of the restrictions **with which he must inevitably be hampered**.*

He had a habit of borrowing, right and left, small sums which might be conveniently forgotten by the borrower, **and which the lender would dislike to ask for**.

*He had a habit of borrowing, right and left, small sums which might be conveniently forgotten by the borrower, **and for which the lender would dislike to ask**.*

Exercise 74D: Diagramming

On your own paper, diagram every word of the following two sentences from *The Strivers' Row Spy*, by Jason Overstreet.

Note to Instructor: These are difficult; give all necessary help.

His disregard for what he was saying, when he was saying it, and whom he was saying it to was alarming.

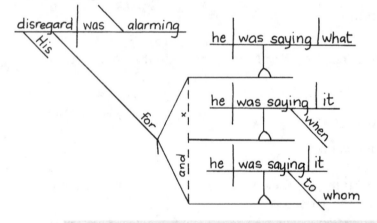

Note to Instructor: The three clauses *what he was saying*, *when he was saying it*, and *whom he was saying it to* are all objects of the preposition *for*. It may help the student if you read her the sentence like this: *His disregard for what he was saying, [for] when he was saying it, and [for] whom he was saying it to was alarming.*

The only possible end of the race problem in the United States to which we can now look without despair is one which embraces the fullest cooperation between white and black in all the phases of national activity.

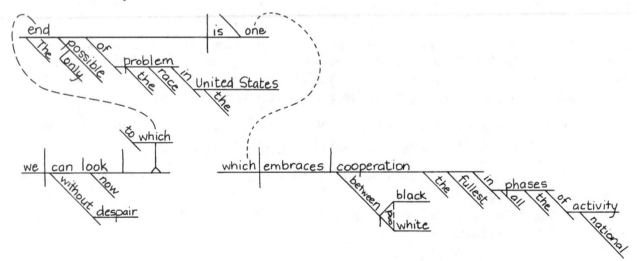

> **Note to Instructor:** The clause *to which we can now look without despair* is adjectival and modifies the noun *end* (the relative pronoun *which* has *end* as its antecedent). The prepositional phrase *to which* is diagrammed as the direct object of the verb *look*, but the student could also choose to diagram the verb as the colloquial *can look to* (with *to* as part of the verb), with *which* as the direct object of the verb.
>
>   The clause *which embraces...national activity* modifies the noun *one* (the second relative pronoun *which* has *one* as its antecedent). In this clause, *white* and *black* serve as nouns (*white [people]* and *black [people]*), and are the compound objects of the preposition *between*.

— LESSON 75 —

Clauses and Phrases
Misplaced Adjective Phrases
Misplaced Adjective Clauses

Exercise 75A: Correcting Misplaced Modifiers

Circle the misplaced adjective clauses and phrases in the following sentences. Draw an arrow to the place where each modifier should be.

My brother blamed the weather for the game cancellation (which was cold and rainy)

The bean stew was for our dinner (simmering away on the stove)

The hen was pecking busily at the weeds in the back yard (with the three fluffy yellow chicks)

The rocks (passing by) could easily fall down onto hikers (balanced along the path)

The northern part of Africa was the home of the greatest Egyptian pharaoh, (which borders the Mediterranean Sea.)

The old deer skeleton had been there for months and months (lying beside the hiking trail)

The grocery store clerk called her supervisor (who had run out of change)

The hiker decided to go back to her group, (afraid to lose the way)

The little girl ran happily home after talking to the librarian (carrying her books in a backpack)

After the tourist paid for the map, he tucked the yellow-edged paper into his pocket (with the pictures on it)

They said that the whole group had gotten lost together (from their hotel)

All around the outside of the house (which keeps the sun away from the large outer) (windows) runs a screened porch.

Original Sentences

My brother blamed the weather, which was cold and rainy, for the game cancellation.

The bean stew simmering away on the stove was for our dinner.

The hen with the three fluffy yellow chicks was pecking busily at the weeds in the back yard.

The rocks balanced along the path could easily fall down onto hikers passing by.

The northern part of Africa, which borders the Mediterranean Sea, was the home of the greatest Egyptian pharaoh.

The old deer skeleton lying beside the hiking trail had been there for months and months.

The grocery store clerk who had run out of change called her supervisor.

The hiker, being afraid that she might lose her way, decided to go back to her group.

Carrying her books in a backpack, the little girl ran happily home after talking to the librarian.

After the tourist paid for the map, he tucked the yellow-edged paper with the pictures on it into his pocket.

They said that the whole group from their hotel had gotten lost together.

All around the outside of the house runs a screened porch which keeps the sun away from the large outer windows.

Exercise 75B: Diagramming

Each of the following sentences contains a misplaced clause or phrase. On your own paper, diagram each sentence correctly, and then read the corrected sentence out loud to your instructor. These sentences are taken from *Grimm's Fairy Tales*!

Note to Instructor: The corrected sentences follow each incorrect sentence in italics.

The tailor with a black patch on her back had three strong sons and one goat.
   The tailor had three strong sons and one goat with a black patch on her back.

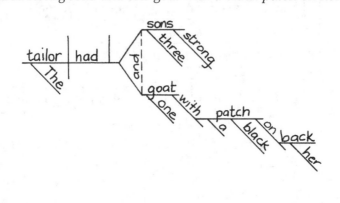

When Rapunzel, which lay in a forest and had neither stairs nor door, was twelve years old, the Witch shut her into a tower.

> *When Rapunzel was twelve years old, the Witch shut her into a tower, which lay in a forest and had neither stairs nor door.*

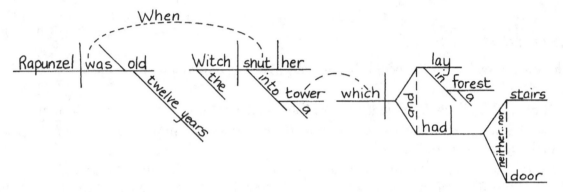

Sleeping beside the fire, he called the other dwarves, and all of them were astonished to see Snow White who ran up.

> *He called the other dwarves, who ran up, and all of them were astonished to see Snow White sleeping beside the fire.*

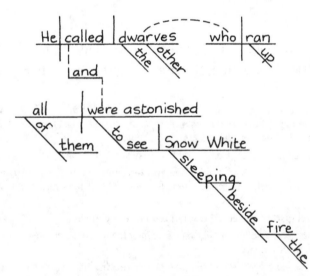

— LESSON 76 —

Noun, Adjective, and Adverb Clauses
Restrictive and Non-Restrictive Modifying Clauses

Exercise 76A: Clause Review

The following sentence is the beginning of *Pride (A Pride and Prejudice Remix)*, by Ibi Zoboi.
  Complete these steps:

1) Find and circle the dependent clauses. Label each one as adjective, adverb, or noun.
2) Identify and underline the subordinating word. If the subordinating word is understood, insert it and then underline it.
3) For the adverb and adjective clauses, draw a line from the subordinating word back to the word modified. For the noun clauses, identify the part of the sentence that each clause is serving as.
4) Diagram the sentence on your own paper.

> **Note to Instructor:** Read through the notes below before the student begins work, and provide all necessary help. This sentence is intended to be challenging!

It's a truth universally acknowledged that when rich people move into the hood, where it's a little bit broken and a little bit forgotten, the first thing they want to do is clean it up.

> **Note to Instructor:** The main clause of the sentence is *It's a truth universally acknowledged.* This is followed by the dependent clause *that when rich people move into the hood, where it's a little bit broken and a little bit forgotten, the first thing they want to do is clean it up.*
>
> The subject and predicate of that dependent clause is *the first thing...is.*
>
> This is a noun clause acting as an appositive and renaming *truth.* (What is the truth? *The first thing is*). The infinitive with understood *to* is *[to] clean it up*; it acts as a predicate nominative renaming *thing.*
>
> Within this noun clause are three additional dependent clauses.
>
> The clause *where it's a little bit broken and a little bit forgotten* is an adjective clause introduced by a relative adverb modifying *hood.*
>
> The clause *[that] they want to do* is an adjective clause modifying *thing* with the understood subordinating word *that.* The infinitive *to do* is acting as a direct object of the verb *want.*
>
> The clause *when rich people move into the hood* is an adverb clause modifying the verb *want.* (When do they want? When they move in.)

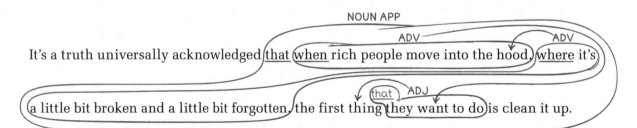

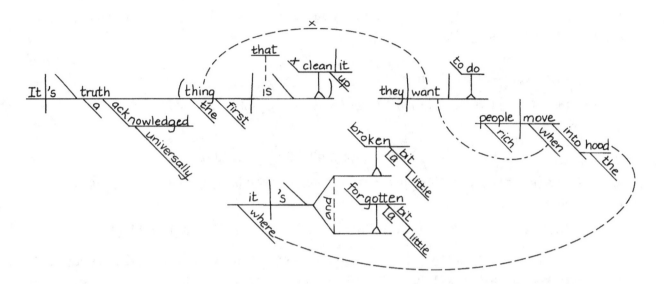

Note to Instructor: The relationship between *It's a truth universally acknowledged* and *that when rich people...clean it up* may not be clear to the student. I have diagnosed the overall dependent clause as appositive because it renames *truth* (the dependent clause *is* the truth). However, the student would not be necessarily wrong to label the whole dependent clause following *acknowledged* as an adjective clause. In that case, the subject and predicate of the clause would be diagrammed as follows, with the remaining three modifying clauses diagrammed in the same way as the preceding diagram. The clause would be labelled *ADJ* with an arrow going back to *truth*. Whichever option the student chooses, discuss the other approach and ask for the student's reaction. This will help the student continue to sharpen their judgment, as well as acknowledge that the English language doesn't always fit neatly into categories!

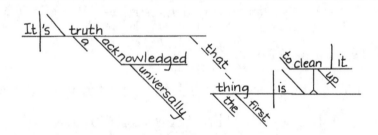

Exercise 76B: Non-Restrictive Clauses and Missing Commas

In the following sentences (some slightly condensed from the original), underline each dependent clause. Place commas around each non-restrictive clause. Use the proofreader's mark: ⌄. Leave sentences with restrictive clauses as they are.

From *Pride: A Pride and Prejudice Remix*, by Ibi Zoboi

In no time, Marisol <u>who's two years younger</u> is standing right beside me.

It's Darius <u>who has a firm grip on my arm</u>.

He plops down in his usual spot on the recliner chair and grabs an old Howard Zinn book <u>that he's read a hundred times</u>.

Now it looks like something <u>that belongs in the suburbs, with its wide double doors, sparkling windows, and tiny manicured lawn</u>.

From *Pride and Prejudice*, by Jane Austen

And with a low bow he left her to attack Mr. Darcy_, <u>whose reception of his advances she eagerly watched</u>.

Mr. Bennet was among the earliest of those <u>who waited on Mr. Bingley</u>.

But there is one of her sisters sitting down just behind you_, <u>who is very pretty, and I dare say, very agreeable</u>.

Mr. Collins invited them to take a stroll in the garden, <u>which was large and well laid out</u>.

But, my dear sister, can I be happy, even supposing the best, in accepting a man <u>whose sisters and friends are all wishing him to marry elsewhere</u>?

Between Elizabeth and Charlotte there was a restraint <u>which kept them mutually silent on the subject</u>.

Exercise 76C: Restrictive Clauses and Unnecessary Commas

In the following sentences, underline each dependent clause. Some dependent clauses may have other dependent clauses within them—double underline clauses within clauses!

Delete the incorrect commas that have been placed around restrictive adjective clauses. Use proofreader's marks: ___ℓ. Leave sentences with non-restrictive clauses as they are.

From *Kingdom of Souls*, by Rena Barron

The few girls_ℓwho speak Tamaran_ℓask me <u>what it's like living so far away in the Almighty Kingdom</u>.

It's the name_ℓ<u>my mother calls the street peddlers in the market, the ones</u>_ℓ <u>who sell worthless good luck charms</u>.

I speak for he_ℓ<u>who has no beginning and no end</u>.

Grandmother nods, takes the bowl, and passes it to Sukar, <u>who swallows hard</u>.

"Don't worry, daughter," he says, folding the sleeves of my orange-and-blue kaftan, <u>which matches his own</u>.

A part of me is anxious to return home, <u>where I'm not so much of an utter failure</u>.

From *Louisa the Poisoner*, by Tanith Lee

March Mire lay at the heart of the great moors, a swamp so dangerous_ℓ<u>that none but fools would venture into it, and seldom did they come out</u>. There were however local legends of persons_ℓ<u>who lived within the mire itself</u>, creatures_ℓ<u>that knew the two or three safe paths across the mud</u>.

The other portion of the leather strap had remained with the police whistle, <u>which the lone policeman had blown</u>.

He sat down at the long table facing Louisa, and the wardress, <u>whom Louisa had charmed the most</u>, stood well back at the door.

The lady, <u>to whom you refer</u>, is here in the court?

Louisa had appeared devoted to Lord Maskullance, <u>in whom possibly she had alone confided</u>.

Constructing Sentences

— LESSON 77 —

Constructing Sentences

Exercise 77A: Making Sentences out of Clauses and Phrases

The independent clauses below are listed in order and make up a story—but they're missing all their supporting pieces.

On your own paper, rewrite the story by attaching the dependent clauses and phrases in Lists 2 and 3 to the independent clauses in List 1 to make complete sentences. You may insert dependent clauses that act as adjectives or adverbs into the beginning, middle, or end of independent clauses (usually by putting them right before or after the word they modify), and you may change any capitalization or punctuation necessary. But do not add or delete words.

The first sentence has been constructed for you.

Crossing out each clause or phrase as you use it will help you not to repeat yourself!

List 1. Independent Clauses

~~Daedalus of Athens was the most skilful man.~~
His statues were so lifelike.
His buildings were the envy.
Minos chose Daedalus.
Daedalus travelled to Crete and built the Labyrinth.
Daedalus himself barely found the way out.
King Minos refused.
Daedalus built a pair of wings and a smaller pair.
The wings were made.
Together, father and son rose and began to fly.
But Icarus became too confident and flew.
The waxed cords began to melt.
His wings fell, and he plunged.

List 2. Dependent Clauses

because he could not leave by either land or sea
that they almost walked and spoke
that was full of winding passages
who saw them
when the Labyrinth was finished
as he drew closer to the sun
which was a monster with the head and shoulders of a bull and the body of a man

List 3. Phrases
of his time
for himself
for his son Icarus
~~an architect, sculptor, and stoneworker~~
higher and higher
of all
because of his fame
the king of Crete
a complicated maze
to allow Daedalus
to his death
of bird feathers
into the air
towards home
ignoring his father's calls
from his shoulders
into the ocean
to make a prison
held together with waxed linen cords
for the Minotaur
to return to Athens
across the ocean

FIRST SENTENCE
Daedalus of Athens was the most skillful man of his time—an architect, sculptor, and stoneworker.

> **Note to Instructor:** The original sentences are provided below (in chronological order). However, any sentences that the student assembles are acceptable as long as they make sense.

Daedalus of Athens was the most skillful man of his time—an architect, sculptor, and stoneworker. His statues were so lifelike that they almost walked and spoke. His buildings were the envy of all who saw them.

Because of his fame, Minos, the king of Crete, chose Daedalus to make a prison for the Minotaur, which was a monster with the head and shoulders of a bull and the body of a man. Daedalus travelled to Crete and built the Labyrinth, a complicated maze that was full of winding passages. When the Labyrinth was finished, Daedalus himself barely found the way out.

King Minos refused to allow Daedalus to return to Athens. Because he could not leave by either land or sea, Daedalus built a pair of wings for himself and a smaller pair for his son Icarus. The wings were made of bird feathers held together with waxed linen cords. Together, father and son rose into the air and began to fly across the ocean, towards home.

But Icarus became too confident and flew higher and higher, ignoring his father's calls. As he drew closer to the sun, the waxed cords began to melt. His wings fell from his shoulders, and he plunged into the ocean to his death.

— LESSON 78 —
Simple Sentences
Complex Sentences

Exercise 78A: Identifying Simple and Complex Sentences

In the sentences below, underline each subject once and each predicate twice. (Find the subjects and predicates in both independent and dependent clauses.) In the blank at the end of each sentence, write *S* for simple or *C* for complex.

These sentences are taken from the novel *Dread Nation*, by Justina Ireland. This novel, a creative cross between a historical novel and a fantasy, is set in the days just after the Civil War—when zombies have infested the southern countryside. The heroine, Jane McKeene, is a student at Miss Preston's School of Combat for Negro Girls, where she is learning to fight the zombie plague.

I swallow a groan and raise the scythe a few inches higher.   S

Miss Duncan waits until I'm about to scream from the holding before she gives me a small nod and turns back to the class.   C

I shake my arms out, one after another, willing the burn to go away.   S

So while I do believe Miss Duncan is a fine instructor, I do not believe that she is human.   C

I lift my weapon, focusing on Miss Duncan and trying to decide if she is indeed a revenant instead of thinking about the deep burning in my poor scrawny arms.   C

I slash the scythe across the empty air until my arms feel like overcooked green beans, limp and wobbly.   C

She is a crack shot with a rifle, invaluable in a long-range capacity.   S

Miss Anderson says the papers say he's going to cure the undead plague!   C

The crown jewel of my collection is the well-oiled Remington single-action, the close-range gun of choice for Miss Preston's girls.   S

Ruthie shakes her head and latches her tiny hand on my skirt, pulling me in the direction of Miss Preston's office.   S

During the Great Discord, right after the dead began to walk and before the Army finally got the shambler plague under control, the building was empty.   C

Ruthie pulls me through the main foyer and down into the left wing of the building, to the big office at the end.   S

Rumor is that Miss Preston's people had gone west to the Minnesota Territory before the war but came back when the undead got the better of them.   C

Exercise 78B: Forming Complex Sentences

On your own paper, rewrite each pair of simple sentences as a single complex sentence. The first is done for you. You will need to add a subordinating word to one of the sentences in each pair to turn it into a dependent clause.

In the last two sets of sentences, try to combine all three simple sentences into one complex sentence!

There may be more than one way to rewrite each sentence. Just make sure that your sentence is grammatical and reads well.

The original sentences are from *The Zombie Survival Guide: Complete Protection from the Living Dead*, by Max Brooks.

Zombies have caught fire.
Zombies will neither notice nor react to the engulfing flames in any way.

> Zombies who have caught fire will neither notice nor react to the engulfing flames in any way.

There are hundreds of thousands of lethal compounds in this world.
It is impossible to discuss them all.

> As there are hundreds of thousands of lethal compounds in this world, it is impossible to discuss them all.

Never forget.
The body of the undead is, for all practical purposes, human.

> Never forget that the body of the undead is, for all practical purposes, human.

A human body dies.
Its flesh is immediately set upon by billions of microscopic organisms.

> When a human body dies, its flesh is immediately set upon by billions of microscopic organisms.

A human body has been dead longer than twelve to eighteen hours.
A human body will be rejected as food.

> A human body that has been dead longer than twelve to eighteen hours will be rejected as food.

It has been suggested.
Zombies possess night vision.
This fact explains their skill at nocturnal hunting.

> It has been suggested that zombies possess night vision, a fact that explains their skill at nocturnal hunting.

A zombie's body is severely damaged.
It will continue to attack.
Nothing remains.

> Even if a zombie's body is severely damaged, it will continue to attack until nothing remains.

Exercise 78C: Diagramming

On your own paper, diagram the following four sentences. The sentences come from traditional Irish songs, which are reproduced here in italics so that you have context.

Beside each diagram, write the number of vertical lines dividing subjects from predicates, along with the label *S* for simple or *C* for complex.

The sentences are not difficult, but there may be a couple of interesting challenges here for you!

The Kilkenny Cats

There once were two cats of Kilkenny,
Each thought there was one cat too many.
So they fought and they fit,
And they scratched and they bit,
Till, excepting their nails
And the tips of their tails,
Instead of two cats, there weren't any.

Each thought there was one cat too many.

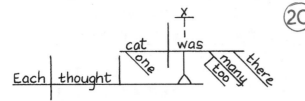

> **Note to Instructor:** The noun clause *[that] there was one cat too many* is introduced by an understood subordinating conjunction and is the direct object of the verb *thought*. The expression *one too many* is idiomatic. The answer diagram takes *many* as an adverb (answering the question *how many?*) modifying the predicate, but the student could also diagram *many* as an adverb modifying *one*. If the student diagrams it beneath *cat*, point out that *cat* is singular and *many* is plural, so it is probably not an adjective modifying *cat*.

They scratched and bit until, instead of two cats, there weren't any.

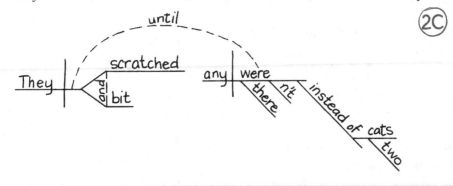

> **Note to Instructor:** In this sentence, *instead of* functions as a single preposition. However, the student could also choose to diagram the prepositional phrase *of two cats* as the object of the preposition *instead*.

Michael Finnigan

There was a boy called Michael Finnigan,
He grew whiskers on his chin-igan.
The wind came out and blew them in again.
Poor old Michael Finnigan, begin again.

There was an old man named Michael Finnigan,
Who went off fishing with a pinnigan.
He caught a fish, but it fell in again.
Poor old Michael Finnigan, begin again.

There was an old man named Michael Finnigan,
Who caught a cold and couldn't get well again.
Then he died, and had to begin again.
Poor old Michael Finnigan, begin again!

The wind came out and blew them in again.

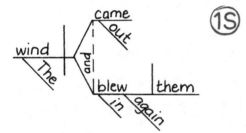

There was an old man named Michael Finnigan who caught a cold and couldn't get well again.

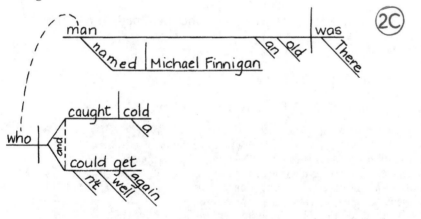

> **Note to Instructor:** The phrase *get well* is tricky! I have diagrammed it here with *well* as an adverb modifying *get*, but the student might also be tempted to diagram it as a predicate adjective (describing *who*) or even as a direct object of *get*. However, *get* never functions as a linking verb, and this meaning of *well* never functions as a noun. If the student chooses either of these options, do not penalize her, but point out that *well* can only be an adjective or adverb and that *get* is not a linking verb.

— LESSON 79 —
Compound Sentences
Run-on Sentences
Comma Splice

Exercise 79A: Forming Compound Sentences

Choose at least one independent clause from Column 1 and at least one independent clause from Column 2. Using correct punctuation and adding coordinating conjunctions as needed, combine the clauses into a compound sentence. (You may use more than two clauses, as long as your sentence makes sense!) Write your new compound sentences on your own paper. Use every clause at least once.

These clauses are taken from compound sentences written by Ernest Hemingway in his classic story *The Old Man and the Sea.*

Column 1	Column 2
I am a boy.	His head and back were dark purple.
The old man had taught the boy to fish.	He had no way of judging the time.
They sat on the Terrace.	In the sun the stripes on his sides showed wide and a light lavender.
Can you really remember that?	The boy loved him.
The newspaper lay across his knees.	The weight of his arm held it there in the evening breeze.
The old man went out the door.	Many of the fishermen made fun of the old man.
He was bright in the sun.	I must obey him.
The moon did not rise now until late.	Did I just tell it to you?
He was not angry.	The boy came after him.

Note to Instructor: The following sentences (the originals) are possible answers; accept any grammatical sentences that the student offers. These should *only* make use of the coordinating conjunctions *and, or, nor, for, so, but, yet.* Watch out for subordinating conjunctions such as *before, while, because, after,* etc. Use of subordinating conjunctions transforms a clause from independent to dependent and makes the sentence complex rather than compound.

No clauses should be joined with a comma splice (a comma without a coordinating conjunction), but all sentences can make use of either a semicolon (with or without a coordinating conjunction) or a comma with a coordinating conjunction.

I am a boy and I must obey him.

The old man had taught the boy to fish and the boy loved him.

They sat on the Terrace and many of the fishermen made fun of the old man and he was not angry.

Can you really remember that or did I just tell it to you?

The newspaper lay across his knees and the weight of his arm held it there in the evening breeze.

The old man went out the door and the boy came after him.

He was bright in the sun and his head and back were dark purple and in the sun the stripes on his sides showed wide and a light lavender.

The moon did not rise now until late and he had no way of judging the time.

Exercise 79B: Correcting Run-on Sentences (Comma Splices)

Using proofreader's marks (∧ to insert a coordinating conjunction, ⌄ to insert a comma, ⌄ to insert a semicolon), correct each of the run-on sentences below.

These are also taken from Ernest Hemingway's classic story *The Old Man and the Sea*.

The line was going out fast but steadily the fish was not panicked.

I'll keep yours and mine together on ice, we can share them in the morning.

He waited with the line between his thumb and his finger, watching it and the other lines at the same time, the fish might have swum up or down.

He was still sleeping on his face the boy was sitting by him watching him.

The old man leaned the mast with its wrapped sail against the wall the boy put the box and the other gear beside it.

But I have hurt them both badly neither one can feel very good.

The old man carried the mast on his shoulder, the boy carried the wooden box with the coiled, hard-braided brown lines, the gaff and the harpoon with its shaft.

The position actually was only somewhat less intolerable he thought of it as almost comfortable.

> **Note to Instructor:** The original sentences are found below; the connecting punctuation and/or coordinating conjunctions are bolded for your reference. The student may choose to use either a semicolon or a comma and a coordinating conjunction, in each of the bolded places.
>
> Ernest Hemingway preferred *and* without punctuation to form his compound sentences! When the student is finished, ask her to read the originals out loud. Point out how often Hemingway chooses to use the simple *and* with no comma or semicolon, and how this creates a forward-flowing staccato rhythm to his sentences.

The line was going out fast but steadily **and** the fish was not panicked.

I'll keep yours and mine together on ice **and** we can share them in the morning.

He waited with the line between his thumb and his finger, watching it and the other lines at the same time, **for** the fish might have swum up or down.

He was still sleeping on his face **and** the boy was sitting by him watching him.

The old man leaned the mast with its wrapped sail against the wall **and** the boy put the box and the other gear beside it.

But I have hurt them both badly **and** neither one can feel very good.

The old man carried the mast on his shoulder **and** the boy carried the wooden box with the coiled, hard-braided brown lines, the gaff and the harpoon with its shaft.

The position actually was only somewhat less intolerable; **but** he thought of it as almost comfortable.

Exercise 79C: Diagramming

On your own paper, diagram every word of the following sentences from Ernest Hemingway's *The Old Man and the Sea*.

There was no pot of yellow rice and fish and the boy knew this too.

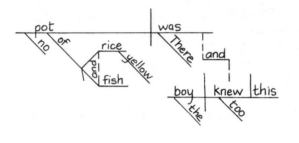

The line rose slowly and steadily and then the surface of the ocean bulged ahead of the boat and the fish came out.

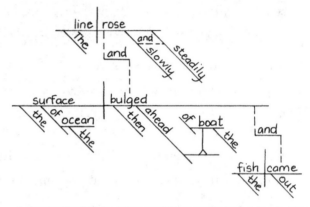

Note to Instructor: The student could also choose to diagram *ahead of* as a single compound preposition with *boat* as the object of the preposition.

They had eaten with no light on the table and the old man took off his trousers and went to bed in the dark.

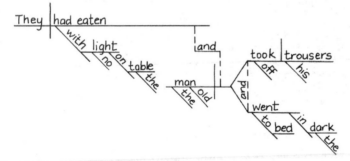

The sail was patched with flour sacks and, furled, it looked like the flag of permanent defeat.

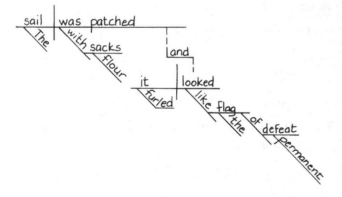

— LESSON 80 —

Compound Sentences
Compound-Complex Sentences
Clauses with Understood Elements

Exercise 80A: Analyzing Complex-Compound Sentences

The sentences below are all complex-compound sentences. For each sentence, carry out the following steps:

a) Cross out each prepositional phrase.

b) Circle any dependent clauses. Label them as *ADJ*, *ADV*, or *NOUN*. Draw a line from adjective and adverb clauses to the word modified. Label noun clauses with the part of the sentence that they function as.

c) Underline the subject of each independent clause once and the predicate twice.

d) Draw a vertical line between each simple and/or complex sentence.

e) Insert missing words (if any).

The first sentence has been done for you. Be careful—some dependent clauses may be within other dependent clauses!

These sentences are taken from a very famous nineteenth-century memoir called *Two Years Before the Mast*. The author, Richard Henry Dana Jr., left his college studies in 1834 and enlisted as a sailor on a merchant ship that was travelling from Boston, all the way around South America, back up to California. "Before the mast" was an expression that meant "where the common sailors sleep."

Early ~~in the morning~~ she was overhauling us a little, but after the rain came on and [ADV] the wind grew lighter, we began to leave her astern.

It was now the middle ~~of April,~~ the southeaster season was nearly over, and the light, regular winds, (which blow ~~down the coast)~~ [ADJ] began to set steadily in, ~~during the latter part of each day~~.

> **Note to Instructor:** If the student asks why the first two independent clauses (*It was now the middle of April* and t*he southeaster season was nearly over*) are linked with only a comma and not also a coordinating conjunction, explain that there are three independent clauses in this compound-complex sentence (the third is the *light, regular winds…began to set steadily in…*), and the rule that says that three items in a series can be connected by commas also applies to independent clauses! If the third independent clause were not present, the first two clauses would be a comma splice. Because the third clause is present, and *is* connected with both a comma and a coordinating conjunction, the sentence is correct.

~~Among other bad practices,~~ he frequently slept ~~on his watch,~~ and, having been discovered asleep ~~by the captain,~~ he was told (that he would be turned off duty [NOUN DO] (if he did it again) [ADV].

> **Note to Instructor:** We have here interpreted *off* as an adverb modifying *would be turned*, with *duty* as the direct object of the verb. However, there are two other legitimate ways to interpret the phrase: *off* could be part of an idiomatic verb (*turn off*) with *duty* as the direct object; or *off* could be acting as a preposition with the object *duty*, so that *off duty* would be a prepositional phrase modifying *would be turned*.

Whatever your feelings may be) you must make a joke of everything at sea; and if you were to fall from aloft and be caught in the belly of a sail, and thus saved from instant death, it would not do to look at all disturbed, or to treat it seriously.

> **Note to Instructor:** The adverbial dependent clause *if you were to....instant death* has one subject (*you*), which has three verbs: *were*, *be caught*, and *saved*.

Some of the watch were asleep, and the others were quiet, so that there was nothing to break the illusion, and I stood leaning over the bulwarks, listening to the slow breathings of the mighty creatures,— now one breaking the water just alongside, whose black body I could see through the fog; and again another, which I could just hear in the distance, —until the low and regular swell seemed like the heaving of the ocean's mighty bosom to the sound of its own heavy and long drawn respirations.

> **Note to Instructor:** The student might also decide that the adverbial clause *so that there.... illusion* modifies the verb *were* (in the independent clause *the others were quiet*). In both cases, it is adverbial, so there is room for judgment.

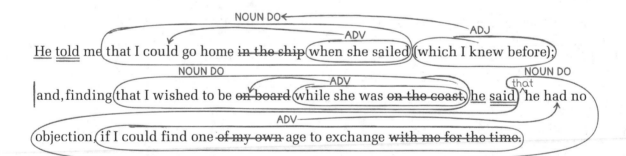

He told me that I could go home in the ship when she sailed (which I knew before); and, finding that I wished to be on board while she was on the coast, he said he had no objection, if I could find one of my own age to exchange with me for the time.

> **Note to Instructor:** The tricky part of this sentence is the clause *which I knew before*. The student might want to include it as a sub-clause of the larger noun clause *that I could go home in the ship when she sailed*, which acts as the direct object of *told* (the pronoun *me* is the indirect object). However, point out that what the speaker actually knew before was the entire noun clause *that I could go home in the ship when she sailed*, so the adjective clause modifies the entire noun clause and is not part of it.
>
> The second noun clause is the direct object of the participle *finding*.

Exercise 80B: Constructing Complex-Compound Sentences

From each set of independent clauses, construct a single complex-compound sentence. You may turn any of the clauses into dependent clauses by adding subordinating words, insert any other words necessary, omit unnecessary words, and make any other needed changes, but try to keep the original meaning of each clause. You must use every clause in the set!

You may turn a clause into a prepositional phrase or another form, as long as your resulting sentence has at least two independent clauses and one dependent clause and contains all of the information in the listed clauses.

These sets of clauses are based on sentences from the opening chapter of the sea adventure novel *Master and Commander*, by Patrick O'Brian. The main character, Jack Aubrey, is a lieutenant in the British navy during the Napoleonic Wars (1803-1815). He is also an amateur musician. In this first chapter, he is waiting to find out if he will be given a ship to captain, and he also attends a chamber music concert.

Write your new sentences on your own paper. The first has been done for you.

> **Note to Instructor:** Each set of independent clauses is followed by the original compound-complex sentence. Others are possible—accept any grammatical answer that has at least two independent and one dependent clause (and incorporates all the information!).

He found something.
His hand was high in the air, beating time.
He lowered it, clenched his mouth shut and looked down at his feet.
The music was over.

> He found that his hand was high in the air, beating time; he lowered it, clenched his mouth shut and looked down at his feet until the music was over.

It was a witty, agreeable minuet, no more.
It was succeeded by a curiously difficult, almost harsh last movement.
That piece seemed to be on the edge of saying something of the very greatest importance.

> It was a witty, agreeable minuet, no more; but it was succeeded by a curiously difficult, almost harsh last movement, a piece that seemed to be on the edge of saying something of the very greatest importance.

Jack Aubrey's face instantly changed from friendly ingenuous communicative pleasure to an expression of somewhat baffled hostility.
He could not but acknowledge something.
He had been beating the time.
He had certainly done so with perfect accuracy.
In itself the thing was wrong.

> Jack Aubrey's face instantly changed from friendly ingenuous communicative pleasure to an expression of somewhat baffled hostility; he could not but acknowledge that he had been beating the time; and although he had certainly done so with perfect accuracy, in itself the thing was wrong.

It was difficult to tell his age.
He had that kind of face.
That kind of face does not give anything away.
He was wearing a wig, a grizzled wig, apparently made of wire, and quite devoid of powder.
He might have been anything between twenty and sixty.

> It was difficult to tell his age, for not only had he that kind of face that does not give
> anything away, but he was wearing a wig, a grizzled wig, apparently made of wire, and
> quite devoid of powder; he might have been anything between twenty and sixty.

The volume of sound died away to the single whispering of a fiddle.
The steady hum of low conversation had never stopped at the back of the room.
The steady hum of low conversation threatened to drown it.
A soldier exploded in a stifled guffaw.
Jack looked angrily around.

> The volume of sound died away to the single whispering of a fiddle, and the steady hum
> of low conversation that never stopped at the back of the room threatened to drown it;
> a soldier exploded in a stifled guffaw and Jack looked angrily around.

His anger could not for the moment find any outward expression.
His anger took on the form of melancholy.
He thought of his shipless state.
He thought of half and whole promises made to him and broken.
He thought of the many schemes.
He had built up many schemes on visionary foundations.

> As it could not for the moment find any outward expression, his anger took on the form
> of melancholy; he thought of his shipless state, of half and whole promises made to him
> and broken, and of the many schemes he had built up on visionary foundations.

Exercise 80C: Diagramming

On your own paper, diagram the following sentences from Ernest Hemingway's *The Old Man and
the Sea*. Next to your diagram, label each sentence as compound (*C*), complex (*CX*), or compound-
complex (*CCX*).

For an hour the old man had been seeing black spots before his eyes and the sweat salted his eyes
and salted the cut over his eye and on his forehead.

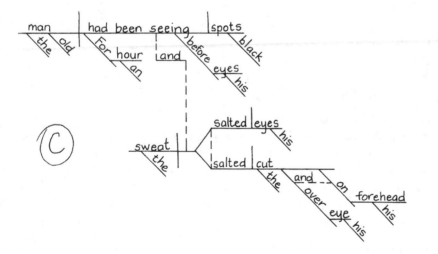

But when the strain showed the fish had turned to come toward the boat, the old man rose to his feet and started the pivoting and the weaving pulling that brought in the line he gained.

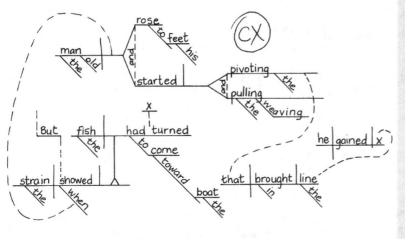

Note to Instructor: When a sentence begins with a coordinating conjunction, diagram it as you would any other coordinating conjunction, but without the connection to another sentence (show the student the *But* on the diagram if necessary).

Although there are four dependent clauses in this sentence, there is only one independent clause, so it is a complex, not complex-compound, sentence. There are two understood *thats* in the dependent clauses, indicated above.

The adjective clause *that brought in the line [that] he gained* modifies both of the object participles *pivoting* and *pulling*, but it is acceptable for the student to link the clause with *pulling* only; however, show the student the diagram and point out that it modifies both participles.

He settled comfortably against the wood and took his suffering as it came and the fish swam steadily and the boat moved slowly through the dark water.

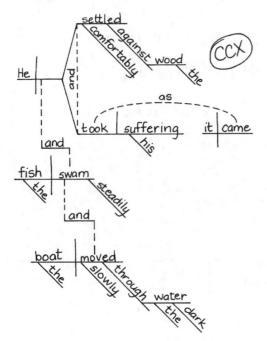

Note to Instructor: This sentence has three independent clauses and only one dependent clause, but that makes it complex-compound.

Conditions

— LESSON 81 —

Helping Verbs
Tense and Voice
Modal Verbs

Exercise 81A: Using *Do, Does,* and *Did*

In the blanks provided, rewrite the bolded verbs in the form described in brackets. Use the appropriate form of the helping verb along with any interrogatives or negatives necessary.

Don't forget that you may have to change the form of the verb! The first one is done for you.

These sentences are slightly adapted from Daniel Defoe's *Journal of the Plague Year*, an account of the 1665 bubonic plague that decimated the city of London.

When I speak of rows of houses being shut up, I **mean** shut up by the magistrates.
[Turn into a negative statement]

    When I speak of rows of houses being shut up, I <u>do not mean</u> shut up by the magistrates.

The making of so many fires, as above, **consumed** an unusual quantity of coals.
[Provide emphasis]

    The making of so many fires, as above, <u>did consume</u> an unusual quantity of coals.

This hardship **exposed** me to any disaster.   [Turn into a negative statement]

    This hardship <u>did not expose</u> me to any disaster.

Any body **goes** by water these times.   [Change into a question]

    <u>Does</u> any body <u>go</u> by water these times?

I **remember** how many died in the house itself.   [Turn into a negative statement]

    I <u>do not remember</u> how many died in the house itself.

You **stop** us on the king's highway, and pretend to deny us.   [Change into a question]

    <u>Why do</u> you <u>stop</u> us on the king's highway, and pretend to deny us <u>?</u>

But the next town behind me will, by the same rule, deny me leave to go back, and so they **starve** me between them.   [Provide emphasis]

But the next town behind me will, by the same rule, deny me leave to go back, and so they <u>do starve</u> me between them.

Our horsemen cannot pass with our baggage that way; it **leads** into the road that we want to go.   [Turn into a negative statement]

   Our horsemen cannot pass with our baggage that way; it <u>does not lead</u> into the road that we want to go.

"Well, but," says I to him, "you **left** her the four shillings too."   [Change into a question]

   "Well, but," says I to him, "<u>did</u> you <u>leave</u> her the four shillings too?"

The young woman, her mother, and the maid had been abroad on some occasion, though I **remember** what.   [Turn into a negative statement]

   The young woman, her mother, and the maid had been abroad on some occasion, though I <u>do not remember</u> what.

The magistrates **moderated and eased** families upon many occasions in this case. [Provide emphasis]

   The magistrates <u>did moderate and [did] ease</u> families upon many occasions in this case.

But still my friend's observation was just, and it **appeared** that the people **recovered** faster and more in number.   [Provide emphasis]

   But still my friend's observation was just, and it <u>did appear</u> that the people <u>did recover</u> faster and more in number.

For though it is true that all the people **went** out of the city of London, yet I may venture to say that in a manner all the horses did.   [Turn into a negative statement]

   For though it is true that all the people <u>did not go</u> out of the city of London, yet I may venture to say that in a manner all the horses did.

This is one of the reasons why I believed then, and **believe** still, that the shutting up houses thus by force was of little or no service in the whole.   [Provide emphasis]

   This is one of the reasons why I believed then, and <u>do believe</u> still, that the shutting up houses thus by force was of little or no service in the whole.

The mourners **went** about the streets indeed, for nobody put on black or made a formal dress of mourning for their nearest friends.   [Turn into a negative statement]

   The mourners <u>did not go</u> about the streets indeed, for nobody put on black or made a formal dress of mourning for their nearest friends.

First, it is so ordered, that every householder **cause** the street before his door to be clean swept all the week long.   [Provide emphasis]

   First, it is so ordered, that every householder <u>do cause</u> the street before his door to be clean swept all the week long.

Exercise 81B: Modal Verbs

Fill in the blanks below with an appropriate helping verb (*should, would, may, might, must, can, could*) to form a modal verb. There may be more than one correct answer for each sentence. Use each helping verb at least once.

These sentences are taken from the anonymously written *A General History of the Pyrates, From Their First Rise and Settlement in the Island of Providence, to the Present Time.* Back in the author's day (the late seventeenth and early eighteenth centuries), writers capitalized any words that they thought were important—so we've kept the original capitalization in these excerpts. (Also, Defoe spelled *pirate* as *pyrate*, which is pronounced in exactly the same way!)

After you finish the exercise, be sure to read the original sentences in the *Answer Key*.

> **Note to Instructor:** The original sentences are found below. Accept any helping verbs that make sense! Be sure to help the student compare her answers with the original verbs below. Ask her which sentences sound best.

Caesar commanded that the Prisoners __should__ be brought and executed, according to the Laws in Cases of Pyracy.

You __must__ understand that these Men continually found Favours and Incouragers at Jamaica, and perhaps they are not all dead yet.

The Lords humbly besought her Majesty to use such Methods as she __should__ think proper for taking the said Island into her Hands.

Their Vessels were so small that they __could__ not attack a Ship of any Force.

He often proceeded to bully the Governor, not that I __can__ discover the least Cause of Quarrel betwixt them.

If such a one has but Courage, he __must__ certainly be a great Man.

How many you __may__ have killed of those that resisted you in the committing of your former Pyracies, I know now.

However, the Governor dissembled, received the Pyrates Invitation civilly, and promised that he and the rest __would__ go.

In the beginning he was very averse to this sort of Life, and __would__ certainly have escaped from it, had a fair Opportunity presented itself.

There are many Harbours to which Pyrates __may__ securely resort without Fear of Discovery from the Inhabitants.

Why __would__ Men, honestly disposed, give their Votes for such a Captain?

It came into his Head that the Tankard __might__ prove of some Use to him.

As to the Lives of our two female Pyrates, we __must__ confess they may appear a little Extravagant.

I understand how to navigate a Ship, and I __can__ soon teach you to steer.

He __could__ say little in Defence of himself.

It cannot be supposed that such a Man of War as this __could__ undertake any considerable Voyage, or attempt any extraordinary Enterprize.

Exercise 81C: Verb Tense and Voice

For each sentence below, underline each verb phrase (in both dependent and independent clauses) and identify the tense and voice of the verb. For state-of-being verbs that are neither active nor passive in voice, identify the tense and write *state-of-being*. Mark modal verbs as *perfect present modal*, *active* (or *passive*) or *simple present modal*, *active* (or *passive*). The first sentence is done for you.

These sentences are taken from *Treasure Island*, by Robert Louis Stevenson.

simple past, active   simple present modal, active   perfect past, active

Every day when he came back from his stroll he would ask if any seafaring men had gone by along the road.

simple past, state-of-being   perfect past, active

That was Flint's treasure that we had come so far to seek.

perfect present, active   simple present, state-of-being

I have seen him wringing his hands after such a rebuff, and I am sure the annoyance and the
simple past, active   perfect present modal, active

terror he lived in must have greatly hastened his early and unhappy death.

perfect present   simple past,   simple past,
modal, active   active   active

You may imagine how I felt when I heard this abominable old rogue addressing another in the very
perfect past, active

same words of flattery as he had used to myself.

perfect present modal, active   simple past, state-of-being

Probably I should have told the whole story to the doctor, for I was in mortal fear lest the captain
simple present modal, active

should repent of his confessions.

perfect past, passive

The captain had been struck dead by thundering apoplexy.

progressive past, active   simple past, active

My heart was beating finely when we two set forth in the cold night upon this dangerous venture.

simple present, passive

The ship is bought.

simple past, state-of-being   simple present modal, active   perfect present modal, active

The thing was extremely small, even for me, and I can hardly imagine that it could have floated

with a full-sized man.

Now, to tell you the truth, from the very first mention of Long John in Squire Trelawney's letter
perfect past, active   simple present modal, active

I had taken a fear in my mind that he might prove to be the very one-legged sailor whom I
perfect past, active

had watched for so long at the old Benbow.

— LESSON 82 —

Conditional Sentences
The Condition Clause
The Consequence Clause

Exercise 82A: Identifying Conditional Sentences

Some of the sentences in this exercise are conditional sentences—and others are not! Identify each conditional sentence by writing a *C* in the margin. For each conditional sentence, label the clauses as *condition* or *consequence*.

These sentences are taken from the collection *The Oxford Book of Japanese Short Stories*, edited by Theodore William Goossen.

consequence   condition
I would be so happy if you could come with me to the mountain.   C

Though twenty years had passed, Konko could still see Nichiyo's expression clearly.

condition   consequence
If you're not here, I suppose they'll make me do the work of two.   C

> **Note to Instructor:** This sentence contains three clauses: *If you're not here, I suppose...work of two*, and within that consequence clause, the noun clause *[that] they'll make me...of two*, the direct object of the verb *suppose*.

condition
Unless one managed to get into one of the cars—at the risk of life and limb—   C
consequence
one would have to wait additional long hours.

I was attracted to things that had something of an impoverished beauty about them.

condition   consequence
If the four had been making a pilgrimage to some nearby temple, their appearance   C
would not have been extraordinary.

As soon as she saw him come in, she gave the command she had prepared for him.

On the ground, still locked, lay the steel shackle that had been fastened to the
elephant's hind leg, as though the elephant had slipped out of it.

Let's go and see if your father's had any luck.

condition   consequence
If only I could sew you a nice kimono, it would be a happy day.   C

Exercise 82B: Tense in Conditional Sentences

Fill in each blank below with the correct tense and form of the verb in brackets. Some sentences may have more than one possible correct answer.

These sentences are drawn from the anthologies *The Oxford Book of American Short Stories*, edited by Joyce Carol Oates, and *The World's Greatest Short Stories*, edited by James Daley.

Don't forget that the consequence clause might come before the condition clause!

First conditional sentences

If the speeches __are__ [state of being] successful, MacPherson __takes__ [take] all the credit.

If we __do meet__ [meet] again, why, we __shall smile__ [smile].

> **Note to Instructor:** *If we meet again, why, we will smile* is also acceptable.

If I __speak__ [speak] the truth it __will be__ [state of being] my wife and my children who will pay in hardships for my outspokenness.

Snakes __won't hurt__ [negative form of hurt] you unless you __hurt__ [hurt] them.

We' __ll go__ [go] before six o'clock if you __want__ [want] to sleep.

If you __must shatter__ [shatter] this hour of peace, __think__ [think] of the mark on the wall.

Second conditional sentences

If Gabriel ever __broke__ [break] the silence of the North, they __would stand__ [stand] together, hand in hand, before the great White Throne.

If, after reaching home, he __found__ [find] himself at any time in want of aid, a letter from him __would be__ [state of being] sure of a reply.

If I __did__ [do] that, I __should catch__ [catch] myself out, and stretch my hand at once for a book in self-protection.

> **Note to Instructor:** The helping verb *should* can also be *could* or *would*.

Third conditional sentences

If he and she __had been living__ [progressive form of *live*] in those days he __would have seen__ [see] ever so clearly the Cause for that fighting.

They __would__ perhaps __have remained__ [remained] with him longer, if those pushing up behind them __had not made__ [negative form of make] a longer peaceful observation impossible.

They __would not have had__ [negative form of *have*] a more perfect day for a garden-party if they __had ordered__ [order] it.

If someone __had died__ [die] there normally, we __would__ still __be having__ [progressive form of *have*] our party.

Exercise 82C: Diagramming

On your own paper, diagram these sentences, taken from J. R. R. Tolkien's *The Two Towers*. A conditional clause should be diagrammed like any other dependent clause.

Unless our enemies rest also, they will leave us far behind, if we stay to sleep.

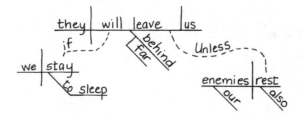

None could pass the Teeth of Mordor and not feel their bite, unless they were summoned by Sauron, or knew the secret passwords that would open the Morannon, the black gate of his land.

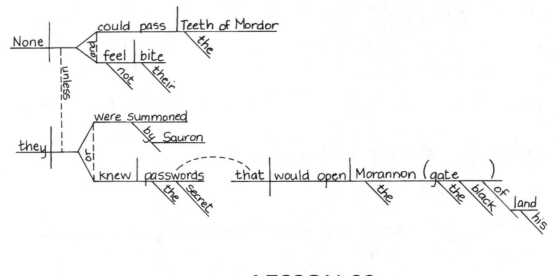

— **LESSON 83** —

Conditional Sentences

The Subjunctive

Exercise 83A: Subjunctive Forms in Folk Tales

Fill in each blank with the correct state-of-being verb. These sentences are taken from the tales collected by the Brothers Grimm.

If I __were__ to fall from one of these great clods, I should undoubtedly break my neck.

I __was__ going to split the tree to get a little wood for cooking.

"Ah me!" cried the wife, "'if I __were__ but a thousand feet beneath the earth!"

But she set to work so nimbly, and pulled the lace so tight, that Snowdrop's breath was stopped, and she fell down as if she __were__ dead.

He was undecided, and knew not if he were worthy of this.

But as the king and queen had only twelve golden dishes for them to eat out of, they were forced to leave one of the fairies out.

And they were married that very day, and the soldier was chosen to be the king's heir.

He has taken the chickens which I was just going to serve up, off the dish, and has run away with them!

I wish you were a raven and would fly away; then I should have a little peace!

The countryman then began to tell his tale, and said he was going to take the goose to a christening.

I think if I were to take another draught it would do me no harm.

When she was emptying the beans into the pan, one dropped without her observing it, and lay on the ground beside a straw.

When he came to the sea, it looked blue and gloomy, though it was very calm.

As they came near the brook they saw something like a large grasshopper jumping towards the water, as if it were going to leap in.

Exercise 83B: Correct Verb Forms in Complex Sentences

In each pair of verb forms, cross out the incorrect form. These sentences are taken from Kate DiCamillo's modern fairy tale *The Tale of Despereaux: Being the Story of a Mouse, a Princess, Some Soup, and a Spool of Thread.*

The darkness had a physical presence as if it (was̶/were) a being all its own.

And so the prisoner took the cloth and draped it around his shoulders as if it (was̶/were) a cloak.

She (was/wer̶e̶) a natural-born cynic who lived in defiance of contracts!

I hope that the hair on the back of your neck stood up as you thought of Mig's fate and how it would be if it (was̶/were) your own.

And so he (was/wer̶e̶) reading the story as if it (was̶/were) a spell and the words of it, spoken aloud, could make magic happen.

When Despereaux stepped from the last stair onto the dungeon floor, Botticelli called out to him as if he (was̶/were) a long-lost friend.

"There is a rat in my soup" (was̶/were) the last words she uttered.

The king stamped his foot harder, and then harder still, so it seemed as if the whole castle, the very world, (was̶/were) shaking.

Terrible howls issued from the dark place, as if the castle itself (was̶/were) weeping.

But as soon as the princess said this, her mother (was/wer̶e̶) gone.

So the mouse raised his head and squared his shoulders and pushed the spool of thread forward again, into the kitchen, where he saw, too late, that there (was/wer̶e̶) a light burning.

Reader, if you (was̶/were) standing in the dungeon, you would certainly hear all of these disturbing and ominous sounds.

If I (was̶/were) standing in the dungeon, I would hear these sounds.

His paws (was̶/were) shaking and his muscles (was/were) jumping and the place where his tail should be (was/wer̶e̶) throbbing.

— LESSON 84 —

Conditional Sentences

The Subjunctive

Moods of Verbs

Subjunctive Forms Using *Be*

Exercise 84A: Parsing Verbs

In the following sentences from the classic short story "The Yellow Wallpaper," by Charlotte Perkins Gilman, underline each predicate, in both main clauses and dependent clauses. Above each, write the tense, voice, and mood of the verb.

> **Tenses:** Simple past, present, future; progressive past, present, future; perfect past, present, future
>
> **Voice:** Active, passive (or state-of-being)
>
> **Mood:** Indicative, subjunctive, imperative, modal, subjunctive/modal

Something to look out for: sometimes one helping verb will actually help out two different verbs! The first example of this has been done for you. Note that both verbs are modal (we have inserted the understood helping verb in brackets).

simple present, state-of-being, indicative   simple present, active, indicative

It <u>is</u> very seldom that mere ordinary people like John and myself <u>secure</u> ancestral halls for the summer.

simple present, active, modal   simple present, active, modal

A colonial mansion, a hereditary estate, I <u>would say</u> a haunted house, and <u>[would] reach</u> the height

progressive present, active, modal

of romantic felicity—but that <u>would be asking</u> too much of fate!

simple future, active, indicative   simple present, active, indicative

Still I <u>will</u> proudly <u>declare</u> that there <u>is</u> something queer about it.

simple present, passive, modal

Else, why <u>should</u> it <u>be let</u> so cheaply?

simple present, active, indicative   simple past, active, indicative   simple past, active, indicative   simple past, active, indicative

I <u>don't</u> <u>like</u> our room a bit. I <u>wanted</u> one downstairs that <u>opened</u> on the piazza and <u>had</u> roses all

simple present, active, modal

over the window, and such pretty old-fashioned chintz hangings! but John <u>would</u> not <u>hear</u> of it.

> **Note to Instructor:** Although the first verb uses the helping verb *do*, it is neither modal nor emphatic because the helping verb acts to make the verb negative.

simple present,   simple present, state-of-being,   simple present, active,
active, indicative   subjunctive   modal

I <u>think</u> sometimes that if I <u>were</u> only well enough to write a little it <u>would relieve</u> the press of ideas

simple present, active,
modal

and <u>rest</u> me.

> **Note to Instructor:** The final verb has the understood helping verb *[would] rest*.

simple present,   simple present,
active, indicative   active, modal

I <u>wish</u> I <u>could get</u> well faster.

simple present,
active, modal

But I <u>must</u> not <u>think</u> about that.

simple present,   simple present,   simple present,   simple present,
active, indicative   active, subjunctive   active, subjunctive   state-of-being, indicative

Even when I <u>go</u> to ride, if I <u>turn</u> my head suddenly and <u>surprise</u> it—there <u>is</u> that smell!

perfect present,   simple past,
active, indicative   active, indicative

Such a peculiar odor, too! I <u>have spent</u> hours in trying to analyze it, to find what it <u>smelled</u> like.

simple past,   simple past,   simple present,
active, indicative   active, indicative   active, modal

Then he <u>took</u> me in his arms and <u>called</u> me a blessed little goose, and said he <u>would go</u> down cellar

simple past,   simple present,
active, subjunctive   active, modal

if I <u>wished</u>, and <u>have</u> it whitewashed into the bargain.

> **Note to Instructor:** The final verb has the understood helping verb *[would] have*.

Exercise 84B: Forming Subjunctives and Modals

Fill in the blanks in the following sentences, from the classic novella *The Haunting of Hill House*, by Shirley Jackson, with the correct verb form indicated in brackets.

> **Note to Instructor:** Any modal helping verbs (*should, might,* etc.) can be used in place of *would* as long as the finished sentence makes sense.

I think that I __would like__ [simple present active modal of *like*] this better if I __had__ [simple past active subjunctive of *have*] the blankets over my head.

If I __hadn't seen__ [perfect past active subjunctive of *see*, negative form] Hill House, __would__ I __be__ [simple present state-of-being modal] so unfair to these people?

You __should have seen__ [perfect present active modal of *see*] the ham they had.

If it __hadn't happened__ [perfect past active subjunctive of *happen*, negative form] you __would__ never __have come__ [perfect present active modal of *come*] to Hill House.

What a farmer's wife you __might have made__ [perfect present active modal of *make*].

Eleanor, wondering if she __were__ [simple past state-of-being subjunctive] really here at all, and not dreaming of Hill House from some safe spot impossibly remote, looked slowly and carefully around the room.

Hill House was left jointly to the two sisters, who __must have been__ [perfect present state-of-being modal] quite young ladies by then.

He looked as though he __were__ [simple past state-of-being subjunctive] doggedly counting to a hundred.

Perhaps if I _don't mention_ [simple present active subjunctive of *mention*, negative form] Hill House I will not be doing wrong.

She brought her hand up to the heavy iron knocker that had a child's face, determined to make more noise and yet more, so that Hill House _might be_ [simple present state-of-being subjunctive] very sure she was there.

If we _let_ [simple present active subjunctive of *let*] you go off wandering by yourself we'd very likely never find you again.

For a few minutes she _has been persuaded_ [perfect present passive modal of *persuade*] to believe that nothing had happened.

Exercise 84C: Diagramming

On your own paper, diagram the following sentences, from *Wide Sargasso Sea*, by Jean Rhys.

If some of the flowers were battered, the others smelt sweeter, the air was bluer and sparkling fresh.

Reality might disconcert her, bewilder her, hurt her, but it would not be reality.

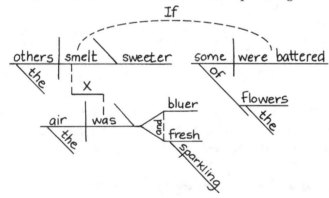

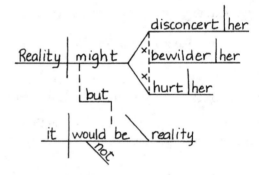

It must have rained heavily during the night for the red clay was very muddy.

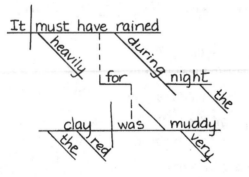

— REVIEW 7 —

Weeks 19-21

Topics
Phrases and Clauses
Adjective, Adverb, and Noun Clauses
Pronouns
Mood: Modal, Subjective, Imperative, Indicative
Conditional Sentences

Review 7A: Improving Sentences with Phrases

In the blanks below, supply phrases that meet the descriptions in brackets. You may supply more than one phrase in any blank, as long as at least one phrase fulfills the requirements (often, additional prepositional phrases may be needed). The first is done for you.

The original sentences are taken from Edith Nesbit's classic collection of tales, *The Book of Dragons*.

This is a challenging assignment—prepare to spend some time on it!

When you are finished, compare your sentences with the originals in the *Answer Key*.

> **Note to Instructor:** This is a difficult exercise, but it will begin to move the student towards using grammatical knowledge to construct more interesting sentences, while also giving a model from an excellent writer. If the student gets stuck, provide her with the first word or two of the original phrase.
>
> Many of these phrases contain additional prepositional or participle phrases. It is not necessary for the student to add multiple phrases as long as her sentence makes sense.
>
> When the student is finished, ask her to read her sentences out loud first, followed by Nesbit's original sentence. Encourage her to listen carefully to both sentences.

adverbial prepositional phrase answering the question *where*
The Queen and the Princess were feeding the goldfish <u>in the courtyard fountains</u>

adverbial prepositional phrase answering the question *how*
<u>with crumbs of the Princess's eighteenth birthday cake</u>, when the King came into the

adjectival participle phrase describing the raven
courtyard, looking as black as thunder, with his black raven <u>hopping after him</u>.

adverbial prepositional phrase describing to   adverbial prepositional phrase describing
what extent Nurse let go   how Lionel bolted off
The minute Nurse let go <u>for a moment</u> Lionel bolted off <u>without waiting for his clean</u>

<u>handkerchief</u>, and in the drawing room there were two very grave-looking gentlemen in red robes

adjectival prepositional phrase describing the gold coronets
with fur, and gold coronets <u>with velvet sticking up out of the middle like the cream in the very</u>

<u>expensive jam tarts</u>.

adjectival past participle phrase describing the hedge
There was a great hedge at the end of this field, <u>all covered with snow and icicles</u>; but the children
found a place where there was a hole, and as no bears or wolves seemed to be just in that part of
the hedge, they crept through and scrambled out of the frozen ditch on the other side.

225

adjectival present participle phrase describing the road
For in front of them, running straight and smooth right away to the Northern Lights , lay a great

adjectival present participle phrase describing the trees
wide road of pure dark ice, and on each side were tall trees all sparkling with white frost , and

adjectival past participle phrase describing the strings of stars
from the boughs of the trees hung strings of stars threaded on fine moonbeams , and shining so

prepositional phrase acting as a predicate adjective describing *like*
brightly that it was like a beautiful fairy daylight .

adverbial prepositional phrase answering the question *where*
And as the dragon came out of the dungeon , following Johnnie and Tina into the bright

adverbial prepositional phrase answering the question *where*
gold and blue of their wedding day , he blinked his eyes as a cat does in the sunshine, and

he shook himself, and the last of his plates dropped off, and his wings with them, and he was
prepositional phrase acting as the predicate adjective describing *he*
just like a very, very extra-sized cat .

adjectival present participle phrase describing the dragon
For there, plain to be seen, was the dragon, as big as a barge, glowing ike a furnace ,

adjectival present participle   adjectival present participle
phrase describing the dragon   phrase describing the dragon
and spitting fire and showing his shining teeth .

Review 7B: Improving Sentences with Clauses

Rewrite each sentence on your own paper, adding a dependent clause that meets the description in brackets. The first is done for you, with explanation provided.

The original sentences are taken from *My Father's Dragon*, by Ruth Stiles Gannett. When you are finished, compare your sentences with the originals in the *Answer Key*.

Note to Instructor: This is a difficult exercise, but it will begin to move the student towards using grammatical knowledge to construct more interesting sentences, while also giving a model from an excellent writer. If the student gets stuck, provide him with the first two or three words of the original clause.
   When the student is finished, ask him to read his sentence out loud first, followed by Gannett's original sentence. Encourage him to listen carefully to both sentences.

adjective clause describing *mane*
A lion was prancing about clawing at his mane, which was all snarled and full of blackberry twigs .

adverb clause describing *went* and answering the question *when*
When everything was packed my father and the cat went down to the docks to the ship.

adverb clause describing *laughed* and answering the question *why*
My father and the dragon laughed themselves weak because it was such a silly sight .

adjective clause describing *clearing* and introduced by a relative adverb
It was the boar coming back from the big clearing where the tigers were chewing gum .

noun clause acting as a direct object
A pale moon came out from behind the clouds and my father could see where the voice was
coming from .

adverb clause describing *grew* and answering the question *when*
It grew louder and louder as he got nearer to the island .

noun clause acting as a predicate nominative

Why, this is just exactly <u>what we've needed all these years</u> !

noun clause acting as a direct object

The cat had told him <u>that tigers were especially fond of chewing gum</u> ,

adjective clause modifying a noun within the noun clause
<u>which was very scarce on the island</u> .

Review 7C: Conditional Clauses

Label the following sentences as first, second, or third conditional by writing *1*, *2*, or *3* in the blank next to each one. Underline each conditional clause. Circle each consequence clause.

These sentences are taken from *Searching for Dragons*, by Patricia C. Wrede.

<u>If she could guess his name,</u> (she could keep the baby)   1

<u>If he hadn't been such a do-gooder,</u> (I wouldn't be in this mess)   3

<u>And if I can't find her there,</u> (I'll swing through the Enchanted Forest on the way back.)   1

<u>If you're fool enough to travel through the Mountains of Morning without a companion,</u> (that's not my concern)   1

(Mendanbar didn't like to think of what might happen) <u>if Kazul stayed missing for long.</u>   2

(He would have to apologize to the gargoyle sooner or later,) <u>unless he could figure out a way to muffle the noise while he worked.</u>   1

<u>If you'd really thought Kazul was here,</u> (you wouldn't have come at all.)   3

(Vanquish that, Cimorene)—<u>if you can!</u>   1

(It would cause a lot of trouble) <u>if I melted the King of the Enchanted Forest in the middle of Kazul's living room.</u>   2

<u>If it came to a fight,</u> (the Enchanted Forest and the Mountains of Morning would be very evenly matched.)   2

<u>But if I figure it out,</u> (I'll let you know)   1

(So he kept the sword in the armory) <u>unless he could think of an excuse to use it.</u> 2

Review 7D: Pronoun Review

The following sentences are taken from Patricia Wrede's *Dealing with Dragons*. Circle every pronoun. Label each as personal (*PER*), possessive (*POSS*), reflexive (*REF*), intensive (*INT*), demonstrative (*DEM*), interrogative (*INTER*), relative (*REL*), or indefinite (*IND*). Beside this label, add the abbreviation for the part of the sentence (or clause) that the pronoun serves as: adjective (*ADJ*), subject (*SUBJ*), predicate adjective (*PA*), direct object (*DO*), indirect object (*IO*), or object of the preposition (*OP*). (Intensive pronouns will not have one of these parts of speech—they act as appositives, which you'll cover in Lesson 94 if this is your first time through this course.)

　　The first has been done for you.

　　　　　　　　　　　　　　　　　PER　　　　　　　　　　　PER　　　POSS
　　　　　　　　　　　　　　　　　SUBJ　　　　　　　　　　DO　　　ADJ

Cimorene was quite sure that (they) were only taking (her) because (her) fairy godmother had told

　PER　　　　　　IND　　　　　　　　　　　　　　PER　　　　　PER　　　　　　　　　　　　REF
　IO　　　　　　　SUBJ　　　　　　　　　　　　　OP　　　　　SUBJ　　　　　　　　　　　OP

(them) that (something) had better be done about (her) and soon. (She) kept this opinion to (herself).

> **Note to Instructor:** The noun clause *that something had better be done about her, and soon* is the direct object of the predicate *had told*; the pronoun *them* is the indirect object.

PER　　　　　　　　　　　　　　　　　　　　　　　　　　　　　　　　　PER　　POSS
SUBJ　　　　　　　　　　　　　　　　　　　　　　　　　　　　　　　　DO　　ADJ

(She) was beginning to feel much less frightened, for the gray-green dragon reminded (her) of (her)

　　　　　　REL　　　　　　　　　　　　　　　　　　　　　REL　　PER
　　　　　　SUBJ　　　　　　　　　　　　　　　　　　　　OP　　SUBJ

great uncle, (who) was old and rather hard of hearing and of (whom) (she) was rather fond.

　　　　　　　　IND　　PER　　　　　　　　　DEM
　　　　　　　　SUBJ　OP　　　　　　　　　　OP

There weren't very (many) of (them) printed, and a lot of (those) were lost in a flood a few years later.

　　　　DEM　　　　　　　　　　　POSS
　　　　ADJ　　　　　　　　　　　OP

"How is (that) fireproofing spell of (yours) coming?" Morwen asked.

　　　　　　　　　　　　　　　　　　　IND　　　PER
　　　　　　　　　　　　　　　　　　　SUBJ　　OP

Fortunately the fireproofing spell was still in effect, and (neither) of (them) even felt warm, though

　　　　　　POSS
　　　　　　ADJ

Alianora lost the ends of (her) sleeves and Cimorene's hemline rose six scorched inches.

PER　　　　　　　　　　　POSS　　　　　　　　　　　　　　　　　　　　REL
SUBJ　　　　　　　　　　ADJ　　　　　　　　　　　　　　　　　　　　SUBJ

(She) felt a little warm, and (her) clothes had been reduced to a few charred rags, but (that) was

　　　　　REL
　　　　　SUBJ

nothing compared to (what) might have happened.

　　PER
　　SUBJ　　　　　　　　　　　　　　　　　　POSS
　　　　　　　　　　　　　　　　　　　　　　OP

If (you)'re that low on dried feverfew, take some of (mine).

DEM
SUBJ

(This) wasn't getting anywhere.

　　IND　　　　　　　　　　　　　　　　PER　　　　　　　　　　　　　　　REL
　　DO　　　　　　　　　　　　　　　　SUBJ　　　　　　INT　　　　　　　SUBJ

A (few) like the wolfsbane and feverfew, (she) could gather (herself) from the herbs (that) grew on the slopes of the mountains.

PER
SUBJ
                                                                    PER   IND   PER
                                                                    SUBJ   DO   SUBJ

(She) was certain that the man was a wizard, though (she) had never met (one) before, and (she) did not

                    IND   PER   REL   PER
                    OP   SUBJ   OP   SUBJ

want to agree to (anything) until (she) was sure of (what) (she) was agreeing to.

PER   INTER   PER
SUBJ   SUBJ   PN

"If (it) wasn't a wizard, (who) was (it)?" the dragon at the far end of the table asked.

> **Note to Instructor:** It is also possible to interpret the second *it* as the subject (*PER SUBJ*) and *who* as the predicate nominative (*INTER PN*).

Review 7E: Parsing

In the sentences below, underline every verb or verb phrase that acts as the predicate of a clause (dependent or independent). Label each verb with the correct tense, voice, and mood.

> **Tenses:** Simple past, present, future; progressive past, present, future; perfect past, present, future
>
> **Voice:** Active, passive (or state-of-being)
>
> **Mood:** Indicative, subjunctive, imperative, modal, subjunctive/modal

The first is done for you.

These sentences are taken from *The Yellow Fairy Book*, by Andrew Lang.

progressive present,   progressive present,
active, indicative   active, indicative

You <u>are looking</u> for the Mother Dragon's mare who <u>is galloping</u> about among the clouds.

simple past,   simple past,
passive, indicative   active, indicative

He <u>was</u> so <u>vexed</u> with his own folly that he <u>did</u> not <u>attempt</u> to explain his conduct, and things

perfect present,   perfect past,
active, modal   active, subjunctive

<u>would have gone</u> badly with him if his friends the fairies <u>had</u> not <u>softened</u> the hearts of his captors.

> **Note to Instructor:** *If his friends the fairies...* is the condition clause with a subjunctive verb, while *and things would have gone...* is the consequence clause with a modal verb.

perfect past,   simple present,
active, indicative   state-of-being, modal

All the neighbouring kings <u>had offered</u> rich rewards to anyone who <u>should be</u> able to destroy the

perfect past,   perfect past,
active, indicative   active, indicative

monster, either by force or enchantment, and many <u>had tried</u> their luck, but all <u>had</u> miserably <u>failed</u>.

simple past,   perfect past,   simple past,
active, indicative passive, indicative   passive, indicative

Once a great forest in which the Dragon <u>lay</u> <u>had been set</u> on fire; the forest <u>was burnt</u> down, but

perfect past,
state-of-being, indicative

the monster <u>had been</u> unhurt.

simple present,   simple present,   simple present,
active, indicative   state-of-being, subjunctive   active, modal

Your prayers and your repentance <u>come</u> too late, and if I <u>were</u> to spare you everyone <u>would think</u> me a fool.

           perfect present,   simple past,   simple past,
           active, indicative   active, indicative   active, indicative

Very long ago, as old people <u>have told</u> me, there <u>lived</u> a terrible monster, who <u>came</u> out of the

      simple past,
      active, indicative

North, and <u>laid</u> waste whole tracts of country, devouring both men and beasts; and this monster

simple past,   simple past,   simple past,
state-of-being, indicative   passive, indicative   passive, modal

<u>was</u> so destructive that it <u>was feared</u> that no living creature <u>would be left</u> on the face of the earth.

    perfect past,   perfect past,   perfect past,
active, indicative   passive, indicative   active, indicative

He <u>told</u> them how the Dragon <u>had been outwitted</u> by his grandmother, and how he <u>had heard</u> from

his own lips the answer to the riddle.

         simple past,   simple present,
      active, indicative   active, modal

The King <u>announced</u> publicly that he <u>would give</u> his daughter in marriage, as well as a large part

                 simple present,
                 active, modal

of his kingdom, to whosoever <u>should free</u> the country from the monster.

         simple past,   simple past,   perfect present,   simple past,
      active, indicative   passive, indicative   active, modal   active, indicative

The Herd-boy <u>did</u> as he <u>was told</u>, and before he <u>could have believed</u> it possible he <u>found</u> himself in

                        simple past,
                    state-of-being, indicative

a big hall, where even the walls <u>were</u> made of pure gold.

         simple past,   simple past,
      active, indicative   active, indicative

The Emperor <u>came</u> himself with his most distinguished knights, and each impostor <u>held</u> up his

                 present progressive,
                 active, subjunctive

arm just as if he <u>were holding</u> something.

Review 7F: Diagramming

On your own paper, diagram every word of the following two sentences from *The Yellow Fairy Book*.

Although the stranger's name and rank were unknown to Rosalie's father, he was really the son of the king of the Golden Isle, which had for capital a city that extended from one sea to another.

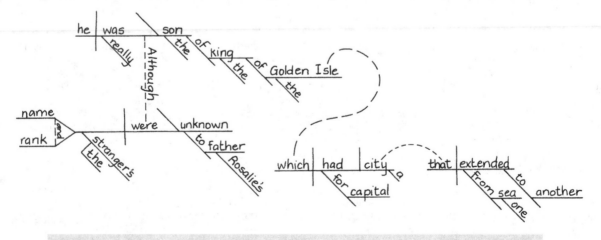

Note to Instructor: The prepositional phrase *for capital* is adverbial because it answers the question *to what extent*. (Golden Isle had a city. To what extent? To the extent that the city was its capital.)

The Fairy entered with them, and warned the Queen that the Wizard King would shortly arrive, infuriated by his loss, and that nothing could preserve the Prince and Princess from his rage and magic unless they were actually married.

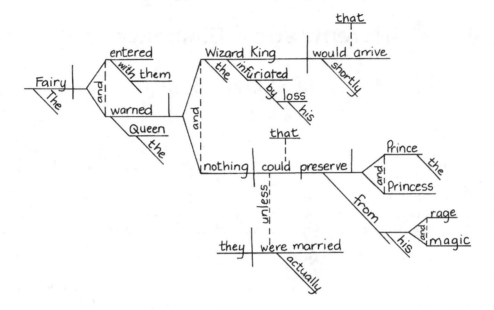

WEEK 22

Parenthetical Elements

— LESSON 85 —

Verb Review

Complete the following chart with the third-person-singular form of the verb indicated in the left-hand column. If you need help, ask your instructor.

Note to Instructor: Ask the student to make her best guess at any forms that confuse her. Then, show her the answers and have her erase (or scratch out) her incorrect answers and write in the correct ones.

INDICATIVE TENSES

		Active	Passive
SIMPLE			
abandon	Past	[he, she, it] abandoned	[he, she, it] was abandoned
paint	Present	[he, she, it] paints	[he, she, it] is painted
pay	Future	[he, she, it] will pay	[he, she, it] will be paid
PROGRESSIVE			
soak	Past	[he, she, it] was soaking	[he, she, it] was being soaked
shut	Present	[he, she, it] is shutting	[he, she, it] is being shut
spread	Future	[he, she, it] will be spreading	[he, she, it] will be being spread
PERFECT			
hug	Past	[he, she, it] had hugged	[he, she, it] had been hugged
wring	Present	[he, she, it] has wrung	[he, she, it] has been wrung
fly	Future	[he, she, it] will have flown	[he, she, it] will have been flown

MODAL TENSES
(would OR should, may, might, must, can, could)

		Active	Passive
SIMPLE			
spring	Present	[he, she, it] would spring	
PERFECT			
sleep	Past	[he, she, it] would have slept	

SUBJUNCTIVE TENSES

		Active	Passive
SIMPLE			
dive	Past	[he, she, it] dove	
sneer	Present	[he, she, it] sneer	

On your own paper, write sentences that use each of the forms above as the predicate of an independent or dependent clause. If you need help (or ideas), ask your instructor.

Note to Instructor: Sample sentences using the forms in the chart are listed below. If the student needs assistance using a particular form, show him the sentence containing that form and then ask him to write a variation of it (different subject, different modifiers, etc.). Students should always be allowed to copy a model when they are confused.

Teri abandoned the bicycle with the flat tire. The bicycle with the flat tire was abandoned by Teri.

Raya paints spectacular pictures of craggy mountains. That picture is painted by Raya.

I will pay a reasonable amount for a good cup of coffee. A reasonable amount will be paid by the customers.

While the shirt was soaking in the dishpan, its owner was being soaked by a sudden rainstorm outside.

The entry gate is shutting too quickly. The entry gate is being shut too quickly.

Soon, snow will be spreading across the whole state. Snow will be being spread by the nor-easter.

Abuela had hugged all of her grandchildren before she even took off her coat. All of the grandchildren had been hugged as soon as they stepped into the room.

She has wrung every single bit of meaning out of that poem. In her paper, that poem has been wrung of every single bit of meaning.

The plane will have flown over seven thousand miles by the time it arrives in New Zealand. The plane will have been flown over seven thousand miles by the pilot and her crew.

If you latched the door, I don't think it would spring open so easily.

The baby would have slept longer if the fireworks hadn't gone off.

If he dove too deeply, he might not come back up again.

Hold your head high, should she sneer at your efforts.

— LESSON 86 —

Restrictive and Non-Restrictive Modifying Clauses
Parenthetical Expressions

Exercise 86A: Restrictive and Non-Restrictive Modifying Clauses

In the following sentences, mark each bolded clause as either *ADV* for adverb or *ADJ* for adjective, and draw an arrow from the clause back to the word modified. Some sentences contain more than one modifying clause—try to identify each one.

Then, identify each adjective clause as either restrictive (*R*) or non-restrictive (*NR*).

Finally, set off all of the non-restrictive adjective clauses with commas. Use the proofreader's mark (⤷) for comma insertion. When you are finished, compare your punctuation with that of the original.

These sentences are very slightly condensed from *The Downstairs Girl*, by Stacey Lee, the story of Jo Kuan, a Chinese-American girl living in Atlanta in the late nineteenth century. The original commas around the non-restrictive clauses have been removed.

It was Robby's mother **who nursed me when I was a baby**.

And it was she **who told Old Gin about the secret basement under the print shop**. [ADJ R]

Whitehall Street, the "spine" of Atlanta, rises well above the treetops with her stately brick and imposing stone buildings—along with the occasional Victorian house **that refuses to give up her seat at the table**. [ADJ R]

She barely traipses in at nine **when the shop opens** and it's not even a quarter past eight. [ADJ NR]

> **Note to Instructor:** The clause is an adjective clause modifying the noun *nine*, introduced by a relative adverb.

Of course, I'd have to split the fee with Robby **whose six-foot height also draws attention, even as he keeps his eyes on the sidewalk**. [ADJ NR] [ADV]

Fluffing up the sleeves of my russet dress, **which have lost their puff and hang like a pair of deflated lungs** I carry myself a block farther to English's Millinery. [ADJ NR]

I set the boxes on our worktable **which is already weighed down with reams of felt**. [ADJ NR]

Servants are routinely blacklisted **when their services come to an end**. [ADV]

I have been admiring the knot embellishment on my friend's hat, and she said it was made by the Chinese girl **who works here**. [ADJ R]

Salt points to the top shelf **where we display the finest offerings** and with a wooden pole, Lizzie retrieves a straw hat in mauve with a cloud of tulle. [ADJ NR]

> **Note to Instructor:** The clause is an adjective clause modifying the noun *shelf*, introduced by a relative adverb.

The Western and Atlantic Railroad was the first of several cuts in the pie **that divided Atlanta into six wards**. [ADJ R]

I hurry to make it through **before it closes**. [ADV]

It was Old Gin **who stayed when the others moved on**. [ADJ R] [ADV]

Exercise 86B: Identifying Parenthetical Expressions

Identify each parenthetical expression as phrase, dependent clause, or complete sentence. These sentences are taken from Charles Darwin's classic account of his five-year round-the-world journey of exploration and discovery, *The Voyage of the Beagle.*

CHALLENGE EXERCISE

Provide a fuller description of each expression. What kind of phrase, clause, or sentence is it? What does it do or modify?

When you are finished, ask your instructor for the fuller explanations. Compare your descriptions to these explanations.

Note to Instructor: As long as the student is able to identify the expression as phrase, dependent clause, or sentence, you may consider the answer correct. The challenge exercise is optional.

Students who are going through this program for the first time may not be familiar with appositives, which are covered in Lesson 94.

dependent clause, adjectival,
modifying Lampyridae

All the fireflies, which I caught here, belonged to the Lampyridae (in which family the English glowworm is included), and the greater number of specimens were of Lampyris occidentalis.

It excited the liveliest admiration that I, a perfect stranger, should know the road (for direction
complete sentence (linked to first sentence by coordinating conjunction for),
explaining why the writer uses the word road instead of direction
and road are synonymous in this open country) to places where I had never been.

phrase, acting as an appositive to rename partridges
We everywhere saw great numbers of partridges (Nothura major).

In the evening the Saurophagus takes its stand on a bush, often by the roadside, and continually repeats without a change a shrill and rather agreeable cry, which somewhat resembles articulate
complete sentence, acting as an appositive to rename Bien te veo
words: the Spaniards say it is like the words "Bien te veo" (I see you well), and accordingly have given it this name.

To begin with, the Polyborus Brasiliensis: this is a common bird, and has a wide geographical
dependent clause, adjectival, modifying savannahs (or La Plata) and
introduced by a relative adverb
range; it is most numerous on the grassy savannahs of La Plata (where it goes by the name of Carrancha), and is far from unfrequent throughout the sterile plains of Patagonia.

We here had the four necessaries of life "en el campo,"—pasture for the horses, water (only
phrase, acting as an appositive to rename water
a muddy puddle), meat and firewood.

It is remarkable that in all the different kinds of glowworms, shining elaters, and various marine

prepositional phrase (introduced by the compound preposition such as), adjective, modifying animals

animals (such as the crustacea, medusae, nereidae, a coralline of the genus Clytia, and Pyrosma), which I have observed, the light has been of a well-marked green colour.

dependent clause, adjectival, modifying salitrales

As long as the ground remains moist in the salitrales (as the Spaniards improperly call them, mistaking this substance for saltpeter), nothing is to be seen but an extensive plain composed of a black, muddy soil, supporting scattered tufts of succulent plants.

dependent clause, adjectival, modifying ostrich

They described it as being less than the common ostrich (which is there abundant), but with a very close general resemblance.

prepositional phrase, adverbial, modifying the adverb Here

Here (at Bahia Blanca) the walls round the houses are built of hardened mud, and I noticed that one, which enclosed a courtyard where I lodged, was bored through by round holes in a score of places.

Exercise 86C: Punctuating Sentences with Parenthetical Expressions

All of the following sentences, taken from Leo Tolstoy's classic novel *Anna Karenina* (translated by Constance Garnett), have misplaced punctuation marks! Draw an arrow from each incorrect mark back to the place where the mark *should be*.

Wasn't it you (and didn't we all appreciate it in you)? who forgave everything, and moved simply by Christian feeling was ready to make any sacrifice?

Though it's a pity to take him from his work (but he has plenty of time!) I must look at his face; will he feel I'm looking at him?

Levin deliberately took out a ten rouble note, and, careful to speak slowly, though losing no time over the business, he handed him the note, and explained that Pyotr Dmitrievitch (what a great and important personage he seemed to Levin now, this Pyotr Dmitrievitch, who had been of so little consequence in his eyes before)! had promised to come at any time.

Dressing without hurry (he never hurried himself, and never lost his self-possession,) Vronsky drove to the sheds.

On the day of the wedding, according to the Russian custom (the princess and Darya Alexandrovna insisted on strictly keeping all the customs,) Levin did not see his betrothed, and dined at his hotel with three bachelor friends, casually brought together at his rooms.

He doesn't believe even in my love for my child, or he despises it (just as he always used to ridicule it.)

She stopped suddenly, and glanced inquiringly at her husband (he did not look at her.)

No one else in Stepan Arkadyevitch's place, having to do with such despair, would have ventured to smile (the smile would have seemed brutal;) but in his smile there was so much of sweetness and almost feminine tenderness that his smile did not wound, but softened and soothed.

And it vaguely came into Levin's mind that she herself was not to blame (she could not be to blame for anything) but what was to blame was her education, too superficial and frivolous. ("That fool Tcharsky: she wanted, I know, to stop him, but didn't know how to.")

As he approached her, his beautiful eyes shone with a specially tender light, and with a faint, happy, and modestly triumphant smile (so it seemed to Levin,) bowing carefully and respectfully over her, he held out his small broad hand to her.

— **LESSON 87** —

Parenthetical Expressions
Dashes

Exercise 87A: Types of Parenthetical Expressions

Identify each parenthetical expression as phrase, dependent clause, or sentence.

These sentences are taken from *A Walk in the Woods*, Bill Bryson's account of his attempt to hike along the Appalachian Trail.

CHALLENGE EXERCISE

Provide a fuller description of each expression. What kind of phrase, clause, or sentence is it? What does it do or modify?

When you are finished, ask your instructor for the fuller explanations. Compare your descriptions to these explanations.

Note to Instructor: This is a challenging assignment—give all necessary help!

From Georgia to Maine, it wanders across fourteen states, through plump, comely hills whose very
phrase
renaming the noun *names*
names—Blue Ridge, Smokies, Cumberlands, Catskills, Green Mountains, White Mountains—seem an invitation to amble.

sentence
providing additional information about the way in which it would be useful

It would be useful (I wasn't quite sure in what way, but I was sure nonetheless) to learn to fend for myself in the wilderness.

The Appalachians are the home of one of the world's great hardwood forests—the expansive relic
phrase
a further expansion on what it means to be a great hardwood forest
of the richest, most diversified sweep of woodland ever to grace the temperate world—and that forest is in trouble.

phrase
past participle phrase acting as an adjective and describing *stories*

I heard four separate stories (always related with a chuckle) of campers and bears sharing tents for
sentence
providing an example of a story of a person being vaporized
a few confused and lively moments; stories of people abruptly vaporized ("tweren't nothing left of him but a scorch mark") by body-sized bolts of lightning when caught in sudden storms on high ridgelines; of tents crushed beneath falling trees, or eased off precipices on ballbearings of beaded rain and sent paragliding onto distant valley floors, or swept away by the watery wall of a flash flood; of hikers beyond counting whose last experience was of trembling earth and the befuddled thought "Now what the—?"

sentence
acting as an adverb, giving more information about the adjective *nine*

At least nine hikers (the actual number depends on which source you consult and how you define a hiker) have been murdered along the trail since 1974.

dependent clause
adverbial, describing the infinitive *to pitch*

Our only apparent option was to pitch our tents—if we could in this wind—crawl in, and hope for the best.

sentence
explaining more about why the narrator didn't expect to buy more equipment

I hadn't expected to buy so much—I already owned hiking boots, a Swiss army knife, and a plastic map pouch that you wear around your neck on a piece of string, so I had felt I was pretty well there—but the more I talked to Dave the more I realized that I was shopping for an expedition.

The mound of provisions that a minute ago had looked so pleasingly abundant and exciting—all
phrase
this could be classified either as adjectival, describing the mound of provisions
or as adverbial, expanding on the adjectives *abundant* and *exciting.*
new! all mine!—suddenly seemed burdensome and extravagant.

I lay saucer-eyed in bed reading clinically precise accounts of people gnawed pulpy in
sentence
telling more about the *noiseless stalking*
their sleeping bags, plucked whimpering from trees, even noiselessly stalked (I didn't know this happened!) as they sauntered unawares down leafy paths or cooled their feet in mountain streams.

Exercise 87B: Punctuating Parenthetical Expressions

On either side of each bolded parenthetical expression, place parentheses, dashes, or commas. There are not necessarily correct answers for these, but compare them to the originals when you have finished.

These sentences are taken from *The Mother Tongue: English and How It Got That Way*, by Bill Bryson.

> **Note to Instructor:** The original versions of Bryson's sentences are below and reflect the author's intentions; any grammatical answers are acceptable, but where the student has chosen different punctuation, ask him to read first his version, and then Bryson's, out loud.

Indeed, Robert Burchfield, editor of the *Oxford English Dictionary*, created a stir in linguistic circles on both sides of the Atlantic when he announced his belief that American English and English English are drifting apart so rapidly that within 200 years the two nations won't be able to understand each other at all.

> **Note to Instructor:** A dash or comma could follow "Indeed," but the sentence cannot begin with parentheses.

For the airlines of 157 nations (**out of 168 in the world**), it is the agreed international language of discourse.

> **Note to Instructor:** If the student chooses to insert a comma after *nations*, the existing comma after *world* will close the parenthetical expression. Dashes cannot be used here because of the existing comma after *world*.

When companies from four European countries—**France, Italy, Germany, and Switzerland**—formed a joint truck-making venture called Iveco in 1977, they chose English as their working language because, as one of the founders wryly observed, "It puts us all at an equal disadvantage."

English is, **in short**, one of the world's great growth industries.

Altogether, about 200,000 English words are in common use, more than in German (**184,000**) and far more than in French (**a mere 100,000**).

> **Note to Instructor:** A dash or comma could follow *Altogether*, but the sentence cannot begin with parentheses (and although a dash is grammatical, it would be awkward).

The Italians even have a word for the mark left on a table by a moist glass (***culacino***) while the Gaelic speakers of Scotland, not to be outdone, have a word for the itchiness that overcomes the upper lip just before taking a sip of whiskey. (**Wouldn't they just?**) It's *sgriob*. And we have nothing in English to match the Danish *hygge* (**meaning "instantly satisfying and cozy"**), the French *sang-froid*, the Russian *glasnost*, or the Spanish *macho*, so we must borrow the term from them or do without the sentiment.

> **Note to Instructor:** Because *Wouldn't they just?* is a complete sentence, it can be set off only with parentheses, not dashes or commas.

Few English-speaking natives, **however well educated**, can confidently elucidate the difference between, **say**, a complement and a predicate or distinguish a full infinitive from a bare one.

A third—**and more contentious**—supposed advantage of English is the relative simplicity of its spelling and pronunciation.

We possess countless examples of pithy phrases—**"life is short," "between heaven and earth," "to go to work"**—which in other languages require articles.

And why, **come to that**, can we be overwhelmed or underwhelmed, but not semi-whelmed or—**if our feelings are less pronounced**—just whelmed?

Moreover, all children everywhere learn languages in much the same way: starting with simple labels (**"Me"**), advancing to subject-verb structures (**"Me want"**), before progressing to subject-verb-emphatics (**"Me want now"**), and so on.

> **Note to Instructor:** A dash or comma could follow *Moreover*, but the sentence cannot begin with parentheses. The parenthetical *Me want* and *Me want now* can be set off by commas or parentheses, but not by dashes because of the commas following *want* and *now*.

Most adults tend (**even when they are not aware of it**) to speak to infants in a simplified, gitchy-goo kind of way.

Exercise 87C: Using Dashes for Emphasis

On your own paper, rewrite the next four sentences, substituting dashes for the underlined punctuation marks and making any other capitalization or punctuation changes needed.

These sentences are taken from Bill Bryson's 2019 book *The Body: A Guide for Occupants.*

Six of these (carbon, oxygen, hydrogen, nitrogen, calcium, and phosphorus) account for 99.1 percent of what makes us, but much of the rest is a bit unexpected.

The cell is full of busy things, ribosomes and proteins, DNA, RNA, mitochrondria, and much other cellular arcana. But none of those are themselves alive. The cell itself is just a compartment, a kind of little room: a cell, to contain them, and of itself is as nonliving as any other room.

DNA exists for just one purpose, to create more DNA.

Original sentences:

Six of these—carbon, oxygen, hydrogen, nitrogen, calcium, and phosphorus—account for 99.1 percent of what makes us, but much of the rest is a bit unexpected.

The cell is full of busy things—ribosomes and proteins, DNA, RNA, mitochrondria, and much other cellular arcana—but none of those are themselves alive. The cell itself is just a compartment—a kind of little room: a cell—to contain them, and of itself is as nonliving as any other room.

DNA exists for just one purpose—to create more DNA.

— LESSON 88 —

Parenthetical Expressions
Dashes
Diagramming Parenthetical Expressions

Exercise 88A: Diagramming Parenthetical Expressions

On your own paper, diagram each of the following sentences.

These sentences are taken from *The Prince of Medicine*, a biography of the Roman physician Galen, written by Susan P. Mattern. (Some have been slightly condensed.) They are meant to be challenging! Do your best, and ask your instructor for help if you get frustrated. When you are finished, compare your answers to the *Answer Key*. (There may be more than one way to diagram these elements.)

Death and mortal illness, in Rome, was not especially associated with old age (and very few of Galen's recorded patients are old), nor even necessarily with childhood.

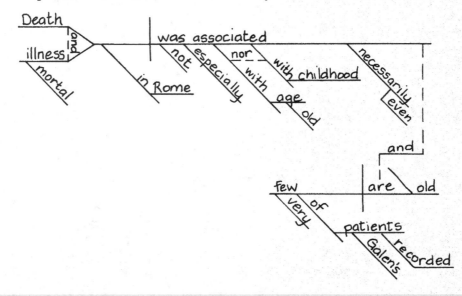

Note to Instructor: The parenthetical expression is a complete sentence that makes the original sentence compound. The student may notice that the writer uses the singular verb *was* as the predicate for the compound subject *death and mortal illness*; this suggests that the writer considers *death and mortal illness* to be a single subject, but grammatically, they have to be diagrammed as two subjects. The prepositional phrase *in Rome* is probably adjectival, given its placement (*death and mortal illness in Rome*), but an argument could be made that it is adverbial and modifies *was associated* (they were associated in Rome). Because *necessarily* is an adverb, it can only modify the verb *was associated*.

Galen and his patients visited the public baths daily or even twice daily (although the wealthiest had private baths in their houses).

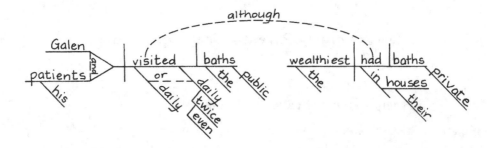

> **Note to Instructor:** The parenthetical expression is an adverbial dependent clause. In this context, *wealthiest* is acting as a noun (it would also be possible to conclude, though, that the subject of the dependent clause is an understood *patients* with *wealthiest* modifying the understood subject, which would be represented by an *x* in the subject space on the dependent clause diagram).

Some gladiatorial epitaphs attest to long records of victories and missions in the career of the deceased—killed finally in the arena perhaps, or, equally likely, dead later from infected wounds, or of other causes.

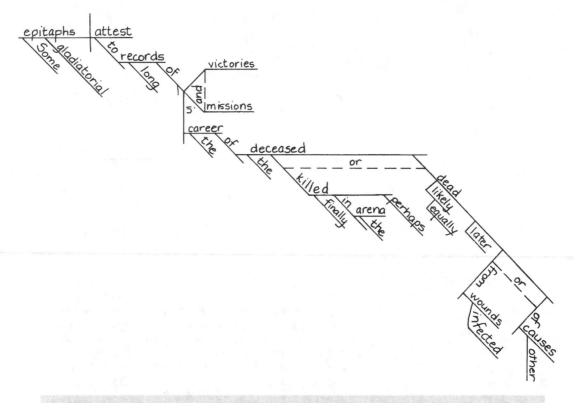

> **Note to Instructor:** The parenthetical expression is an adjectival participial phrase that modifies the noun *deceased*. Within it, the second parenthetical expression *equally likely* modifies the adjective *dead*. Note that the prepositional phrase *in the career…* modifies both *victories* and *missions*, which are themselves the compound objects of the preposition *of*.

One gladiator, a "knight" (these fought on horseback with lances) had a deep and broadly gaping gash across his lower thigh near the kneecap, so Galen was forced ("I dared") to exceed anything he had witnessed his teachers accomplish in drawing the muscles together and stripping the covering (he may mean the epitenon) off of the severed tendons.

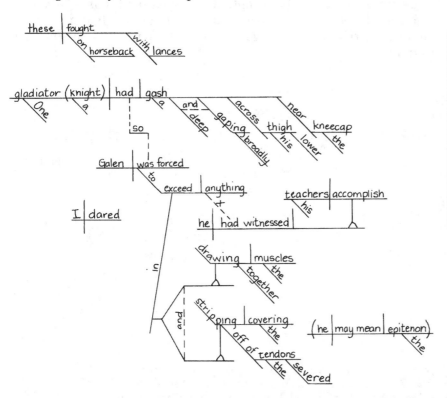

Note to Instructor: This sentence contains several parenthetical expressions. The adjectival clause *these fought on horseback with lances* modifies *knight*. The independent sentences *I dared* and *he may mean the epitenon* are syntactically separate from the main sentence and stand apart. *I dared* is a quotation of Galen's own words.

Galen does not name his teachers—perhaps because their reputations were modest and these names would not have been impressive on their own; he identifies their teachers (except in the case of the Epicurean) and their intellectual affiliation.

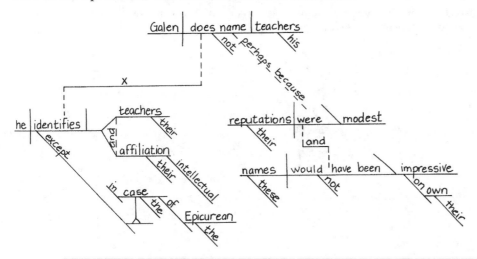

Note to Instructor: The first parenthetical expression *perhaps because their reputations…* is an adverbial dependent clause modifying the verb *does name* and answering the question *why*, with *perhaps because* acting as a compound subordinating conjunction. The second parenthetical expression is a prepositional phrase modifying *identifies*, with another prepositional phrase (*in the case of the Epicurean*) acting as the object of the preposition *except*.

The purpose of the lungs in Galen's system was mainly to ventilate the heart and thus regulate innate heat—an entity emanating from the heart and present from birth (it gradually diminished with age), which, cooking the blood as it arrived from the veins, injected it with vital pneuma that the arteries then distributed around the body.

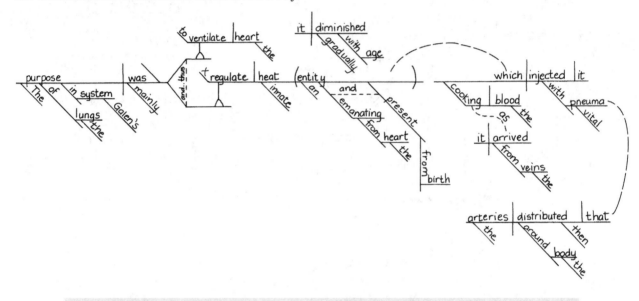

Dialogue and Quotations

— LESSON 89 —

Dialogue

Exercise 89A: Punctuating Dialogue

The excerpt below is from Robert Louis Stevenson's classic novel *The Strange Case of Dr. Jekyll and Mr. Hyde*. Most of the dialogue is missing quotation marks, and some of it is missing ending punctuation as well. Do your best to supply the missing punctuation marks. (Don't use proofreader's marks—just write the punctuation directly into the sentences.)

The passage describes the first encounter of the lawyer Mr. Utterson with the mysterious Mr. Hyde, a man Mr. Utterson has long suspected of committing crimes.

When you are finished, compare your version with the original.

> **Note to Instructor:** The original version is below, with the necessary punctuation marks bolded for your convenience. You may assign the student the task of comparing the original punctuation with her edited version. Ask her to circle any differences with a colored pencil; this will help her pay close attention to the correct punctuation.

The steps drew swiftly nearer, and swelled out suddenly louder as they turned the end of the street. The lawyer, looking forth from the entry, could soon see what manner of man he had to deal with. He was small and very plainly dressed and the look of him, even at that distance, went somehow strongly against the watcher's inclination. But he made straight for the door, crossing the roadway to save time; and as he came, he drew a key from his pocket like one approaching home.

Mr. Utterson stepped out and touched him on the shoulder as he passed. "Mr. Hyde, I think?"

Mr. Hyde shrank back with a hissing intake of the breath. But his fear was only momentary; and though he did not look the lawyer in the face, he answered coolly enough: "That is my name. What do you want?"

"I see you are going in," returned the lawyer. "I am an old friend of Dr. Jekyll's—Mr. Utterson of Gaunt Street—you must have heard of my name; and meeting you so conveniently, I thought you might admit me."

"You will not find Dr. Jekyll; he is from home," replied Mr. Hyde, inserting the key. And then suddenly, but still without looking up, "How did you know me?" he asked.

"On your side," said Mr. Utterson, "will you do me a favour?"

"With pleasure," replied the other. "What shall it be?"

"Will you let me see your face?" asked the lawyer.

Mr. Hyde appeared to hesitate, and then, as if upon some sudden reflection, fronted about with an air of defiance; and the pair stared at each other pretty fixedly for a few seconds. "Now I shall know you again," said Mr. Utterson. "It may be useful."

"Yes," returned Mr. Hyde, "it is as well we have met; and à propos, you should have my address." And he gave a number of a street in Soho.

"Good God!" thought Mr. Utterson, "can he, too, have been thinking of the will?" But he kept his feelings to himself and only grunted in acknowledgment of the address.

"And now," said the other, "how did you know me?"

"By description," was the reply.

"Whose description?"

"We have common friends," said Mr. Utterson.

"Common friends," echoed Mr. Hyde, a little hoarsely. "Who are they?"

"Jekyll, for instance," said the lawyer.

"He never told you," cried Mr. Hyde, with a flush of anger. "I did not think you would have lied."

"Come," said Mr. Utterson, "that is not fitting language."

The other snarled aloud into a savage laugh; and the next moment, with extraordinary quickness, he had unlocked the door and disappeared into the house.

Exercise 89B: Writing Dialogue Correctly

On your own paper, rewrite the following sentences as dialogue, using the past tense for the dialogue tags. Use the notations in parentheses to help you.

You may choose to place dialogue tags before, in the middle, or after dialogue, or to leave the tags out completely. But you must have at least one sentence with a dialogue tag that comes before, at least one sentence with a dialogue tag that comes after, at least one speech with the dialogue tag in the middle, and at least one speech with no dialogue tag at all.

The text in italics is part of the scene and should be included in your final version, but it isn't dialogue.

When you are finished, compare your answers with the original.

This passage was slightly condensed from *The Railway Children*, by Edith Nesbit. The three "railway children" are Robert (Bobbie), Peter, and their youngest sister Phyllis. In this part of the story, they are having the kind of argument that siblings often have—a silly argument that blows up because they're all on edge for another reason!

(Bobbie says) "I was using the rake."
(Peter says)   "Well, I'm using it now."
(Bobbie says)   "But I had it first."
(Peter says) "Then it's my turn now."
        And that was how the quarrel began.
(There is some heated argument and then Peter says) "You're always being disagreeable about nothing."
(Bobbie is holding onto the rake's handle and says) "I had the rake first."

(Peter says) "Don't—I tell you I said this morning I meant to have it. Didn't I, Phil?"

Phyllis said she didn't want to be mixed up in their rows. And instantly, of course, she was.

(Peter says) "If you remember, you ought to say."

(Bobbie says) "Of course she doesn't remember—but she might say so."

(Peter says) "I wish I'd had a brother instead of two whiny little kiddy sisters."

This was always recognised as indicating the high-water mark of Peter's rage.

(Bobbie wants to say) "Don't let's quarrel. Mother hates it so."

But though she tried hard, she couldn't. Peter was looking too disagreeable and insulting.

(Bobbie snaps) "Take the horrid rake, then."

And she suddenly let go her hold on the handle. Peter had been holding on to it too firmly, and he staggered and fell over backward, the teeth of the rake between his feet.

(Before she can stop herself, Bobbie says) "Serve you right."

Mother put her head out of the window, and it wasn't half a minute after that she was in the garden kneeling by the side of Peter.

(Mother says) "Now, are you hurt?"

> **Note to Instructor:** Allow the student to compare his answers with the original text below, but accept any grammatical rewriting.

"I was using the rake," said Bobbie.

"Well, I'm using it now," said Peter.

"But I had it first," said Bobbie.

"Then it's my turn now," said Peter. And that was how the quarrel began.

"You're always being disagreeable about nothing," said Peter, after some heated argument.

"I had the rake first," said Bobbie, holding on to its handle.

"Don't—I tell you I said this morning I meant to have it. Didn't I, Phil?"

Phyllis said she didn't want to be mixed up in their rows. And instantly, of course, she was.

"If you remember, you ought to say."

"Of course she doesn't remember—but she might say so."

Peter said, "I wish I'd had a brother instead of two whiny little kiddy sisters." This was always recognised as indicating the high-water mark of Peter's rage.

Bobbie wanted to say, "Don't let's quarrel. Mother hates it so." But though she tried hard, she couldn't. Peter was looking too disagreeable and insulting.

"Take the horrid rake, then," she snapped. And she suddenly let go her hold on the handle. Peter had been holding on to it too firmly, and he staggered and fell over backward, the teeth of the rake between his feet.

"Serve you right," said Bobbie, before she could stop herself.

Mother put her head out of the window, and it wasn't half a minute after that she was in the garden kneeling by the side of Peter.

"Now," said Mother, "are you hurt?"

Exercise 89C: Proofreading

Using the following proofreader's marks, correct these incorrect sentences. The originals are from *Catching Fire*, by Suzanne Collins.

Insert quotation marks: ⱽ   insert comma: ⌄

insert period: ⊙   insert question mark: ⌄?

insert exclamation point: ↑   delete: ℓ

move punctuation mark: ↰

"You're hideous, you know that, right"? I ask him. Buttercup nudges my hand for more petting, but we have to go⊙"Come on, you".

"Aren't you supposed to be on a train" he asks me.

"They're collecting me at noon" I answer.

"Shouldn't you look better" he asks in a loud whisper? I can't help smiling at his teasing, in spite of my mood. "Maybe a ribbon in your hair or something"? He flicks my braid with his hand and I brush him away.

"Don't worry⊙By the time they get through with me I'll be unrecognizable" I say.

I nudge his shoulder⊙"Get up" I say loudly, because I've learned there's no subtle way to wake him.

"Is everything all right, Katniss" she asks?⊙

"It's fine. We never see it on television, but the president always visits the victors before the tour to wish them luck" I say brightly.

My mother's face floods with relief⊙"Oh. I thought there was some kind of trouble".

> **Note to Instructor:** For your reference, the properly punctuated sentences are below.

"You're hideous, you know that, right?" I ask him. Buttercup nudges my hand for more petting, but we have to go. "Come on, you."

"Aren't you supposed to be on a train?" he asks me.

"They're collecting me at noon," I answer.

"Shouldn't you look better?" he asks in a loud whisper. I can't help smiling at his teasing, in spite of my mood. "Maybe a ribbon in your hair or something?" He flicks my braid with his hand and I brush him away.

"Don't worry. By the time they get through with me I'll be unrecognizable," I say.

I nudge his shoulder. "Get up!" I say loudly, because I've learned there's no subtle way to wake him.

"Is everything all right, Katniss?" she asks.

"It's fine. We never see it on television, but the president always visits the victors before the tour to wish them luck," I say brightly.

My mother's face floods with relief. "Oh. I thought there was some kind of trouble."

— LESSON 90 —

Dialogue
Direct Quotations

Exercise 90A: Punctuating Dialogue

The passage of dialogue below, from L. Frank Baum's *Glinda of Oz*, is missing punctuation. Write in all of the missing punctuation marks (insert them directly rather than using proofreader's marks). When you are finished, compare your answers to the original.

Is that all the Book says asked Ozma.

Every word said Dorothy, and Ozma and Glinda both looked at the Record and seemed surprised and perplexed.

Tell me, Glinda said Ozma, who are the Flatheads

I cannot, your Majesty confessed the Sorceress Until now I never have heard of them, nor have I ever heard the Skeezers mentioned. In the faraway corners of Oz are hidden many curious tribes of people, and those who never leave their own countries and never are visited by those from our favored part of Oz, naturally are unknown to me. However, if you so desire, I can learn through my arts of sorcery something of the Skeezers and the Flatheads.

I wish you would answered Ozma seriously. You see, Glinda, if these are Oz people they are my subjects and I cannot allow any wars or troubles in the Land I rule, if I can possibly help it.

Very well, your Majesty said the Sorceress, I will try to get some information to guide you. Please excuse me for a time, while I retire to my Room of Magic and Sorcery

May I go with you asked Dorothy, eagerly.

No, Princess. was the reply. It would spoil the charm to have anyone present.

So Glinda locked herself in her own Room of Magic and Dorothy and Ozma waited patiently for her to come out again.

> **Note to Instructor:** The original text is found below. You may accept grammatical variations (for example, an exclamation point at the end of a speech rather than a comma or period), but ask the student to compare his version with the original. How does the change in punctuation affect the passage?

"Is that all the Book says?" asked Ozma.

"Every word," said Dorothy, and Ozma and Glinda both looked at the Record and seemed surprised and perplexed.

"Tell me, Glinda," said Ozma, "who are the Flatheads?"

"I cannot, your Majesty," confessed the Sorceress. "Until now I never have heard of them, nor have I ever heard the Skeezers mentioned. In the faraway corners of Oz are hidden many curious tribes of people, and those who never leave their own countries and never are visited by those from our favored part of Oz, naturally are unknown to me. However, if you so desire, I can learn through my arts of sorcery something of the Skeezers and the Flatheads."

"I wish you would," answered Ozma seriously. "You see, Glinda, if these are Oz people they are my subjects and I cannot allow any wars or troubles in the Land I rule, if I can possibly help it."

"Very well, your Majesty," said the Sorceress, "I will try to get some information to guide you. Please excuse me for a time, while I retire to my Room of Magic and Sorcery."

"May I go with you?" asked Dorothy, eagerly.

"No, Princess," was the reply. "It would spoil the charm to have anyone present."

So Glinda locked herself in her own Room of Magic and Dorothy and Ozma waited patiently for her to come out again.

Exercise 90B: Punctuating Direct Quotations

In the sentences below, the authors quote various experts talking and writing about Mars. Write in all of the missing punctuation marks (insert them directly rather than using proofreader's marks). When you are finished, compare your answers to the original sentences.

The camera had fog in it and some of the scan lines failed, causing streaks across the frame. The resolution was awful recalls JPL engineer John Casani. You really couldn't see much. But the images would presumably get better as *Mariner 4* came closer and closer to the planet, imaging it as the sun struck the landscape more obliquely, picking up more contrast.

Upon seeing the pictures, Lyndon Johnson sighed It may be—it may just be—that life as we know it…is more unique than many have thought.

The reality of the cold, hard, desolate world was beyond anything that scientists had imagined, beyond even the imaginations of the great science-fiction writers. Craters? Why didn't we think of craters Isaac Asimov, upon seeing the Mariner 4 images, reportedly asked a friend.

Inside the book, Lowell scrawled Hurry!

    —Sarah Stewart Johnson, *The Sirens of Mars: Searching for Life on Another World*

The key ingredient is water. People often say how amazingly robust life is McKay says. My reaction is the opposite. It always needs water. If we had the trick of learning to live without water, life would be hardier.

They happened upon the Antarctic coastline after "a magical journey of towering mountains and shining glaciers in the memorable phrase of one chronicler of their travels.

But then, Buzz Aldrin has always dreamed of an encore: walking on Mars. I think we can all say with confidence that we are closer to Mars today than we have ever been Aldrin had said earlier that same year.

When Scott and his team happened upon them, they were astounded. The hillsides were covered with a coarse granitic sand strewn with numerous boulders he recorded in his diaries.

    —Elizabeth Howell and Nicholas Booth, *The Search for Life on Mars: The Greatest Scientific Detective Story of All Time*

The camera had fog in it and some of the scan lines failed, causing streaks across the frame. "The resolution was awful," recalls JPL engineer John Casani. "You really couldn't see much." But the images would presumably get better as Mariner 4 came closer and closer to the planet, imaging it as the sun struck the landscape more obliquely, picking up more contrast.

Upon seeing the pictures, Lyndon Johnson sighed, "It may be—it may just be—that life as we know it...is more unique than many have thought."

The reality of the cold, hard, desolate world was beyond anything that scientists had imagined, beyond even the imaginations of the great science-fiction writers. "Craters? Why didn't we think of craters?" Isaac Asimov, upon seeing the Mariner 4 images, reportedly asked a friend.

Inside the book, Lowell scrawled, "Hurry!"

—Sarah Stewart Johnson, *The Sirens of Mars: Searching for Life on Another World*

The key ingredient is water. "People often say how amazingly robust life is," McKay says. "My reaction is the opposite. It always needs water. If we had the trick of learning to live without water, life would be hardier."

They happened upon the Antarctic coastline after "a magical journey of towering mountains and shining glaciers," in the memorable phrase of one chronicler of their travels.

But then, Buzz Aldrin has always dreamed of an encore: walking on Mars. "I think we can all say with confidence that we are closer to Mars today than we have ever been," Aldrin had said earlier that same year.

When Scott and his team happened upon them, they were astounded. "The hillsides were covered with a coarse granitic sand strewn with numerous boulders," he recorded in his diaries.

—Elizabeth Howell and Nicholas Booth, *The Search for Life on Mars: The Greatest Scientific Detective Story of All Time*

Exercise 90C: Attribution Tags

In the following excerpts, taken from Stephen O'Meara and William Sheehan's *Mars: The Lure of the Red Planet*, find and underline the direct quotes that are missing their attribution tags. When you are finished, ask your instructor to check your work.

Then, compare the excerpts with the originals found in the *Answer Key*. Circle each attribution tag in the *Answer Key*.

On paper, *Pathfinder's* purpose was to get something—anything—to land on Mars. "After [that]," project scientist Matthew Golombek said, "whatever we did was pretty much considered gravy."

The most common size was from a few centimeters to about 20 centimeters (8 inches). "We wanted rocks and we got rocks." Ares Vallis was supposed to be a geological wonderland and it was.

The consensus swelled unanimously: "The area shows the effect of catastrophic flooding." Torrents of water, perhaps having a volume equal to that of all the Great Lakes combined, had washed down the valley from the southeast, carved the trough, and deposited the boulders. "In a typical flood like this on Earth," Golombek explained, "we would expect to see big rocks deposited during the first rush of water. Then, as the water volume and speed lessen, we see dust and smaller particles deposited around the rocks."

To make identifying the rocks easier, the scientists quickly began naming them. "Within hours scientists were jostling for position in front of wall-sized prints of the lander's pictures and demanding to name the rocks."

The Assyrians were, moreover, preoccupied with astrological affairs; even more than the Babylonians had been, they were enchanted by the strangely compelling and still potent idea that the motions, positions, and brightnesses of the heavenly bodies in some unfathomable way controlled human destiny. "Astrology connected the life of man so closely with the heavens that the stars and their wanderings began to occupy an important place in his thoughts and activities."

Alas, Aristarchus's idea, like Heracleides', attracted scant attention at the time. "Why did the Greeks develop a heliocentric hypothesis and then let it fall by the wayside?"

The date of the eclipse had been predicted long before by astronomers, and Tycho, as his early biographer Pierre Gassendi wrote, "thought of it as divine that men could know the motions of the stars so accurately that they could long before foretell their places and relative positions."

> **Note to Instructor:** Here are the original paragraphs for the student's reference. After completing the exercises in her workbook, she should circle each attribution tag below.

On paper, Pathfinder's purpose was to get something—anything—to land on Mars. "After [that]," project scientist Matthew Golombek said, "whatever we did was pretty much considered gravy."

The most common size was from a few centimeters to about 20 centimeters (8 inches). "We wanted rocks," Golombek said, "and we got rocks." Ares Vallis was supposed to be a geological wonderland and it was.

The consensus swelled unanimously: "The area," Golombek said, "shows the effect of catastrophic flooding." Torrents of water, perhaps having a volume equal to that of all the Great Lakes combined, had washed down the valley from the southeast, carved the trough, and deposited the boulders. "In a typical flood like this on Earth," Golombek explained, "we would expect to see big rocks deposited during the first rush of water. Then, as the water volume and speed lessen, we see dust and smaller particles deposited around the rocks."

To make identifying the rocks easier, the scientists quickly began naming them. "Within hours," Shirley recalls, "scientists were jostling for position in front of wall-sized prints of the lander's pictures and demanding to name the rocks."

The Assyrians were, moreover, preoccupied with astrological affairs; even more than the Babylonians had been, they were enchanted by the strangely compelling and still potent idea that the motions, positions, and brightnesses of the heavenly bodies in some unfathomable way controlled human destiny. "Astrology connected the life of man so closely with the heavens," wrote historian Anton Pannekoek, "that the stars and their wanderings began to occupy an important place in his thoughts and activities."

Alas, Aristarchus's idea, like Heracleides', attracted scan attention at the time. "Why," William Stahl asks in his entry on Aristarchus in the *Dictionary of Scientific Biography*, "did the Greeks develop a heliocentric hypothesis and then let it fall by the wayside?"

The date of the eclipse had been predicted long before by astronomers, and Tycho, as his early biographer Pierre Gassendi wrote, "thought of it as divine that men could know the motions of the stars so accurately that they could long before foretell their places and relative positions."

Key: **The following attribution quotes should be circled.**
Student: **Do not read this key until you have completed the exercise!**

Paragraph #1: project scientist Matthew Golombek said
Paragraph #2: Golombek said
Paragraph #3: Golombek said AND Golombek explained
Paragraph #4: Shirley recalls
Paragraph #5: wrote historian Anton Pannekoek
Paragraph #6: William Stahl asks in his entry on Aristarchus in the *Dictionary of Scientific Biography*
Paragraph #7: as his early biographer Pierre Gassendi wrote

— **LESSON 91** —

Direct Quotations
Ellipses
Partial Quotations

Exercise 91A: Using Ellipses

The following excerpt is from the classic science history The Age of Invention: A Chronicle of Mechanical Conquest, by Holland Thompson.

The total word count is 576. Using a word processor, retype the passage but condense it so that it has no more than 350 words. Make sure that you don't end up with run-on sentences or fragments!

When you are finished, compare your version with the condensed version found in the *Answer Key*.

From boyhood Franklin had been interested in natural phenomena. His "Journal of a Voyage from London to Philadelphia", written at sea as he returned from his first stay in London, shows unusual powers of exact observation for a youth of twenty. Many of the questions he propounded to the Junto had a scientific bearing. He made an original and important invention in 1749, the "Pennsylvania fireplace," which, under the name of the Franklin stove, is in common use to this day, and which brought to the ill-made houses of the time increased comfort and a great saving of fuel. But it brought Franklin no pecuniary reward, for he never deigned to patent any of his inventions.

His active, inquiring mind played upon hundreds of questions in a dozen different branches of science. He studied smoky chimneys; he invented bifocal spectacles; he studied the effect of oil upon ruffled water; he identified the "dry bellyache" as lead poisoning; he preached ventilation in the days when windows were closed tight at night, and upon the sick at all times; he investigated fertilizers in agriculture. Many of his suggestions have since borne fruit, and his observations show that he foresaw some of the great developments of the nineteenth century.

His fame in science rests chiefly upon his discoveries in electricity. On a visit to Boston in 1746 he saw some electrical experiments and at once became deeply interested. Peter Collinson of London, a Fellow of the Royal Society, who had made several gifts to the Philadelphia Library, sent over some of the crude electrical apparatus of the day, which Franklin used, as well as some contrivances he had purchased in Boston. He says in a letter to Collinson: "For my own part, I never was before engaged in any study that so engrossed my attention and my time as this has lately done."

Franklin's letters to Collinson tell of his first experiments and speculations as to the nature of electricity. Experiments made by a little group of friends showed the effect of pointed bodies in drawing off electricity. He decided that electricity was not the result of friction, but that the mysterious force was diffused through most substances, and that nature is always alert to restore its equilibrium. He developed the theory of positive and negative electricity, or plus and minus electrification. The same letter tells of some of the tricks which the little group of experimenters were accustomed to play upon their wondering neighbors. They set alcohol on fire, relighted candles just blown out, produced mimic flashes of lightning, gave shocks on touching or kissing, and caused an artificial spider to move mysteriously.

Franklin carried on experiments with the Leyden jar, made an electrical battery, killed a fowl and roasted it upon a spit turned by electricity, sent a current through water and found it still able to ignite alcohol, ignited gunpowder, and charged glasses of wine so that the drinkers received shocks. More important, perhaps, he began to develop the theory of the identity of lightning and electricity, and the possibility of protecting buildings by iron rods. By means of an iron rod he brought down electricity into his house, where he studied its effect upon bells and concluded that clouds were generally negatively electrified. In June, 1752, he performed the famous experiment with the kite, drawing down electricity from the clouds and charging a Leyden jar from the key at the end of the string.

> **Note to Instructor:** A sample condensation is shown below. The student may choose to omit different parts of the passage. When she is finished, check her paragraphs for sense and readability. Ask her to read her paragraphs out loud, listening for meaning. Then, allow her to read the sample answer below.
> Each omission must be marked by ellipses.

From boyhood Franklin had been interested in natural phenomena... His active, inquiring mind played upon hundreds of questions in a dozen different branches of science. He studied smoky chimneys; he invented bifocal spectacles; he studied the effect of oil upon ruffled water; he identified the "dry bellyache" as lead poisoning; he preached ventilation in the days when windows were closed tight at night, and upon the sick at all times; he investigated fertilizers in agriculture. Many of his suggestions have since borne fruit...

His fame in science rests chiefly upon his discoveries in electricity... Peter Collinson of London, a Fellow of the Royal Society... sent over some of the crude electrical apparatus of the day, which Franklin used, as well as some contrivances he had purchased in Boston... Franklin's letters to Collinson tell of his first experiments and speculations as to the nature of electricity. Experiments made by a little group of friends showed the effect of pointed bodies in drawing off electricity. He decided that electricity was not the result of friction, but that the mysterious force was diffused through most substances, and that nature is always alert to restore its equilibrium. He developed the theory of positive and negative electricity, or plus and minus electrification...

Franklin carried on experiments with the Leyden jar, made an electrical battery, killed a fowl and roasted it upon a spit turned by electricity, sent a current through water and found it still able to ignite alcohol, ignited gunpowder, and charged glasses of wine so that the drinkers received shocks. More important, perhaps, he began to develop the theory of the identity of lightning and electricity, and the possibility of protecting buildings by iron rods. By means of an iron rod he brought down electricity into his house, where he studied its effect upon bells and concluded that clouds were generally negatively electrified. In June, 1752, he performed the famous experiment with the kite, drawing down electricity from the clouds and charging a Leyden jar from the key at the end of the string.

Exercise 91B: Partial Quotations

On your own paper, rewrite each of the statements below two times. Each rewritten statement must contain a partial quotation. Draw the partial quotation from the bolded sentences that follow each statement. The authors of the bolded sentences are provided for you—be sure to include an attribution tag for each direct quote!

You may change and adapt the statements freely.

At least one of your sentences should contain a very short one- to three-word quote; one should contain a preposition phrase, gerund phrase, participle phrase, or infinitive phrase; and one should quote a dependent clause.

If you need help, ask your instructor to show you sample answers.

Note to Instructor: If the student needs a jump-start, show her *one* of the sample sentences that follow each statement.

The invention of the wheel allowed farmers to haul loads across land easily for the first time.

Before wheeled vehicles were invented, really heavy things could be moved efficiently only on water, using barges or rafts, or by organizing a larger hauling group on land. Some of the heavier items that prehistoric, temperate European farmers had to haul across land all the time included harvested grain crops, hay crops, manure for fertilizer, firewood, building lumber, clay for pottery making, hides and leather, and people.

—David W. Anthony, *The Horse, the Wheel, and Language*

1-3 words

David Anthony writes that the invention of the wheel allowed farmers to haul "really heavy things" across land easily for the first time.

Gerund phrase

The invention of the wheel allowed farmers to haul heavy loads across land easily without "organizing a larger hauling group on land," according to *The Horse, the Wheel, and Language.*

Prepositional phrase

David Anthony tells us that before the invention of the wheel, farmers could only haul heavy loads "on water, using barges or rafts, or by organizing a larger hauling group on land."

Dependent clause

As David Anthony writes, "before wheeled vehicles were invented," farmers could not easily move heavy loads across land.

The physicist Percy Spencer invented the microwave oven while working for the defense contractor Raytheon.

The ever-inventive Percy Spencer opened another important door for Raytheon when he decided to experiment with the well-known warming capacity of the microwaves emitted by magnetrons. Spencer, intrigued by a candy bar that melted in his pocket when he was near an operating magnetron, decided to see what the waves would do to popcorn kernels and was delighted to find that they quickly popped. The next day he exploded an egg by the same means.

> —Alan Earls and Robert Edwards, *Raytheon Company*

1-3 words

According to Alan Earls and Robert Edwards, the physicist Percy Spencer invented the microwave oven after a candy bar "melted in his pocket" while he was working for the defense contractor Raytheon.

Prepositional phrase

In the book *Raytheon Company,* Alan Earls and Robert Edwards write that Percy Spencer invented the microwave after he popped popcorn with a magnetron and then cooked an egg "by the same means."

Participle phrase

According to the book *Raytheon Company,* the physicist Percy Spencer invented the microwave oven after microwaves "emitted by magnetrons" melted a candy bar in his pocket.

Dependent clause

According to Alan Earls and Robert Edwards, the physicist Percy Spencer invented the microwave oven after a candy bar in his pocket melted "when he was near an operating magnetron."

The Internet, a network that connects other networks together, began as ARPANET, a military project linking computers together.

Bob Taylor had been the young director of the office within the Defense Department's Advanced Research Projects Agency overseeing computer research, and he was the one who had started the ARPANET. The project had embodied the most peaceful intentions—to link computers at scientific laboratories across the country so that researchers might share computer resources.

> —Matthew Lyon and Katie Hafner, *Where Wizards Stay Up Late*

1-3 words

The Internet began as ARPANET, a military project linking computers together so that scientists, in the words of Matthew Lyon and Katie Hafner, could "share computer resources."

Infinitive phrase

The book *Where Wizards Stay Up Late* tells us that the Internet began as ARPANET, a military project supervised by a Defense Department director "to link computers at scientific laboratories across the country."

Dependent clause

According to Matthew Lyon and Katie Hafner, the Internet, a network that connects other networks together, began as ARPANET, a military project that "embodied the most peaceful intentions."

Dependent clause

Matthew Lyon and Katie Hafner write that the Internet, a network that connects other networks together, began as ARPANET, a military project linking computers together "so that researchers might share computer resources."

Exercise 91C: Diagramming

On your own paper, diagram every word of the following sentences. These are taken from *Beyond: Our Future in Space*, by Chris Impey. In the chapter where these sentences occur, Impey is discussing the role of Germany's rocket scientists during World War II in developing the technology that would eventually be used in space flight.

Ask your instructor for help if you get stuck! Do your best, and then compare your answers with the *Answer Key*.

The V-2 was far more advanced than any of Goddard's rockets, but he was convinced the Germans had "stolen" his ideas.

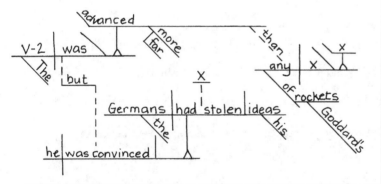

Note to Instructor: We have diagrammed *advanced* as a past participle acting as an adjective, rather than as a passive verb (*was advanced*) because the word can so easily be used alone as an adjective (as in *an advanced class*, an *advanced case*, etc.). By contrast, *was convinced* in the second part of this compound-complex sentence seems more clearly a verb (*he convinces, he is convinced*), and *convinced* is a much less common adjective (*the convinced man* does not sound natural!).

If the student diagrams *was advanced* as a passive verb, accept the answer but explain the reasoning above. The *far more* and the than dotted line would then extend off the predicate line.

Than any of Goddard's rockets is a comparative clause with understood elements: *than any of Goddard's rockets [were advanced]*. If *were advanced* is diagrammed as a passive verb, the predicate of the comparative clause should be diagrammed the same way, as below:

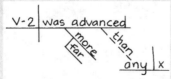

If the student needs a quick review of comparative clauses, look back together at Week 17, Lesson 66.

The clause *[that] Germans had stolen his ideas* acts as the direct object of *was convinced* and has an understood introductory *that*.

The architect of the V-2 was the most controversial figure in the history of rocketry: Wernher von Braun.

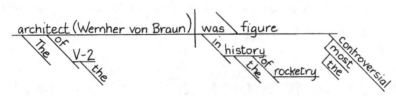

> **Note to Instructor:** The name *Wernher von Braun* may appear parenthetical but is actually an appositive renaming *architect*. It could also be diagrammed as an appositive renaming *figure*.
>
> Students who have not yet completed a *Grammar for the Well-Trained Mind* course may not be familiar with appositives (Lesson 94). They may diagram *figure* and *Wernher von Braun* as compound predicate nominatives renaming *architect*. You can accept this answer as correct.

After seeing film footage of the successful launch of a V-2 prototype, Hitler personally made von Braun a professor—an exceptional honor for a thirty-one-year-old engineer.

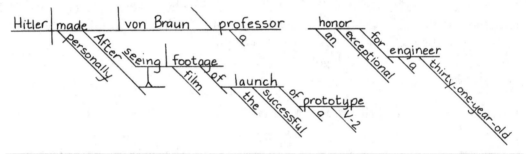

> **Note to Instructor:** The noun *professor* is an object complement (see Week 10, Lesson 40). The preposition *After* has the present participle *seeing* as its object, with *footage* acting as the object of the participle.
>
> The phrase *an exceptional honor for a thirty-one-year-old engineer* refers, in meaning, to the entire sentence (Hitler making von Braun a professor) but does not have a clear grammatical relationship to any major element of the sentence, so must be diagrammed as a parenthetical element.
>
> The adjective *thirty-one-year-old* must be diagrammed as a single compound adjective because the words are all hyphenated together.

Scientists use counterfactual thinking as a high-level skill for developing theories, by asking, "What might be but isn't, and why?"

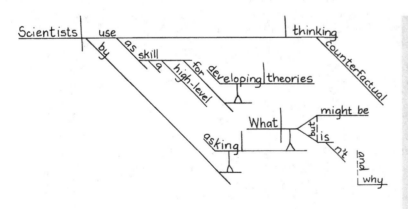

> **Note to Instructor:** *as, for* and *by* are all acting as prepositions in this sentence. In the prepositional phrase *by asking, "What might be but isn't, and why?,"* the present participle *asking* is the object of the preposition, and the clause *What might be but isn't* is the object of the participle. The verbs *might be* and *is* are predicates to the subject *What*, but the phrase *and why* has a semantic but not grammatical relationship to the rest of that clause. We have diagrammed it as a parenthetical element.

— LESSON 92 —

Partial Quotations

Ellipses

Block Quotes

Colons

Brackets

Exercise 92A: Writing Dialogue Correctly

The following speeches, from the classic 1951 novel *All-of-a-Kind Family*, are listed in the correct order but are missing their dialogue tags. On your own paper, rewrite the speeches as dialogue, making use of the dialogue tags below. You must place at least one dialogue tag before a speech, one in the middle of a speech, and one following a speech.

A list of the rules governing dialogue follows, for your reference.

When you are finished, compare your dialogue to the original passage in the *Answer Key.*

All-of-a-Kind Family tells the story of five Jewish girls growing up in New York City in 1912. In this scene, the sisters are plotting a way to save enough money to buy their father a birthday present, something they've never been able to do before.

List 1. Dialogue (in Correct Order)

If we all saved our pennies for the next week, we'd have enough money

I'll save my pennies

But that won't leave us any money to spend for a whole week We won't be able to buy any candy or anything for a whole week?

Well, can't you give up your candy for a week?

What about the library lady? We promised to give her a penny every Friday

Oh, dear, I forgot all about that

Aren't we finished paying for that old book yet?

The library lady said we'd be all paid up in about three weeks

That's just fine! Only Papa's birthday is next week

Maybe she'll let us skip a week

List 2. Dialogue Tags (Not in Correct Order)

Gertie chimed in

Ella said

Ella demanded

said Ella

Sarah reminded them

Sarah said

Henny asked

wailed Henny

Henny retorted

suggested Charlotte

List 3. For Reference: Rules for Writing Dialogue

A dialogue tag identifies the person making the speech.

When a dialogue tag comes after a speech, place a comma, exclamation point, or question mark inside the closing quotation marks.

When a dialogue tag comes before a speech, place a comma after the tag. Put the dialogue's final punctuation mark inside the closing quotation marks.

Speeches do not need to be attached to a dialogue tag as long as the text clearly indicates the speaker.

Usually, a new paragraph begins with each new speaker.

When a dialogue tag comes in the middle of a speech, follow it with a comma if the following dialogue is an incomplete sentence. Follow it with a period if the following dialogue is a complete sentence.

> **Note to Instructor:** The original text, very slightly adapted, is shown below. As long as the above rules are followed, the student's rewritten dialogue does not need to match exactly. Ask the student to point out the differences between her dialogue and the passage below.

"If we all saved our pennies for the next week, we'd have enough money," Ella said.

"I'll save my pennies," Gertie chimed in.

"But that won't leave us any money to spend for a whole week," wailed Henny. "We won't be able to buy any candy or anything for a whole week?"

Ella demanded, "Well, can't you give up your candy for a week?"

"What about the library lady?" Sarah reminded them. "We promised to give her a penny every Friday."

"Oh, dear," said Ella. "I forgot all about that."

Henny asked, "Aren't we finished paying for that old book yet?"

"The library lady said we'd be all paid up in about three weeks," Sarah said.

"That's just fine!" Henny retorted. "Only Papa's birthday is next week."

"Maybe she'll let us skip a week," suggested Charlotte.

Exercise 92B: Using Direct Quotations Correctly

On your own paper, rewrite the following three paragraphs, inserting at least one quote from each of the following three sources into the paragraph. Use the following guidelines:

a) At least one quote must be a block quote.

b) At least one quote must be a complete sentence.

c) At least one quote must be a partial sentence incorporated into your own sentence.

d) Each quote must have an attribution tag.

e) At least one quote must be condensed, using ellipses.

f) You must make at least one change or addition that needs to be put in brackets.

A list of the rules governing direct quotations follows, for your reference.

You may make whatever changes are needed to the paragraphs. When you are finished, compare your paragraphs to the sample answer in the *Answer Key*.

List 1. Paragraphs

Epilepsy: the Greeks called it the "sacred disease," but they were not the first. In Sumer, around 2,000 BCE, a scribe describes an epileptic convulsion.

For nearly a millennium and half, epileptic seizures were thought to be a sign that a god or demon was present. The Babylonians, who followed the Sumerians in the lands between the Tigris and the Euphrates, blamed demons who infested sufferers because of uncleanness. In the Greece of the pre-Socratics, epilepsy was a punishment sent by Poseidon (if the sufferer made hoarse sounds) or the earth-goddess Cybele (if the seizure was stronger on the right side of the body and involved the gnashing of teeth).

Hippocrates, the fifth-century BCE doctor from the Greek island of Kos, off the coast of Asia Minor, disagreed. He argued that disease is caused by purely physical factors that can be discovered by physicians—with epilepsy as Exhibit A.

Unlike priests and sorcerers, Hippocrates bases his explanation of epilepsy on his observations: Men who suffer head injuries are far more likely to suffer unexpected convulsions, so the cause of this syndrome is clearly located in the head. The Greeks were unclear about what exactly went on, up there inside the skull, but the jelly inside the head obviously controlled the body. Convulsions of the muscles and joints obviously began with a problem inside the skull.

List 2. Sources

If his seizure always seizes him in the evening, his eyes are clouded, his ears ring. If a sick man's neck turns to the right, time and again, while his hands and feet are paralysed, his eyes are now closed, now rolling, saliva flows from his mouth, he makes sounds, then it is caused by the hand of the moon-god Shin. He opens his eyes time and time again, he bites his tongue; he does not know himself when it seizes him.

> —A Sumerian scribe, describing an epileptic convulsion around 2,000 BCE

It is thus with regard to the disease called Sacred: it appears to me to be nowise more divine nor more sacred than other diseases, but has a natural cause from which it originates like other affections. Men regard its nature and cause as divine from ignorance and wonder, because it is not at all like to other diseases. And this notion of its divinity is kept up by their inability to comprehend it.

> —Hippocrates, *On the Sacred Disease*

In these ways I am of the opinion that the brain exercises the greatest power in the man. This is the interpreter to us of those things which emanate from the air, when it happens to be in a sound state.

> —Hippocrates, *On the Sacred Disease*

List 3. For Reference: Rules For Using Direct Quotations

When an attribution tag comes after a direct quote, place a comma, exclamation point, or question mark inside the closing quotation marks.

When an attribution tag comes before a direct quote, place a comma after the tag. Put the dialogue's final punctuation mark inside the closing quotation marks.

When an attribution tag comes in the middle of a direct quotation, follow it with a comma if the remaining quote is an incomplete sentence. Follow it with a period if the remaining quote is a complete sentence.

Direct quotes can be words, phrases, clauses, or sentences, as long as they are set off by quotation marks and form part of a grammatically correct original sentence.

An ellipsis shows where something has been cut out of a sentence.

Every direct quote must have an attribution tag.

If a direct quotation is longer than three lines, indent the entire quote one inch from the margin in a separate block of text and omit quotation marks.

If you change or make additions to a direct quotation, use brackets.

> **Note to Instructor:** You will need to check the student's paragraphs against the rules above. The sample answer below is just one way to insert the direct quotations.
>
> If the student needs prompting, allow her to read the sample answer below and then require her to use different parts of the sources in her own rewritten paragraphs.
>
> Notice that the student has not been asked to provide footnotes or in-text citations; the focus of this lesson is on incorporating quotes properly into a piece of written work.

Epilepsy: the Greeks called it the "sacred disease," but they were not the first. In Sumer, around 2,000 BCE, a scribe describes an epileptic convulsion "caused by the hand of the moon-god Shin":

> [the] sick man's neck turns to the right, time and again, while his hands and feet are paralysed, his eyes are now closed, now rolling, saliva flows from his mouth, he makes sounds... he does not know himself when it seizes him.

For nearly a millennium and half, epileptic seizures were thought to be a sign that a god or demon was present. The Babylonians, who followed the Sumerians in the lands between the Tigris and the Euphrates, blamed demons who infested sufferers because of uncleanness. In the Greece of the pre-Socratics, epilepsy was a punishment sent by Poseidon (if the sufferer made hoarse sounds) or the earth-goddess Cybele (if the seizure was stronger on the right side of the body and involved the gnashing of teeth).

Hippocrates, the fifth century BCE doctor from the Greek island of Kos, off the coast of Asia Minor, disagreed. He argued that disease is caused by *purely* physical factors that can be discovered by physicians—with epilepsy as Exhibit A. "This notion of [epilepsy's] divinity," Hippocrates says tartly, "is kept up by [men's] inability to comprehend it."

Unlike priests and sorcerers, Hippocrates bases his explanation of epilepsy on his observations: Men who suffer head injuries are far more likely to suffer unexpected convulsions, so the cause of this syndrome is clearly located in the head. The Greeks were unclear about what exactly went on, up there inside the skull, but the jelly inside the head obviously controlled the body: "The brain exercises the greatest power in the man," Hippocrates explains in *On the Sacred Disease.* Convulsions of the muscles and joints obviously began with a problem inside the skull.

Floating Elements

— LESSON 93 —

Interjections
Nouns of Direct Address
Parenthetical Expressions

Exercise 93A: Using Floating Elements Correctly

On your own paper, rewrite the following sentences in List 1, inserting interjections, nouns of direct address, and parenthetical expressions from List 2. You must use every item in List 2 at least once. Every sentence in List 1 must have at least one insertion.

Interjections may either come before or after sentences on their own, or may be incorporated directly into the sentence.

List 1. Sentences

Now the foxes and chickens will have fun together!
You'll feel much better now.
Why are you weeping?
This journey is the most exciting one we've ever set out on.
The giant has nothing better to do.
That is the loudest screaming I have ever heard!
What can you see out of the window?
I didn't get enough magic soup to eat at dinner.
What will become of Hansel and Gretel?
I will have nothing to do with a talking fish!
This is only a bad dream.

List 2. Interjections, Nouns of Direct Address, Parenthetical Expressions

besides
it seems to me
alas
well
oh ho
there, there
my dear child
my darling
after all
hurrah
bravo
Ji-woo

Note to Instructor: The answers below are samples. Any grammatical, properly punctuated versions of these sentences are acceptable.

Hurrah! Now the foxes and chickens will have fun together!

There, there, you'll feel much better now.

My dear child, why are you weeping?

This journey, it seems to me, is the most exciting one we've ever set out on.

After all, the giant has nothing better to do.

Bravo! That is the loudest screaming I have ever heard!

Well, Ji-woo, what can you see out of the window?

Besides, I didn't get enough magic soup to eat at dinner.

Alas, what will become of Hansel and Gretel?

Oh ho, I will have nothing to do with a talking fish!

My darling, this is only a bad dream.

Exercise 93B: Parenthetical Expressions

In the following pairs of sentences, underline each subject once and each predicate twice (in both independent and dependent clauses). In each pair, cross out the parenthetical expression that is not essential to the sentences. If the expression is used as an essential part of the sentence, circle it and label it with the correct part of the sentence (e.g., *prep phrase acting as adj, subject and predicate*, etc.). If it acts as a modifier, draw an arrow to the word it modifies.

The play, ~~I hesitate to say,~~ is the worst one I've ever seen.

subject and predicate
(and infinitive)

(I hesitate to say) that he flat-out lied, but he certainly misled me.

A hippo, ~~not a crocodile,~~ is the most dangerous animal in the river.

predicate nominative

An alligator (is not a crocodile,) although many people mix them up.

The rocket launch, ~~in my opinion,~~ is doomed to fail.

prepositional phrase
acting as an adverb

That politician has drastically fallen (in my opinion).

subject and predicate
of the dependent adverb clause

(If you please) the king, he may grant your request!

(You) ~~If you please,~~ do not leave muddy tracks all over the marble floor.

Note to Instructor: The dependent clause *If you please the king* is conditional and acts as an adverb modifying the main verb of the independent clause. If the student does not identify the clause as a modifier, don't mark the answer wrong, but point out the function.

~~Darn it,~~ I jammed my finger again!

object of the participle "saying"

(You) Stop saying (darn it)!

Exercise 93C: Diagramming

On your own paper, diagram every word of the following sentences. Several of them can be diagrammed in more than one way—when you're finished, compare your answers with the *Answer Key* and look at the instructor's notes to understand the difference!

These are taken from three novels and a short story by the pioneering speculative fiction writer Octavia Butler.

From *Kindred*

The years hadn't changed her much,
and, of course, they hadn't changed me at all.

No, Dana, I just didn't pay any attention.

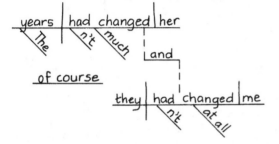

From *Parable of the Sower*

Today is our birthday—my fifteenth and my father's fifty-fifth.

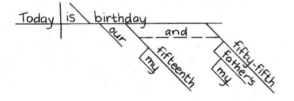

From *Parable of the Talents*

These were stupid affairs—wastes of life and treasure.

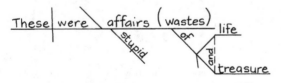

Note to Instructor: The phrase *wastes of life and treasure* could also be diagrammed as a second predicate nominative, making *affairs* and *wastes* compound predicate nominatives renaming *These*. I have diagrammed it as an appositive because it is introduced with a dash rather than connected to the sentence with *and*, but both diagrams are correct.

Students who have not yet gone through a full year of *Grammar for the Well-Trained Mind* may not recognize appositives (covered in the next lesson) and will probably diagram *wastes* as a second predicate nominative.

From "Bloodchild"

He looked young—my brother's age perhaps.

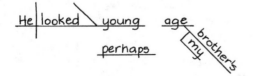

Note to Instructor: The parenthetical element *my brother's age* contains within itself a second parenthetical element, *perhaps*! If the student has already completed another level of this course, you may point out that *my brother's age perhaps* is the particular kind of parenthetical level known as an *absolute* (see Lesson 96).

— LESSON 94 —

Appositives

Exercise 94A: Using Appositives

On your own paper, rewrite each group of sentences below as a single sentence using one or more appositives. You may make any necessary changes to the original sentences.

Note to Instructor: The answers below are samples; other correct answers are possible. However, check to make sure the student has used appositives rather than other grammatical constructions.

The harp is the oldest musical instrument played by humans.
Harps have strings that are plucked with fingers.

Harps, the oldest musical instruments played by humans, have strings that are plucked with fingers.

Alfred the Great was king of the Saxons in the ninth century.
Alfred the Great established the first professorship of music in Britain.

The king of the Saxons in the ninth century, Alfred the Great, established the first professorship of music in Britain.

Troubadors travelled through medieval Europe.
Troubadors were singers of love songs, serenades, rounds, and shepherd's chants.

Troubadors, singers of love songs, serenades, rounds, and shepherd's chants, travelled through medieval Europe.

Palestrina was a sixteenth-century composer.
Palestrina was Italian.
Palestrina came to Rome to study music.
Rome was the greatest city in Italy.

Palestrina, the sixteenth-century Italian composer, came to Rome, the greatest city in Italy, to study music.

Counterpoint is the addition of a second melodic line to an already existing melody.
Both melodic lines move constantly.
The melodic lines are related to each other.

In counterpoint, the addition of a second melodic line to an already existing melody, the two lines move constantly and are related to each other.

Half of Johann Sebastian Bach's compositions are fugues.
Fugues are musical pieces that repeat a theme, using counterpoint.

Fugues, musical pieces that repeat a theme using counterpoint, make up half of Johann Sebastian Bach's compositions.

Exercise 94B: Identifying Appositives

In each of the following sentences, underline the subject(s) once and the predicate(s) twice (in both independent and dependent clauses). Circle each appositive or appositive phrase.

These sentences are taken from the novel *Bel Canto*, by Ann Patchett.

They waited, (father and son) without speaking, until finally the darkness fell and the first breath of music stirred from someplace far below them.

Tiny people, (insects, really) slipped out from behind the curtains, opened their mouths, and with their voices gilded the walls with their yearning, their grief, their boundless, reckless love that would lead each one to separate ruin.

It was his oldest daughter, (Kiyomi) who bought him his first recording of Roxane Coss for his birthday.

It was soaring, (that voice) warm and complicated, utterly fearless.

It was Mr. Hosokawa's selection, (the aria from *Rusalka*) which she had just completed when the lights went out.

He did not seek something achingly obscure, (an aria from *Partenope* perhaps) so as to prove himself an aficionado.

The only music would be after dinner, Roxane Coss and her accompanist, (a man in his thirties from Sweden or Norway with fine yellow hair and beautiful, tapering fingers.)

Two hours before the beginning of Mr. Hosokawa's birthday party, President Masuda, (a native of this country born of Japanese parents) had sent a note of regret saying that important matters beyond his control would prevent him from attending the evening's event.

Into the presidential void, the Vice President, (Ruben Iglesias) stepped forward to host the party.

Exercise 94C: Diagramming

On your own paper, diagram every word of the following five sentences from Exercise 94B.

It was his oldest daughter, Kiyomi, who bought him his first recording of Roxane Coss for his birthday.

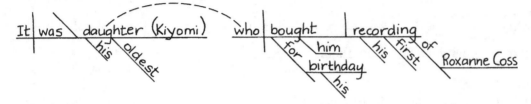

It was soaring, that voice, warm and complicated, utterly fearless.

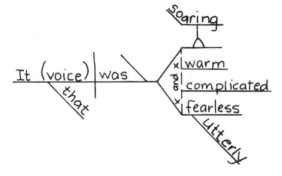

It was Mr. Hosokawa's selection, the aria from *Rusalka*, which she had just completed when the lights went out.

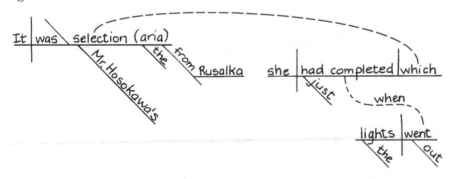

Into the presidential void, the Vice President, Ruben Iglesias, stepped forward to host the party.

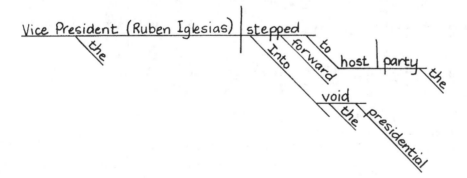

— LESSON 95 —

Appositives

Intensive and Reflexive Pronouns

Noun Clauses in Apposition

Object Complements

Exercise 95A: Reflexive and Intensive Pronoun Review

In the following sentences, taken from poems written by Robert Frost, underline each reflexive or intensive pronoun. Put parentheses around each intensive pronoun. Label each reflexive pronoun with one of the following labels: *DO* (direct object of a verb form), *IO* (indirect object of a verb form), *PN* (predicate nominative), or *OP* (object of a preposition).

For *DO* pronouns *ONLY*, draw an arrow from the label back to the verb or verb form that is affecting it.

He was hard on <u>himself</u>. I couldn't find
That he kept any hours—not for <u>himself</u>.
   —"The Code"

He gave his own poor iliac a wrench
And plunged <u>himself</u> head foremost in the trench.
   —"Haec Fabula Docet"

He lingered for some word she wouldn't say,
Said it at last (<u>himself</u>), "Good-night."
   —"Snow"

I armed <u>myself</u> against such bones as might be
With the pitch-blackened stub of an ax-handle.
   —"The Census-Taker"

I am overtired
Of the great harvest I (<u>myself</u>) desired.
   —"After Apple-Picking"

We could have some arrangement
By which I'd bind <u>myself</u> to keep hands off.
   —"Home Burial"

Nothing to say to all those marriages!

She had made three (<u>herself</u>) to three of his.

    —"Place for a Third"

Then she climbed slowly to her feet,

OP
And walked off, talking to <u>herself</u> or Paul.

    —"Paul's Wife"

OP
Turn the farm in upon <u>itself</u>

            DO
Until it can contain <u>itself</u> no more.

    —"Build Soil"

The earth (<u>itself</u>) is liable to the fate

Of meaninglessly being broken off.

    —"The Lesson for Today"

IO
Make <u>yourself</u> up a cheering song of how

Someone's road home from work this once was.

    —"Directive"

Isn't it pretty much the same idea?

You said (<u>yourself</u>) you weren't avoiding work.

    —"From Plane to Plane"

OP
We'd kept all these years between <u>ourselves</u>

So as to have it ready for outsiders.

    —"The Witch of Coos"

Something we were withholding made us weak

PN
Until we found out that it was <u>ourselves</u>.

    —"The Gift Outright"

Men fumble at the possibilities

OP
When left to guess forever for <u>themselves</u>.

    —"A Masque of Reason"

Exercise 95B: Identifying Appositives

Each of the following sentences, taken from Jay Parini's biography *Robert Frost: A Life*, contains an appositive phrase or clause. Find and underline each appositive. Make sure that you underline the entire appositive!

Draw an arrow from each appositive back to the word or phrase it renames. Finally, label each appositive as *WORD*, *PHRASE*, or *CLAUSE*. A word contains only one grammatical element. A phrase contains modifiers.

Be careful—some of these appositives are clauses, but some are words or phrases that are then *modified* by a clause! That's not the same thing as a clause *acting* as an appositive.

When you are finished, point out to your instructor the sentences where a phrase acting as an appositive is modified by a clause.

> **Note to Instructor:** The sentences where an appositive word or phrase are modified by a clause are marked with an asterisk below.

He was a poet who took nothing for granted, who could cast his thoughts upon the objects

around him, as Emerson—a central figure in Frost's imagination—urged poets to do. *PHRASE*

According to family legend, the poet's brash, talented father, William Prescott Frost, Jr., *WORD* warned the doctor who delivered his son that he would shoot him if anything went wrong.

> **Note to Instructor:** *William Prescott Frost, Jr.* is a single proper noun, not a phrase, because it contains no other grammatical elements.

✳ Will Frost met a young teacher (the only other teacher at this small school) who agreed to give *PHRASE*

him lessons in stenography—a skill he rightly guessed would come in handy when he turned *PHRASE* his hand to journalism.

> **Note to Instructor:** The appositive *skill* is modified by the clause (with understood subordinating word) *[that] he rightly guessed would come in handy when he turned his hand to journalism*. That clause contains another clause, the adverbial *when he turned his hand to journalism*, which modifies the verb *would come*.

Her father, Thomas Moodie, was drowned at sea when she was eight; her mother, Mary, shipped *WORD*   *WORD* Belle off at the age of eleven to a wealthy uncle and aunt in Ohio.

The rumor, that Belle had been the child of an illegitimate relationship, would persist in the *CLAUSE* Frost family.

✳ The Frost children were well looked after by their mother and Aunt Blanche, both experienced *PHRASE* teachers who put a premium on a disciplined, traditional education.

> **Note to Instructor:** The clause *who put a premium on a disciplined, traditional education* modifies the appositive phrase *both experienced teachers*.

When Robbie was five, arrangements were made for him to attend a private kindergarten in the
home of a Russian woman, <ins>Madame Zitska</ins>, even though he had to go halfway across the city of
San Francisco by horse-drawn omnibus to get there.

WORD

✱ On warm Sundays in spring, they often went to the botanical displays at Woodward's Gardens
in the old mission district—<ins>the setting for "At Woodward's Gardens," which Frost published
in 1936</ins>.

PHRASE

> **Note to Instructor:** The appositive *the setting* is modified by the prepositional adjective phrase
> *for "At Woodward's Gardens,"* and the clause *which Frost published in 1936* is an adjectival clause
> modifying *"At Woodward's Gardens."*

Another book of Scottish interest that she introduced to her children was *The Scottish Chiefs*
(1810), <ins>a work of popular history by Jane Porter</ins>.

PHRASE

Robbie liked to set off alone on foot, often hiking to Nob Hill, where the new millionaires—
<ins>men such as Charles Crocker, Leland Stanford, Mark Hopkins and D. D. Colton</ins>—were building
huge Victorian houses as monuments to their own egos, crafting them from the best
imported materials.

PHRASE

✱ Will Frost actually managed to work at the newspaper on May 5, <ins>the day before he died at age
thirty-four</ins>.

PHRASE

> **Note to Instructor:** The appositive word *day* is modified by the adjective clause *before he died at
> age thirty-four.*

In particular, Grandfather Frost, with his flowing white beard and small, wire-rimmed
glasses—<ins>an important man in this working-class community, and a dominant figure in this
small mill town</ins>—seemed austere.

PHRASE

> **Note to Instructor:** The phrase actually contains two appositives, *important man* and *dominant
> figure*, both modified by adjectival prepositional phrases.

Grandmother Frost, <ins>an intense, nervous woman</ins>, was scarcely any warmer.

PHRASE

The undeniable truth, <ins>that her son had a gift for learning</ins>, was clear to Belle Frost by now.

CLAUSE

During the summer of 1889, Frost devoted himself in the evenings and on weekends to reading
books not found in the classical course at Lawrence: <ins>Cooper's *The Deerslayer* and *The Last of
the Mohicans*, Mary Hartwell Catherwood's *The Romance of Dollard*, and Prescott's *History of
the Conquest of Mexico*</ins>.

PHRASE

> **Note to Instructor:** The phrase actually contains three appositives, each one introduced by the
> possessive form of the author's last name.

✸ Elinor was a year and half older than Frost, and had missed a good deal of school owing to
a mysterious disease called "slow fever"—a sickness that entailed fevers and periods of
PHRASE
acute exhaustion.

> **Note to Instructor:** The student could also draw the arrow back to *slow fever*.
>   The appositive phrase contains the adjective clause *that entailed fevers and periods of acute exhaustion*, modifying *sickness*.

✸ Frost sat the Harvard entrance exams in October 1891, as expected, finishing seventh in
English literature, a subject he had never studied formally in school.
PHRASE

> **Note to Instructor:** The appositive *subject* is modified by the adjective clause with understood subordinating word *[that] he had never studied formally in school*.

Frost determined to go his own way, or to seem to go his own way, as in "The Road Not Taken,"
PHRASE
his most famous poem, which he ends with a wry self-critical note that he will be telling
people "with a sigh" that he "took the road less traveled by."

CLAUSE
Frost's new knowledge, that teaching children was not for him, compelled him to search for
other ways to earn a living.

Exercise 95C: Diagramming

On your own paper, diagram every word of these sentences from Exercise 95B.

> **Note to Instructor:** Each sentence contains a challenging element—give all necessary help!

He was a poet who took nothing for granted, who could cast his thoughts upon the objects around
him, as Emerson—a central figure in Frost's imagination—urged poets to do.

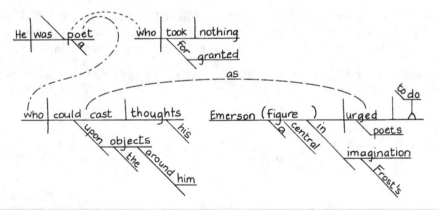

> **Note to Instructor:** In the adverbial clause *as Emerson...to do*, which modifies the verb *could cast*, the infinitive *to do* is what Emerson is actually urging, so serves as the direct object, with *poets* as the indirect object (compare *he threw the poet a ball* to *he urged poets to do*).

Will Frost met a young teacher (the only other teacher at this small school) who agreed to give him lessons in stenography—a skill he rightly guessed would come in handy when he turned his hand to journalism.

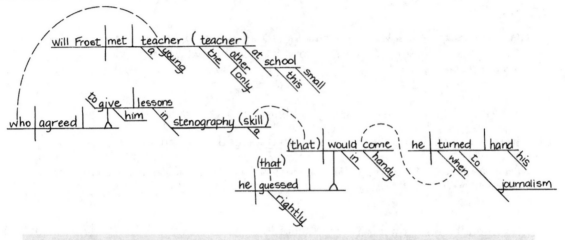

> **Note to Instructor:** The appositive phrase contains two clauses with understood subordinating words: *a skill [that] he rightly guessed [that] would come in handy when he turned his hand to journalism.* The central clause modifies *skill*: *a skill [that] would come in handy when he turned his hand to journalism.* That clause, however, is also the direct object of *[that] he guessed.* If the student struggles, show her the diagram, allow her to study it, and then ask her to reproduce it without looking at the key.

The rumor, that Belle had been the child of an illegitimate relationship, would persist in the Frost family.

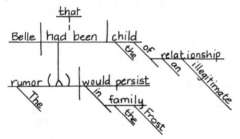

Robbie liked to set off alone on foot, often hiking to Nob Hill, where the new millionaires—men such as Charles Crocker, Leland Stanford, Mark Hopkins and D. D. Colton—were building huge Victorian houses as monuments to their own egos, crafting them from the best imported materials.

> **Note to Student:** In the above sentence, *such as* functions as a single preposition (a synonym for *like*).

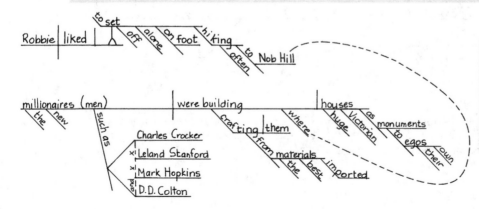

> **Note to Instructor:** The entire clause *where the new millionaires...materials* is an adjective clause describing a place, introduced by the relative adverb *where* (see Lesson 71).

— LESSON 96 —

Appositives
Noun Clauses in Apposition
Absolute Constructions

Exercise 96A: Identifying Absolute Constructions

In the following sentences, taken from *The Princess Bride*, by William Goldman, circle the absolute constructions. Label each absolute construction as *CL* for clause or *PHR* for phrase. For clauses, underline the subject of each clause once and the predicate twice.

PHR
He spoke from inside, (his dark face darkened by shadow.)

PHR   PHR
(Now granted) things had improved since the farm boy had come to slave for him—(no question) the farm boy had certain skills, and the complaints were quite nonexistent now—but that didn't make his the finest cows in Florin.

> **Note to Instructor:** The student may identify the entire compound sentence between the dashes as absolute. You may accept this, but also ask the student to identify the additional absolute contained within this parenthetical expression.

CL
The farm boy did have good teeth, (give credit where credit was due)

> **Note to Instructor:** The absolute construction actually contains two clauses. The subject of the first (main) clause is an understood *you*. The second clause is adverbial and modifies *give*.

PHR   PHR
There was much to be done now, (with Westley gone) and (more than that) ever since the Count had visited, everyone in the area had increased his milk order.

PHR
But travel consumed time, (ships and horses being what they were) and the time away from Florin was worrying.

> **Note to Instructor:** The absolute construction itself is a phrase, but within that phrase, the clause *what they were* renames *ships* and *horses*.

CL
This double door (it might be noted,) was at the south end of the room.

PHR
At 8:23:55 Prince Humperdink rose roaring, (the veins in his thick neck etched like hemp)

PHR
The Great Square of Florin City was filled as never before, (awaiting the introduction of Prince Humperdink's bride-to-be, Princess Buttercup of Hammersmith.)

> **Note to Instructor:** *The Great Square* is not *awaiting*; the people in it were *awaiting*, so the participle phrase is not grammatically connected to the rest of the sentence.

PHR

There were, (to be sure) some who, while admitting she was pleasing enough, were withholding judgement as to her quality as a queen.

Buttercup did not know how long she was out, but they were still in the boat when she blinked,

PHR

(the blanket shielding her)

Exercise 96B: Appositives, Modifiers, and Absolute Constructions

The sentences below, taken from *Strong Poison*, by the British mystery novelist Dorothy Sayers, each contain phrases or clauses set off by dashes. Some are appositives, some are modifiers, and some are absolute constructions. Identify them by writing *APP*, *MOD*, or *AC* above each one. For appositives and modifiers, draw an arrow back to the word being renamed or modified.

AC

Since that time—and she is now twenty-nine years old—she has worked industriously to keep herself.

APP

At this point the elderly spinster on the jury was seen to be making a note—a vigorous note, to judge from the action of her pencil on the paper.

AC

The dates of these occasions cannot be ascertained with any certainty—they were informal parties—but there is some evidence that there was a meeting towards the end of March.

APP

After the third attack—the one in May—the doctor advises Boyes to go away for a change, and he selects the northwest corner of Wales.

MOD

A very cold letter, you may think—almost hostile in tone.

MOD

I shall not have to keep your attention very much longer, but I do ask for it at this point, specially— though you have been attending most patiently and industriously all the time—because now we come to the actual day of the death itself.

> **Note to Instructor:** If the student labels this clause as *AC*, you may accept the answer, but point out that since it is a dependent clause, it is more likely to be functioning as an adverb, modifying the predicate *do ask*.

APP

The omelette—the only dish which did not go out to the kitchen—was prepared by Philip Boyes himself and shared by his cousin.

At 9:15 Boyes leaves Mr. Urquhart's house in Woburn Square, and is driven in a taxi to the house

AC

where Miss Vane has her flat, No. 100 Doughty Street—a distance of about half a mile.

AC

Now you have been told—and the medical witnesses all agree in this—that if a person takes arsenic, a certain proportion of it will be deposited in the skin, nails and hair.

The prisoner had the means—the arsenic—^{APP} she had the expert knowledge, and she had the opportunity to administer it.

And the girl—who has got rather fed up with him—^{MOD} thinks of a grand scoop that will make both of them best-sellers.

She took everything—money, jewels, horses, carriages, all the rest of it—^{APP} and turned it into good consolidated funds.

Well, the long and short of it was that the eldest sister, Jane—the one who married the schoolmaster—^{APP} would have nothing to do with the family black sheep.

> **Note to Instructor:** The *sister* is the *one who married*. The *Jane* is *the one who married* doesn't make sense unless there is more than one Jane (there is more than one sister). *Jane* is another appositive renaming *sister*.

Poisoning is a passion that grows upon you—like drink or drugs.^{MOD}

> **Note to Instructor:** *Like drink or drugs* is a prepositional phrase acting as an adjective. What kind of passion? A passion like drink or drugs.

Exercise 96C: Diagramming

On your own paper, diagram every word of the following sentences, taken from the mystery novel *Murder Must Advertise*, by Dorothy Sayers.

Miss Rossiter and Miss Parton are our guardian angels—type our copy, correct our grammar, provide us with pencils and paper and feed us on coffee and cake.

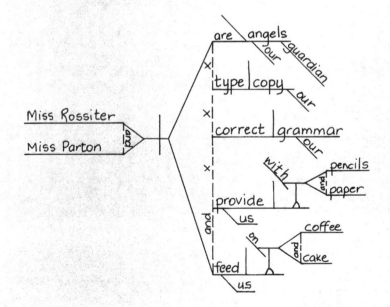

Like a cat, which, in his soft-footed inquisitiveness, he rather resembled, he made himself acquainted with his new home.

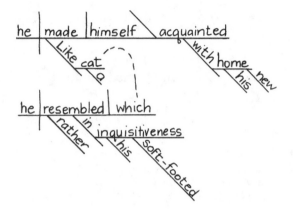

What disgusting stuff cauliflower could be—a curdle of cabbage!

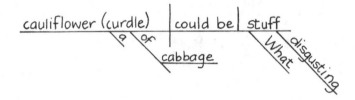

This pencil—a natty scarlet, as you observe, with gold lettering—didn't come from any of Darling's branches.

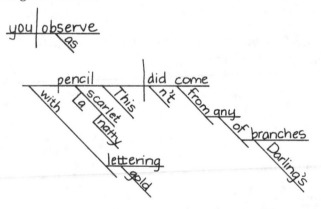

Note to Instructor: In the absolute construction *as you observe*, the word *as* could also be diagrammed as a subordinating word. We have diagrammed it as an adverb because the clause has no grammatical connection to the rest of the sentence.

— REVIEW 8 —

Weeks 22-24

Topics
Parenthetical Expressions
Dashes, Colons, and Brackets
Dialogue and Dialogue Tags
Direct Quotations and Attribution Tags
Ellipses and Partial Quotations
Block Quotes
Interjections
Nouns of Direct Address
Appositives
Noun Clauses in Apposition
Absolute Constructions

Review 8A: Definition Fill-in-the-Blank

You learned many definitions in the past three weeks! Fill in the blanks in the definitions below with one of the terms from the list. Many of the terms will be used more than once.

> **Note to Instructor:** Allow the student to look back through the workbook and find definitions as necessary; the value of the exercise comes in the student's completing each definition, whether from memory or not.

commas	comma	parentheses
line space	dashes	coordinating conjunction
semicolon	colon	paragraph
appositive	appositives	absolute construction
period	attribution tag	exclamation point
parenthetical expression	interjections	dialogue tag
question mark	brackets	ellipses
restrictive modifying clause	nouns of direct address	quotation marks
nonrestrictive modifying clause	closing quotation marks	short parenthetical expressions

 Dashes can enclose words that are not essential to the sentence.

 Dashes can also be used singly to separate parts of a sentence.

 Commas make a parenthetical element a part of the sentence.

 Dashes emphasize a parenthetical element.

 Parentheses minimize a parenthetical element.

279

The independent clauses of a compound sentence must be joined by a __comma__ and a __coordinating conjunction__, a __semicolon__, or a __semicolon__ and a __coordinating conjunction__. They cannot be joined by a __comma__ alone.

A __restrictive modifying clause__ defines the word that it modifies. Removing the clause changes the essential meaning of the sentence.

A __nonrestrictive modifying clause__ describes the word that it modifies. Removing the clause doesn't change the essential meaning of the sentence.

__Parentheses__ can enclose words that are not essential to the sentence.

A __parenthetical expression__ often interrupts or is irrelevant to the rest of the sentence. Punctuation goes inside the __parentheses__ if it applies to the __parenthetical expression__; all other punctuation goes outside the __parentheses__.

A __parenthetical expression__ only begins with a capital letter if it is a complete sentence with ending punctuation.

A __parenthetical expression__ can also be set off by commas.

__Short parenthetical expressions__ such as the following are usually set off by commas: *in short, in fact, in reality, as it were, as it happens, no doubt, in a word, to be sure, to be brief, after all, you know, of course.*

Only a __nonrestrictive modifying clause__ should be set off by commas.

An __appositive__ is a noun, pronoun, or noun phrase that usually follows another noun and renames or explains it. __Appositives__ are set off by __commas__.

A dependent clause can act as an __appositive__ if it renames the noun that it follows.

When a __dialogue tag__ comes before a speech, place a __comma__ after the tag. Put the dialogue's final punctuation mark inside the __closing quotation marks__.

__Ellipses__ show where something has been cut out of a sentence.

A second or third quote from the same source does not need another __attribution tag__, as long as context makes the source of the quote clear.

Direct quotes can be words, phrases, clauses, or sentences, as long as they are set off by __quotation marks__ and form part of a grammatically correct original sentence.

If a direct quotation is longer than three lines, indent the entire quote one inch from the margin in a separate block of text and omit __quotation marks__.

If you change or make additions to a direct quotation, use __brackets__.

When using word processing software, leave an additional __line space__ before and after a block quote.

Block quotes should be introduced by a __colon__ (if preceded by a complete sentence) or a __comma__ (if preceded by a partial sentence).

__Interjections__ express sudden feeling or emotion. They are set off with __commas__ or stand alone with a closing punctuation mark.

__Nouns of direct address__ name a person or thing who is being spoken to. They are set off with __commas__. They are capitalized only if they are proper names or titles.

An ___absolute construction___ has a strong semantic relationship but no grammatical connection to the rest of the sentence.

Speeches do not need to be attached to a ___dialogue tag___ as long as the text clearly indicates the speaker.

Usually, a new ___paragraph___ begins with each new speaker.

When a ___dialogue tag___ comes in the middle of a speech, follow it with a ___comma___ if the following dialogue is an incomplete sentence. Follow it with a ___period___ if the following dialogue is a complete sentence.

When an ___attribution tag___ comes after a direct quote, place a ___comma___, ___exclamation point___, or ___question mark___ inside the closing quotation marks.

When an ___attribution tag___ comes before a direct quote, place a ___comma___ after the tag. Put the dialogue's final punctuation mark inside the ___closing quotation marks___.

When an ___attribution tag___ comes in the middle of a direct quotation, follow it with a ___comma___ if the remaining quote is an incomplete sentence. Follow it with a ___period___ if the remaining quote is a complete sentence.

Every direct quote must have an ___attribution tag___.

Review 8B: Punctuating Restrictive and Non-Restrictive Clauses, Compound Sentences, Interjections, Parenthetical Expressions, Items in Series, and Nouns of Direct Address

The sentences below contain restrictive clauses, nonrestrictive clauses, interjections, parenthetical expressions, items in series, and nouns of direct address. Some are compound sentences. But all of them have lost their punctuation! Insert all necessary punctuation directly into the sentences (use the actual punctuation marks rather than proofreader's marks).

These sentences are taken from the story "Hansel and Gretel," found in *Grimms' Fairy Tales*, collected by the nineteenth-century German folklorists Jacob Grimm and Wilhelm Grimm, translated into English by Edgar Taylor and Marian Edwardes.

O, you fool, then we must all four die of hunger!

The moon shone brightly, and the white pebbles which lay in front of the house glittered like real silver pennies.

> **Note to Instructor:** Although it is not necessarily incorrect to link short independent clauses together with just a coordinating conjunction, rather than a comma and a coordinating conjunction, the comma here follows the rule that the student has already learned.

Now, children, lay yourselves down by the fire and rest; we will go into the forest and cut some wood.

Hansel took his little sister by the hand and followed only the pebbles which shone like newly-coined silver pieces.

> **Note to Instructor:** *The pebbles which shone like newly-coined silver pieces* are the only pebbles referred to in this sentence, so this is a restrictive clause.

On the way into the forest Hansel crumbled the bread which had been given him, and he often threw a morsel on the ground.

> **Note to Instructor:** *The bread which had been given him* is the only possible bread that he could crumble, so this is a restrictive clause.

When the moon came they set out, but they found no crumbs; the many thousands of birds which fly about in the woods and fields had picked them all up.

> **Note to Instructor:** The two independent clauses *they set out* and *they found no crumbs* are linked by a comma and coordinating conjunction, as the rule states. The *birds which fly about in the woods and fields* picked up the crumbs, not other birds, so this is a restrictive clause.

Hansel, who liked the taste of the roof, tore down a great piece of it, and Gretel pushed out the whole of one round window-pane, sat down, and enjoyed herself with it.

> **Note to Instructor:** The clause *who liked the taste of the roof* is nonrestrictive. Gretel carries out three actions in a series (*pushed, sat down, enjoyed*), so each should be set off by a comma.

Oh, you dear children, who has brought you here?

The old woman had only pretended to be so kind; she was in reality a wicked witch, who lay in wait for children, and had only built the little house of bread in order to entice them there.

> **Note to Instructor:** The adjective clause *who lay in wait* is ambiguous; in the original, it is a nonrestrictive clause set off by commas, but the student could identify it as restrictive. Accept either answer, but point out the ambiguity.

Get up, lazy thing, fetch some water, and cook something good for your brother; he is in the stable outside, and is to be made fat.

> **Note to Instructor:** There are three commands in a series (*get up, fetch, cook*), all separated by commas. The comma after *outside* appears in the original but is optional.

Gretel began to weep bitterly, but it was all in vain, for she was forced to do what the wicked witch commanded.

> **Note to Instructor:** There are three independent clauses, each set off with a comma and coordinating conjunction (*Gretel began to weep, it was all in vain, she was forced*).

Hansel, however, stretched out a little bone to her, and the old woman, who had dim eyes, could not see it.

> **Note to Instructor:** The adjective clause *who had dim eyes* is nonrestrictive.

She pushed poor Gretel out to the oven, which was already shooting up flames of fire.

> **Note to Instructor:** There is only one *oven*, whether or not it is *shooting up flames of fire*, so this clause is nonrestrictive.

Then Gretel gave her a push that drove her far into the oven, and shut the iron door, and fastened the bolt which was on it.

> **Note to Instructor:** The three actions in a series (*gave her a push, shut the iron door, fastened the bolt*) are separated by commas. The adjective clause *that drove her far into the oven* is restrictive.

Gretel, however, ran like lightning to Hansel; she opened his little shed and let him out.

Their father had not known one happy hour since he had left the children in the forest; the cruel stepmother, as it happened, was dead.

Then all anxiety was at an end, and they lived together in perfect happiness.

Review 8C: Dialogue

In the following passage from "How the Camel Got His Hump" (from the *Just So Stories,* by Rudyard Kipling), all of the punctuation around, before, and after the lines of dialogue is missing. Insert all necessary punctuation directly into the sentences (use the actual punctuation marks rather than proofreader's marks).

There is a special challenge in the excerpt! If you can't find it, your instructor will point it out to you.

> **Note to Instructor:** The original punctuation is below, but you may accept any appropriate ending punctuation.

In the beginning of years, when the world was so new and all, and the Animals were just beginning to work for Man, there was a Camel, and he lived in the middle of a Howling Desert because he did not want to work; and besides, he was a Howler himself. So he ate sticks and thorns and tamarisks and milkweed and prickles, most 'scruciating idle; and when anybody spoke to him he said, "Humph!"

> **Note to Instructor:** This exclamation point could also be a period.

Presently the Horse came to him on Monday morning, with a saddle on his back and a bit in his mouth, and said, "Camel, O Camel, come out and trot like the rest of us."

"Humph!" said the Camel; and the Horse went away and told the Man.

> **Note to Instructor:** Here and following, the exclamation point after *Humph* could also be a comma.

Presently the Dog came to him, with a stick in his mouth, and said, "Camel, O Camel, come and fetch and carry like the rest of us."

"Humph!" said the Camel; and the Dog went away and told the Man.

Presently the Ox came to him, with the yoke on his neck and said, "Camel, O Camel, come and plough like the rest of us."

"Humph!" said the Camel; and the Ox went away and told the Man.

At the end of the day the Man called the Horse and the Dog and the Ox together, and said, "Three, O Three, I'm very sorry for you (with the world so new-and-all); but that Humph-thing in the Desert can't work, or he would have been here by now, so I am going to leave him alone, and you must work double-time to make up for it."

That made the Three very angry (with the world so new-and-all), and they held a palaver, and an *indaba*, and a *punchayet*, and a pow-wow on the edge of the Desert; and the Camel came chewing on milkweed *most* 'scruciating idle, and laughed at them. Then he said, "Humph!" and went away again.

Presently there came along the Djinn in charge of All Deserts, rolling in a cloud of dust (Djinns always travel that way because it is Magic), and he stopped to palaver and pow-pow with the Three.

"Djinn of All Deserts," said the Horse, "is it right for any one to be idle, with the world so new-and-all?"

"Certainly not," said the Djinn.

"Well," said the Horse, "there's a thing in the middle of your Howling Desert (and he's a Howler himself) with a long neck and long legs, and he hasn't done a stroke of work since Monday morning. He won't trot."

"Whew!" said the Djinn, whistling, "that's my Camel, for all the gold in Arabia! What does he say about it?"

> **Note to Instructor**: Although the exclamation point after *Whew* could also be a comma, this is clearly an exclamation, so an exclamation point is preferable.

"He says, 'Humph!'" said the Dog, "and he won't fetch and carry."

> **Note to Instructor:** The student may not know that when you place a quote within another quote, you use single quotation marks to set it off. Also note that when a quote and a quote-within-a-quote end simultaneously, you use the single and double quotes together. If the student simply puts quote marks around the entire speech beginning *He says...* , accept it but point out the original punctuation above (and in the quote below).

"Does he say anything else?"

"Only 'Humph!' and he won't plough," said the Ox.

"Very good," said the Djinn. "I'll humph him, if you will kindly wait a minute."

> **Note to Instructor:** The period after *Djinn* could also be a comma.

The Djinn rolled himself up in his dust-cloak, and took a bearing across the desert, and found the Camel most 'scruciatingly idle, looking at his own reflection in a pool of water.

"My long and bubbling friend," said the Djinn, "what's this I hear of your doing no work, with the world so new-and-all?"

"Humph!" said the Camel.

The Djinn sat down, with his chin in his hand, and began to think a Great Magic, while the Camel looked at his own reflection in the pool of water.

"You've given the Three extra work ever since Monday morning, all on account of your 'scruciating idleness," said the Djinn; and he went on thinking Magics, with his chin in his hand.

"Humph!" said the Camel.

"I shouldn't say that again if I were you," said the Djinn. "You might say it once too often."

Review 8D: Parenthetical Expressions, Appositives, Absolute Constructions

Each one of the sentences below contains an element not closely connected to the rest of the sentence: parenthetical, appositive, or absolute.

In each sentence, find and circle the unconnected element (word, phrase, or clause). Above it, write *PAR* for parenthetical, *APP* for appositive, or *AB* for absolute.

In the blank at the end of the sentence, note whether the element is set apart with commas (*C*), parentheses (*P*), dashes (*D*), or some other mark (*O*).

These are taken from "A Boyhood in Scotland," a personal essay by the great nineteenth-century nature writer John Muir.

One fine day, (as the story goes) when the bell was ringing gently, the pirate
put out to the rock.   C

This happened (I think) before I was sent to school.   <u>C</u>
[AB above "I think"]

I couldn't imagine what the doctor, (a tall, severe-looking man in black) was
doing to my brother.   <u>C</u>
[APP above "a tall, severe-looking man in black"]

When I was a little boy at Mungo Siddons's school, a flower-show was held
in Dunbar, and I saw a number of the exhibitors carrying large handfuls of
dahlias, (the first I had ever seen)   <u>C</u>
[APP above "the first I had ever seen"]

Our bedroom was adjacent to the ghost room, which had in it a lot of chemical
apparatus—(glass tubing, glass and brass retorts, test-tubes, flasks, etc)—and we
thought that those strange articles were still used by the old dead doctor.   <u>D</u>
[APP above "glass tubing..."]

David (not to be outdone) crawled up to the top of the window-roof and got
bravely astride of it; but in trying to return he lost courage and began to cry.   <u>P</u>
[PAR above "not to be outdone"]

> **Note to Instructor:** The line between absolute and parenthetical element is fuzzy. This
> could be classified as either, but I have chosen parenthetical because of the punctuation.

(After attaining the manly, belligerent age of five or six years) very few of my
schooldays passed without a fist fight.   <u>C</u>
[AB above "the manly, belligerent age of five or six years"]

> **Note to Instructor:** This is an absolute because the underlined participle phrase has no
> grammatical connection to any other element in the sentence. It cannot modify *few* or
> *schooldays* because neither of those nouns has attained the age of five or six years.

We even carried on war, (class against class) in those wild, precious minutes.   <u>C</u>
[AB above "class against class"]

Every boy owned some sort of craft whittled from a block of wood and trimmed
with infinite pains—(sloops, schooners, brigs, and full-rigged ships, with their
sails and string ropes properly adjusted and named for us by some old sailor.)   <u>D</u>
[APP above "sloops, schooners..."]

Our most exciting sport, (however) was playing with gunpowder.   <u>C</u>
[PAR above "however"]

Like squirrels that begin to eat nuts before they are ripe, we began to eat apples
about as soon as they were formed, causing (of course) desperate gastric
disturbances to be cured by castor oil.   <u>P</u>
[PAR above "of course"]

Our portions were consumed in about a couple of minutes; (then off to school.)   <u>O</u>
[AB above "then off to school"]

We had hens in our back yard, and on the next Saturday we managed to swallow
a couple of raw eggs apiece, (a disgusting job)   <u>C</u>
[APP above "a disgusting job"]

> **Note to Instructor:** The noun phrase *a disgusting job* renames the participle *to swallow,* which here
> acts as a noun (the object of the predicate *managed*) and so can be renamed by another noun.

APP

These were my first excursions—(the beginnings of lifelong wanderings)   D

Review 8E: Direct Quotations

In the following two excerpts from two different books about hoaxes and conspiracies, the bolded quotations have not been properly punctuated. Rewrite the paragraphs on your own paper or with your own word processor. (You do not need to include the author and title information!) Punctuate and space the quotations properly.

When you are finished, circle any places where words have been left out of the direct quotations. Underline any places where words or punctuation has been added to the direct quotations. Then compare your answers with the original.

Donna Henes, a self-proclaimed **artist and ritual-maker,** gathered about a hundred people in New York City to publicly stand eggs up at the exact moment of the vernal equinox on March 20, 1983. This event was covered by the *New Yorker* magazine, and a story about it appeared in its April 4, 1983 issue, describing how Ms. Henes handed out eggs to the onlookers, making them promise not to stand any up before the appointed time. Around 11:39 PM she upended an egg and announced **Spring is here**

Everyone in the crowd, us included, got busy balancing eggs the *New Yorker* effused. **Honest to God, it works** The unnamed reporter was not so convinced, however, as to swallow this line whole.

   –Philip C. Plait, *Bad Astronomy: Misconceptions and Misuses Revealed, from Astrology to the Moon Landing "Hoax"*

It's also tempting to simply label conspiracy theories as either "mainstream" or "fringe." Journalist Paul Musgrave referenced this dichotomy when he wrote in the *Washington Post* **Less than two months into the administration, the danger is no longer that Trump will make conspiracy thinking mainstream. That has already come to pass... [S]uch untruths may now be driving government policy in realms as disparate as immigration policy and civil rights.** What Musgrave is talking about is a fairly small shift in a dividing line on the conspiracy spectrum.

   –Slightly adapted from Mick West, *Escaping the Rabbit Hole: How to Debunk Conspiracy Theories Using Facts, Logic, and Respect*

Note to Instructor: The original punctuation is shown below. Ask the student to compare her version with this one, and point out any differences.

Donna Henes, a self-proclaimed "artist and ritual-maker," gathered about a hundred people in New York City to publicly stand eggs up at the exact moment of the vernal equinox on March 20, 1983. This event was covered by the *New Yorker* magazine, and a story about it appeared in its April 4, 1983 issue, describing how Ms. Henes handed out eggs to the onlookers, making them promise not to stand any up before the appointed time. Around 11:39 PM she upended an egg and announced, "Spring is here."

"Everyone in the crowd, us included, got busy balancing eggs," the *New Yorker* effused. "Honest to God, it works." The unnamed reporter was not so convinced, however, as to swallow this line whole.

   –Philip C. Plait, *Bad Astronomy: Misconceptions and Misuses Revealed, from Astrology to the Moon Landing "Hoax"*

It's also tempting to simply label conspiracy theories as either "mainstream" or "fringe." Journalist Paul Musgrave referenced this dichotomy when he wrote in the *Washington Post*:

> Less than two months into the administration, the danger is no longer that Trump will make conspiracy thinking mainstream. That has already come to pass⊙ [S]uch untruths may now be driving government policy in realms as disparate as immigration policy and civil rights.

What Musgrave is talking about is a fairly small shift in a dividing line on the conspiracy spectrum.

> –Slightly adapted from Mick West, *Escaping the Rabbit Hole: How to Debunk Conspiracy Theories Using Facts, Logic, and Respect*

> **Note to Instructor:** The words *Washington Post* could also be followed by a comma.

Review 8F: Diagramming

On your own paper, diagram every word of the following sentences from the first chapter of the novel *When We Were Orphans*, by the British novelist Kazuo Ishiguro (the 2017 winner of the Nobel Prize in literature).

Each sentence contains words set off by a dash, but each of these function as a different part of the sentence. Be ready to explain to your instructor briefly how the different words set off by dashes function!

Ask for help if necessary.

Eventually he flopped down into the sofa, and we were able to exchange news—our own and that of old schoolfriends.

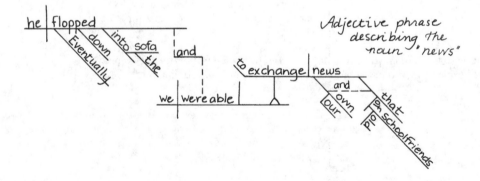

After a while, I grew angry—at myself, at Osbourne, at the whole proceedings.

I did not notice until later—one needs a second magnifying glass to read the engraving—that it was manufactured in Zurich in 1887.

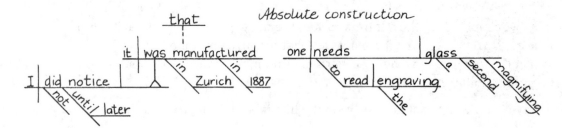

I believe it was at this point I finally assented to his suggestion for the evening—an evening which, as I shall explain, was to prove far more significant—and showed him out.

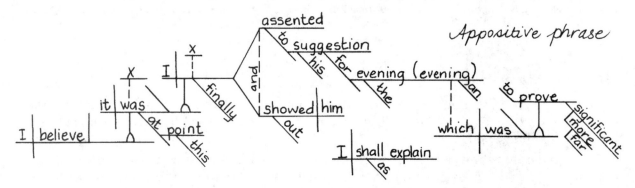

> **Note to Instructor:** This sentence contains two subordinate clauses with understood subordinating words, as shown below. The first clause, *it was at this point...showed him out,* is the direct object of the predicate *believe.* Within that clause, *at this point* is an adverbial prepositional clause answering the question *when*, and the clause *[that] I finally assented...and showed* is a predicate nominative renaming it.
>
> In addition, the appositive phrase *an evening which...significant* contains an absolute within itself—a very tricky construction! The phrase itself remains an appositive, however, renaming the first occurrence of *evening.*
>
> "I believe [that] it was at this point [that] I finally assented to his suggestion for the evening—an evening which, as I shall explain, was to prove far more significant—and showed him out."

WEEK 25

Complex Verb Tenses

— LESSON 97 —

Verb Tense, Voice, and Mood
Tense Review (Indicative)
Progressive Perfect Tenses (Indicative)

Exercise 97A: Review of Indicative Tenses

The following partially completed chart shows the active and passive tenses of the regular verb *help* (in the third-person singular), the irregular verb *leave* (in the third-person plural), and the irregular verb *send* (in the first-person singular). Review your indicative tenses by completing the chart now.

			Active	Passive
SIMPLE TENSES				
	help	Past	he helped	he was helped
	leave		they left	they were left
	send		I sent	I was sent
	help	Present	he helps	he is helped
	leave		they leave	they are left
	send		I send	I am sent
	help	Future	he will help	he will be helped
	leave		they will leave	they will be left
	send		I will send	I will be sent
PROGRESSIVE TENSES				
	help	Past	he was helping	he was being helped
	leave		they were leaving	they were being left
	send		I was sending	I was being sent
	help	Present	he is helping	he is being helped
	leave		they are leaving	they are being left
	send		I am sending	I am being sent
	help	Future	he will be helping	he will be being helped
	leave		they will be leaving	they will be being left
	send		I will be sending	I will be being sent

			Active	**Passive**
PERFECT TENSES				
	help *leave* *send*	Past	he had helped they had left I had sent	he had been helped they had been left I had been sent
	help *leave* *send*	Present	he has helped they have left I have sent	he has been helped they have been left I have been sent
	help *leave* *send*	Future	he will have helped they will have left I will have sent	he will have been helped they will have been left I will have been sent

Exercise 97B: Parsing Verbs

Identify the tense, voice, and mood of each underlined verb. You may abbreviate (*PROG, PERF, SIMP, PAST, PRES, FUT* for tense; *ACT, PASS, ST-OF-BE* for voice; *IND, SUBJ, MOD* for mood).

The first is done for you.

These sentences have been slightly adapted from *The Old Curiosity Shop*, by Charles Dickens.

SIMP PAST, ACT, IND   PROG PERF PAST, ACT, IND
She added that there was no harm in what she had been doing, but it was a great secret—a secret
                SIMP PAST, ACT, IND
which she did not even know herself.

> **Note to Instructor:** The verb *did know* is not modal—the helping verb *did* is used in order to create a negative.

                        PERF PAST, PASS, SUBJ
If no such suspicion had been awakened by his speech, his wiry hair, dull eyes, and sallow face
PERF PRES, ST-OF-BE, MOD
would still have been strong witnesses against him.

> **Note to Instructor:** This is a third conditional sentence. If the student has trouble identifying the mood of the verbs, ask him to look back at the charts in Lessons 82 and 83.

There were suits of mail standing like ghosts in armour here and there, fantastic carvings,
                        PERF PRES, PASS, MOD
tapestry and strange furniture that might have been designed in dreams.

    PERF PRES, PASS, IND   PERF PRES, ACT, IND
I have been rendered uneasy by what you said the other night, and can only plead that I have done
all for the best.

        SIMP PRES, ACT, IND   PERF PRES, ST-OF-BE, MOD
"I'm sorry I have an appointment in the city," said Quilp, looking at his watch, "or I should have
been very glad to have spent half an hour with you."

                        PERF FUT, ACT, IND
"Wait until dusk," returned Mr Groves. "You will have eaten your suppers by then."

PROG PERF PASS, ACT, IND

Yet it was strange that she <u>had been imagining</u> this figure so very distinctly.

FUT PERF, ACT, IND

Unless my aunt sends me a remittance, I <u>shall have gone</u> without a room for the night.

PRES PROG, ACT, IND   PERF PRES, ACT, IND

"She <u>is sleeping</u> soundly," he said, "but no wonder. Angel hands <u>have strewn</u> the ground deep with snow."

SIMP PRES, PASS, MOD   PERF PAST, ACT, IND

She wished they <u>could be told</u> how much she thought about them, and how she <u>had watched</u> them

SIMP PAST, ACT, IND

as they <u>walked</u> together, by the river side at night.

SIMP FUT, PASS, IND

You <u>shall</u> not <u>be permitted</u> to fly in the face of your superiors in this exceedingly gross manner!

Exercise 97C: Completing Sentences

Complete the following sentences by providing an appropriate verb in the tense and voice indicated beneath each blank. (All verbs are in the indicative mood.)

Note to Instructor: As long as the verbs are in the correct tense, any verbs that make sense are acceptable.

The little lake on the edge of the farm <u> has been shrinking </u> for the last few years, as the
progressive perfect present, active
weather has gotten hotter and dryer.

The rebel leader <u> has been involved </u> in four different attempts to take over the government
perfect present, passive
of her country.

For the last twelve hours, the ultra-marathoner <u> has been running </u> through the desert.
progressive perfect present, active

By tomorrow, the enormous birthday cake <u> will have been baked </u> and <u> frosted </u>.
perfect future, passive (compound!)   perfect future, passive

By tomorrow night, the entire cake <u> will have been eaten </u> by hungry guests.
perfect future, passive

By the time I go to college, I <u> will have been learning </u> grammar for ten years!
progressive perfect future, active

The flower <u> is blooming </u> better than ever, since it <u> has been growing </u> in the full sunlight.
progressive present, active   progressive perfect present, active

Unless the borrower has completed the application, his debt <u> will </u> not <u> have been forgiven </u>
perfect future, passive
in time for him to take out another loan.

For years before the pandemic began, poor tenants <u> had been being evicted </u> at every
progressive perfect past, passive
possible opportunity.

The gigantic towers   <u>have been being built</u>   for years, and they still aren't ready for tenants to
progressive perfect present, passive
move in!

— LESSON 98 —

Simple Present and Perfect Present Modal Verbs
Progressive Present and Progressive Perfect Present Modal Verbs

Exercise 98A: Parsing Verbs

In the following sentences from *Moby-Dick*, by Herman Melville, find and underline each modal
verb. Write the tense and voice of each modal verb above it. (For state-of-being verbs, the voice is
simply *state-of-being*.) The first is done for you.

simple present, passive   simple present, active
Ahab gave orders that not an oar <u>should be used</u>, and no man <u>must speak</u> but in whispers.

simple present, active
But in the foamy confusion of their mixed and struggling hosts, the marksmen <u>could</u> not always

<u>hit</u> their mark; and this brought about new revelations of the incredible ferocity of the foe.

simple present, active
Beelzebub himself <u>might climb</u> up the side and step down into the cabin to chat with the captain,
simple present, active
and it <u>would</u> not <u>create</u> any unsubduable excitement in the forecastle.

perfect present, state-of-being
Meanwhile, the whale he had struck must also <u>have been</u> on its travels.

simple present, active
For who <u>could tell</u> but what the next morning, as soon as I popped out of the room, the harpooneer
progressive present, active
<u>might be standing</u> in the entry, all ready to knock me down!

One packed rush was made to the side, and every eye counted every ripple, as moment followed
simple present, passive
moment, and no sign of either the sinker or the diver <u>could be seen</u>.

perfect present, state-of-being
A nose to the whale <u>would have been</u> impertinent.

perfect present, active
What just before <u>might have seemed</u> to him a thing most momentous, now seems but a part of the
general joke.

perfect present, active
For one of them <u>may have received</u> a transfer of letters from some third, and now far remote
simple present, state-of-being
vessel; and some of those letters <u>may be</u> for the people of the ship she now meets.

perfect present, passive

Some at least of the imaginative impressions about to be presented <u>may have been shared</u> by most men.

simple present, active

To accomplish his object Ahab <u>must use</u> tools.

perfect present, passive

The lines, of which, hardly an instant before, not one hand's breadth <u>could have been gained</u>, were now in long quick coils flung back all dripping into the boats.

That for six thousand years—and no one knows how many millions of ages before—the

progressive perfect present, active

great whales <u>should have been spouting</u> all over the sea—this is surely a noteworthy thing.

simple present, active   simple present, active

The headsman <u>should stay</u> in the bows from first to last; he <u>should</u> both <u>dart</u> the harpoon and the

simple present, passive

lance, and no rowing whatever <u>should be expected</u> of him, except under circumstances obvious to any fisherman.

Exercise 98B: Forming Modal Verbs

Fill in the blanks with the missing modal verbs. Using the helping verbs indicated, put each action verb provided into the correct modal tense.

Around the reef, we __could see__ fish of every luminous color that __could be imagined__ .

    helping verb: could   helping verb: could
    simple present active of *see*   simple present passive of *imagine*

Sharks __can raise__ their bodies out of the water, but only partly, and only with great effort.

    helping verb: can
    simple present active of *raise*

Our guide __must have been convincing__ , because the entire party decided to scuba dive down into the cold depths of the ocean.

    helping verb: must
    progressive perfect present active of *convince*

Huge bull sharks, we later learned, __may have been seen__ as close as fifty yards off our private beach.

    helping verb: may
    perfect present passive of *see*

I __might have expected__ the catastrophe that followed!

    helping verb: might
    perfect present active of *expect*

Before our vacation was finished, we __would be mourning__ the loss of nearly all of our colleagues!

    helping verb: would
    progressive present active of *mourn*

To be so aggressive, the sharks ___must have been being starved___ for food for many weeks before we arrived on the scene.

> helping verb: must
> progressive perfect present passive of *starve*

The epic battle between swimmers and sharks ___would be retold___ again and again over the coming years.

> helping verb: would
> simple present passive of *retell*

Magazine subscribers the world over ___would be reading___ about our struggle against the bull sharks for years to come, and the story ___may have destroyed___ the popularity of Shark Bay for all time.

> helping verb: would   helping verb: may
> progressive present active of *read*   perfect present active of *destroy*

— LESSON 99 —

Modal Verb Tenses
The Imperative Mood
The Subjunctive Mood
More Subjunctive Tenses

Exercise 99A: Complete the Chart

Fill in the missing forms on the following chart. Use the verbs indicated above each chart, in order. The first form on each chart is done for you.

INDICATIVE
(aggravate, build, dazzle, forget, bless, hurry, interrupt, keep, leave, lighten, murder, twist)

Indicative Tense	Active Formation	Examples	Passive Formation	Examples
Simple present	Add *-s* in third-person singular	I aggravate he, she, it aggravates	*am/is/are* + past participle	I am aggravated you are aggravated he, she, it is aggravated
Simple past	Add *-d* or *-ed*, or change form	I built	*was/were* + past participle	I was built you were built

Indicative Tense	Active Formation	Examples	Passive Formation	Examples
Simple future	+ *will* OR *shall*	they will dazzle	*will be* + past participle	it will be dazzled

Progressive present	*am/is/are*
	 +
	 present participle
		I am forgetting
		 you
		  are forgetting
		 he, she, it
		  is forgetting
			am/is/are being
			 +
			 past participle
				I
				 am being forgotten
				 you
				 are being forgotten
				 he, she, it
				 is being forgotten

Progressive past	*was/were*
	 +
	 present participle
		I was blessing
		 you
		  were blessing
		 he, she, it
		  was blessing
			was/were being
			 +
			 past participle
				I was being blessed
				 you
				  were being blessed
				 he, she, it
				  was being blessed

Progressive future	*will be* + present participle	I will be hurrying	*will be being* + past participle	it will be being hurried

Perfect present	*has/have*
	 +
	 past participle
		I have interrupted
		 you
		  have interrupted
		 he, she, it
		  has interrupted
			has/have been
			 +
			 past participle
				I have been
				 interrupted
				 you
				  have been
				 interrupted
				 he, she, it
				  has been
				 interrupted

Perfect past	*had*
	 +
	 past participle
		they
		  had kept
			had been
			 +
			 past participle
				you
				  had been kept

Perfect future	*will have* + past participle	we will have left	*will have been* + past participle	they will have been left

Indicative Tense	Active Formation	Examples	Passive Formation	Examples
Progressive perfect present	*have/has been* + present participle	I have been lightening he, she, it has been lightening	*have/has been being* + past participle	I have been being lightened he, she, it has been being lightened
Progressive perfect past	*had been* + present participle	you had been murdering	*had been being* + past participle	you had been being murdered
Progressive perfect future	*will have been* + present participle	you will have been twisting	*will have been being* + past participle	they will have been being twisted

MODAL
(avoid, freeze, poison, try)

Note to Instructor: Student's choice of modal helping verb may vary. *Should, would, may, might, must, can,* and *could* are all acceptable.

Modal Tense	Active Formation	Examples	Passive Formation	Examples
Simple present	modal helping verb + simple present main verb	I could avoid you might avoid he, she, it may avoid	modal helping verb + *be* + past participle	I might be avoided they can be avoided
Progressive present	modal helping verb + *be* + present participle	I should be freezing	modal helping verb + *be* + *being* + past participle	it may be being frozen
Perfect present	modal helping verb + *have* + past participle	you could have poisoned	modal helping verb + *have* + *been* + past participle	it might have been poisoned

Modal Tense	Active Formation	Examples	Passive Formation	Examples
Progressive perfect present	modal helping verb + *have been* + present participle	I _may have been trying_	modal helping verb + *have been being* + past participle	we _should have been being tried_

IMPERATIVE
(chase, mock)

Imperative Tense	Active Formation	Examples	Passive Formation	Examples
Present	Simple present form without subject	_Chase_ ! _Mock_ !	*be* + past participle	_Be chased_ ! _Be mocked_ !

SUBJUNCTIVE
(capture, deceive, destroy, gather, honor, scold, tweak, underestimate)

Subjunctive Tense	Active Formation	Examples	Passive Formation	Examples
Simple present	No change in any person	I _capture_ you _capture_ he, she, it _capture_ we _capture_ you _capture_ they _capture_	*be* + past participle	I _be captured_ they _be captured_
Simple past	**Same as indicative:** Add -*d* or -*ed*, or change form	I _deceived_ you _deceived_ he, she, it _deceived_	*were* + past participle	it _were deceived_

Subjunctive Tense	Active Formation	Examples	Passive Formation	Examples
Progressive present	**Same as indicative:** *am/is/are* + present participle	I am destroying / you are destroying / he, she, it is destroying	**Same as indicative:** *am/is/are being* + past participle	I am being destroyed / you are being destroyed / he, she, it is being destroyed
Progressive past	*were* + present participle	I were gathering / you were gathering / he, she, it were gathering	*were being* + past participle	I were being gathered / you were being gathered / he, she, it were being gathered
Perfect present	**Same as indicative:** *has/have* + past participle	I have honored / he, she, it has honored / they have honored	**Same as indicative:** *has/have been* + past participle	I have been honored / he, she, it has been honored / they have been honored
Perfect past	**Same as indicative:** *had* + past participle	we had scolded	**Same as indicative:** *had been* + past participle	we had been scolded
Progressive perfect present	**Same as indicative:** *have/has been* + present participle	I have been tweaking / you have been tweaking / he, she, it has been tweaking	**Same as indicative:** *have/has been being* + past participle	I have been being tweaked / you have been being tweaked / he, she, it has been being tweaked
Progressive perfect past	**Same as indicative:** *had been* + present participle	you had been underestimating	**Same as indicative:** *had been being* + past participle	you had been being underestimated

Exercise 99B: Parsing

Write the mood, tense, and voice of each underlined verb above it. The first is done for you.

These sentences are taken from *The Great Brain*, by John D. Fitzgerald.

subjunctive   modal
past   present
state-of-being   active

If there <u>were</u> one man in all of Adenville who <u>would order</u> the first water closet ever seen in town, that man had to be Papa.

modal   modal
present   present
active   state-of-being

You <u>would think</u> a man smart enough to be an editor and publisher <u>would be</u> smart enough not to let himself be swindled.

indicative
progressive past
active

We <u>were beating</u> with sticks on Mamma's washtubs, pretending to be drummers in a band.

indicative   indicative
perfect past   progressive past
active   active

Aunt Bertha, who <u>had lived</u> with us since the death of her husband, <u>was greasing</u> a bread pan with bacon rinds.

indicative
perfect past
passive

I was positive that Papa <u>had been swindled</u> again on another crazy invention.

indicative
progressive perfect past
active

Papa came home for lunch with Sweyn, who <u>had been helping</u> at the newspaper office.

indicative   modal
simple past   progressive present
active   active

I <u>thought</u> ahead to the time when I <u>would be graduating</u> from the sixth grade in Adenville, like

Sweyn would in June of that year.

imperative   imperative
present   present
active   active

"You <u>go</u> round up ten more kids. <u>Tell</u> them they not only get to see the digging of the first

indicative
simple future
passive

cesspool for a water closet for a penny, but also that they <u>will be served</u> refreshments."

modal
perfect present
active

With his great brain I knew he <u>could have influenced</u> me, but he didn't even try.

modal   modal
present   perfect present
active   active

You <u>can bet</u> Mr. Thompson <u>would have made</u> it his business to find out why.

modal
present
active

I knew from the color of the sign that Howard <u>must have</u> the mumps.

modal
perfect present
state-of-being
They knew Jimmie Peterson <u>must have been</u> in on it, but I didn't say so.

modal
perfect present
active
He said that the current is so swift it <u>could have carried</u> them all to their deaths.

subjunctive
past
active
"It is all right, Mamma," Tom said, as if he <u>led</u> ten kids into our kitchen every day.

modal   subjunctive
perfect present   perfect past
active   active
I <u>would have gone</u> with them if Uncle Mark <u>had asked</u> me.

— LESSON 100 —

Review of Moods and Tenses
Conditional Sentences

Exercise 100A: Conditional Sentences

Identify the following sentences (taken from the popular South Korean novel *Kim Jiyoung, Born 1982*, written by Cho Nam-Joo, translated into English by Jamie Chang) as first, second, or third conditional by writing a *1*, *2*, or *3* in the blank next to each.

If Grandma had been alive, she would have ripped into Eunyoung.   3

If you like someone, you're friendlier and nicer to them.   1

And if I work, don't you spend my pay, too?   1

If she ever came across another part-time job that offered the hours
and pay she wanted, she would take it, regardless of what it was.   2

It'll ruin this company's reputation if word gets around in the field.   1

I can apologize if I came on too strong.   2

If the woman hadn't said that to her, Jiyoung would have lived in
fear for even longer.   3

If you catch a falling snowflake and make a wish, it comes true.   1

Even if they do manage to find new work, it is quite common for them to
end up with jobs that are more menial than their previous employment.   1

Exercise 100B: Parsing

Write the correct mood, tense, and voice above each underlined verb. These sentences are taken from *A Book of Myths*, by Jean Lang.

indicative, simple past,
state-of-being

indicative,
simple past, passive

It <u>was</u> a sunless world in which land, air, and sea <u>were mixed</u> up together.

indicative,
simple past, active

The East Wind <u>rushed</u> across the Ægean Sea, seizing the sails with cruel grasp and casting them

subjunctive, simple past,
state-of-being

in tatters before it, snapping the mast as though it <u>were</u> but a dry reed by the river.

modal,
perfect present, passive

Before its furious charge, even the heart of a hero <u>might have been stricken</u>.

subjunctive, simple past,
active

modal, simple present,
active

If I <u>boasted</u>, by my boast I <u>must stand</u>.

modal,
perfect present, active

Prometheus knew that at any moment he <u>could have brought</u> his torment to an end.

modal,
perfect present, active

The children said farewell to Lîr, who <u>must have wondered</u> at the tears that stood in Finola's eyes.

indicative,
simple past, state-of-being

modal,
perfect present, passive

So sure <u>were</u> they of that love from the very first moment that it seemed as though they <u>must have been born</u> loving one another.

indicative,
progressive perfect past, active

The day before their hurried flight from Erin, Ainle and Ardan <u>had been playing</u> chess with Conor, the king.

indicative,
simple past, passive

An embassy <u>was sent</u> by the king to the oracle of Apollo.

indicative,
simple future, passive

All your strength <u>will be wanted</u> to hold the horses in.

indicative,
perfect past, state-of-being

modal, perfect present,
state-of-being

He told her all that <u>had been</u>, all that <u>might have been</u>.

indicative,
simple future, active

You <u>will have</u> a little grave apart to yourself.

modal,
simple present, active

imperative,
simple present, active

If by a miracle I <u>should return</u>, <u>look</u> you to yourself, Roland!

Exercise 100C: Diagramming

On your own paper, diagram every word of the following sentences from *The Complete Idiot's Guide to Game Theory,* by Edward Rosenthal. (You may not be interested in game theory, but you should still be able to understand the grammar of these sentences!)

If you need help, ask your instructor.

Often in this book we have relied on games having a certain set of rules that the players must follow.

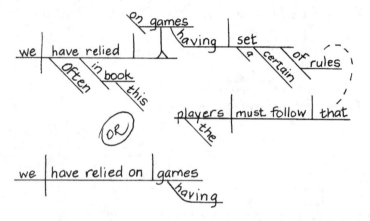

> **Note to Instructor:** The verb *rely* can take the prepositional phrase *on games having...* as its object—or *have relied on* can be diagrammed as a single compound verb, with *games* as its object. In either case, the present participle *having* modifies *games.*
>
> | The subordinate clause *that the players must follow* most likely refers directly to the object of the preposition *rules* [*rules that the players must follow*], but it is not grammatically incorrect for the student to diagram it as referring to the object of the present participle *set.*

On the other hand, if you simply divided up the $120 equally, neither you, Jennifer, nor Dan should have any worries about getting a raw deal.

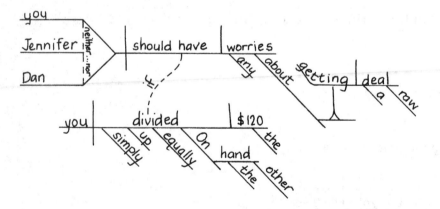

> **Note to Instructor:** The verb *divided up* could also be diagrammed as a single compound verb. *$120* here serves as a noun (the direct object of the predicate *divided [up]*).

If one of the players gets greedy and plays one defection too many, the other player will employ a so-called trigger strategy: to defect forever after.

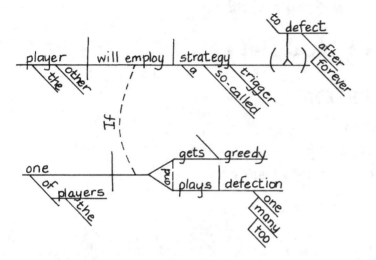

> **Note to Instructor:** Although this sentence has a straightforward cause/consequence clause structure, it also has a few oddities. The infinitive *to defect* is the appositive of the direct object *strategy*; *forever after* has here been diagrammed as the adverb *after* modified by the adverb *forever*, but the two words could also be diagrammed on a single line modifying *to defect* as a compound adverb. The same is true of the phrase *one too many*—accept any diagram that puts those three words beneath *defection*, but show the student the diagram above.
>
> This is an idiosyncratic use of the verb *gets* as a linking verb! The student may have difficulty with this usage. Accept a diagram that diagrams *gets* as an action verb and *greedy* as an adverb, but show the student the diagram above as another possible option.

WEEK 26

More Modifiers

— LESSON 101 —

Adjective Review
Adjectives in the Appositive Position
Correct Comma Usage

Exercise 101A: Identifying Adjectives

Underline every adjective (including verb forms used as adjectives) in the following sentences, from *The Custom of the Country*, by Edith Wharton.

Draw an arrow from each adjective to the word it modifies.

Above each adjective, write *DESC* for descriptive or *POSS* for possessive. Then, label each as in the attributive (*ATT*) or appositive (*APP*) position.

Do not underline articles! There are just too many of them.

Mrs. Heeny, a stout professional-looking person in a waterproof, her rusty veil thrown back, and a shabby alligator bag at her feet, followed the mother's glance with good-humoured approval.

Her pale soft-cheeked face, with puffy eyelids and drooping mouth, suggested a partially-melted wax figure which had run to double-chin.

Mr. Spragg, having finished the last course of his heterogeneous meal, was adjusting his gold eyeglasses for a glance at the paper when Undine trailed down the sumptuous stuffy room, where coffee-fumes hung perpetually under the emblazoned ceiling and the spongy carpet might have absorbed a year's crumbs without a sweeping.

About them sat pallid families, richly dressed, and silently eating their way through a bill-of-fare which seemed to have ransacked the globe for gastronomic incompatibilities; and in the middle of the room a knot of equally pallid waiters, engaged in languid conversation, turned their backs by common consent on the persons they were supposed to serve.

304

Presently her attention was drawn to a lady in black who was examining the pictures through a tortoise-shell eyeglass adorned with diamonds and hanging from a long pearl chain.

The realities lay about him now: the books jamming his old college bookcases and overflowing on chairs and tables; sketches too—he could do charming things, if only he had known how to finish them!—and, on the writing-table at his elbow, scattered sheets of prose and verse; charming things also, but, like the sketches, unfinished.

His imagination, peopled with such varied images and associations, fed by so many currents from the long stream of human experience, could hardly picture the bareness of the small half-lit place in which his wife's spirit fluttered.

Exercise 101B: Punctuation Practice

The sentences below are missing all of their punctuation marks! Using everything you have learned about punctuation, insert correct punctuation. You may simply write the punctuation marks in, rather than using proofreader's marks.

These sentences are taken from the modern gothic novel *The Haunting of Hill House*, by Shirley Jackson, first published in 1959.

Each of these people then received a letter from Dr. Montague extending an invitation to spend all or part of a summer at a comfortable country house old but perfectly equipped with plumbing electricity central heating and clean mattresses.

His aunt who was the owner of Hill House was fond of pointing out that her nephew had the best education the best clothes the best taste and the worst companions of anyone she had ever known she would have leaped at any chance to put him safely away for a few weeks.

It was made of gray stone grotesquely solid jammed hard against the wooden side of the house with the insistent veranda holding it there.

On either side of them the trees silent relinquished the dark color they had held paled grew transparent and stood white and ghastly against the black sky.

They could hear the laughter of the children and the affectionate amused voices of the mother and father the grass was richly thickly green the flowers were colored red and orange and yellow the sky was blue and gold and one child wore a scarlet jumper and raised its voice again in laughter tumbling after a puppy over the grass.

Within walls continued upright bricks met neatly floors were firm and doors were sensibly shut silence lay steadily against the wood and stone of Hill House and whatever walked there walked alone.

Each of these people, then, received a letter from Dr. Montague extending an invitation to spend all or part of a summer at a comfortable country house, old, but perfectly equipped with plumbing, electricity, central heating, and clean mattresses.

Note to Instructor: The commas around *then* set the word off as a parenthetical element. It is not incorrect for the student to interpret *then* as an adverb modifying *received*, in which case the commas are not needed.

The comma after *old* is optional, but the comma before it is essential.

The comma after *heating* is an Oxford comma.

His aunt, who was the owner of Hill House, was fond of pointing out that her nephew had the best education, the best clothes, the best taste, and the worst companions of anyone she had ever known; she would have leaped at any chance to put him safely away for a few weeks.

Note to Instructor: The clause following *aunt* is a nonrestrictive adjective clause and must be set off by commas.

The comma after *taste* is an Oxford comma.

The clause *[that] she had ever known* is restrictive and should not be set off by commas.

It was made of gray stone, grotesquely solid, jammed hard against the wooden side of the house, with the insistent veranda holding it there.

Note to Instructor: The subject *It* is followed by three phrases acting as adjectives in the appositive position: *grotesquely solid* (adjective phrase), *jammed hard...house* (past participle phrase acting as an adjective), and *with....there* (prepositional phrase acting as an adjective).

On either side of them the trees, silent, relinquished the dark color they had held, paled, grew transparent and stood white and ghastly against the black sky.

Note to Instructor: The appositive adjective *silent* comes between the subject *trees* and the predicate *relinquished*.

The series of three predicates *relinquished*, *paled*, and *grew* are separated by commas.

A comma could also follow *transparent* to separate the fourth predicate (that would be an Oxford comma), but the author has here made the choice to tie the predicates *grew* and *stood* more closely together.

The appositive adjectives *white and ghastly* could also be set off with commas.

The introductory prepositional phrase *On either side of them* could also be followed by a comma.

They could hear the laughter of the children and the affectionate, amused voices of the mother and father; the grass was richly, thickly green, the flowers were colored red and orange and yellow, the sky was blue and gold, and one child wore a scarlet jumper and raised its voice again in laughter, tumbling after a puppy over the grass.

Note to Instructor: Because the adjectives *affectionate* and *amused* could be reversed, a comma is necessary to separate them. The same is true of *richly* and *thickly*.

The semicolon after *father* is placed there by the author in order to segment off the first sentence (what the narrators can hear) from the series of four sentences that all describe what they can see. It could, however, be a comma.

The next four clauses (*grass was*, *flowers were*, *sky was*, *child wore... and raised*) are items in a series, separated by commas. The comma after *gold* is an Oxford comma.

Within, walls continued upright, bricks met neatly, floors were firm, and doors were sensibly shut; silence lay steadily against the wood and stone of Hill House, and whatever walked there, walked alone.

> **Note to Instructor:** The comma after *Within* is a tricky one! *Within* is an adverb modifying *continued* (*walls continued upright within*). Since it has been shifted to the beginning of the sentence for rhetorical emphasis, a comma prevents misunderstanding.
>
> The four short independent clauses *walls continued upright, bricks met neatly, floors were firm*, and *doors were sensibly shut* are items linked by commas. The *and* before the final clause is preceded by an Oxford comma.
>
> The semicolon after *shut* could be a comma. The author has used a semicolon because the *and* before *doors were sensibly shut* indicates that it is the last item in a series, so the clause *silence lay steadily* begins a new series.
>
> The comma between *there* and *walked alone* is optional and exists to prevent misunderstanding.

Exercise 101C: Diagramming

On your own paper, diagram the following sentences from the modern gothic stories *Revenge: Eleven Dark Tales*, by Yoko Ogawa, translated by Stephen Snyder.

Each sentence has a different variation of items in a series, separated by commas. When you're finished diagramming, try to tell your instructor what they are.

Each sentence also has a different kind of element set off by a dash! Also try to tell your instructor what grammatical function each of these elements serves.

The light in the glass display case was pleasant and soft, the pastries looked beautiful, and the stool was quite comfortable—I liked the place, in spite of the service.

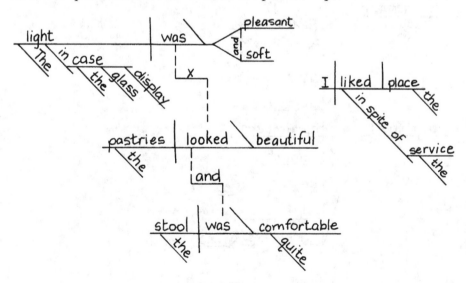

> **Note to Instructor:** The items in a series are the three independent clauses *light was pleasant and soft*, *pastries looked*, and *stool was*.
>
> The element set off by a dash is an absolute construction, related by meaning but not grammatically to the first part of the sentence.
>
> *In spite of* here functions as a single preposition.

She rearranged her scarf, tapped the toe of her shoe, and anxiously fidgeted with the clasps on a black leather wallet—apparently used to collect her accounts.

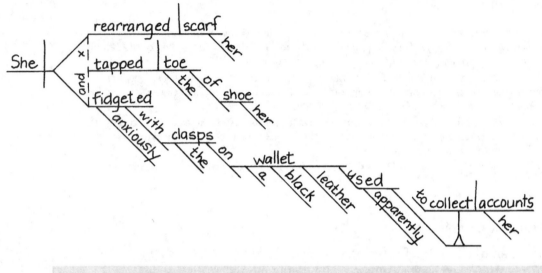

> **Note to Instructor:** The items in the series are the three predicates *rearranged*, *tapped*, and *fidgeted*.
> The element set off by a dash is the past participle phrase *apparently used to collect her accounts*, which functions as an adjective modifying *wallet*.

First, I turned off our refrigerator and emptied it: last night's potato salad, ham, eggs, cabbage, cucumbers, wilted spinach, yogurt, some cans of beer, pork—I pulled everything out and threw it aside.

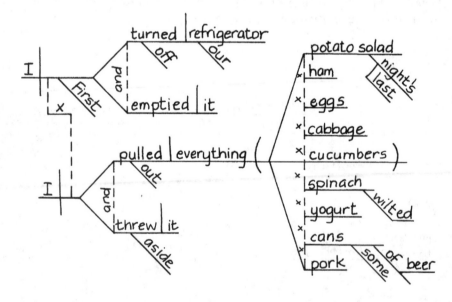

> **Note to Instructor:** The items in the series are the nine appositives renaming *everything*.
> The element set off by a dash is the second independent clause in this compound sentence. The appositives actually precede the dash, but rename the direct object of the first predicate in that clause, *pulled*.

— LESSON 102 —

Adjective Review

Pronoun Review

Limiting Adjectives

Exercise 102A: Identifying Adjectives

The following excerpts are taken from the novel *Madam, Will You Talk?* by the modern gothic writer Mary Stewart.

Underline every word that acts as an adjective.

Do not include phrases or clauses acting as adjectives. Also, do not include articles. (There are just too many!)

Label each one using the following abbreviations:

Descriptive Adjectives		**Limiting Adjectives**	
Regular	*DA-R*	Possessives	*LA-P*
Present participles	*DA-PresP*	~~Articles~~	~~LA-A~~
Past participles	*DA-PastP*	Demonstratives	*LA-D*
		Indefinites	*LA-IND*
		Interrogatives	*LA-INT*
		Numbers	*LA-N*

                  DA-PastP   DA-R   LA-N
A <u>white-painted</u> <u>trellis</u> wall separated the court on <u>one</u> side from the street, and beyond it people,

                                                      LA-P   DA-R
mules, cars, buses, moved about <u>their</u> business up and down the <u>narrow</u> thoroughfare. But inside

        DA-PastP   DA-R   DA-R   DA-R
the <u>vine-covered</u> trellis it was very <u>still</u> and <u>peaceful</u>. The gravel between the <u>little</u> chairs was

carefully raked and watered; shade lay gently across the tables.

> **Note to Instructor:** The compound adjectives *white-painted* and *vine-covered* are labelled as past participles because they are forms of the verbs *to paint* and *to cover*. The words *raked* and *watered* are passive verbs (the gravel *was raked* and *was watered*), not past participles acting as adjectives.

LA-P   DA-R   DA-R
<u>His</u> face, which had, even in the <u>slight</u> courtesies of small-talk, betrayed humour and a <u>quick</u>

                                                              DA-R LA-IND   DA-R
intelligence at work, seemed suddenly to mask itself, to become <u>older</u>. <u>Some</u> <u>impalpable</u> burden

                            LA-P   DA-R   DA-R
almost visibly dropped on to <u>his</u> shoulders. One was <u>conscious</u>, in spite of the <u>sensitive</u> youth of

LA-P   LA-D   DA-R   DA-R
<u>his</u> mouth, and <u>those</u> <u>childish</u> <u>thin</u> wrists and hands, of something that could meet and challenge

        DA-R   LA-P DA-R
a quite <u>adult</u> destiny on <u>its</u> <u>own</u> ground, strength for strength.

                          DA-R
The couple under the <u>palm</u> tree might have sat anywhere for the portrait of Suburban England

        DA-PastP   DA-R
Abroad. <u>Dressed</u> as only the British can dress for a <u>sub-tropical</u> climate—that is, just as they

                              DA-R   DA-PresP LA-P   DA-R
would for a fortnight on the <u>North-East</u> coast of England—they sat <u>sipping</u> <u>their</u> drinks with <u>wary</u>

              LA-P   DA-R *or* LA-N   DA-R

enjoyment, and eyeing <u>their</u> <u>seventeen-year-old</u> daughter with the sort of expression that <u>barnyard</u>

                                                   DA-PresP

fowls might have if they suddenly hatched a flamingo. For she was <u>startling</u> to say the least of

                DA-R   DA-R DA-R

it. She would have been <u>pretty</u> in a <u>fair</u> <u>English</u> fashion, but she had seen fit to disguise herself

        LA-P   DA-R DA-R   LA-N   LA-P

by combing <u>her</u> hair in a <u>flat</u> <u>thick</u> mat down over <u>one</u> side of <u>her</u> face. From behind the curtain

        LA-N   DA-PastP   DA-R

appeared <u>one</u> eye, <u>blue-shadowed</u> to an <u>amazing</u> appearance of dissipation.

> **Note to Instructor:** The proper noun *Suburban England Abroad* has been treated as a single noun, but the student could also label *Suburban* and *Abroad* as *DA-R*. The compound adjective *seventeen-year-old* can be labelled as either *DA-R* or *LA-N* (both are correct).

Exercise 102B: Analysis

The passage above shows you how a good writer uses adjectives: a mix of colorful descriptive adjectives and sparer, simpler limiting adjectives.

    The total word count of the excerpt is 270 words. Now count each type of adjective and fill out the following chart.

> **Note to Instructor:** This exercise is intended to engage statistically inclined thinkers in a way that grammar usually doesn't. You may certainly skip it if the student finds this sort of calculation frustrating or unhelpful.
>
>   The figures below are based on *Suburban England Abroad* as a single compound noun and *seventeen-year-old* as *LA-N* (rather than *DA-R*).

Descriptive Adjectives

Regular	26
Present participles	2
Past participles	4

Total Descriptive Adjectives __32__

Total Adjectives Used __47__

Limiting Adjectives

Possessives	9
~~Articles~~	═══
Demonstratives	1
Indefinites	1
Interrogatives	0
Numbers	4

Total Limiting Adjectives __15__

Good prose can't be reduced to *just* formulas—but formulas can give you some extra help in writing well. The total word count of the excerpt is 270 words. You can figure out what fraction of the total word count is taken up by adjectives by dividing the total word count by the total number of adjectives used. Work that sum now, and ask your instructor for help if necessary.

$$\begin{array}{r} 5\ \text{r.35} \\ 47\overline{\smash{)}270} \end{array}$$

    The calculation above tells you that 1 out of every __5 (or 6)__ [insert answer to division problem!] words in this passage is an adjective. In other words, adjectives do not make up more than about 1/__5 or 1/6__ of this descriptive writing.

> **Note to Instructor:** The remainder of 35 means that 1 out of 6 is a better measure of the adjective's occurrence! Accept either answer, though.

Now let's look at the relationship between limiting and descriptive adjectives. Complete the following division problem:

$$\text{[number of limiting adjectives]} \quad 15 \overline{)32}^{\,2\text{ r. }2} \quad \text{[number of descriptive adjectives]}$$

The calculation above tells you that 1 out of every __2 –3__ [insert answer to second division problem!] adjectives used is a limiting adjective.

Ask your instructor to share the last part of this exercise with you.

> **Note to Instructor:** Share the following conclusion with the student.

So, about 1/5 or 1/6 of Mary Stewart's words are adjectives (one out of every 5 or 6 words). Of those adjectives, between 1/3 and 1/2 are limiting (one out of every 2 or 3 adjectives). The rest are descriptive.

Exercise 102C: Using Adjectives

On your own paper, rewrite the passage below. It is taken from Mary Stewart's modern Gothic novel *Thunder on the Right*—but most of the adjectives (except for articles) have been removed. The blanks show where adjectives should go. Some of the blanks represent two adjectives!

Follow these guidelines:

- Use at least one compound, hyphenated adjective.
- Use at least one indefinite adjective.
- Use at least two present participles acting as adjectives.
- Use at least two past participles acting as adjectives.
- Use at least two adjectives in one of the blanks.
- Use at least one possessive adjective.

It was a _____ afternoon. The road lifted _____ length before them along the hillside, the valley _____ itself in curve after curve. The road was, to begin with, narrowly _____, with _____ meadows _____ sharply to the stream bed on the right, to rise again beyond the water in _____ pastures where cattle grazed with slowly _____ bells. The valley twisted toward the south, and before them the _____ barrier of _____ peaks which barred it had, miraculously, parted, and now valley and road were cupped between _____ slopes _____, _____ in sunlight, toward still more _____ crests of blue that brushed the sky. And these, _____ with distance, _____ in with snow and shadow against the _____ fingers of cloud that clung to them were, unbelievably, but the _____ ridges of the _____ barriers beyond... She turned off the road into the track—it was little more—that climbed the _____ valley. She walked steadily, and soon, as she rounded a curve of the track, she saw, _____ distance ahead of her, set back against the mountainside to the left, the _____ walls of the convent. A _____ tower jutted up to catch the sunlight, vividly _____ against a rampart of pines beyond, and, even as Jennifer glimpsed it and guessed _____ nature, she heard, _____ out of the _____ wind, the _____ sound of a bell. She tilted her head to listen, _____, her _____ being pierced, _____ through, _____ with a _____ delight. But presently the _____ beauty of that _____ note, insisting beat by beat upon the strangeness of the place, took her with a _____ sensation, part pleasure and part fear, and wholly _____. To her, suddenly, in that _____ haunt of bells and _____ waters, the mission on which she was bound seemed to lose reality.

> **Notes to Instructor:** The original passage is found below. The required elements are labelled for your reference.
>
> When the student has finished, show her the original.
>
> If she gets frustrated, show her one or more lines of the original and encourage her to use a thesaurus. Also encourage her to have fun; this is a challenging exercise but it should also be a chance for her to exercise her creativity!

                                           possessive

It was a <u>golden</u> afternoon. The road lifted <u>its</u> length before them along the hillside,

present participle

the valley <u>unfolding</u> itself in curve after curve. The road was, to begin with, narrowly

past participle   *two adjectives*   *present participle*

<u>enclosed</u>, with <u>steep green</u> meadows <u>falling</u> sharply to the stream bed on the right, to

                                  present participle

rise again beyond the water in <u>sheer</u> pastures where cattle grazed with slowly <u>tolling</u> bells.

                              compound, hyphenated

The valley twisted toward the south, and before them the <u>great</u> barrier of <u>dim-green</u> peaks

which barred it had, miraculously, parted, and now valley and road were cupped between

compound, hyphenated   *present participle*

<u>pine-clothed</u> slopes <u>roaring</u>, <u>rich</u> in sunlight, toward still more <u>distant</u> crests of blue

                          past participle

that brushed the sky. And these, <u>faint</u> with distance, <u>etched</u> in with snow and shadow

against the <u>long</u> fingers of cloud that clung to them were, unbelievably, but the <u>first</u> ridges

of the <u>greater</u> barriers beyond... She turned off the road into the track—it was little more—

that climbed the <u>smaller</u> valley. She walked steadily, and soon, as she rounded a curve of the

        indefinite

track, she saw, <u>some</u> distance ahead of her, set back against the mountainside to the left,

  two adjectives   *two adjectives*

the <u>high white</u> walls of the convent. A <u>small square</u> tower jutted up to catch the sunlight,

vividly <u>white</u> against a rampart of pines beyond, and, even as Jennifer glimpsed it and

           present participle   *compound, hyphenated*

guessed <u>its</u> nature, she heard, <u>floating</u> out of the <u>thyme-laden</u> wind, the <u>silver</u>

             present participle   *past participle*

sound of a bell. She tilted her head to listen, <u>smiling</u>, her <u>whole</u> being pierced, <u>rinsed</u>

    present participle

through, <u>tingling</u> with a <u>keen</u> delight. But presently the <u>very</u> beauty of that <u>pure</u>

two adjectives

<u>passionless</u> note, insisting beat by beat upon the strangeness of the place, took her with a

<u>new</u> sensation, part pleasure and part fear, and wholly <u>dreamlike</u>. To her, suddenly, in

          present participle

that <u>high</u> haunt of bells and <u>tumbling</u> waters, the mission on which she was bound seemed

to lose reality.

— LESSON 103 —

Misplaced Modifiers
Squinting Modifiers
Dangling Modifiers

Exercise 103A: Correcting Misplaced Modifiers

Circle each misplaced modifier and draw an arrow to the place in the sentence that it should occupy.

We watched our daughter drive away (through the window).

The shopowner chased after the thief (filled with indignation).

The singer was standing in the lobby (with an armful of flowers)

> **Note to Instructor:** The modifier *with an armful of flowers* is most naturally an adverbial phrase modifying *standing* (how was the singer standing?) but could also be an adjective phrase modifying *singer*, in which case the arrow should go to the space between *singer* and *was*.]

We all decided to meet up for a Labor Day picnic (in May)

> **Note to Instructor:** The phrase *in May* refers to the time of the decision, not the time of the picnic, and so can go either immediately before or after the main clause *We all decided*.

(Weeping and afraid) the vast dark kitchen was cold and frightening to the lost child.

I had just gotten up when I caught sight of a wolf (wearing a bathrobe)

> **Note to Instructor:** The phrase *wearing a bathrobe* describes *I* but can either go before the subject or just after the predicate.

The horses were finally corralled by the animal handlers (galloping wildly across the field)

(Burnt to a crisp,) the campers did not enjoy the s'mores as much as they had hoped.

(Piled full of mushrooms) with thyme sauce, I passed the platter to my dinner guests.

The exhausted man threw himself into the hammock (gasping for air)

Exercise 103B: Clarifying Squinting Modifiers

Circle each squinting modifier. On your own paper, rewrite each sentence twice, eliminating the ambiguity by moving the squinting modifier to produce sentences with two different meanings. Insert commas and change capitalization/punctuation as needed. (And be aware—you might be able to eliminate the ambiguity by simply changing punctuation!)

> **Note to Instructor:** Explanatory notes follow where needed; use these at any point that the student is confused.

Sprinting up hills (quickly) builds up your cardiovascular endurance.

> Sprinting quickly up hills builds up your cardiovascular endurance.
> Sprinting up hills builds up your cardiovascular endurance quickly.

Screaming at the top of your lungs (often) upsets other people.

> Often, screaming at the top of your lungs upsets other people.
> **OR**
> Screaming at the top of your lungs upsets other people often.

> **Note to Instructor:** Both of these sentences mean that the upset happens often when (any) screaming occurs.

> Screaming often at the top of your lungs upsets other people.

> **Note to Instructor:** This means that the screaming occurs often, and only then does the upset occur.

She told us that she went for a long jog (after she finished the chocolate cake.)

> After she finished the chocolate cake, she told us that she went for a long jog.
> She told us that, after she finished the chocolate cake, she went for a long jog.

Let's be sure that we celebrate the play's ending (with a big party.)

> Let's be sure that we celebrate, with a big party, the play's ending.
> Let's be sure that we celebrate the play that ends with a big party.

> **Note to Instructor:** Does the ending (which will be celebrated) have a big party in it, or is the big party a celebration of the ending?

Our director said that we seemed too nervous (during the rehearsal.)

> During the rehearsal, our director said that we seemed too nervous.

> **Note to Instructor:** This means that the director made the observation during the rehearsal.

> Our director said that, during the rehearsal, we seemed too nervous.
> **OR**
> Our director said that we seemed, during the rehearsal, too nervous.

> **Note to Instructor:** This means that at some undefined point the director said that the actors were nervous while they were rehearsing.

Actors who get nervous (rarely) turn out be superstars.

> Actors who rarely get nervous turn out to be superstars.

> > **Note to Instructor:** This means that actors who usually don't get nervous turn out to be superstars.

> Rarely, actors who get nervous turn out to be superstars.
> Actors who get nervous turn out rarely to be superstars.
> Actors who get nervous turn out to be superstars rarely.

> > **Note to Instructor:** All three of these sentences mean that actors who do get nervous generally do NOT become superstars.

If you jog (slowly) you will get faster and faster.

> If you jog slowly, [then] you will get faster and faster.

> > **Note to Instructor:** This means that slow jogging leads to speeding up. The insertion of *then* is optional but it helps to clarify the meaning a little more than just the comma.

> If you jog, you will slowly get faster and faster.

> > **Note to Instructor:** This means that jogging (at any speed) eventually, but slowly, leads to speeding up.

I explained to my son (when the lightning struck) he would need to be careful.

> When the lightning struck, I explained to my son [that] he would need to be careful.
> I explained to my son [that] he would need to be careful when the lightning struck.

> > **Note to Instructor:** The insertion of *that* in both rewritten sentences is optional but will help to clarify the meaning of sentences. In the first, the explanation happens when the lightning struck; in the second, the explanation happens before the lightning strikes (in the indeterminate future).

Exercise 103C: Rewriting Dangling Modifiers

On your own paper, rewrite each of these sentences twice, using each of the strategies described in the lesson. You should feel free to change and add verbs and other words, as long as the meaning of the sentence remains the same.

The first is done for you! Notice that the first answer supplies the missing subject that the modifier describes, while the second turns the dangling modifier into a dependent clause.

These have been adapted from *The Disappearing Spoon and Other True Tales of Madness, Love, and the History of the World from the Periodic Table of the Elements*, by Sam Kean.

When you've finished rewriting your sentences, your instructor will show you the originals.

> **Note to Instructor:** Answers may vary; as long as they follow the rules in "How to Fix a Dangling Modifier", you may accept different versions. The first answer in each set provides the missing noun that the dangling modifier should modify; the second turns the dangling modifier into a clause.
>
> > After you have checked the student's versions, show him the original sentences.
> >
> > If the student cannot figure out the answers, show him one of the rewritten sentences, and ask him to rewrite the sentence using the other strategy.

Lying there with the glass stick under my tongue, the thermometer would slip from my mouth when I would answer an imagined question out loud, and shatter on the hardwood floor.

> Lying there with the glass stick under my tongue, I would answer an imagined question out loud, and the thermometer would slip from my mouth and shatter on the hardwood floor.

> As I was lying there with the glass stick under my tongue, I would answer an imagined question out loud, and the thermometer would slip from my mouth and shatter on the hardwood floor.

ORIGINAL SENTENCE

Lying there with the glass stick under my tongue, I would answer an imagined question out loud, and the thermometer would slip from my mouth and shatter on the hardwood floor, the liquid mercury in the bulb scattering like ball bearings.

Lusting for gold, mercury was considered the most potent and poetic substance in the universe by medieval alchemists.

> Lusting for gold, medieval alchemists considered mercury to be the most potent and poetic substance in the universe.

> Medieval alchemists who lusted for gold considered mercury to be the most potent and poetic substance in the universe.

ORIGINAL SENTENCE

Medieval alchemists, despite their lust for gold, considered mercury the most potent and poetic substance in the universe.

First presented with the jumble of the periodic table, mercury was found nowhere.

> First presented with the jumble of the period table, I looked for mercury and found it nowhere.

> When I was first presented with the jumble of the periodic table, mercury was found nowhere.

ORIGINAL SENTENCE

When first presented with the jumble of the periodic table, I scanned for mercury and couldn't find it there.

Force-feeding people a mercury chloride sludge, their teeth and hair fell out from this pet treatment.

> Force-feeding people a mercury chloride sludge until their teeth and hair fell out, the doctor adopted this pet treatment for any disease.

> Because the doctor force-fed people a mercury chloride sludge, their teeth and hair fell out from this pet treatment.

ORIGINAL SENTENCE

The doctor's pet treatment, for any disease, was a mercury chloride sludge that he force-fed people, often until their teeth and hair fell out.

Dredging around in the steamy vats, their hair and wits were gradually lost (like the mad hatter in *Alice in Wonderland*), because hat manufacturers once used a bright orange mercury wash to separate fur from pelts.

> Dredging around in the steam vats, hatters gradually lost their hair and wits (like the mad hatter in Alice in Wonderland), because hat manufacturers once used a bright orange mercury wash to separate fur from pelts.

When hatters dredged around in the steamy vats, they gradually lost their hair and wits (like the mad hatter in Alice in Wonderland), because hat manufacturers once used a bright orange mercury wash to separate fur from pelts.

ORIGINAL SENTENCE

Hat manufacturers once used a bright orange mercury wash to separate fur from pelts, and the common hatters who dredged around in the steamy vats, like the mad one in Alice in Wonderland, gradually lost their hair and wits.

— LESSON 104 —

Degrees of Adjectives
Comparisons Using *More*, *Fewer*, and *Less*

Exercise 104A: Positive, Comparative, and Superlative Adjectives

Use the following chart to review spelling rules for forming degrees of adjectives. Fill in the missing forms. Then, fill in the blank in each sentence with each adjective indicated in brackets (properly spelled!).

The sentences are all drawn from Anne Bronte's classic novel *The Tenant of Wildfell Hall*.

Spelling Rules:

If the adjective ends in *-e* already, add only *-r* or *-st*.

noble	nobler	noblest
pure	purer	purest
fine	finer	finest

If the adjective ends in a short vowel sound and a consonant, double the consonant and add *-er* or *-est*.

red	redder	reddest
thin	thinner	thinnest
flat	flatter	flattest

If the adjective ends in *-y*, change the *y* to *i* and add *-er* or *-est*.

hazy	hazier	haziest
muddy	muddier	muddiest

Her sister, Mary, was several years older , several inches taller , and of a larger , coarser build—a plain, quiet, sensible girl, who had patiently nursed their mother, through her last long, tedious illness, and been the housekeeper, and family drudge, from thence to the present time. [in order, the comparatives of *old*, *tall*, *large*, and *coarse*]

If you persist, I must regard you as my deadliest foe. [the superlative of *deadly*]

None of our gentlemen had the smallest pretensions to a literary taste, except Mr. Hargrave; and he, at present, was quite contented with the newspapers and periodicals of the day. [the superlative of *small*]

Arthur was clad in his ___plainest___ clothes, and wrapped in a coarse woolen shawl. [the superlative of *plain*]

We must defer the enjoyment of your hospitality till the return of ___longer___ days and ___warmer___ nights. [in order, the comparatives of *long* and *warm*]

But I shall say no more against her: I see that she was actuated by the best and ___noblest___ motives in what she has done; and if the act is not a wise one, may heaven protect her from its consequences! [the superlative of *noble*]

It was a ___younger___ , ___slighter___ , ___rosier___ beauty—lovely indeed, but with far less dignity and depth of soul—without that indefinable grace, that keenly spiritual yet gentle charm, that ineffable power to attract and subjugate the heart—my heart at least. [in order, the comparatives of *young*, *slight*, and *rosy*]

Yesterday morning, one of October's ___brightest___ , ___loveliest___ days, Milicent and I were in the garden enjoying a brief half-hour together with our children, while Annabella was lying on the drawing-room sofa, deep in the last new novel. [in order, the superlatives of *bright* and *lovely*]

She was, and I believe still is, one of the ___happiest___ and ___fondest___ wives in England. [in order, the superlatives of *happy* and *fond*]

When she was returned to the silence and solitude of her own home, it would be my ___fittest___ opportunity. [the superlative of *fit*]

If a cold ensued, the ___severer___ the better—it would help to account for the sullen moods and moping melancholy likely to cloud my brow for long enough. [comparative of *severe*]

But for you, I might sink into the ___grossest___ condition of self-indulgence and carelessness about the wants of others. [the superlative of *gross*]

Exercise 104B: Forming Comparisons

Rewrite each set of independent clauses so that they form a comparative sentence making use of *more*, *less*, *fewer*, and/or comparative forms. The first is done for you.

When you are finished, ask your instructor to show you the original sentences, which are taken from the nonfiction book *No Filter: The Inside Story of Instagram*, by Sarah Frier.

The first is done for you.

Note to Instructor: Some of the sentences have been slightly shortened—be sure to show the student both the shortened sentence and the original full-length sentence where provided.

The student's sentences do not need to be identical as long as they incorporate a comparison.

A user went out more times.
They got more virtual prizes.

The more times a user went out, the more virtual prizes they got.

Facebook got bigger.
Facebook had more power to shape global politics.

> But the bigger Facebook got, the more it had the power to shape global politics.

Instagram grew bigger.
Users strived for followers, likes, and comments.

> The bigger Instagram grew, the more its users strived for followers, likes, and comments.

Original sentence: The bigger Instagram grew, the more its users strived for followers, likes, and comments, because the rewards of achieving them—through personal validation, social standing, and even financial reward—were tremendous.

Instagram's network got stronger.
Instagram's network became an alternative to Facebook for restaurant menus.

> The stronger Instagram's network got, the more it would become an alternative to
> Facebook for restaurant menus.

Original sentence: The stronger Instagram's network got, the more it would become an alternative to Facebook for restaurant menus, so a user could search for an ingredient like "tuna" and find all the places that served it.

He made the deal faster.
Systrom was less likely to call someone who would give advice unfavorable to Facebook.

> But the faster he made the deal, the less likely Systrom was to call someone who would
> give advice unfavorable to Facebook.

Original sentence: But the faster he made the deal, the less likely Systrom was to call someone who would give advice unfavorable to Facebook—or a counteroffer.

A network became bigger.
The unintended consequences of its decisions grew bigger.

> The bigger a network became, the bigger the unintended consequences of its decisions.

Original sentence: Facebook had proved that the bigger a network became, the bigger the unintended consequences of its decisions.

More people joined the product.
They produced more content.
There were more slots in the news feed for brands to place ads.

> And the more people who joined the product, and the more content they produced, the
> more slots there would be in the news feed for brands to place ads.

Exercise 104C: Using *Fewer* and *Less*

Complete the sentences by filling in each blank with either *fewer* or *less*.

The original sentences are taken from David Kirkpatrick's nonfiction book *The Facebook Effect: The Inside Story of the Company That Is Connecting the World*.

But he couldn't understand why Zuckerberg thought Facebook, which had far __fewer__ users at that point, was worth several times what he'd paid for MySpace.

If Accel invested it would be very intimately involved, which might mean less freedom.

It and its business partners learn a lot about us, but in general we know far less about it and exactly how the company is using our data.

That was tough enough to deal with in the quaint days of the News Feed controversy, when Facebook had fewer than 10 million users.

Though it had fewer features than Thefacebook, it was experiencing a similar stratospheric uptake—by the end of the month about two-thirds of undergraduates had registered.

Its strategy was to go after less snooty schools that the elite Thefacebook hadn't yet targeted.

They typically had fewer users at each new campus so they could add more schools without putting as much demand on their systems as Thefacebook's hordes did.

At other moments the phrase made even less sense.

Some consumer-oriented companies now put less emphasis on their website and more on their Facebook page.

Exercise 104D: Diagramming

On your own paper, diagram every word of the following sentences from *The Green Fairy Book*, by Andrew Lang.

    The second, third, and fourth sentences all contain challenges (although not related to the comparison elements!). Do your best, and ask your instructor for help if you need it.

> **Note to Instructor:** On sentences 2, 3, and 4, provide all necessary help!

The more he howled the more the others laughed.

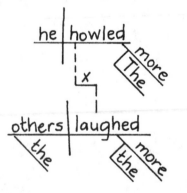

The more he walked towards the light the further away it seemed.

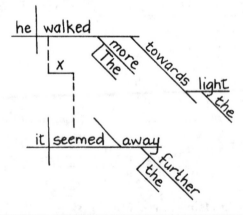

> **Note to Instructor:** The identity of *away* may be difficult for the student. In this sentence, *seemed* is a linking verb, connecting the subject *it* with the adjective *away*. The adverb *further* modifies the predicate adjective *away*.

Her stepmother's heart wasn't in the least touched, and the more the poor girl did, the more she asked her to do.

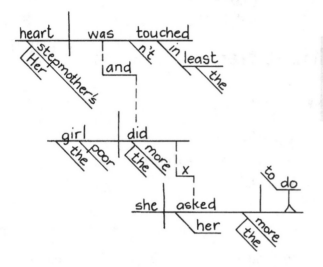

While I do my household tasks you had better stay in bed, since the more one sleeps the less one need eat.

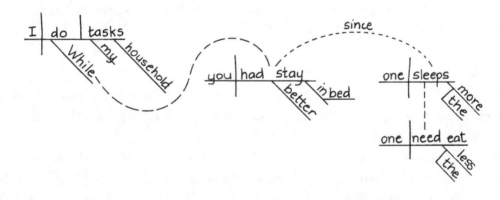

Double Identities

— LESSON 105 —

Clauses with Understood Elements
Than as Conjunction, Preposition, and Adverb
Quasi-Coordinators

Exercise 105A: Comparisons Using *Than*

Each of the following sentences, taken from *The Autobiography of Charles Darwin*, by (who else?) Charles Darwin, contains a comparison clause introduced by *than* and missing some of its words. Using carets, do your best to insert the missing words.

> **Note to Instructor:** The student's phrasing may differ.
> Each comparison clause must have a subject and predicate. Words in brackets fill the clauses out; if the student does not include them, do not mark the answer wrong. However, when the student is finished, ask him to compare his work to the answers below.

was [bad for my mind]

Nothing could have been worse for the development of my mind than Dr. Butler's school^, as it was strictly classical, nothing else being taught, except a little ancient geography and history.

In connection with pleasure from poetry, I may add that in 1822 a vivid delight in scenery was first awakened in my mind, during a riding tour on the borders of Wales, and this has lasted

has lasted

longer than any other aesthetic pleasure^.

left [a picture on my mind]

Nothing has left a more vivid picture on my mind than these evenings at Maer^.

appears [to be hopeless]

On first examining a new district nothing can appear more hopeless than the chaos of rocks^; but by recording the stratification and nature of the rocks and fossils at many points, always reasoning and predicting what will be found elsewhere, light soon begins to dawn on the district, and the structure of the whole becomes more or less intelligible.

I discovered, though unconsciously and insensibly, that the pleasure of observing and reasoning

was [high]

was a much higher one than that of skill and sport^.

I saw

I saw more of Lyell than^of any other man, both before and after my marriage.

A man with a mind more highly organised or better constituted than mine^, **was organized** would not, I suppose, have thus suffered; and if I had to live my life again, I would have made a rule to read some poetry and listen to some music at least once every week; for perhaps the parts of my brain now atrophied would thus have been kept active through use.

> **Note to Instructor:** In the clause *mine [was organized]*, *mine* serves as a possessive pronoun rather than a possessive adjective and acts as the subject of the clause, with *was organized* as the passive verb completing the clause.

Exercise 105B: Identifying Parts of the Sentence

In the following sentences, from *How Star Wars Conquered the Universe: The Past, Present, and Future of a Multibillion Dollar Franchise*, by Chris Taylor, identify each bolded word or phrase as *SC* for subordinating conjunction, *QC* for quasi-coordinator, *PREP* for preposition, *ADJ* for adjective, or *ADV* for adverb.

> **Note to Instructor:** The student only needs to insert the labels below. Additional notes are for your reference; use them to help the student as needed.

SC is intelligent and adept
She is more intelligent and adept **than** Buck^.

SC
No sooner had he sat on the stone **than** he was up with a yell, and running down the trail.

ADV
There are multiple Vaders in every garrison, and naturally no event should have **more than** one Vader.

> **Note to Instructor:** The adverb compound modifier describes the adjective *one*.

ADV
There was, Sean discovered, **more than** enough iron in the Earth's core to construct two million Death Stars.

SC
$16 million was a better outcome **than** anyone around Lucas could imagine, save for Spielberg.

ADV
In 1978, the company sold **more than** forty-two million Star Wars items; the majority, twenty-six million, were action figures.

QC
The Internet had barely become a gathering place for Star Wars fans, **let alone** Stormtrooper costume owners.

QC
Foster had also written the novelization of *Dark Star*—**not to mention** a whopping ten Star Trek novelizations based on that franchise's animated series.

ADJ
Leigh Brackett died **less than** a month later.

SC   was dark
On the other hand, the new film was a darker beast **than** its predecessor^, a fairy tale of the grimmer, Grimm variety.

Something often forgotten today is that many members of the audience were **less than** okay with such openended endings.
ADV

Once again, the comedic target was something **other than** Star Wars.
PREP

PREP
Other than that, the Force is largely a mystery.

This time it was a freak avalanche **rather than** a freak desert storm.
QC

QC
Lucas added a wisecracking, two-headed announcer to the pod race, **rather than** have Jabba the Hutt himself introduce the racers.

Exercise 105C: Diagramming

On your own paper, diagram every word of the following sentences, taken from the original *Star Wars Trilogy* novels by George Lucas.

But there was nothing to see other than the darkening expanses of snow and ice.

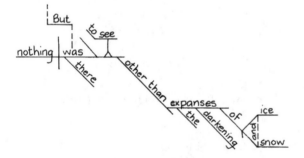

Once forward, he fell rather than sat in the pilot's seat and immediately began checking readouts and gauges.

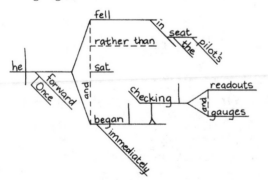

Note to Instructor: The subject *he* is followed by three predicates: *fell, sat,* and *began*. The first two are linked with the quasi-coordinator, the third by *and*. The adverb *forward* (modified by *once*) modifies all three predicates (all three actions happened once he was forward).

It's the ship that made the Kessel run in less than twelve standard timeparts!

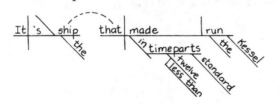

The sleekly elongated ship was larger and even more ominous than the five wedge-shaped Imperial Star Destroyers guarding it.

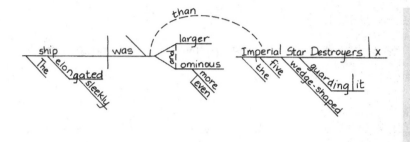

Note to Instructor: The student may extend the dotted line with *than* from *ominous* rather than from the predicate line before the compound branch (as above). Do not mark this as incorrect, but point out that that ship was both larger AND more ominous than the Imperial Star Destroyers, so the comparison applies to both predicate adjectives.

— LESSON 106 —

The Word *As*

Quasi-Coordinators

Exercise 106A: Identifying Parts of the Sentence

In the following sentences, find and underline every adverb, preposition, conjunction, and quasi-coordinator. Then label each as *ADV* for adverb, *PREP* for preposition, *CC* for coordinating conjunction, *SC* for subordinating conjunction, and *QC* for quasi-coordinator. Remember that a quasi-coordinator can be a short phrase as well as a single word.

These sentences are taken from the classic science fiction novel *The First Men in the Moon*, by H. G. Wells.

Note to Instructor: Where a subordinating conjunction introduces a subordinate clause with understood elements, those elements have been inserted below. The student does not need to insert those elements—they are included for your reference.

He had his watch <u>out</u> <u>as</u> I came <u>up</u> <u>to</u> him.
            ADV SC   ADV PREP

Nothing clears <u>up</u> one's ideas <u>so</u> <u>much</u> <u>as</u> explaining them.^ clears them up
          ADV   ADV ADV SC

The great point, <u>as</u> I insisted, was to get the thing done.
             SC

He looked <u>as</u> damaged and pitiful <u>as</u> any living creature I have <u>ever</u> seen.^ looked damaged and pitiful
      ADV   SC   ADV

The sky outside was <u>as</u> black <u>as</u> the darkness <u>within</u> the sphere,^ <u>but</u> the shape <u>of</u> the open window was black
           ADV   SC   PREP   CC   PREP
was marked <u>by</u> an infinite number <u>of</u> stars.
       PREP   PREP

I was half-inclined to go <u>back</u> <u>into</u> the moon <u>without</u> him, <u>rather than</u> seek him <u>until</u> it was
                  ADV PREP   PREP   QC   SC
<u>too</u> late.
ADV

PREP   SC   ADV   CC
For a time, whether it was long or short I do not know, there was nothing but blank darkness.

                                                     ADV   PREP   PREP
Men have watched this planet systematically with telescopes for over two hundred years.

ADV   PREP   CC   PREP   CC
Instantly my coat tails were over my head, and I was progressing in great leaps and bounds, and

PREP   PREP
against my will, towards him.

ADV   PREP   PREP   CC   PREP   CC PREP   CC
Then I hauled the blanket from beneath my feet and got it about me and over my head and eyes.

                       ADV CC   PREP   PREP   PREP   PREP
He turned me about and pointed to the brow of the eastward cliff, looming above the haze about

       ADV   SC   PREP   was light
us, scarce lighter than the darkness of the sky.^

                 ADV ADV   SC
I twisted my head round as well as my bonds would permit.

Exercise 106B: Diagramming

On your own paper, diagram every word of the following sentences, very slightly adapted from *A History of Chemistry*, written by Bernadette Bensaude-Vincent and Isabelle Stengers, translated by Deborah van Dam.

Ask for help if you need it!

Note to Instructor: Provide all necessary help.

As early as the beginning of the eighteenth century, Olivier de Serres had pointed out the presence of sugar in beets.

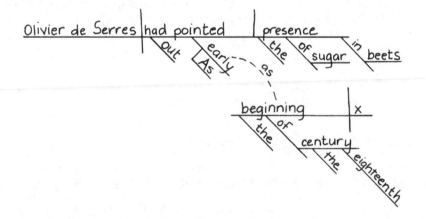

Note to Instructor: The comparative clause *as the beginning of the eighteenth century [was]* contains an understood predicate and modifies the adverb *early*.

In Alexandria, crossroads of culture and commerce, "chemistry" as a body of knowledge and experience devoted to retrieving a legacy, to deciphering, reconstructing, and transmitting a lost science, was born.

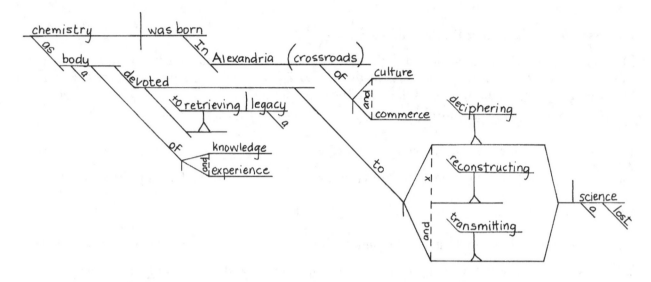

Note to Instructor: The past participle *devoted*, which modifies *body*, is modified by two prepositional phrases. Both occurrences of the preposition *to* have present participles as the objects of the prepositions. The second *to* has three objects (*deciphering, reconstructing, transmitting*), all of which have the same object: *science*.

An apparently more modest path was to use the method of the "table makers," as they were called, not as a condensed and convenient way to present chemical knowledge, but as an end in itself.

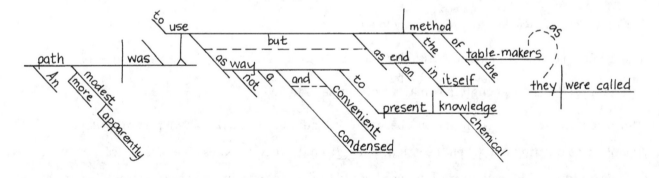

Note to Instructor: In the diagram, *apparently* modifies *modest*, but it could also be diagrammed as modifying *more* (it is both *apparently more modest* and *more apparently modest*). The two prepositional phrases *as a way* and *as an end* are both adverbial and modify the infinitive *to use* (which itself serves as the predicate nominative renaming *path*). The subordinate clause *as they were called* modifies the noun *table-makers*.

— LESSON 107 —

Words That Can Be Multiple Parts of Speech

Exercise 107A: Identifying Parts of Speech

Identify the part of speech of each underlined word by writing the correct abbreviation above it: *N* (noun), *PRO* (pronoun), *V* (verb), *ADJ* (adjective), *ADV* (adverb), *PREP* (preposition), *CC* (coordinating conjunction), or *SC* (subordinating conjunction).

These sentences are taken from the novel *Hard Times*, by Charles Dickens.

He had virtually retired from the wholesale hardware trade <u>before</u>[SC] he built Stone Lodge, and was <u>now</u>[ADV] looking <u>about</u>[ADV] <u>for</u>[PREP] a suitable opportunity of making an arithmetical figure in Parliament.

Not that a ditch was new <u>to</u>[PREP] me, <u>for</u>[CC] I was born <u>in</u>[PREP] a ditch.

<u>As</u>[SC] she straightened her own figure, and held <u>up</u>[ADV] her head in adapting her action <u>to</u>[PREP] her words, the idea crossed Stephen <u>that</u>[SC] he had seen this old woman <u>before</u>[ADV], and had not <u>quite</u>[ADV] liked her.

When Tom appeared <u>before</u>[PREP] dinner, <u>though</u>[SC] his mind seemed heavy <u>enough</u>[ADV], his body was <u>on</u>[PREP] the alert; and he appeared <u>before</u>[SC] Mr. Bounderby came <u>in</u>[ADV].

I have been uneasy <u>for</u>[PREP] the consequences of his being <u>so</u>[ADV] involved, <u>but</u>[CC] I have kept these secrets <u>until</u>[PREP] <u>now</u>[N], <u>when</u>[SC] I trust them <u>to</u>[PREP] your honour.

<u>Now</u>[ADV] that I have asked you <u>so</u>[ADV] much, tell me the <u>end</u>[N].

O Tom, Tom, do we <u>end</u>[V] <u>so</u>[ADV], <u>after</u>[PREP] all my love!

I beg your pardon, sir, <u>for</u>[PREP] being troublesome—but—have you had any letter <u>yet</u>[ADV] <u>about</u>[PREP] me?

<u>As</u>[ADV] soon <u>as</u>[SC] I was big <u>enough</u>[ADV] to run <u>away</u>[ADV], of course I ran <u>away</u>[ADV].

She sat at the window, <u>when</u>[SC] the sun began to sink <u>behind</u>[PREP] the smoke; she sat there, <u>when</u>[SC] the smoke was burning red, <u>when</u>[SC] the colour faded <u>from</u>[PREP] it, <u>when</u>[SC] darkness seemed to rise slowly <u>out</u>[ADV] of the ground, and creep <u>upward</u>[ADV], upward, up to the house-tops, <u>up</u>[PREP] the church steeple, <u>up</u>[PREP] <u>to</u>[PREP] the summits of the factory chimneys, up to the sky.

She was <u>so</u>[ADV] constrained, and yet <u>so</u>[ADV] careless; <u>so</u>[ADV] reserved, and <u>yet</u>[ADV] <u>so</u>[ADV] watchful; so cold and proud, and <u>yet</u>[ADV] <u>so</u>[ADV] sensitively ashamed of her husband's braggart humility.

<u>As</u>[ADV] Stephen had <u>but</u>[ADV] a <u>little</u>[ADJ] <u>while</u>[N] <u>ago</u>[ADJ] instinctively addressed himself to her, <u>so</u>[CC] she <u>now</u>[ADV] instinctively addressed herself to Rachael.

> **Note to Instructor:** In this sentence, *while* functions as a noun representing a certain space of time; *little* and *ago* both modify the noun *while*; and *but* functions as an adverb modifying the adjective *little*.

ADJ   CC   ADV   PREP
All her wildness and passion had subsided; but, though softened, she was not in tears.

             CC   PREP
He went his way, but she stood on the same spot, rubbing the cheek he had kissed with her

           SC
handkerchief, until it was burning red.

ADV ADV   ADV ADV   PREP N   ADV ADV
The more I spoke to him, the more he hid his face; and at first he shook all over.

         ADV SC   ADV ADJ
He darted on until he was very near this figure.

Exercise 107B: Diagramming

On your own paper, diagram every word of the following sentences from *Hard Times*.
   If you need help, ask your instructor!

He wanted nothing but his whip.

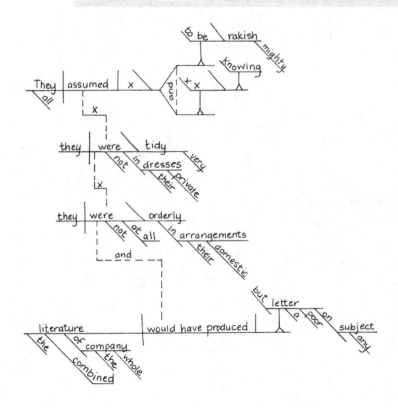

Note to Instructor: In this sentence, *but* is a preposition with the object *whip*, and the prepositional phrase modifies the noun *nothing*.

They all assumed to be mighty rakish and knowing, they were not very tidy in their private dresses, they were not at all orderly in their domestic arrangements, and the combined literature of the whole company would have produced but a poor letter on any subject.

Note to Student: The first independent clause of the sentence contains two understood elements. If you cannot find them, ask your instructor for help! (This is a difficult clause.)

Note to Instructor: The first independent clause contains an understood direct object, with the infinitive phrases to be *mighty rakish and [to be] knowing* serving as objective complements (*They all assumed [themselves] to be mighty rakish and [to be] knowing*). The student will probably first attempt to diagram the infinitive phrases as direct objects of *assumed*, but point out that *assumed to be rakish* doesn't make sense: there's a missing object (the reflexive pronoun) that *to be rakish* modifies.

In the third independent clause, *at* is a preposition with the object *all* (functioning as a noun).

In the final independent clause, *but* again functions as a preposition, but this time the prepositional phrase *but a poor letter* serves as the direct object of the verb *would have produced*.

I have explained to Miss Louisa—this is Miss Louisa—the miserable but natural end of your late career; and you are to expressly understand that the whole of that subject is past, and is not to be referred to any more.

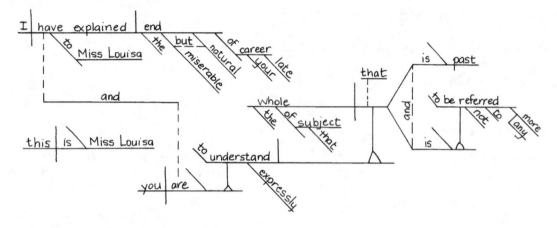

> **Note to Instructor:** The clause *this is Miss Louisa* is an absolute construction. The infinitive *to understand* acts as a predicate adjective describing *you* and following the linking verb *are*. The clause *that the whole...any more* acts as the object of the infinitive *to understand*. Within that clause, *past* and the infinitive phrase *to be referred...* both act as predicate adjectives describing *whole*.

That could hardly be, she knew, until an hour past midnight; but in the country silence, which did anything but calm the trouble of her thoughts, time lagged wearily.

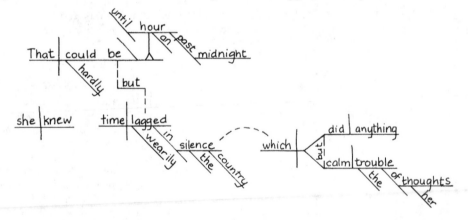

> **Note to Instructor:** The clause *she knew* is an absolute construction.
>
> In the first clause, the prepositional phrase *until an hour past midnight* acts as a predicate adjective describing *That*.
>
> In the dependent clause *which did... thoughts, but* acts as a coordinating conjunction linking the compound verbs *did* and *calm*, both of which are followed by direct objects. This is an unusual construction—if the student chooses another solution, do not mark it wrong, but ask her to compare her diagram with the diagram above.

— LESSON 108 —

Nouns Acting as Other Parts of Speech
Adverbial Noun Phrases

Exercise 108A: Nouns

These sentences are taken from the memoir *Bird by Bird: Some Instructions on Writing and Life*, by Anne Lamott. Identify the part of the sentence that each noun plays by labelling it as *S* for subject, *PN* for predicate nominative, *APP* for appositive, *DO* for direct object, or *OP* for object of the preposition.

               OP   OP
It doesn't come from <u>outside</u> or <u>above</u>.

 S   OP   S   OP
<u>Books</u> were revered in our <u>house</u>, and great <u>writers</u> admired above <u>everyone</u> else.

                 DO   OP
Keep moving; let them spend some <u>time</u> together, let them jam for a <u>while</u>.

          DO   OP   DO   OP   OP
I always show my <u>work</u> to one or two <u>people</u> before sending a <u>copy</u> to my <u>editor</u> or <u>agent</u>.

   PN   PN
It is <u>work</u> and <u>play</u> together.

         DO   OP   OP   APP   OP
We found my <u>parents</u> rejoicing over the <u>arrival</u> of my dad's new <u>novel</u>, the first <u>copy</u> off the <u>press</u>.

                OP   S   OP
Every so often at a writing <u>conference</u>, <u>people</u> get taken aside by wonderful <u>writers</u> who love their
DO   OP
<u>story</u> and who help them in some pivotal <u>way</u>.

     S   PN   PN
A moral <u>position</u> is not a <u>slogan</u>, or wishful <u>thinking</u>.

Exercise 108B: Nouns as Other Parts of Speech

Each of the following sets of sentences is missing one of the nouns from the exercise above—but the noun is also functioning as a part of speech!

    Your task: figure out which noun can fill every blank.

    When you are done, label the part of speech of each word in the blanks (*N* for noun, *ADJ* for adjective, *ADV* for adverb, *PREP* for preposition, *V* for verb, *SC* for subordinating conjunction). The first is partially done for you.

    The sentences are taken from Anne Lamott's memoir *Traveling Mercies: Some Thoughts on Faith*.

COPY
  V
<u>Copy</u>   it down and tape it to the refrigerator.

    One day not long after, she sidled up to me at school and asked me if I had an extra
N
<u>copy</u>   of the book I wrote about being a mother.

__outside__

    After breakfast, he went off to swim with a friend, and I went __outside__ [ADV] to look at the mountain peak in daylight.

    I just remembered that sometimes you start with the __outside__ [N] and you get it right.

    __Outside__ [PREP] the windows were trees and roses, the eastern shores of San Francisco Bay, blue waters, blue sky: birds, life, motion, stillness.

__above__

    He pointed to where a hawk hung just __above__ [PREP] the wall of cliffs which runs the length of the beach.

    From up __above__ [N] it looked fertile and abandoned, surrounded by nondescript suburban houses and anonymous buildings.

    Mt. Tamalpais loomed __above__ [ADV], and we hiked her windy trails many weekends.

__while__

    I sat in the movie theater and cried for a __while__ [N].

    It became clear that Sam would need me to hold onto him __while__ [SC] we were in the water.

    I suddenly remembered the cave where the prophet Elijah hung out __while__ [ADV] waiting to be either killed by Ahab or saved by God.

__work__

    My father believes in hard __work__ [N]

    We lurched and crashed along until finally we nosed right into the greasy __work__ [ADJ] deck of the tire shop.

    I lay on my bed pretending to read but watching him __work__ [V]: he is a very slow writer, looking like a thoughtful old person with arthritis and bad vision.

__way__

    It made me feel helpless in the best possible __way__ [N].

    The laughter rose from __way__ [ADJ] below, from below my feet.

    Let me put it this __way__ [ADV], Annie.

Exercise 108C: Identifying Parts of Speech

Identify the part of speech of each underlined word by writing the correct abbreviation above it:
N (noun), *ADV-N* (adverbial noun), *PRO* (pronoun), *V* (verb), *ADJ* (adjective), *ADV* (adverb), *PREP*
(preposition), *CC* (coordinating conjunction), *CorrC* (correlative conjunction), *SC* (subordinating
conjunction), or *QC* (quasi-coordinator). Not all labels may be used!

These sentences are taken from *Writing Down the Bones*, by Natalie Goldberg.

The new roller pens that are <u>out</u> <u>now</u> are fast too, but there's a slight loss of control.
(ADJ ADV)

> **Note to Instructor:** In this sentence, *out* follows a linking verb and so functions as a predicate
> adjective describing *pens* (which pens? the *out* pens).

<u>Sometimes</u>, instead of writing in a notebook, you might want to directly type <u>out</u> your thoughts.
(ADV ... ADV)

<u>Out</u> of this fertile soil <u>bloom</u> our poems and stories.
(PREP ... V)

> **Note to Instructor:** The preposition *Out* has as its object the second prepositional phrase *of*
> *this fertile soil*. All together, the prepositional phrase *Out of this fertile soil* is adverbial and modifies
> *bloom* (answering the question *where?*).

Don't hold too <u>tight</u>; allow it to come <u>out</u> <u>how</u> it needs to <u>rather than</u> trying to control it.
(ADV ... ADV ADV ... QC)

> **Note to Instructor:** This is a colloquial use of the adjective form *tight* rather than the adverbial
> form *tightly*, but the word still modifies the verb *hold*.
>
> The adverb *how* modifies *needs* and also works to subordinate the adverbial clause *how it needs*
> *to come out*, which modifies *allow* and answers the question *how*.

I've bought <u>hundreds</u> <u>over</u> the <u>years</u>.
(N PREP N)

They know <u>what</u> <u>well</u> the water they <u>drink</u> comes <u>from</u>, <u>that</u> their cat who ran away two <u>years</u> ago
will not return.
(ADJ N ... V ... PREP SC ... ADV-N)

> **Note to Instructor:** If the student marks *from* as an adverb, point out that there is an inversion
> in this noun clause: *They know [the water they drink comes from what well]*. The noun *well* is the object
> of the preposition *from*.

<u>Read</u> a <u>lot</u>, listen <u>well</u> and <u>deeply</u>, and <u>write</u> a <u>lot</u>.
(V N ... ADV ADV ... V N)

I try to fill a notebook a <u>month</u>.
(ADV-N)

<u>Within</u> a <u>month</u> <u>one</u> of the stories was accepted by a very <u>fine</u> magazine.
(PREP N PRO ... ADJ)

<u>That</u> <u>day</u> in the studio my conscious mind was frustrated and had no idea <u>that</u> I had written
(ADJ N ... SC)
<u>anything</u> <u>good</u>, but <u>below</u> my discursive, critical thoughts <u>that</u> buzz <u>around</u> <u>like</u> a swarm of
(PRO ADJ PREP ... PRO ADV PREP)
mosquitoes, my hand was busy recording <u>first</u> thoughts and writing a very <u>present</u> piece.
(ADJ ... ADJ)

SC   ADV ADV   ADJ

If you begin <u>too</u> <u>exactly</u>, you will stay <u>precise</u> but never hit the exact mark that makes the words

           PREP   N   N   N

vibrate with the truth that goes <u>through</u> the <u>present</u>, <u>past</u>, and <u>future</u>.

> **Note to Instructor:** In this sentence, the verb *stay* functions as a linking verb, with *precise* as the predicate adjective describing the subject *you*.

      ADV   V   ADJ   ADJ N

You can sit <u>down</u> and <u>time</u> yourself and add to the original work that <u>second</u>, third, or <u>fourth</u> <u>time</u>

you wrote on something.

        SC   SC V   ADJ   N

People will react <u>however</u> they want; and <u>if</u> you <u>write</u> poetry, get used to <u>no</u> reaction at <u>all</u>.

                   SC

If you find yourself checking the clock too much <u>as</u> you write, say to yourself you are going to

     SC ADJ CC ADJ   ADJ   SC

keep writing <u>until</u> <u>three</u> (<u>or</u> <u>four</u> or five) pages, <u>both</u> sides, are filled or <u>until</u> the cake is baked.

ADJ ADJ N PREP   ADJ

<u>All</u> <u>that</u> <u>heat</u> goes <u>into</u> the making of <u>that</u> cake.

             PRO   ADJ

A writer must say yes to life, to <u>all</u> of life: the <u>water</u> glasses, the Kemp's half-and-half, the ketchup

on the counter.

                             N

If the class is too large and it will take up too much <u>time</u>, we alternate the people who will read

PREP   N CC   V ADV ADJ N

<u>after</u> each <u>round</u>, <u>so</u> you might <u>read</u> <u>every</u> <u>other</u> <u>time</u> instead of every time.

                          ADV PREP

The piece I read I later typed up and entitled "Slow Seeing the World Go <u>Round</u>," <u>about</u> my

          N   PREP

grandmother drinking <u>water</u>, raising children, and leaving the world <u>without</u> socks, salamis,

 N

or <u>salt</u>.

Exercise 108D: Adverbial Noun Phrases

Fourteen of the following sentences, from Stephen King's *On Writing*, contain adverbial nouns or adverbial noun phrases (possibly more than one!). The rest do not.

 Circle each adverbial noun or noun phrase, and draw an arrow from the circle to the word modified. The first is done for you.

She gave birth to Joe (less than three hours later)

Most of the nine months I should have spent in the first grade I spent in bed.

> **Note to Instructor:** The noun *months* is the object of the preposition *of*.

The money the sisters sent her (each month) covered the groceries but little else.

(That year) my brother David jumped ahead to the fourth grade and I was pulled out of school entirely.

I would be paid sixty-four hundred dollars (a year,) which seemed an unthinkable sum after earning a dollar-sixty (an hour) at the laundry.

We talked for another half an hour, but I don't remember a single word of what we said.

> **Note to Instructor:** The compound noun *half an hour* is the object of the preposition *for.*

There was no sense of exhilaration, no buzz—(not that day)—but there was a sense of accomplishment that was almost as good.

It occurs to me, in a muddled sort of way, that (an hour before) I was taking a walk and planning to pick some berries in a field that overlooks Lake Kezar.

At one moment I had none of this; at the next I had all of it.

> **Note to Instructor:** The noun *moment* is the object of the preposition *At.*

I drove (home) had a brief nap, and then set out on my usual walk.

If I don't write (every day) the characters begin to stale off in my mind—they begin to seem like characters instead of real people.

I was only passing the time on a late spring afternoon, but (two months later) *Cavalier* magazine bought the story for two hundred dollars.

> **Note to Instructor:** The noun *afternoon* is the object of the preposition *on.*

According to the story, a friend came to visit him (one day) and found the great man sprawled across his writing desk in a posture of utter despair.

> **Note to Instructor:** The adverbial noun phrase *one day* could also be taken to modify the verb *came.*

I'd usually find that treasured tee-shirt or my favorite Nikes deep under the bed (months later) looking sad and abandoned among the dust kitties.

I should have stayed (home) I think; going for a walk (today) was a really bad idea.

(Ten years or so later,) after I'd sold a couple of novels, I discovered "The Night of the Tiger" in a box of old manuscripts and thought it was still a perfectly respectable tale, albeit one obviously written by a guy who had only begun to learn his chops.

My wife has put up with a lot from me over the years, but her sense of humor stretches only so far.

> **Note to Instructor:** The noun *years* is the object of the preposition *over*.

He looks at himself (a moment longer) in the mirror, lips pink and eyes bleak, then slowly returns to the table.

Exercise 108E: Diagramming

On your own paper, diagram every word of the following sentences, slightly adapted from Exercise 108D.

The money the sisters sent her each month covered the groceries but little else.

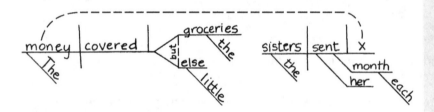

> **Note to Instructor:** The pronoun *else* is the second direct object of the verb *covered*. The noun clause *[that] the sisters sent her each month* modifies *money* and contains an understood relative pronoun: *the sisters sent her [money] each month*.

There was no sense of exhilaration, no buzz—not that day—but there was a sense of accomplishment that was almost as good.

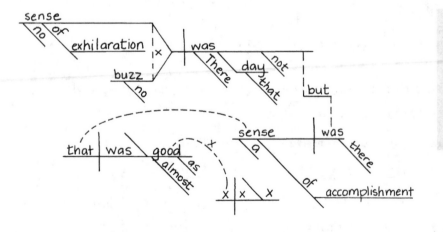

> **Note to Instructor:** The comparative clause that ends the sentence contains a final clause made up of understood elements: *a sense of accomplishment that was almost as good [as the sense was good]*. You may need to point the student back to Lesson 106 to review.

I should have stayed home, I think; going for a walk today was a really bad idea.

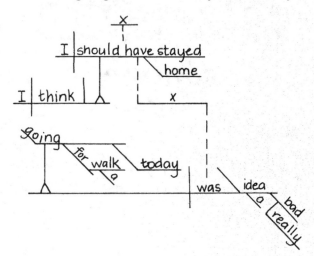

Ten years later, after I'd sold a couple of novels, I discovered "The Night of the Tiger" in a box of old manuscripts and thought it was still a perfectly respectable tale, albeit one obviously written by a guy who had only begun to learn his chops.

> **Note to Student:** The word *albeit* is a conjunction (but not a commonly used one!).

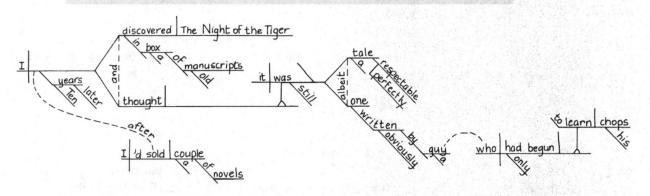

> **Note to Instructor:** The adverbial noun phrase *Ten years later* and the adverbial clause *after I'd sold a couple of novels* modify both verbs (*discovered* and *thought*). The infinitive *to learn* is the object of the verb *had begun*.

— REVIEW 9 —
Weeks 25-27

Topics
Progressive Perfect Indicative Tenses
Progressive Present and Progressive Perfect Present Modal Verbs
Conditional Sentences
Adjectives in the Appositive Position
Correct Comma Usage
Limiting Adjectives
Misplaced, Squinting, and Dangling Modifier Comparisons
Using *More*, *Fewer*, and *Less* Quasi-Coordinators
Words That Can Be Multiple Parts of Speech
Nouns Acting as Other Parts of Speech
Adverbial Nouns

Review 9A: Definition Fill-in-the-Blank

In the last three weeks, you learned (and reviewed) even more definitions than in Weeks 22, 23, and 24! Fill in the blanks in the definitions below with one of the terms from the list. Many of the terms will be used more than once.

abstract noun	active	adjective
adjectives	adverb	adverbial noun
adverbs	apostrophe	appositive
attributive	cardinal numbers	clause
comma	commas	comparative
compound modifiers	compound preposition	coordinating conjunction
dangling modifier	demonstrative adjectives	demonstrative pronouns
descriptive adjective	fewer	first conditional
future	imperative	indefinite adjectives
indefinite pronouns	indicative	interrogative adjectives
interrogative pronouns	less	misplaced modifier
modal	noun	ordinal numbers
passive	past	past participle
perfect	perfect past	perfect present
plural	positive	possessive adjective
predicative	present	progressive
progressive perfect	progressive present	quasi-coordinators
second conditional	simple	simple present
singular	squinting modifier	state-of-being
subjunctive	subordinating conjunction	superlative
third conditional		

338

Cardinal numbers represent quantities (one, two, three, four . . .).

Ordinal numbers represent order (first, second, third, fourth . . .).

Demonstrative pronouns demonstrate or point out something. They take the place of a single word or a group of words.

Demonstrative adjectives modify nouns and answer the question _Which one?_

Indefinite pronouns are pronouns without antecedents.

Indefinite adjectives modify nouns and answer the questions _Which one?_ and _How many?_

A _descriptive adjective_ tells what kind.

A _descriptive adjective_ becomes an _abstract noun_ when you add -_ness_ to it.

A _possessive adjective_ tells whose.

A _noun_ becomes an _adjective_ when it is made possessive.

Form the possessive of a _singular_ noun by adding an _apostrophe_ and the letter _s_.

Form the possessive of a _plural_ noun ending in -_s_ by adding an _apostrophe_ only.

Form the possessive of a _plural_ noun that does not end in -_s_ as if it were a _singular_ noun.

Indicative verbs express real actions.

Subjunctive verbs express situations that are unreal, wished for, or uncertain.

Imperative verbs express intended actions.

Modal verbs express possible actions and situations that have not actually happened.

The present passive imperative is formed by adding the helping verb _be_ to the _past participle_ of the verb.

The present passive subjunctive is formed by pairing _be_ with the _past participle_ of a verb.

Use the simple past subjunctive _state-of-being_ verb, plus an infinitive, to express a future unreal action.

First conditional sentences express circumstances that might actually happen. The predicate of the condition clause is in a _present_ tense. The predicate of the consequence clause is an _imperative_ or is in a _present_ or _future_ tense.

Second conditional sentences express circumstances that are contrary to reality. The predicate of the condition clause is in a _past_ tense. The predicate of the consequence clause is in the _simple_ or _progressive present_ modal tense.

Third conditional sentences express past circumstances that never happened. The predicate of the condition clause is in the _perfect past_ tense. The predicate of the consequence clause is in the _perfect present_ modal or _simple present_ modal tense.

An _adjective_ that comes right before the noun it modifies is in the _attributive_ position.

An __adjective__ that follows the noun it modifies is in the __predicative__ position.

__Appositive__ adjectives directly follow the word they modify.

When three or more nouns, adjectives, verbs, or adverbs appear in a series, they should be separated by __commas__ .

More than and *less than* are __compound modifiers__ .

An __adverbial noun__ tells the time or place of an action, or explains *how long*, *how far*, *how deep*, *how thick*, or *how much*. It can modify a verb, __adjective__ or __adverb__ .

An __adverbial noun__ plus its modifiers is an __adverbial noun__ phrase.

A __misplaced modifier__ is an adjective, adjective phrase, adverb, or adverb phrase in the wrong place.

A __squinting modifier__ can belong either to the sentence element preceding or the element following.

A __dangling modifier__ has no noun or verb to modify.

A __coordinating conjunction__ joins equal words or groups of words together.

A __subordinating conjunction__ joins unequal words or groups of words together.

__Quasi-coordinators__ link compound parts of a sentence that are unequal. __Quasi- coordinators__ include *rather than*, *sooner than*, *let alone*, *as well as*, and *not to mention*.

When three or more items are in a list, a __coordinating conjunction__ before the last term is usual but not necessary.

When three or more items are in a list and a __coordinating conjunction__ is used, a __comma__ should still follow the next-to-last item in the list.

When two or more adjectives are in the __attributive__ position, they are only separated by __commas__ if they are equally important in meaning.

__Interrogative pronouns__ take the place of nouns in questions.

__Interrogative adjectives__ modify nouns.

The __positive__ degree of an adjective describes only one thing.

The __comparative__ degree of an adjective compares two things.

The __superlative__ degree of an adjective compares three or more things.

Most regular adjectives form the __comparative__ by adding *-r* or *-er*.

Most regular adjectives form the __superlative__ by adding *-st* or *-est*.

Many adjectives form their __comparative__ and __superlative__ forms by adding the word *more* or *most* before the adjective instead of using *–er* or *–est*. In __comparative__ and __superlative__ adjective forms, the words *more* and *most* are used as __adverbs__ .

Use ___fewer___ for concrete items and ___less___ for abstractions.

In comparisons using *more . . . fewer* and *more . . . less*, *more* and *less* can act as either ___adverbs___ or ___adjectives___ and *the* can act as an ___adverb___.

In comparisons using two comparative forms, the forms may act as either ___adverbs___ or ___adjectives___, and *the* can act as an ___adverb___.

When *than* is used in a comparison and introduces a ___clause___ with understood elements, it is acting as a ___subordinating conjunction___.

Other than is a ___compound preposition___ that means "besides" or "except."

In a sentence with an ___active___ verb, the subject performs the action.

In a sentence with a ___passive___ verb, the subject receives the action.

A ___simple___ verb simply tells whether an action takes place in the past, present, or future.

A ___progressive___ verb describes an ongoing or continuous action.

A ___perfect___ verb describes an action which has been completed before another action takes place.

A ___progressive perfect___ verb describes an ongoing or continuous action that has a definite end.

Review 9B: Parsing

Above each underlined verb, write the complete tense, the voice (or note *state-of-being*), and the mood. The first verb is done for you.

These sentences are from *Salamandastron: A Tale of Redwall*, by Brian Jacques.

perfect past,   perfect past,
active, indicative active, indicative

Many and many a long season <u>had come</u> and <u>gone</u> since that fateful midwinter day in the

Southwest Lands.

> **Note to Instructor:** The helping verb *had* also helps the verb *gone*: *...a long season had come and [had] gone.*

simple past,   perfect past,
active, indicative   state-of-being, indicative

Above the tideline <u>stood</u> the great citadel of Salamandastron, the mountainous shell that <u>had</u> once

simple past,
state-of-being, indicative

<u>been</u> a volcano when the world <u>was</u> young.

perfect past,
passive, indicative

Through countless ages <u>it had been ruled</u> by the mysterious badger Lords and their friends, the hares of the Long Patrol.

simple present,   simple present,
active, indicative   passive, indicative

I <u>know</u> for a fact that the center of that mountain <u>is packed</u> with gold, silver, jewels, armor,

simple past,
active, subjunctive

swords, encrusted shields and all manner of wonderful weapons. Just think, if you <u>owned</u> a fifth

progressive present,   progressive present,
active, modal   active, modal

part of all that, every creature in the land <u>would be bowing</u> their heads and <u>fighting</u> to kiss

your footpaws.

> **Note to Instructor:** The helping verb *would be* also helps the verb *fighting*: *...would be bowing their heads and [would be] fighting to kiss.*

simple present,
active, modal

Now I think that between five warriors like ourselves we <u>could manage</u> to slip a dagger in his ribs

progressive present,
active, indicative

while we<u>'re congratulating</u> him on a job well done.

perfect present,
passive, modal

It <u>should have been worn</u> by your brother Urthstripe.

perfect past,
passive, indicative

The previous night <u>had been spent</u> swapping life stories with their new friends.

perfect present,
active, modal

You <u>must have chirruped</u> like a cricket too early.

simple past,   perfect past,
active, indicative   active, indicative

Samkim <u>covered</u> his eyes, realizing what <u>had happened</u>.

perfect past,   perfect past,
active, subjunctive   active, modal

If I <u>had known</u> that Ferahgo was in the area of my son's home I <u>would</u> never <u>have gone</u> out into the

woodland that day to gather snowdrops.

perfect present progressive,   perfect present,
active, indicative   active, indicative

Lately I <u>have been saying</u> strange poems and singing songs that I <u>have</u> never even <u>heard</u> before—

most of you have heard me.

> **Note to Instructor:** The helping verbs *have been* also help the verb *singing*: *...have been saying strange poems and [have been] singing songs.*

simple future,   simple future,
active, indicative   state-of-being, indicative

That way the only place it <u>will have</u> left to run <u>will be</u> straight into this pool.

past perfect,
passive, indicative

Salamandastron <u>had been breached</u>—the horde of Ferahgo was within the mountain.

perfect past progressive,
active, indicative

Since dawn King Glagweb <u>had been peering</u> over the edge of the pit, watching Mara intently.

simple present,   simple present,

state-of-being, subjunctive   active, modal

I want this poisoner myself, but if we <u>are</u> to capture him we <u>must act</u> with all speed.

progressive present,

active, subjunctive

If the spirit of Redwall <u>is trying</u> to tell us something, then the least we can do is listen!

perfect present,

active, modal

Hey, Migroo, they <u>might've gone</u> this way.

Review 9C: Provide the Verb

Complete each song line or stanza by providing an appropriate verb in the tense indicated. You may want to use the chart in Lesson 99 for reference.

If there are two blanks for a single verb, the helping verb (or verbs) is divided from the main verb by another part of the sentence.

If you can't think of a verb, ask your instructor for help.

When you are finished, compare your answers to the original lines.

Note to Instructor: The original verbs are inserted below. You may accept any answers that make sense. Show the student the original lines after she completes the exercise.

Note to Student: The following lines are all taken from popular musicals.

present progressive, active, indicative

I ___am___ not ___throwing___ away my shot!

—*Hamilton*

present perfect, active, indicative

___Have___ I actually ___understood___?

—*Wicked*

simple past, passive, indicative

They ___were followed___ by rows and rows of the finest virtuosos, the cream of ev'ry famous band.

—*The Music Man*

simple present,   simple present,

active, indicative   active, modal

I ___wish___ you ___would tell___ me why.

—*Frozen*

perfect present, active, indicative

We ___should___ never ___have taken___ you in in the first place!

—*Les Miserables*

present, active,   present, active,

imperative   imperative

___Climb___ every mountain, ___search___ high and low.

—*The Sound of Music*

simple future, active, indicative
Who ___will buy___ this wonderful morning?
　　—*Oliver*

perfect present, active, indicative
A new day ___has begun___.
　　—*Cats*

perfect past, active, indicative
But the moon ___had disappeared___, and so had Christopher MacGill.
　　—*Brigadoon*

progressive past, active, indicative
Well, I ___was wandering___ along by the banks of the river, when seven fat cows came up out of
the Nile.
　　—*Joseph and the Amazing Technicolor Dreamcoat*

Note to Student: The following lyrics are all from nineteenth century operettas (short, usually comic operas that also include spoken dialogue) by playwright W. S. Gilbert and composer Arthur Sullivan.

May that which now is the far-off horizon
simple future, active, indicative
(But which ___will___ then ___become___ the middle distance),
In fruitful promise be exceeded only
perfect future, active, indicative
By that which ___will have opened___, in the meantime,
Into a new and glorious horizon!
　　—*The Sorcerer*

perfect past, passive, indicative
Unspeak the oaths that never ___had been spoken___,
simple present, passive, modal
And break the vows that never ___should be broken___!
　　—*Utopia Limited*

perfect present, passive, indicative
Well, he ___has been discovered___,
perfect present, active, indicative
and my father ___has brought___ me here to claim his hand.
　　—*The Gondoliers*

simple present, passive, modal
I ___should be___ much ___hurt___ if I thought it was.
　　—*The Gondoliers*

simple present, passive, subjunctive
If from my sister I ___were torn___,
It could be borne—

I should, no doubt, be horrified,

  simple present, active, modal

But I   <u>could bear</u>   it.

    —*The Gondoliers*

              perfect present, passive, modal

Our views   <u>may have been</u>   hastily   <u>formed</u>   on insufficient grounds.

    —*The Gondoliers*

With a pleasure that's emphatic,

We retire to our attic

             perfect present, passive, indicative

With the gratifying feeling that our duty   <u>has been done</u> !

    —*The Gondoliers*

                  simple past, passive, indicative

When you were a prattling babe of six months old you   <u>were married</u>   by proxy to no less a personage than the infant son and heir of His Majesty the immeasurably wealthy King of Barataria!

    —*The Gondoliers*

Review 9D: Identifying Adjectives and Punctuating Items in a Series

In the following poem, "The Cremation of Sam McGee," by Robert Service, carry out the following three steps:

a) Underline once and label all adjectives (except for articles), using the following abbreviations:

Descriptive Adjectives		Limiting Adjectives	
Regular	DA-R	Possessives	LA-P
Present participles	DA-PresP	~~Articles~~	~~LA-A~~
Past participles	DA-PastP	Demonstratives	LA-D
Infinitives	DA-Inf	Indefinites	LA-IND
		Interrogatives	LA-INT
		Numbers	LA-N

b) Circle all adjectives that are in the predicate or in the predicative position and draw an arrow from each back to the noun it modifies.

c) Identify proper adjectives as *DA-R Prop.*

        DA-R   DA-R

There are <u>strange</u> things done in the <u>midnight</u> sun

By the men who moil for gold;

  DA-R PROP   DA-R

The <u>Arctic</u> trails have their <u>secret</u> tales

               LA-P

That would make <u>your</u> blood run cold;

                   DA-R

The Northern Lights have seen <u>queer</u> sights,

DA-R
But the queerest they ever did see

LA-D
Was that night on the marge of Lake Lebarge

I cremated Sam McGee.

> **Note to Instructor:** The adjective *queerest* modifies the understood repetition of the noun *sights*: *The Northern Lights have seen queer sights, but the queerest [sight] they ever did see.*

Now Sam McGee was from Tennessee, where the cotton blooms and blows.

LA-P
Why he left his home in the South to roam round the Pole God only knows.

DA-R
He was always cold, but the land of gold seemed to hold him like a spell;

> **Note to Instructor:** The verb *seemed* here is an active verb, modified by the adverbial infinitive *to hold.*

DA-R
Though he'd often say in his homely way that he'd "sooner live in hell."

LA-P   DA-R PROP
On a Christmas Day we were mushing our way over the Dawson trail.

LA-P   LA-P   LA-PastP
Talk of your cold! through the parka's fold it stabbed like a driven nail.

LA-P
If our eyes we'd close, then the lashes froze, till sometimes we couldn't see;

DA-R   DA-R
It wasn't much fun, but the only one to whimper was Sam McGee.

LA-D DA-R   LA-P
And that very night as we lay packed tight in our robes beneath the snow,

DA-R
And the dogs were fed, and the stars o'erhead were dancing heel and toe,

LA-D
He turned to me, and, "Cap," says he, "I'll cash in this trip, I guess;

LA-P DA-R
And if I do, I'm asking that you won't refuse my last request."

DA-R
Well, he seemed so low that I couldn't say no: then he says with a sort of moan:

DA-PastP
"It's the cursèd cold, and it's got right hold till I'm chilled clean through to the bone.

> **Note to Instructor:** *I'm chilled* is a present passive verb (active, *I chill*; passive, *I am chilled*). If the student labels *chilled* as a DA-PastP adjective, do not mark this wrong, but point out that it is more naturally read as a passive verb.

DA-R   LA-P DA-R   DA-R
Yet 'taint being dead, it's my awful dread of the icy grave that pains:

> **Note to Instructor:** We have labelled *dead* as a predicate adjective, because the clause *'taint being dead* is a poetic condensation of *It ain't being dead*, a dialect version of *It isn't being dead*. If the student does not identify *dead* as an adjective, do not mark her wrong, but show her this explanation.

LA-PDA-R
So I want you to swear that, foul or fair, you'll cremate my last remains."

LA-P DA-R   DA-inf.
A pal's last need is a thing to heed, so I swore I would not fail;

                                                                                      DA-R
And we started on at the streak of dawn, but God! he looked ghastly (pale)

                                                                LA-P
He crouched on the sleigh, and he raved all day of his home in Tennessee;

And before nightfall a corpse was all that was left of Sam McGee.

> **Note to Instructor:** In this sentence, *all* is an indefinite pronoun rather than an indefinite adjective; *was left* is a passive form of the verb *leave*, rather than a linking verb followed by a predicate adjective.

                                       LA-D
There wasn't a breath in that land of death, and I hurried, horror driven,

                     DA-R   DA-PastP
With a corpse (half-hid) that I couldn't get rid because of a promise (given;)

                                                              LA-P
It was lashed to the sleigh, and it seemed to say: "You may tax your brawn and brains,

                                                     LA-D DA-R
But you promised true, and it's up to you to cremate those last remains."

              DA-PastP   DA-PastP   LA-PLA-P DA-R
Now a promise (made) is a debt (unpaid,) and the trail has its own stern code.
              DA-Inf   LA-P   DA-R   LA-P   LA-D
In the days (to come) though my lips were (dumb) in my heart how I cursed that load.
  DA-R DA-R   DA-R
In the long, long night, by the lone firelight, while the huskies, round in a ring,
       LA-P   DA-R
Howled out their woes to the homeless snows—O God! how I loathed the thing!

  DA-R   LA-D DA-R
And every day that quiet clay seemed to heavy and heavier grow;

> **Note to Instructor:** The verb *seemed* here is an active verb, modified by the adverbial infinitive *to grow*.

                                                               DA-R
And on I went, though the dogs were spent and the grub was getting (low)

> **Note to Instructor:** *were spent* is a passive form of the verb *to spend*, not a linking verb with predicate adjective.

            DA-R   DA-R
The trail was (bad) and I felt half (mad) but I swore I would not give in;
                    DA-R
And I'd often sing to the hateful thing, and it hearkened with a grin.

Till I came to the marge of Lake Lebarge, and a derelict there lay;

It was jammed in the ice, but I saw in a trice it was called the "Alice May."

                                              LA-P DA-R
And I looked at it, and I thought a bit, and I looked at my frozen chum:

                          DA-R   LA-P
Then, "Here," said I, with a sudden cry, "is my cre-ma-tor-eum."

LA-IND   DA-R   DA-R
Some planks I tore from the cabin floor, and I lit the boiler fire;
LA-IND
Some coal I found that was lying around, and I heaped the fuel higher;

The flames just soared, and the furnace roared—<u>such</u> a blaze you seldom see;

> **Note to Instructor:** The noun *blaze* is the direct object of the verb *see* and is modified by *such* and *a*.

And I burrowed a hole in the <u>glowing</u> coal, and I stuffed in Sam McGee.

Then I made a hike, for I didn't like to hear him sizzle so;

And the heavens scowled, and the huskies howled, and the wind began to blow.

It was <u>icy</u> cold, but the <u>hot</u> sweat rolled down <u>my</u> cheeks, and I don't know why;

And the <u>greasy</u> smoke in an <u>inky</u> cloak went streaking down the sky.

I do not know how long in the snow I wrestled with <u>grisly</u> fear;

But the stars came out and they danced about ere again I ventured near;

I was sick with dread, but I bravely said: "I'll just take a peep inside.

I guess he's cooked, and it's time I looked," ... then the door I opened wide.

And there sat Sam, looking cool and calm, in the heart of the furnace roar;

> **Note to Instructor:** This is an unusual construction—the present participle *looking* acts as an adjective modifying the noun *Sam*, but also functions as a linking verb connecting the adjectives *cool* and *calm* to *Sam*.

And he wore a smile you could see a mile, and he said: "Please close <u>that</u> door.

It's fine in here, but I greatly fear you'll let in the cold and storm—

Since I left Plumtree, down in Tennessee, it's the <u>first</u> time I've been warm."

Review 9E: Correcting Modifiers

The following sentences all have modifier problems!

Rewrite each sentence correctly on your own paper, and be ready to explain the solution out loud to your instructor. You may need to add or delete words or phrases—as long as the sentence makes sense, that's fine. There may be more than one way to fix each sentence.

> **Note to Instructor:** Use the explanations below to prompt the student if necessary. These sentences may also be rewritten/corrected in other ways as long as the central error is corrected.

Bleating noisily, the farm was filled with the sounds of sheep.

Bleating noisily, the sheep filled the farm with sound.

OR

Because the ewes were bleating noisily, the farm was filled with the sounds of sheep.

Explanation: The participle phrase bleating noisily *is modifying the farm. The farm isn't bleating—the sheep are!*

Between cows and sheep, sheep are definitely the most loud animal.

Between cows and sheep, sheep are definitely the louder animal.

> *Explanation: This sentence needs a double correction! When you are comparing only two items (cows and sheep), you should use the comparative form, not the superlative form. The correct comparative form of* loud *is* louder, *not* more loud *(and the correct superlative form would be* loudest *rather than* most loud.

However, ducks win the prize for the annoyingest animal.

However, ducks win the prize for the most annoying animal.

> *Explanation: The correct superlative form of* annoyingest *is* most annoying.

After being fed, the farm is much quieter.

After the animals are fed, the farm is much quieter.

OR

After being fed, the animals on the farm are much quieter.

> *Explanation: The adverbial phrase* After being fed *has no verb to modify! The student can either change it into an adverbial clause that has its own subject and predicate, or can transform it into an adjective phrase by inserting a noun for the phrase to modify (animals).*

That big white duck in the nest that is busy laying an egg is the oldest duck in the pen.

That big white duck that is busy laying an egg in the nest is the oldest duck in the pen.

> *Explanation: The big white duck is laying an egg—not the nest!*

The biggest sheep in the paddock who butts the other sheep is a bully.

The biggest sheep in the paddock is a bully who butts the other sheep.

OR

The biggest sheep who butts the other sheep in the paddock is a bully.

> *Explanation: Technically, the paddock is butting the other sheep! The clause* who butts the other sheep *needs to clearly modify* biggest sheep.

That ram knocked down the fence because he is the powerfullest animal in the pasture.

That ram knocked down the fence because he is the most powerful animal in the pasture.

> *Explanation: The correct superlative form of* powerful *is* most powerful. *We assume that there are more than two animals in the pasture, so the superlative rather than comparative form is appropriate.*

Wandering through the farm, the smell of all the manure was overpowering me!

Wandering through the farm, I was overpowered by the smell of all the manure!

OR

As I wandered through the farm, the smell of all the manure was overpowering!

> *Explanation: The participle phrase* Wandering through the farm *modifies* smell, *which is not wandering through the farm!*

The chickens seemed to require less scoops of grain than the ducks.

The chickens seemed to require fewer scoops of grain than the ducks.

OR

The chickens seemed to require less grain than the ducks.

> *Explanation: The noun* scoops *represents a quantity that can be counted, so it should be modified by* fewer *rather than* less. *The noun* grain *cannot easily be counted, so* less *would be appropriate if the noun* scoops *were removed.*

That horse is the beautifullest of all the horses with the white mane and tail.

That horse with the white mane and tail is the most beautiful of all the horses.

> *Explanation: This sentence requires two corrections! The superlative form of* beautiful *is* most beautiful, *not* beautifullest. *The prepositional phrase* with the white mane and tail *is placed so that it modifies* all, *but should be moved so that it clearly modifies* that horse *(since it is singular and not plural, it cannot modify* all, *which is plural).*

The mare with the chestnut foal in the front paddock asked for treats when I walked by.

In the front paddock, the mare with the chestnut foal asked for treats when I walked by.

> *Explanation: Although this sentence isn't grammatically incorrect, the meaning is unclear. The foal is in the front paddock, but where is the mare?*

To run a successful farm, fields have to be planted on time and properly fertilized.

To run a successful farm, a farmer has to plant fields on time and properly fertilize them.

OR

On a successful farm, fields have to be planted on time.

> *Explanation: The infinitive phrase* To run a successful farm *doesn't have a clear word to modify! Who is running the farm? The student can either provide a noun, or change the infinitive phrase into an adverbial phrase modifying the verb.*

The pigs are pastured the most far away from the farmhouse.

The pigs are pastured the farthest away from the farmhouse.

> *Explanation: The proper form of* far *is* farthest, *not* most far.

> **Additional Note to Instructor:** Technically, the forms *far, farther,* and *farthest* refer to distance in space (as in the sentence above), while the forms *far, further,* and *furthest* refer to non-physical distance (as in "That was the furthest thing from my mind"). However, this is a distinction that seems to be disappearing from English. Point it out to the student, but do not mark the sentence wrong.

The spotted pig with the huge jowls I was afraid of seemed like it might jump out of the pen and attack me.

I was afraid of the spotted pig with the huge jowls because it seemed like it might jump out of the pen and attack me.

OR

The spotted pig I was afraid of had huge jowls, and it seemed like it might jump out of the pen and attack me.

> *Explanation: The speaker is afraid of the pig, not just the pig's jowls! When the clause* I was afraid of *is moved, the final clause beginning* because *needs to be modified as well.*

After walking around the farm, afternoon tea with cream scones satisfied my hunger.

> After walking around the farm, I had afternoon tea with cream scones to satisfy my hunger.
> OR
> After I walked around the farm, afternoon tea with cream scones satisfied my hunger.

> > *Explanation: The phrase* After walking around the farm *sounds as if the afternoon tea is walking around the farm! It should be turned into a clause, or supplied with a better word to modify* (I).

Review 9F: Identifying Adverbs

In the following sentences, taken from *The Shepherd's Life*, by James Rebanks, carry out the following steps:

a) Underline each word, phrase, or clause that is acting as an adverb.

b) Draw a line from the word/phrase/clause to the verb form, adjective, or adverb modified.

c) Above the word or phrase, note whether it is a regular adverb (*ADV*), an adverbial noun or noun phrase (*AN*), a prepositional phrase (*PrepP*), an infinitive phrase (*INF*), a present participle phrase (*PresP*), a past participle phrase (*PastP*), an adverbial clause (*C*), or a relative adverb introducing an adjective clause (*RA*).

Remember: Within a phrase or clause acting as an adverb, there might also be an adverb modifying an adjective or verb form. Underline these adverbs a second time. There might even be a third adverb or adverbial phrase in some phrases and clauses—underline those three times! And keep your eyes open for the one sentence that might need four underlinings—or possibly five.

The earth spins <u>through the vastness of space</u>. The grass comes and goes <u>with the warmth of the sun</u>. *[PrepP, PrepP]*

We farm <u>in a valley called Matterdale</u>, <u>between the first two rounded fells that emerge on your left as you travel west on the main road from Penrith</u>. *[PrepP, PrepP, C, ADV, PrepP]*

There is a stolen moment <u>each early summer</u> <u>when I climb that fell and sit with my sheepdogs and have half an hour to take the world in</u>. *[AN, C, PrepP, INF, ADV]*

The swallows explode <u>outwards</u> <u>from the barn door</u>. They fledged <u>a couple of days ago</u>, and whole families head <u>out</u> <u>to the fields</u>, <u>where they hawk all day over the grass and thistles</u>. Fingers of pink and orange light are <u>now</u> creeping <u>over the fell sides</u>. *[ADV, PrepP, AN, ADV, PrepP, RA, AN, PrepP, ADV, PrepP]*

> **Note to Instructor:** We have marked *out* as a single adverb, and *to the fields* as a prepositional phrase modifying *out*. However, the student could also mark the entire phrase *out to the fields* as an adverbial prepositional phrase, with *out* as the adverb and the prepositional phrase *to the fields* serving as the object of the preposition.

PrepP · PrepP · PrepP · ADV · PrepP

I drive through the village past cars being pushed into drives by folk who've just returned from

PastP · PrepP · PrepP

trying to get to work in the local town, beaten by the snow.

> **Note to Instructor:** There are five levels of adverbial words and phrases here! The prepositional phrase *through the village* modifies *drive*.
>
> The entire prepositional phrase *past cars being pushed into drives by folk who've just returned from trying to get to work in the local town, beaten by the snow* modifies *drive* as well.
>
> Within that prepositional phrase, the additional prepositional phrases *into drives* and *by folk who've just returned from trying to get to work in the local town, beaten by the snow* modify the adjectival past participle *being pushed* (which itself describes *cars*).
>
> Within that second long prepositional phrase, the prepositional phrase *from trying to get to work in the local town* and the past participle *beaten by the snow* both modify the verb *returned*.
>
> Within *from trying to get to work in the local town*, the prepositional phrase *in the local town* modifies *to get*.
>
> Within *beaten by the snow*, the prepositional phrase *by the snow* modifies the past participle *beaten*.

PrepP · PrepP · ADV · INF · PrepP

Two or three of us are sent up the left-hand side of the fell, after Joe, to sweep out the sheep across

PrepP · ADV · AN · INF · AN

the fell to the right, with one of us peeling off to hold them that way every half mile or so.

> **Note to Instructor:** There are two adverbial nouns in the second infinitive phrase. The phrase *that way* is unusual, but it answers the question *where*, and the noun *way* is thus acting as an adverb.

C · ADV

One of the other shepherd's dogs nips my hand as I push the sheep through.

C · AN · PrepP

When the last ones are sorted, the shepherds walk their sheep home for clipping.

ADV · ADV · PrepP · PrepP

Sometimes I am left alone somewhere on the mountain, waiting for the others.

> **Note to Instructor:** *Somewhere* is a preposition, and the prepositional phrase *on the mountain* is the object of the preposition.

Review 9G: Comma Use

The following sentences have lost all of their commas. Insert commas directly into the text (no need to use proofreader's marks) wherever needed.

These sentences were taken from *The Secret Life of Cows*, by Rosamund Young.

Note to Instructor: The original sentences are below; you may accept variations as long as they follow the rules of comma use. Circled commas are optional.

Cows are individuals, as are sheep, pigs, and hens, and, I dare say, all the creatures on the planet, however unnoticed, unstudied, or unsung.

If, when a young calf tries to eat some hay, it is repeatedly pushed away by bigger, stronger cattle, and it then works out that, by squeezing in under its mother's chin, it will be able to eat in peace, that seems to me an example of useful practical intelligence.

At our farm, Kite's Nest, the calves stay with their mothers for as long as they choose.

Cows can be highly intelligent or slow to understand: friendly, considerate, aggressive, docile, inventive, dull, proud, or shy.

Where cattle have adequate living space, freedom from competition for food, licence to roam freely, and, above all, where they can live in family groups in which there is a preponderance of mature animals, immunity to lung and stomach worms can be established.

Calves play games together, copying and learning constantly.

In *The Shepherd's Calendar*, John Clare wrote, "The ass... will eager stoop/to pick the sprouting thistle up."

Farmed birds should be allowed to follow their behavioural instincts, grow at their natural rate, eat safe food, and live dignified lives.

When hens are healthy and happy, their feathers shine, their eyes are bright and alert, and they spend all day being as busy as bees: pecking, grazing, chopping, pulling, running, investigating, digging, playing, and singing contentedly.

It is widely accepted that animals such as cats, dogs, and horses, usually kept in small numbers and given individual attention, are capable of exhibiting symptoms of boredom and unhappiness, that they can pine and grieve and show signs of feeling unwell.

When we have had occasion to treat a farm animal as a pet, because of illness, accident, or bereavement, it has exhibited great intelligence, a huge capacity for affection, and an ability to fit in with an unusual routine.

Review 9H: Conjunctions

In the following sentences, from the short story collection *Tales of Men and Ghosts,* by Edith Wharton, find and circle every conjunction. Label each as coordinating (*C*), compound coordinating (*COMC*), subordinating (*SUB*), compound subordinating (*CSUB*), coordinating correlative (*CC*), subordinating correlative (*SC*), or quasi-coordinator (*QC*).

                          SUB
His attempts at self-destruction were (as) futile as his snatches at fame!

> **Note to Instructor:** The first *as* is an adverb modifying the adjective *futile*. The second *as* subordinates the clause with understood elements *his snatches at fame [were futile]*.

                                            CC   CC
He stood a little way off, looking down at her with a gaze that was (both) hesitating (and) constrained.

> **Note to Instructor:** In this sentence, *that* is a relative pronoun referring back to *gaze*, not a subordinating conjunction.

                       CSUB   C
He had spoken painfully at first, (as if) there were a knot in his throat; (but) each time he repeated the words he found they were easier to say.

  C SUB
(But) (as) he walked away, his fears dispelled, the sense of listlessness returned on him.

SUB   SUB
(As) he did so he noticed (that) the reporter was accompanied by a tall man with grave compassionate eyes.

                                                       QC
I had always wanted to do her some service, to justify myself in my own eyes (rather than) hers;
C
(and) here was a beautiful embodiment of my chance.

                      SUB   COMC
He was as inexpressive (as) he is to-day, (and yet) oddly obtrusive: one of those uncomfortable presences whose silence is an interruption.

                      QC   SUB
It was his face, really, (rather than) his words, that told her, (as) she furtively studied it, the tale of
    C
failure (and) slow discouragement which had so blurred its handsome lines.

                                                                  C   SUB
For a time he was content to let himself go on the tranquil current of this existence; (but) (although) his auditors gave him for the most part an encouraging attention, which, in some, went the length of really brilliant and helpful suggestion, he gradually felt a recurrence of his old doubts.

                SC
At length he discovered (that) on certain days visitors from the outer world were admitted to his
      C   C   C
retreat; (and) he wrote out long (and) logically constructed relations of his crime, (and) furtively slipped them into the hands of these messengers of hope.

Neave *wanted* what he appreciated—wanted it with his touch and his sight⟨as well as⟩ with his imagination.
^{QC}

I thought this shrewd of Archie,⟨as well as⟩ generous;⟨and⟩I saw the wisdom of Dredge's course.
^{QC}   ^C

Of course she laid stress on the fact⟨that⟩his ideas were the object of her contemplation;⟨but⟩he was pleasantly aware, from the lady's tone,⟨that⟩she guessed him to be⟨neither⟩old⟨nor⟩ridiculous.
^{SC}   ^{SC}   ^C ^{CC} ^{CC}

Review 9I: Identifying Independent Elements

The following sentences, taken from the novel *Austenland,* by Shannon Hale, all contain independent elements: absolutes (*ABS*), parenthetical expressions (*PE*), interjections (*INT*), nouns of direct address (*NDA*), appositives (*APP*), and/or noun clauses in apposition (*NCA*).

Locate, underline, and label each one. If an independent element occurs within another independent element, underline it twice.

Jane's mother, <u>Shirley,</u> came to visit and brought along Great-Aunt Carolyn.
^{APP}

"<u>Really,</u> <u>Jane,</u> I don't know how you survive here," said Shirley, picking the brittle leaves from among the sallow green ones.
^{INT}   ^{NDA}

I'm sure your poor aunt wants to relax, but it's like a sauna in here <u>and not a moment of silence</u>— <u>traffic, car alarms, sirens nonstop.</u>
^{ABS}
^{ABS (PE)}

> **Note to Instructor:** The sentence contains two absolutes. The absolute *and not a moment of silence* refers to Jane's apartment *(it)* in meaning, but does not have a grammatical connection. The absolute *traffic, car alarms, sirens nonstop* expands on the lack of silence but grammatically renames neither *moment* nor *silence*. The second absolute could also be categorized as a parenthetical expression.

She took a scolding stance, <u>hand on hip.</u>
^{ABS}

Carolyn smiled, <u>her uncountable cheek wrinkles gathered into a few deeper ones.</u>
^{ABS}

Hours later, when the nameless driver stopped the car and opened her door, Jane found herself in the quaint, green, rolling countryside she recognized from travel brochures, <u>the sky as cloudy as all English October skies ought to be,</u> and the ground, <u>of course,</u> unpleasantly damp.
^{ABS}
^{PE}

Let me assure you that we will still do all in our power to make your visit, <u>such as it is,</u> enjoyable.
^{PE}

Mrs. Wattlesbrook settled down to quiz her on the items of study—<u>how to play the card games whist and speculation,</u> <u>general etiquette,</u> <u>current events of the Regency period,</u> and so on.
^{ABS}
^{ABS}   ^{ABS}

APP
Mrs. Wattlesbrook was reminding Jane of Miss April, the spiteful, tight-bunned, glossy-lipped, stick-cracking ballet teacher of her elementary school years.

Review 9J: Words with Multiple Identities

In the following sentences, taken from the Jane Austen novel *Persuasion*, identify each bolded word as a noun (*N*), verb (*V*). adverb (*ADV*), adjective (*ADJ*), pronoun (*PRO*), preposition (*PREP*), subordinating conjunction (*SC*), or coordinating conjunction (*CC*).

PREP ADJ   N   ADV
He was **at that time** a very young man, **just** engaged in the study of the law; and Elizabeth found
N   N
him extremely agreeable, and every **plan** in his **favour** was confirmed.

V
I am not particularly disposed to **favour** a tenant.

PREP   PREP   N   SC   N   ADJ
Depend **upon** me **for** taking **care that** no tenant has **more** than his **just** rights.

ADJ   V
For you **alone**, I think and **plan**.

ADV   V
It would be going **only** to multiply trouble to the others, and **increase** his own distress; and a
ADV
much better scheme followed and was acted **upon**.

V   ADJ
She ventured to **hope** he did not always read **only** poetry.

ADJ   V   CC
All equality of alliance must **rest** with Elizabeth, **for** Mary had merely connected herself with an
ADJ   ADJ   ADJ
old country family of respectability and large fortune, and had therefore given **all** the honour and
received none.

N
The **country** round Lyme is very fine.

ADV ADV PRO   N
He could plainly see **how old all** the **rest** of his family and acquaintance were growing.

SC   SC ADJ
He would go, **though** I told him **how ill** I was.

PREP   PRO
Like many other great moralists and preachers, she had been eloquent on a point in **which** her
ADV
own conduct would **ill** bear examination.

> **Note to Instructor:** *Which* is a relative pronoun introducing the subordinate clause *in which her own conduct would ill bear examination* and referring back to *point*.

SC   CC   N
Anne felt **that** she had gained nothing **but** an **increase** of curiosity.

V PREP PRO   SC
I am sure neither Henrietta nor I should **care at all** for the play, **if** Miss Anne could not be with us.

> **Note to Instructor:** The prepositional phrase *at all* modifies *care* and acts as an adverb. In this context, *all* is a pronoun which serves as the object of the preposition *at*.

                                                                                    ADJ
Mrs. Musgrove was giving Mrs. Croft the history of her eldest daughter's engagement, and **just** in
ADJ   PRO
that inconvenient tone of voice **which** was perfectly audible while it pretended to be a whisper.

> **Note to Instructor:** The adjective *just* modifies the noun *tone* (*in just that tone*). The relative pronoun *which* introduces the subordinate clause and refers back to *tone*.

SC   ADJ PRO   ADJ PRO
If I could explain to you **all this**, and **all that** a man can bear and do, and glories to do, for the
                   ADJ
sake of **these** treasures of his existence!

> **Note to Instructor:** The pronoun *that* is the object of the compound verb *bear* and *do* and is modified by the adjective *all*.

      ADJ   CC   PRO   ADV
In the **quieter** professions, there is a toil and a labour of the mind, **if** not of the body, **which seldom** leaves a man's looks to the natural effect of time.

Review 9K: Phrases, Clauses, and Absolutes

The following paragraph, from Charles Dickens' novel *Barnaby Rudge*, is made up of one single sentence! This exercise should give you a sense of just how an accomplished writer can string together MANY different sentence elements to create a vivid scene.

First, read the sentence as it was written, in paragraph form. (You might want to read it out loud.)

There he sat, watching his wife as she decorated the room with flowers for the greater honour of Dolly and Joseph Willet, who had gone out walking, and for whom the tea-kettle had been singing gaily on the hob full twenty minutes, chirping as never kettle chirped before; for whom the best service of real undoubted china, patterned with divers round-faced mandarins holding up broad umbrellas, was now displayed in all its glory; to tempt whose appetites a clear, transparent, juicy ham, garnished with cool green lettuce-leaves and fragrant cucumber, reposed upon a shady table, covered with a snow-white cloth; for whose delight, preserves and jams, crisp cakes and other pastry, short to eat, with cunning twists, and cottage loaves, and rolls of bread both white and brown, were all set forth in rich profusion; in whose youth Mrs V. herself had grown quite young, and stood there in a gown of red and white: symmetrical in figure, buxom in bodice, ruddy in cheek and lip, faultless in ankle, laughing in face and mood, in all respects delicious to behold—there sat the locksmith among all and every these delights, the sun that shone upon them all: the centre of the system: the source of light, heat, life, and frank enjoyment in the bright household world.

Then, look at the version of the sentence that follows. Each part of the sentence has been placed on a separate line. For each part, point out the following:

- Identity: Is it a phrase, clause, independent element (*IND*)—or other?

- Type: If it's a phrase, is it prepositional (*PrepP*), present participle (*PresP*), past participle (*PastP*), or infinitive (*INF*)? If it's a clause, is it independent (*IND*) or subordinate (*SUB*)? And if it's *other*, how would you describe it?

- Part of speech: Then, identify whether the part serves as an adjective (*ADJ*), adverb (*ADV*), appositive (*APP*), noun—or something else.

- Finally, in the last blank, if the part modifies, renames, or otherwise relates to another word in the sentence, list that word.

We have completed a few of the blanks below, to show you how it's done.

There are two things to keep in mind! First, a sentence part might contain other elements (for example, a past participle phrase might contain a prepositional phrase), but only identify the main sentence part on each line; don't worry about any other phrases contained within it. See the first completed example below—the clause *There he sat* contains the adverbial present participle phrase *watching his wife*, but there is no need to identify this separately.

Second, a couple of the parts are divided by yet another part! Where that happens, we have placed ellipses to connect the parts together.

Take some time over this. Ask your instructor for help if necessary. And, if you get frustrated, just remember—we could have asked you to diagram this sentence!

Note to Instructor: Offer all help and accept any reasonable answers! This is an exploration into the ways that English grammar can help writers paint a vivid scene.

	Identity	Type	Part of Speech	Related to (if any) (modifies or renames)
There he sat, watching his wife	clause	ind	main	none
as she decorated the room	clause	sub	adv	watching
with flowers	phrase	prep	adv	decorated
for the greater honour of Dolly and Joseph Willet,	phrase	prep	adv	decorated
who had gone out walking,	clause	sub	adj	Dolly and Joseph Willet
and for whom the tea-kettle had been singing gaily on the hob	clause	sub	adj	Dolly and Joseph Willet
full twenty minutes,	phrase	adverbial noun	noun	had been singing
chirping as never kettle chirped before;	phrase	pres part	adv	had been singing

Note to Instructor: The present participle phrase contains within in the subordinate clause *as never kettle chirped before*, which acts as an adverb modifying *chirping*, but there is no need for the student to identify this. The present participle *chirping* governs the phrase and sets its identity.

	Identity	Type	Part of Speech	Related to (if any) (modifies or renames)
for whom the best service of real undoubted china... was now displayed	clause	sub	adj	Dolly and Joseph Willet
patterned with divers round-faced mandarins	phrase	past part	adj	china
holding up broad umbrellas,	phrase	pres part	adj	mandarins
in all its glory;	phrase	prep	adv	was displayed

Note to Instructor: The phrase *in all its glory* may confuse the student since it is separated in this list from the clause it modifies, but point her back to the original paragraph so that she can see that it follows *was displayed*.

to tempt whose appetites	phrase	inf	adv	reposed

Note to Instructor: The adverbial phrase comes long before the verb it modifies!

a clear, transparent, juicy ham... reposed	clause	ind	main	none

Note to Instructor: There are four main clauses in this compound-complex sentence; three are separated by semicolons, and the fourth is set off by a dash.

garnished with cool green lettuce-leaves and fragrant cucumber	phrase	past part	adj	ham
upon a shady table,	phrase	prep	adv	reposed
covered with a snow-white cloth;	phrase	past part	adj	table
for whose delight,	phrase	prep	adv	set forth

Note to Instructor: The adverbial phrase comes long before the verb it modifies!

preserves and jams, crisp cakes and other pastry, short to eat... and cottage loaves, and rolls of bread both white and brown, were all set forth	clause	ind	main	noun

Note to Instructor: This third main clause is also set off by a semicolon and has six subjects paired with the predicate set *forth*.

with cunning twists	phrase	prep	adj	pastry
in rich profusion;	phrase	prep	adv	set forth
in whose youth Mrs V. herself had grown quite young, and stood there	clause	sub	adj	Dolly and Joseph Willet

Note to Instructor: Although the student may find this sentence difficult to follow at first reading, this grammatical analysis should help make the meaning clear: in the presence of the young couple, Mrs. V. herself has begun to feel and act younger. If the student is confused, provide all necessary help.

	Identity	Type	Part of Speech	Related to (if any) (modifies or renames)
in a gown of red and white:	phrase	prep	adv	stood
symmetrical in figure,	phrase	adj	adj	Mrs. V

> **Note to Instructor:** This phrase and the next three are all adjective phrases—adjectives in the predicative position followed by a modifying prepositional phrase, all describing the same subject.

	Identity	Type	Part of Speech	Related to (if any)
buxom in bodice,	phrase	adj	adj	Mrs. V
ruddy in cheek and lip,	phrase	adj	adj	Mrs. V
faultless in ankle,	phrase	adj	adj	Mrs. V
laughing in face and mood,	phrase	pres part	adj	Mrs. V
in all respects delicious to behold—	phrase	prep	adj	Mrs. V
there sat the locksmith	clause	ind	main	noun

> **Note to Instructor:** This final main clause is set off by a dash. You may need to explain to the student that *the locksmith* is the *he* of the very first main clause.

	Identity	Type	Part of Speech	Related to (if any)
among all and every these delights,	phrase	prep	adv	sat
the sun	phrase	other	app	locksmith

> **Note to Instructor:** It is also acceptable for the student to identify *the sun*'s type as *other*—it is simply an appositive, renaming *locksmith* (he is the sun that shone upon them all). There are three appositives renaming *locksmith*: *—sun, centre,* and *source,* —but the other two appositives contain additional modifying elements and so can be more easily identified as phrases.

	Identity	Type	Part of Speech	Related to (if any)
that shone upon them all:	clause	sub	adj	sun
the centre of the system:	phrase	other	app	locksmith
the source of light, heat, life, and frank enjoyment	phrase	other	app	locksmith
in the bright household world.	phrase	prep	adj	source

Still More Verbs

— LESSON 109 —

Hortative Verbs
Subjunctive Verbs

Exercise 109A: Identifying Hortative Verbs

Speechmakers are often exhorting their readers—so they tend to use many hortative verbs! In the following sentences, underline every element of each hortative verb (*let* or *may*, any other helping verbs, and the main verb). Above the underlined verb, identify it as state-of-being (*SB*), active (*A*), or passive (*P*). If the person or thing being exhorted is present in the sentence, circle the noun or pronoun that identifies him/her/it, and identify it as *S* for subject or *O* for object.

Be careful—some sentences may have no hortative verbs at all!

The first is done for you.

Let (tyrants) fear!

—"Speech to the Troops at Tilbury," Elizabeth I

And let (me) warn you that it is dangerous to copy the example of a nation whose crimes, towering up to heaven, were thrown down by the breath of the Almighty, burying that nation in irrevocable ruin!

In the fervent aspirations of William Lloyd Garrison, I say, and let every (heart) join in saying it:
God speed the year of jubilee
The wide world o'er!

If I do forget, if I do not faithfully remember those bleeding children of sorrow this day, "may my right (hand) forget her cunning, and may my (tongue) cleave to the roof of my mouth!"

You may rejoice, I must mourn.

> **Note to Instructor:** The verb *may rejoice* is modal, not hortative.

—"What to the Slave Is the Fourth of July?," Frederick Douglass

Let (him) remember also that the worth of the ideal must be largely determined by the success with which it can in practice be realized.

Let (us) try to level up, but let (us) beware of the evil of leveling down.

Long may (you) carry yourselves proudly as citizens of a nation which bears a leading part in the teaching and uplifting of mankind.

Let (those) who have, keep, let (those) who have not, strive to attain, a high standard of cultivation and scholarship. Yet let (us) remember that these stand second to certain other things.

> **Note to Instructor:** You may need to point out to the student that *who have* and *who have not* are both adjective clauses *modifying those*, and that the hortative verbs are *let keep* and *let strive*, not *let have*.

—"Citizenship in a Republic," Theodore Roosevelt

Before you discuss the resolution, let (me) place before you one or two things.

May (it) be that the reins will be placed in the hands of the Parsis, for instance—as I would love to see happen—or they may be handed to some others whose names are not heard in the Congress today.

> **Note to Instructor:** The verb *may be handed* is a passive modal verb, not hortative.

Let (me) however, hasten to assure that I am the same Gandhi as I was in 1920.

—"Quit India," Mahatma Gandhi

But let the (men) of Hartford imagine that they were not in the position of being voters at all, that they were governed without their consent being obtained, that the legislature turned an absolutely deaf ear to their demands, what would the men of Hartford do then?

—"Freedom or Death," Emmeline Pankhurst

You are hemmed in on all sides; all your plans are clearer than the day to us; let (me) remind you of them.

With malice toward none, with charity for all, with firmness in the right as God gives us to see the right, let (us) strive on to finish the work we are in, to bind up the nation's wounds, to care for him who shall have borne the battle and for his widow and his orphan, to do all which may achieve and cherish a just and lasting peace among ourselves and with all nations.

Both parties deprecated war, but one of them would make war rather than let the nation survive, and the other would accept war rather than let it perish, and the war came.

> **Note to Instructor:** In this sentence, both occurrences of *let* are action verbs in comparative clauses (*one would make rather than [one would] let, other would accept rather than [other would] let*).

— "Second Inaugural Address," Abraham Lincoln

Wherefore, O conscript fathers, let the (worthless) be gone,—let (them) separate themselves from the good,—let (them) collect in one place,—let (them) as I have often said before, be separated from us by a wall; let (them) cease to plot against the consul in his own house,—to surround the tribunal of the city pretor,—to besiege the senate-house with swords,—to prepare brands and torches to burn the city; let (it) in short, be written on the brow of every citizen, what his sentiments are about the republic.

> — "The First Oration Against Catiline," Cicero

Exercise 109B: Rewriting Indicative Verbs as Hortative Verbs

Hortative verbs also appear frequently in song lyrics! In the lines below, the statements and commands in bold type originally contained hortative verbs. On your own paper, rewrite each bolded clause so that the main verbs are hortative. Then, compare your answers with the original.

If you need help, ask your instructor.

Note to Instructor: Each excerpt with bolded clauses is followed by the original, hortative version. Accept any reasonable answers, but ask the student to read both her rewritten sentences and the originals out loud, listening carefully to both.

It will happen that the shadow's call will fly away.

> May it be the shadow's call will fly away.
>> —"May It Be," Enya

They will talk, if they want to!

> Let them talk, if they want to!
>> —"Let Them Talk," Little Willie John

The river will run,
The dreamers will wake the nation.

> Let the river run,
> Let all the dreamers wake the nation.
>> —"Let the River Run," Carly Simon

The rough times ahead will become triumphs in time.

> May the rough times ahead become triumphs in time.
>> —"The Irish Wedding Song," Ian Betteridge

She will defend our laws, and ever give us cause
To sing with heart and voice, God save the Queen!

> May she defend our laws, and ever give us cause
> To sing with heart and voice, God save the Queen!
>> —"God Save the Queen," Anon.

He can sink or **he can swim**,

He doesn't care for me, and I don't care for him.

Let him sink or let him swim,

He doesn't care for me, and I don't care for him.

—"Let Him Go, Let Him Tarry," Trad.

Exercise 109C: Diagramming

On your own paper, diagram every word of each sentence. These come from speeches made by three nineteenth-century women who fought for women's *suffrage*—the right for women to vote. This right was not granted to American women until 1920, just one hundred years ago.

May these statements lead you to reflect upon this subject, that you may know what woman's condition is in society—what her restrictions are, and seek to remove them.

—Lucretia Mott, "Discourse on Woman" (1849)

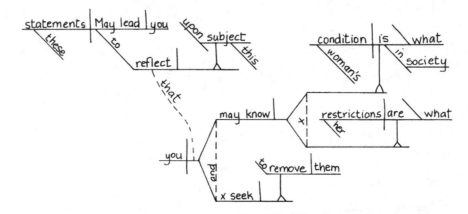

> **Note to Instructor:** The dependent clause *that you may know...seek to remove them* is adverbial and answers the question *why* (Why reflect upon this subject? So that you may know). The subject of the clause, *you*, has two predicates—*that you may know [and may] seek*. The first predicate has two clauses acting as its direct object, while the second has an infinitive phrase as its direct object.

And let not woman hesitate to enter upon the work before her from any fear of transcending the bounds of her sphere.

—Amelia Bloomer, "Most Terribly Bereft" (1855)

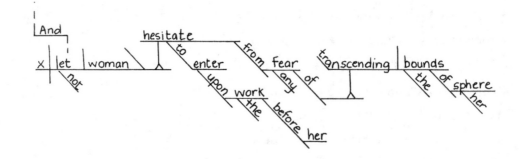

Let it be remembered, finally, that it has ever been the pride and boast of America that the rights for which she contended were the rights of human nature.

—Susan B. Anthony, quoting James Madison in "Is It a Crime to Vote?" (1872)

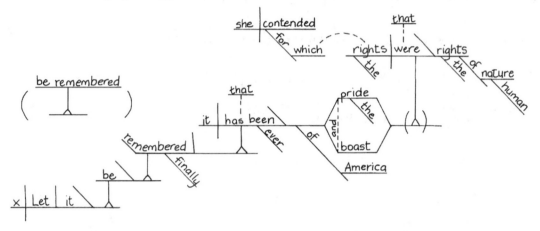

> **Note to Instructor:** We have diagrammed *be remembered* as a linking verb followed by a past participle, but it could also be diagrammed as a single verb (as in the parentheses). The rest of the sentence is the same. *Pride* and *boast* are both modified by the prepositional phrase *of America*, and both nouns are renamed by the appositive clause *that the rights... human nature.* Within that clause, the adjective clause *for which she contended* modifies *rights*, and the relative pronoun *which* refers back to *rights*.

— LESSON 110 —

Transitive Verbs

Intransitive Verbs

Sit/Set, Lie/Lay, Rise/Raise

Ambitransitive Verbs

Exercise 110A: Ambitransitive Verbs

Each one of the sentences below (adapted from the book *African Folk Tales*, edited by Hugh Vernon-Jackson) contains at least one ambitransitive verb. For each sentence, carry out the following steps:

a) Underline the action verbs that are acting as predicates (in both independent and subordinate clauses), and label each one as *TR* for transitive or *INTR* for intransitive.

b) Circle the direct object of each active transitive verb. Remember that clauses and phrases can act as objects and subjects, as well as single words.

c) Choose two sentences with transitive verbs. On your own paper, rewrite them so that the verb becomes passive. You may need to supply additional subjects or other parts of speech!

d) Choose two sentences with intransitive verbs. Rewrite them so that the verbs become transitive. You may need to supply additional objects or other parts of speech!

But as he washed(it) it broke.

TR
You have broken the (calabash) and I am glad.

TR   TR
Now, the tortoise knew (that crocodile eggs have a delicious (flavour))

TR   TR   INTR
Unless you do (what) I say, your mouth and nose will never open again!

INTR   TR
The frightened animal suddenly kicked out and opened a (rift) in the earth beneath him.

TR   TR
Pay no (attention) to (what) the old woman said!

TR   INTR
If you do not give me the (treasure) you will pay!

TR
The leopards drove each forked (stick) into the ground.

TR   INTR   INTR
He picked up the (reins) clucked to the horse, and drove away.

TR
The three rascals played a (trick) on the donkey.

INTR
The tiger cubs played until they were tired.

TR
Ali gave the traveller (one) of the remaining camels.

TR
You ate my (cake) without asking my permission!

INTR   INTR
The she-goat and her children were hungry, and so they sat down and ate.

TR
Please help (us) with our camels!

INTR   INTR
The traveller shouted, but no one helped.

TR
He shouted his (pain) to the sky.

Note to Instructor: The student's two rewritten sentences should resemble two of the following.

c)

But, as it was washed by him, it broke.

The calabash has been broken by you, and I am glad.

Now, that crocodile eggs have a delicious flavour was known by the tortoise.

Unless what is said by me is done by you, your mouth and nose will never open again!

The frightened animal suddenly kicked out and a rift was opened in the earth beneath him.

No attention should be paid to what was said by the old woman!

If the treasure is not given to me by you, you will pay!

Each forked stick was driven by the leopards into the ground.

The reins were picked up by him, he clucked to the horse, and he drove away.

A trick was played by the three rascals on the donkey.

One of the remaining camels was given to the traveller by Ali.

My cake was eaten by you without your asking my permission!

We must be helped with our camels, please!

His pain was shouted to the sky.

> **Note to Instructor:** The student's rewritten sentences should resemble two of the following:

d)

But as he washed it, he broke it.

Unless you do what I say, you will never open your mouth and nose again!

The frightened animal suddenly kicked the ground and opened a rift in the earth beneath him.

If you do not give me the treasure, you will pay me!

He picked up the reins, clucked his tongue at the horse, and drove the cart away.

The tiger cubs played games until they were tired.

The she-goat and her children were hungry, and so they sat themselves down, and ate dinner.

The traveller shouted his pain, but no one helped him.

Exercise 110B: The Prefix *Ambi-*

Using a dictionary or thesaurus, find two more words using the prefix *ambi-* where the prefix carries the meaning of "both." On your own paper, write the words and their definitions, and then use each correctly in a sentence. If the word is too technical for you to write an original sentence, you may locate a sentence using an internet search and write it down.

> **Note to Instructor:** These are sample answers; the student's answers may vary. Make sure that the words the student chooses carry the meaning of *both* rather than *around*, another possible meaning of the prefix *ambi-* (so: *ambivalent*, but not *ambiance* or *ambition*).
>
> If the student has completed previous levels of this course, make sure that she picks different answers than she chose in previous years!

ambilateral: affecting both sides

The patient's muscle weakness was ambilateral.

ambilevous: having awkwardness at completing manual tasks with both right and left hands

The ambilevous child couldn't open the toy box with either hand.

ambiloquent: regularly speaking to both sides at once, "double tongued"

That politician is the most ambiloquent leader since Machiavelli.

ambipolar: having both positive and negative charge carriers

Ambipolar diffusion is important in redistributing magnetic flux. (From *Issues in Astronomy and Astrophysics*)

ambisextrous: used by or suitable for any gender, unisex

That particular salon specializes in ambisextrous haircuts.

ambisinister: equally clumsy with both hands

The ambisinister cook dropped the tureen of soup, cut both hands with his paring knife, and burned his left elbow while trying to turn on the burner with his right hand.

ambisyllabic: a word with a single sound that is shared by two different syllables

The word *apple* is ambisyllabic, because the *p* sound belongs to both the first and the last syllable.

ambitendency: contradictory behaviors rising out of conflicting thoughts or impulses

Her ambitendency appeared when she put out her hand for a handshake, drew it away, put it back out, and then withdrew it again.

ambivalent: having mixed feelings or more than one feeling, having trouble choosing between two different options

The six-year-old felt ambivalent about the family's enormous new dog.

ambivert: someone who is both introverted and extroverted

Ambiverts make good salespeople because they enjoy talking to customers but don't overwhelm them with too much attention.

Exercise 110C: Diagramming

On your own paper, diagram every word of the following quotations.

When you are finished, label each action verb occupying a predicate space with *T* for transitive or *INT* for intransitive.

> **Note to Instructor:** You may need to remind the student that a passive verb is transitive, because the subject receives the action of the verb.

Live in the sunshine, swim the sea, drink the wild air.
—Ralph Waldo Emerson

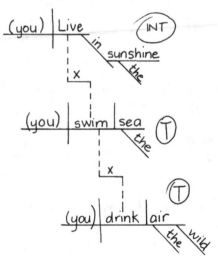

If you set your goals ridiculously high and it's a failure, you will fail above everyone else's success.
    —James Cameron

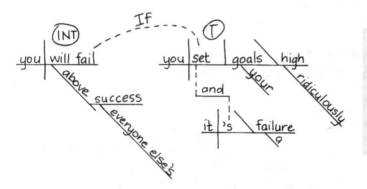

Note to Instructor: We have diagrammed *everyone else's* as a single compound adjective because neither *everyone* nor *else's* makes sense as a single adjective modifying *success*. If the student diagrams either *everyone* or *else's* as a modifier to *success* with the other word modifying it, accept the answer but show the student our solution as well.

I have learned over the years that when one's mind is made up, this diminishes fear.
    —Rosa Parks

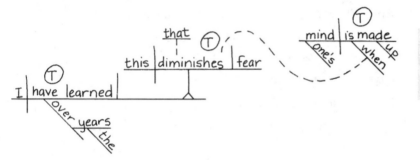

Note to Instructor: The noun clause *that when one's mind... fear* is the direct object of the verb *learn*, which here is a transitive verb.

The best and most beautiful things in the world cannot be seen or even touched—they must be felt with the heart.
    —Helen Keller

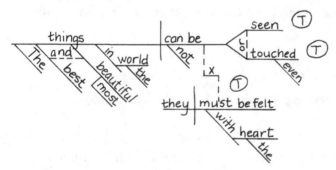

Note to Instructor: The helping verbs *can be* help out both *seen* and *touched* and make both verbs passive, so that *things* receives the action of both verbs.

In three words I can sum up everything I've learned about life: it goes on.
    —Robert Frost

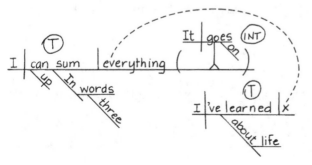

Note to Instructor: We have diagrammed the clause *it goes on* as an appositive renaming *everything*, but it could also be diagrammed as an independent element to the left of the main diagram.

— LESSON 111 —

Ambitransitive Verbs
Gerunds and Infinitives
Infinitive Phrases as Direct Objects
Infinitive Phrases with Understood *To*

Exercise 111A: Infinitives and Other Uses of *To*

In the following sentences, from Olaudah Equiano's eighteenth-century memoir *The Interesting Narrative of the Life of Olaudah Equiano, or Gustavas Vassa, the African, Written By Himself,* underline every phrase that incorporates the word *to*. For infinitives, underline just the infinitive itself; for prepositional phrases, underline just the preposition and its object (and any words that come between them); for verb phrases, underline the entire verb.

- Label each phrase as *INF* for infinitive, *PREP* for prepositional, or *V* for verb.

- For infinitives, further identify the phrase as *S* for subject, *DO* for direct object, *PA* for predicate adjective, *PN* for predicate nominative, *ADJ* for adjective, or *ADV* for adverb.

- For prepositional phrases, label the object of the preposition as *OP*.

- For verb phrases, parse the verb, giving tense, voice, and mood.

- For infinitive adjective and adverb phrases, draw an arrow back to the word modified.

  The first is done for you.

People generally think those memoirs only worthy to be read or remembered which abound in great or striking events, those, in short, which in a high degree excite either admiration or pity: all others they consign to contempt and oblivion.

That part of Africa, known by the name of Guinea, to which the trade for slaves is carried on, extends along the coast above 3400 miles, from the Senegal to Angola, and includes a variety of kingdoms.

All are taught the use of these weapons; even our women are warriors, and march boldly out to fight along with the men.

This speech seemed to confound him; he began to recoil: and my heart that instant sunk within me.

Indeed such were the horrors of my views and fears at the moment, that, if ten thousand worlds had been my own, I would have freely parted with them all to have exchanged my condition with that of the meanest slave in my own country.

INF PN   INF DO   INF PA
I inquired of these what was <u>to be done</u> with us; they gave me <u>to understand</u> we were <u>to be carried</u>
PREP   OP   INF ADV
<u>to these white people's country</u> <u>to work</u> for them.

INF DO   INF DO
I at that time began <u>to understand</u> him a little, and refused <u>to be called</u> so, and told him
as well as I could that I would be called Jacob; but he said I should not, and still called
INF DO   PREP   OP
me Gustavus; and when I refused <u>to answer</u> <u>to my new name</u>, which at first I did, it gained me
INF ADV
many a cuff; so at length I submitted, and was obliged <u>to bear</u> the present name, by which I have
been known ever since.

> **Note to Instructor:** The infinitive *to bear* cannot be the direct object of *was obliged* because it is a
> passive verb.

V present active modal   PREP OP
I am sensible I <u>ought to entreat</u> your pardon for addressing <u>to you</u> a work so wholly devoid of
literary merit!

INF ADJ
I now thought my condition much mended; I had sails <u>to lie</u> on, and plenty of good victuals
INF ADJ   PREP OP
<u>to eat</u>; and every body on board used me very kindly, quite contrary <u>to what</u> I had seen of any
INF DO
white people before; I therefore began <u>to think</u> that they were not all of the same disposition.

PREP OP
When I came <u>to Spithead</u>, I found we were destined for the Mediterranean, with a large fleet,
INF ADV PREP OP
which was now ready <u>to put</u> <u>to sea</u>.

INF ADJ   INF ADV   INF ADV   INF ADV
I now knew what it was <u>to work</u> hard; I was made <u>to help</u> <u>to unload</u> and <u>load</u> the ship.

> **Note to Instructor:** In the noun clause *what it was to work hard*, *it* is the subject and *what* the
> predicate nominative; *to work* modifies *what*.
>   In the infinitive pair *to unload and load*, the *to* serves both verb forms.

PREP   OP   OP
<u>To my no small surprise, and very great joy</u>, the captain confirmed every syllable that I had said:
INF DO
and even more; for he said he had tried different times <u>to see</u> if I would make any attempt of this
kind, both at St. Eustatia and in America, and he never found that I made the smallest.

Exercise 111B: Diagramming

On your own paper, diagram every word of the following sentences from *Common Sense*, by Thomas Paine. Ask for help if you need it!

To God, and not to man, are all men accountable on the score of religion.

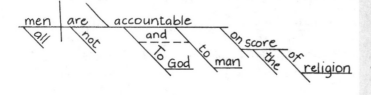

Note to Instructor: Although the adverb *not* refers only to one of the proposed scenarios (*all men are accountable to God, all men are not accountable to men*), it should be diagrammed beneath the verb since *not* does not usually function as an adjective, and so cannot modify *man*.

To unite the sinews of commerce and defense is sound policy; for when our strength and our riches play into each other's hand, we need fear no external enemy.

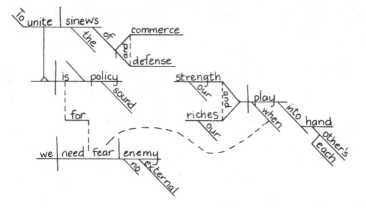

Note to Instructor: The verb phrase *need fear* is unusual—in this predicate, *need* is acting as a helping verb to form the complete predicate *need fear*. (You can point out to the student that *fear* is clearly an action verb, not a direct object—the meaning of the clause is *we don't fear the enemy*, not *we need fear*).

For as in absolute governments the King is law, so in free countries the law ought to be King; and there ought to be no other.

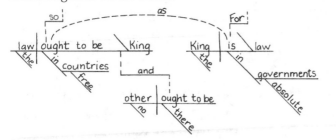

Note to Instructor: Although we have diagrammed *For* as a conjunction introducing the first clause, the student could also diagram *For as* as a single compound subordinating conjunction on the dotted line where *as* is located.

The primary clause in this sentence is *So law ought to be King*, and *so* is diagrammed as an initial conjunction.

When we are planning for posterity, we ought to remember, that virtue is not hereditary.

Note to Student: This last sentence has several challenging elements in it! Do your best and ask for help as needed.

We are endeavoring, and will steadily continue to endeavor, to separate and dissolve a connexion which hath already filled our land with blood; and which, while the name of it remains, will be the fatal cause of future mischiefs to both countries.

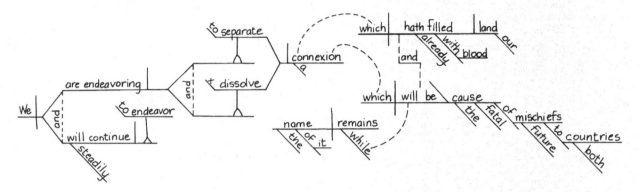

> **Note to Instructor:** The independent clause *We are endeavoring, and will steadily continue to endeavor* has a single subject and a compound predicate (*are endeavoring* and *will continue*). The first predicate, *are endeavoring*, has two direct objects: the infinitives *to separate* and *[to] dissolve*. Those two direct objects share a single object: *connexion*.
>
> The two adjective clauses introduced by *which* both modify *connexion* and are also connected by the coordinating conjunction *and*.

— LESSON 112 —

Principal Parts
Yet More Troublesome Verbs

Exercise 112A: Verb Definitions

For each definition, choose the best term from the word bank. Write it into the blank next to the definition.

imperative	present participle	second principal part
third principal part	transitive verb	modal
subjunctive	gerund	hortative
first principal part	ambitransitive verb	progressive verb
infinitive	perfect verb	simple verb
intransitive verb	indicative	

Describes an ongoing or continuous action	progressive verb
Expresses intended actions	imperative
Expresses action that is received by some person or thing	transitive verb
Affirms or declares what actually is	indicative
Present participle acting as a noun	gerund
Expresses situations that are unreal, wished for, or uncertain	subjunctive

A verb form ending in *-ing*	present participle
Encourages or recommends an action	hortative
Can be either transitive or intransitive	ambitransitive verb
The simple present (first-person singular)	first principal part
Expresses possible actions	modal
Describes an action which has been completed before another action takes place	perfect verb
The same as the simple past verb form	second principal part
Formed by combining *to* and the first-person singular present form of a verb	infinitive
Expresses action that is not received by any person or thing	intransitive verb
Simply tells whether an action takes place in the past, present, or future	simple verb
The perfect past verb form, minus helping verbs	third principal part

Exercise 112B: Using Troublesome Verbs Correctly

In the following sentences from the anonymous collection *English Fairy Tales*, fill in the blanks.

The first blank (above the sentence) should be filled in with the first principal part of the correct verb: *lie* or *lay* in the first set of sentences, *sit* or *set* in the second set, and *rise* or *raise* in the third set.

You will be able to tell from the context of the sentence whether you should use the transitive verbs *lay*, *set*, and *raise* (if the verb is passive, or has a direct object), or the intransitive verbs *lie*, *sit*, and *rise* (if the action of the verb is not passed on to any other word in the sentence).

The second blank (in the sentence itself) should be filled in with the correct form of that verb.

simple present active indicative of _lie_
Here _lies_ Tom Thumb, King Arthur's knight,
Who died by a spider's cruel bite.

simple past active indicative of _lie_
He _lay_ down on the ground, and shading his eyes with one hand, looked up into the sky, and pointed heavenwards with the other hand.

simple past active indicative of _lie_
On went Johnny-cake, and by-and-by he came to a fox that _lay_ quietly in a corner of the fence.

simple present active indicative of _lay_
Wife, bring me the hen that _lays_ the golden eggs.

simple past active indicative of _lay_
Mr. Vinegar, you foolish man, you blockhead, you simpleton; you went to the fair, and _laid_ out all your money in buying a cow.

The Laidly Worm crawled and crept, and crept and crawled till it reached the Heugh or rock of the
simple present active indicative of _lie_
Spindlestone, round which it coiled itself, and _lay_ there basking with its terrible snout in the air.

simple past active indicative of lie

So at last she lifted the frog up on to her lap, and it lay there for a time.

> Wash me, and comb me,
>
> simple present active imperative of lay
>
> And lay me down softly.
>
> simple present active imperative of lay
>
> And lay me on a bank to dry,
>
> That I may look pretty,
>
> When somebody passes by.

simple past active indicative of lie

And then she lay down upon the bed of the Little, Small, Wee Bear; and that was neither too high at the head, nor at the foot, but just right.

simple present active imperative of lie

Get off your horse and lie down.

simple past active indicative of lay

One came up roaring with open mouth to devour him, when he struck it with his wand, and laid it in an instant dead at his feet.

His mother, who was very sorry to see her darling in such a woeful state, put him into a teacup,
simple past active indicative of lay
and soon washed off the batter; after which she kissed him, and laid him in bed.

simple past active indicative of lay

The Brownie at Hilton Hall would play at mischief, but if the servants laid out for it a bowl of cream, or a knuckle cake spread with honey, it would clear away things for them, and make everything tidy in the kitchen.

**

active infinitive of sit

And they had each a chair to sit in; a little chair for the Little, Small, Wee Bear; and a middle-sized chair for the Middle Bear; and a great chair for the Great, Huge Bear.

Well, who should be there but her master's son, and what should he do but fall in love
simple past active indicative of set
with her the minute he set eyes on her.

> simple present active imperative of sit
>
> But sit ye down; but woe, O, woe,
>
> That ever ye were born,
>
> For come the King of Elfland in,
>
> Your fortune is forlorn.

The king was so charmed with his address that he ordered a little chair to be made, in order that
simple present active modal of sit
Tom might sit upon his table, and also a palace of gold, a span high, with a door an inch wide, to live in.

simple present active indicative of sit

Jack was so lazy that he would do nothing but bask in the sun in the hot weather, and sit by the corner of the hearth in the winter-time.

simple past active indicative of set

So she took them in, and set them down before the fire, and gave them milk and bread;

active infinitive of sit

now Katie was a very brave girl, so she offered to sit up with him.

perfect past active indicative of set

However, the last day of the last month he takes her to a room she'd never set eyes on before.

simple past active indicative of set

She came to the stile, set down the candles, and proceeded to climb over.

simple past active indicative of sit

And after they were married all the company sat down to the dinner.

passive infinitive of set

Mr. Fitzwarren ordered a chair to be set for him, and so he began to think they were making game of him.

simple past active indicative of sit

She sat down on a stool in the kitchen, and law! how she did cry!

simple past active indicative of sit

And all the day the girl sat trying to think of names to say to it when it came at night.

simple past active indicative of sit

He travelled till he came to a big stone, and there he sat down to rest.

**

simple present active indicative of rise

As twelve o clock rings, however, the sick prince rises , dresses himself, and slips downstairs.

simple past active indicative of raise

Mr. Fox cursed and swore, and drew his sword, raised it, and brought it down upon the hand of the poor lady.

simple past active indicative of rise

So Kate gave him a third bite, and he rose quite well, dressed himself, and sat down by the fire.

active infinitive of raise

Childe Rowland was just going to raise it to his lips, when he looked at his sister and remembered why he had come all that way.

active infinitive of rise

Dick now tried to rise , but was obliged to lie down again, being too weak to stand, for he had not eaten any food for three days.

simple present active modal of rise

Then the fairies would fan him till he could rise again and go on dancing.

simple past active indicative of rise
It rose to the boy's knees and still more water was poured.

King Arthur and his whole court were so sorry at the loss of their little favourite that they went
      simple past active indicative of raise
into mourning and raised a fine white marble monument over his grave.

Exercise 112C: More Principal Parts

Fill in the chart below with the missing principal parts of each verb. (You may use a dictionary if necessary.) Some are regular, and some are irregular.

Then, in the sentences below from Ben Bova's science fiction novel *Neptune*, fill in the blanks with the correct verb, in the tense, mood, and voice indicated in brackets at the end of each sentence. Each verb is used one time.

	First Principal Part **Present**	Second Principal Part **Past**	Third Principal Part **Past Participle**
I	am	was	been
	read	read	read
	withstand	withstood	withstood
	eat	ate	eaten
	live	lived	lived
	notify	notified	notified
	inform	informed	informed
	change	changed	changed
	test	tested	tested
	choose	chose	chosen
	find	found	found
	see	saw	seen
	take	took	taken
	breathe	breathed	breathed
	pull	pulled	pulled
	detain	detained	detained

We ___should have taken___ some of the fishes and other organisms down there for analysis. [perfect present, active, modal]

The mission ___will take___ nearly a century to get there. [simple future, active, indicative]

We ___should have tested___ them to see if they have elevated levels of potassium or sulfur. [perfect present, active, modal]

It ___must have been___ devastating. [perfect present, state-of-being, modal]

As calmly as if she ___were reading___ from a textbook, Francine went on. [past progressive, active, subjunctive]

Even the built-in desk opposite the small sofa was clear of papers or any other sign that someone ___had been living___ in this suite for weeks. [perfect past progressive, active, indicative]

They ___had___ all ___been___ already ___notified___ of this meeting. [perfect past, passive, indicative]

He wanted to breathe the same air she ___would be breathing___. [progressive present, active, modal]

We have considered the possibility, and we ___have found___ that this idea of an alien invasion is pure conjecture! [perfect present, active, indicative]

I believe he ___might___ well ___have chosen___ cryonic preservation once he realized his submersible was beyond recovery. [perfect present, active, modal]

Darby ___has seen___ to it that you won't be here to plead your case. [perfect present, active, indicative]

Once the planet Uranus was found by William Herschel in 1781, studies of its motion indicated that it ___was being pulled___ slightly out of its predicted orbit by the gravitational tug of an unseen, more distant planet. [progressive past, passive, indicative]

Its walls ___had withstood___ invading armies and rebelling Hungarians for many centuries. [perfect past, active, indicative]

The creatures of Neptune's deep ocean ___had eaten___ almost everything. [perfect past, active, indicative]

I ___am being detained___ aboard this station against my will! [progressive present, passive, indicative]

I ___have___ not ___been informed___ of any emergency. [perfect present, passive, indicative]

But he ___might have changed___ course. [perfect present, active, modal]

Still More About Clauses

— LESSON 113 —

Clauses and Phrases

Exercise 113A: Phrases and Clauses

Identify each circled set of words as *PH* for phrase or *CL* for clause.

- Then, identify the part of the sentence (*S, DO, IO, OP, PN, PA, ADV, ADJ*) that each set of words functions as.

- For phrases, further identify the phrase as *PREP* (prepositional), *INF* (infinitive), *PRESP* (present participle), or *PASTP* (past participle).

- For clauses, underline the subject once and the predicate twice.

- For adjective and adverb phrases and clauses, draw an arrow to the word modified.

Some of the phrases and clauses might have another clause with them! If you find these clauses, tell your instructor about them.

All of these sentences are taken from *Raggedy Andy Stories*, by Johnny Gruelle.

CL ADJ

Raggedy Andy did not know his age, but he remembered many things that had happened

CL ADV

years and years and years ago, when he and Raggedy Ann were quite young.

CL ADV

But why should one worry one's rag head about one's age when all one's life has been

PH ADJ PASTP

one happy experience after another, with each day filled with love and sunshine?

PH INF DO

It was only when all the dolls had stopped to rest and put the feathers back into the

CL DO

pillow cases that Raggedy Andy discovered he had lost one of his arms in the scuffle.

PH ADV PRESP

Raggedy Andy stood upon the stove and watched the candy, (dipping into it every once

CL DO   PH ADV PRESP

in a while) to see (if it had cooked long enough,) and (stirring it with the large spoon.)

> **Note to Instructor:** The noun clause *if it had cooked long enough* serves as the direct object of the infinitive *to see.*

PH ADV PREP   CL ADV

All the dolls gathered (about the platter) on the floor, and (while Raggedy Andy cut the

paper into neat squares,) the dolls wrapped the taffy in the papers.

PH ADV PREP

Then the taffy was put into a large bag, and (with much pulling and tugging) it was finally

CL ADJ

dragged up into the nursery, (where a window faced out toward the street.)

> **Note to Instructor:** The clause is an adjective clause introduced by a relative adverb.

PH ADJ PASTP

A wooden horse, (covered with canton flannel and touched lightly with a paint brush)

PH ADV INF

dipped in black paint (to give him a dappled gray appearance,) was one of the presents.

CL ADV   PH DO PRESP

Then, (as all the dolls' merry laughter rang out,) Raggedy Andy stopped (rubbing his hands,)

PH ADV PRESP   PH ADV PREP

and (catching Raggedy Ann about the waist,) he went skipping (across the nursery floor)

CL ADV

with her, whirling so fast (neither saw they had gone out through the door until it was too late.)

> **Note to Instructor:** The adverbial clause *neither saw...late* contains two additional clauses: the noun clause *they had gone* out through the door, which is the direct object of *saw,* and the adverb clause *until it was too late,* which modifies *saw* and answers the question *when.*

PH ADV PRESP

All the dolls took turns (putting their ears to the mouth of the beautiful shell.)

PH ADJ PASTP   PH ADJ PRESP

The coloring (consisted of dainty pinks, creamy whites and pale blues,) (all running

together just as the coloring in an opal runs from one shade into another.)

> **Note to Instructor:** The *PH ADJ PRESP* phrase contains an adverbial clause modifying the participle *running*: *just as the coloring in an opal runs from one shade into another.*

Exercise 113B: Diagramming

On your own paper, diagram every word of the following sentences, taken from *Sweets: A History of Candy*, by Tim Richardson.

> **Note to Instructor:** Give all necessary help!

In 1866 Fry launched a dark chocolate bar filled with a mint fondant: Fry's Chocolate Cream.

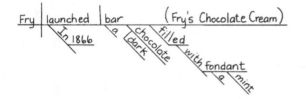

These bars are not modern versions of Fry's original plain bars, but of the second important innovation in chocolate-bar history: the bar that is not all chocolate.

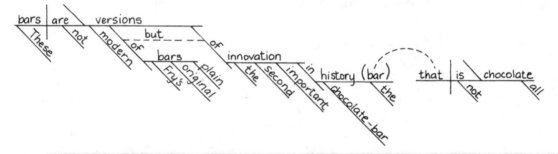

> **Note to Instructor:** The two prepositional phrases *of Fry's original plain bars* and *of the second important innovation in chocolate-bar history* both modify the noun *versions*: *These bars are not modern versions of Fry's original plain bars, but [are versions] of the second important innovation in chocolate-bar history*. The student could also make the argument that the two predicates—the existing *are* and the understood *are*—could be diagrammed as a compound predicate, with the first prepositional phrase modifying the existing predicate nominative *versions*, and the second phrase modifying the understood predicate nominative. Our solution is simpler, but the other is also acceptable.
>
> The *bar* following the colon is an appositive renaming *innovation*, and the adjective clause *that is not all chocolate* modifies it.

In 1913, the Swiss chocolatier Jules Sechaud created the technology for making moulded chocolate shells into which fondant could be poured (as opposed to simply dipping hard centres in chocolate) and the chocolate assortment was transformed.

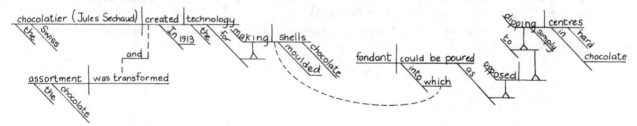

> **Note to Instructor:** This sentence has multiple participial modifiers! *Making moulded chocolate shells* is the object of the preposition *for* (and *moulded* is a past participle, the British spelling of the verb *to mold*). Within the adjectival clause *into which... in chocolate*), *as* acts as a preposition, with the past participle *opposed* as its object, and the prepositional phrase *to dipping...* as the object of *opposed*. In that prepositional phrase, *to* is the preposition and the present participle *dipping* is the object of the preposition.

The citizens of every country believe that their own chocolate is "real" chocolate, and that anything else is an inferior version.

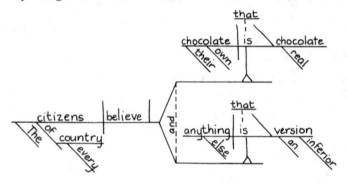

The breakfast tradition of chocolate with churros (long fried pastries) can be found in a cafe or two in many Spanish towns today, and the visitor used to pre-sweetened eating chocolate might be surprised to find that one adds sugar to this drink, as one might with coffee.

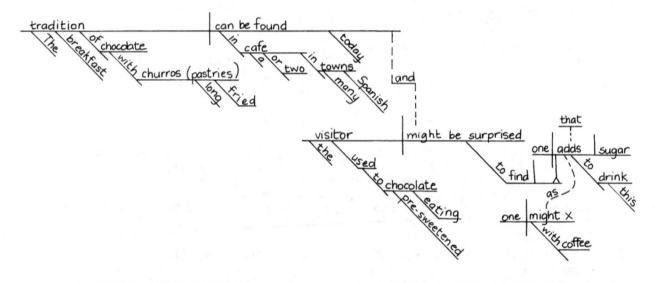

Note to Instructor: In the phrase *or two*, *or* is acting as a preposition, not a conjunction. The student could, however, also argue that *or* is acting as a conjunction linking *a* and *two* as adjectives modifying *cafe*; you may also accept this interpretation.

The clause *that one adds sugar to this drink* is the object of the infinitive *to find*. The clause *as one might [find] with coffee* is adverbial and modifies *adds*.

The past participle phrase *used to pre-sweetened eating chocolate* is adjectival and modifies *visitor*.

— LESSON 114 —

Restrictive and Non-Restrictive Modifying Clauses
Punctuating Modifying Clauses
Which and *That*

Exercise 114A: Restrictive and Non-Restrictive Adjective Clauses

Find every adjective clause in the following sentences, taken from *T. Rex and the Crater of Doom* by Walter Alvarez, and then follow these steps:

a) Underline each adjective clause.

b) Circle the relative pronoun that introduces each clause.

c) Draw an arrow from the pronoun back to the word modified.

d) Label each clause as *R* for restrictive or *NR* for nonrestrictive.

e) Draw an asterisk or star next to each sentence that does not follow the *which/that* rule.

We come into this world in ignorance of everything (that) happened before we were born.

The normal circulation of the ocean, (which) delivered oxygen to its depths, slowed down as a result of the warming.

*Looking back across the abyss of time (which) separates us from the Cretaceous, we can somehow feel nostalgia for a long-lost world, one which had its own rhythm and harmony.

*The Solar System abounds in comets and asteroids, some even bigger than the one (which) was nearing Earth on that day 65 million years ago.

Even if the impact site had been on oceanic crust (that) had been subducted, tsunami erosion of the surrounding continental margins might reveal where the crater had been.

*A few of these asteroids and comets are diverted into orbits (which) cross that of the Earth.

*The 108-megaton impact of the comet (which) ended the Cretaceous was therefore equivalent to the explosion of 10,000 times the entire nuclear arsenal of the world (although the impact explosion was not nuclear).

Throughout the decade of the 1980s, more and more evidence was discovered (that) supported the impact theory for the KT extinction, but the impact site remained frustratingly elusive.

But land above sea level is the main site of erosion, (which) levels hills and mountains and removes sediment previously deposited.

✳Before long, unmanned probes to other planets and moons sent back images (which) made it clear
that impact craters are the rule in the solar system, not the exception. [R]

Exceptions like the scablands of eastern Washington, (which) seemed to require catastrophic [NR]
causes, were explained away or ignored.

✳The energy escapes in the form of photons (which) ricochet around inside the star, sustaining the [R]
pressure (that) keeps the gravity of the star from shrinking it to a much smaller size. [R]

> **Note to Instructor:** Technically, *which ricochet around inside the star... shrinking it to a much smaller size* is one restrictive adjective clause describing *photon*, and *that keeps... smaller size* is a second restrictive adjective clause within it. The student may choose to underline the entire clause and double underline the second clause; accept either way of marking the sentence.

✳It was a suggestion (that) sounded reasonable to astronomers, who have photographed supernovas, [R]
and to physicists, who understand the nuclear processes that make stars explode.

Exercise 114B: Dependent Clauses Within Dependent Clauses

The following sentences all contain dependent clauses that have other dependent clauses within them.

Underline the whole of each one of these dependent clauses (including additional dependent clauses that act as nouns or modifiers within it). Draw a box around the subject of the main dependent clause, and underline its predicate twice. In the right-hand margin, write the abbreviation for the part of the sentence that the main dependent clause is fulfilling: *N-SUB* for a noun clause acting as subject, *N-PN* for predicate nominative, *N-DO* for direct object, *N-OP* for object of the preposition, *N-APP* for appositive, and then *ADJ* for adjective and *ADV* for adverb. For adjective and adverb clauses, draw a line from the label back to the word in the main independent clause that is modified.

Then, circle any additional clauses that fall within the main dependent clause. Label each clause, above the circle, in the same way: *N-SUB* for a noun clause acting as subject, *N-PN* for predicate nominative, *N-DO* for direct object, *N-OP* for object of the preposition, *N-APP* for appositive, and then *ADJ* for adjective and *ADV* for adverb. For adjective and adverb clauses, draw a line from the label back to the word in the main dependent clause modified.

The first is done for you.

These are all taken from *Fire in the Sky: Cosmic Collisions, Killer Asteroids, and the Race to Defend Earth*, by Gordon L. Dillow.

Because meteorites are usually named for the town closest to (where they are found,) the [ADV]
meteorites collected by Volz and others came to be known as Canyon Diablo meteorites—
and soon "Canyon Diablos" were featured in every important meteorite collection. [ADV]

Barringer eventually learned that the meteorites found around the crater also contained small
percentages of platinum and iridium, (which are rare in the Earth's crust but relatively abundant [ADJ]
in asteroids.) [N–DO]

Strangely enough, while deciding that Meteor Crater was not the result of a cosmic impact, N–DO

Gilbert got the notion that the craters on the Moon were the result of cosmic impacts, not ADJ

volcanos as everyone thought.

> **Note to Instructor:** The noun clause *that Meteor Crater...impact* is the object of the present
> participle *deciding*, which itself is the object of the preposition *while* (the entire prepositional
> phrase, including the clause, is adverbial and modifies *got*.)

I'll admit that given the breadth and scope of the universe, it seems likely that there is life N–DO

somewhere beyond our own little planet.

> **Note to Instructor:** The past participle phrase *given the breadth and scope of the universe* is part of
> the noun clause introduced by *that*. It modifies the predicate of the noun clause, *seems*.
> The predicate adjective *likely* follows the linking verb *seems* and describes the subject of the
> noun clause, *it*.

It's been said that time transforms the improbable into the certain, that anything that can ADV

happen will happen, given enough time.

> **Note to Instructor:** The clause cannot be a direct object because *has been said* is a passive verb.

The problem is that because asteroids don't reflect much sunlight, they're hard to spot even

with powerful telescopes, especially the smaller ones—which may be a good thing for our N–PN

peace of mind.

It was at that moment that he came up with an idea, an almost breathtakingly audacious idea, N–PN

one that he would pursue for the next quarter century.

For example, when a Great Comet appeared in 1910 a French scientist warned that when Earth ADV

passed through the comet's tail it would be enveloped in deadly cyanogen gas, which could N–DO

"possibly snuff out all life on the planet."

Exercise 114C: Diagramming

On your own paper, diagram every word of the following three sentences. If you need help, ask your instructor.

These are from *The Asteroid Threat: Defending Our Planet from Deadly Near-Earth Objects*, by William E. Burrows. They describe the massive meteor that struck near the Russian city of Chelyabinsk on February 15, 2013.

Note to Instructor: Give all necessary help!

The asteroid—which had become a meteor when it plunged into the atmosphere and then meteorites when the wall of air broke it into large fragments—was about fifty-six feet in diameter, weighed more than seven thousand tons, and was made of rock that was probably laced with nickel and iron.

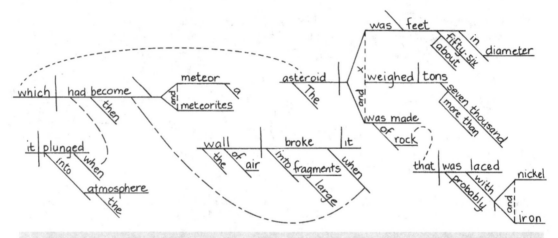

Note to Instructor: This is an interesting example of a sentence whose full meaning can't quite be conveyed by a diagram. The two adverb *clauses when it plunged into the atmosphere* and *when the wall of air broke it into large fragments* both grammatically modify the predicate of the adjective clause *which had... fragments*, but they actually refer to two different times of *becoming*. It would not be incorrect to diagram the predicate of the adjective clause as two separate verbs, the second being understood, with one adverb clause modifying each verb: *which had become a meteor when it plunged into the atmosphere and then [had become] meteorites when the wall of air broke it into large fragments*. However, we have chosen the simpler option.

The numbers *fifty-six feet* (modified by *about*) and *seven thousand tons* (modified by the compound modifier *more than*) can also be diagrammed as single compound nouns.

The Comprehensive Nuclear-Test-Ban Treaty Organization reported that the sound wave registered on sensors from Greenland to Antarctica, making it the largest ever detected by its network.

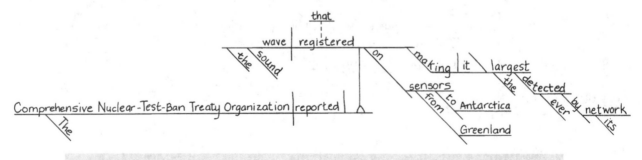

Note to Instructor: The pronoun *it* is the object of the present participle *making*, and *largest* is the object complement.

The force of the explosion was deeply frightening to those who saw and felt it because it showed them, in the most dramatic way, how vulnerable living creatures and their habitats are to the indomitable violence of nature.

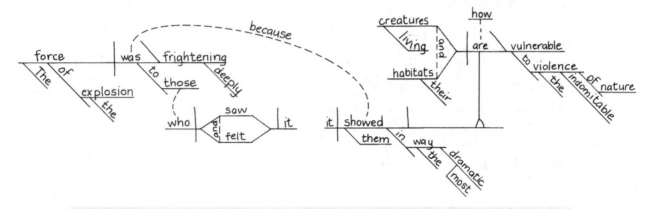

> **Note to Instructor:** The noun clause *how vulnerable... nature* is the object of the verb *showed*; the pronoun *them* is the indirect object.

— LESSON 115 —

Conditional Sentences

Conditional Sentences as Dependent Clauses
Conditional Sentences with Missing Words
Formal *If* Clauses

Exercise 115A: Conditional Clauses

In the following sentences from *Mansfield Park,* by Jane Austen, circle every conditional sentence. This may mean circling the entire sentence, circling only the part of it that makes up the conditional-consequence clause set, or circling the conditional and consequence clauses separately if they are divided by other words.

After you have circled the conditional sentences, underline twice and then parse the predicate in each conditional and consequence clause.

Finally, write a *1, 2,* or *3* in the blank to indicate *first, second,* or *third conditional.*

The first is done for you.

Whatever I can do, as you well know, I am always ready enough to do for the good of

those I love; and, though I could never feel for this little girl the hundredth part of the

regard I bear your own dear children, nor consider her, in any respect, so much my own,

I should hate myself if I were capable of neglecting her.

simple present, active, modal

simple present, state-of-being, subjunctive

1

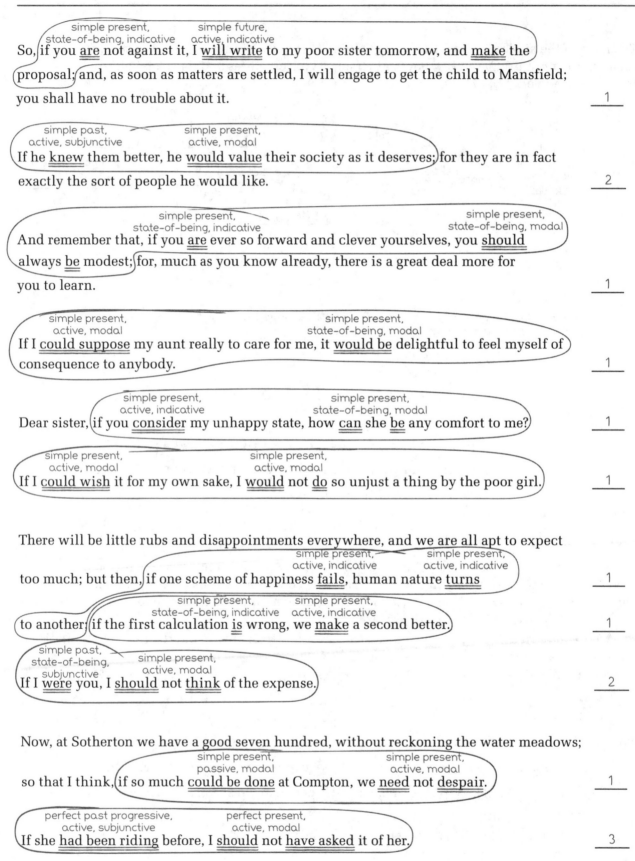

simple present,
state-of-being, indicative   *simple future,*
                                 active, indicative

So, if you <u>are</u> not against it, I <u>will write</u> to my poor sister tomorrow, and <u>make</u> the proposal; and, as soon as matters are settled, I will engage to get the child to Mansfield; you shall have no trouble about it.   1

simple past,   *simple present,*
active, subjunctive   *active, modal*

If he <u>knew</u> them better, he <u>would value</u> their society as it deserves; for they are in fact exactly the sort of people he would like.   2

simple present,   *simple present,*
state-of-being, indicative   *state-of-being, modal*

And remember that, if you <u>are</u> ever so forward and clever yourselves, you <u>should</u> always <u>be</u> modest; for, much as you know already, there is a great deal more for you to learn.   1

simple present,   *simple present,*
active, modal   *state-of-being, modal*

If I <u>could suppose</u> my aunt really to care for me, it <u>would be</u> delightful to feel myself of consequence to anybody.   1

simple present,   *simple present,*
active, indicative   *state-of-being, modal*

Dear sister, if you <u>consider</u> my unhappy state, how <u>can</u> she <u>be</u> any comfort to me?   1

simple present,   *simple present,*
active, modal   *active, modal*

If I <u>could wish</u> it for my own sake, I <u>would</u> not <u>do</u> so unjust a thing by the poor girl.   1

There will be little rubs and disappointments everywhere, and we <u>are</u> all apt to expect too much; but then, if one scheme of happiness <u>fails</u>, human nature <u>turns</u>

simple present,   *simple present,*
active, indicative   *active, indicative*
                                                                                                  1

to another, if the first calculation <u>is</u> wrong, we <u>make</u> a second better.

simple present,   *simple present,*
state-of-being, indicative   *active, indicative*
                                                                                                  1

simple past,
state-of-being,   *simple present,*
subjunctive   *active, modal*

If I <u>were</u> you, I <u>should</u> not <u>think</u> of the expense.   2

Now, at Sotherton we have a good seven hundred, without reckoning the water meadows;

simple present,   *simple present,*
passive, modal   *active, modal*

so that I think, if so much <u>could be done</u> at Compton, we <u>need</u> not <u>despair</u>.   1

perfect past progressive,   *perfect present,*
active, subjunctive   *active, modal*

If she <u>had been riding</u> before, I <u>should</u> not <u>have asked</u> it of her.   3

simple present, state-of-being,
modal, subjunctive

simple present,
active, modal

<u>Should</u> her disposition <u>be</u> really bad, we <u>must</u> not, for our own children's sake,

<u>continue</u> her in the family; but there is no reason to expect so great an evil.   1

simple present,
state-of-being, subjunctive

simple present,
active, modal

My dear Edmund, if you <u>were</u> but in orders now, you <u>might perform</u> the

ceremony directly.   2

simple present,
active, imperative

simple present,
active, indicative

<u>Don't</u> <u>act</u> yourself, if you <u>do</u> not <u>like</u> it, but don't expect to govern everybody else.   1

And though Dr. Grant is most kind and obliging to me, and though he is really a gentleman,
and, I dare say, a good scholar and clever, and often preaches good sermons, and is very
respectable, *I* see him to be an indolent, selfish *bon vivant*, who must have his palate consulted
in everything; who will not stir a finger for the convenience of any one; and who, moreover,

simple present,
active, indicative

simple present,
state-of-being, indicative

if the cook <u>makes</u> a blunder, <u>is</u> out of humour with his excellent wife.   1

Exercise 115B: Diagramming

On your own paper, diagram every word of the following sentences from *Mansfield Park*. Do
your best, and ask your instructor for help if you need it. (You might want to use some scratch
paper as well.)

If he is to die, there will be two poor young men less in the world; and with a fearless face and
bold voice would I say to any one, that wealth and consequence could fall into no hands more
deserving of them.

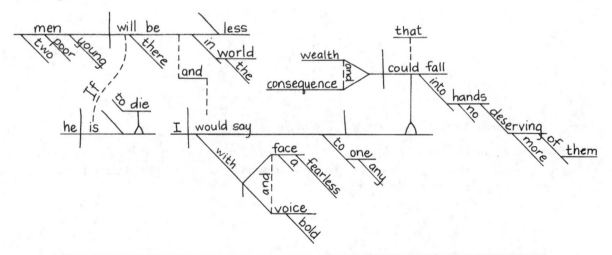

Note to Instructor: In this sentence, *less* is a predicate adjective (not an adverb), following
the linking verb *will be*.

In the subordinate clause *If he is to die*, the infinitive *to do* acts as a predicate adjective
describing *he* and following the linking verb *is*.

Were you even less pleasing—supposing her not to love you already (of which, however, I can have little doubt)—you would be safe.

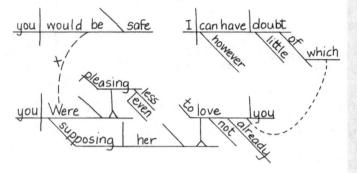

Note to Instructor: In this sentence, *less* is an adverb, describing the present participle *pleasing* (which is acting as a predicate adjective describing *you*).

In the adverbial present participle phrase *supposing her not to love you...*, *her* is the object of the present participle, and the infinitive phrase *to love you already* is the object complement.

In the subordinate clause *of which, however, I can have little doubt*, the relative pronoun *which* refers to the entire concept *not to love you already*, so it is connected to the line on which that phrase stands.

A most scandalous, ill-natured rumour has just reached me, and I write, dear Fanny, to warn you against giving the least credit to it, should it spread into the country.

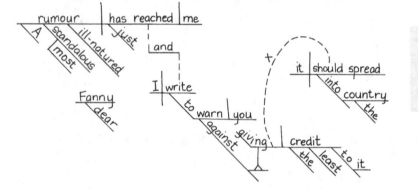

Note to Student: This sentence has an unusual connection between condition and consequence! Do your best to find it, and then ask your instructor for an explanation.

—**LESSON 116**—

Words That Can Be Multiple Parts of Speech
Interrogatives
Demonstratives
Relative Adverbs and Subordinating Conjunctions

Exercise 116A: Words Acting as Multiple Parts of Speech

Use these sentences, taken from *The Middle Moffat*, by Eleanor Estes, to identify the parts of speech that the bolded words can serve as. The first blank is filled in for you. Fill in the blanks with the correct labels from the following list:

conjunction	interjection	preposition	adverb
adjective	noun	pronoun	verb

The **middle** Moffat was going to be the **middle** bear.   adjective

The **middle** of the earth was a mysterious place like the **middle** of the night, and the **middle** of the ocean, too, where there very likely were waterspouts, whirlpools, and mermaids.   noun

Mama was making all the costumes, **even** the bear heads.

Maybe she had grown up some, too, and she hadn't **even** known it.

Of course, Mama would have to sit out front there with the regular people, **even** though she had made the costumes.

To **even** things up, Janey could join the basketball team.

She was pointing **right** straight at that little parlor organ.

She hoped she was doing some good for the **right** side.

Sylvie could play the organ with **both** hands and the hands played different parts.

They always went to school together and they came home together, too, **both** at noon time and in the afternoon.

For weeks the teacher had talked of little **else** in school.

But where **else** could she keep the photographs of all her nephews?

She would try it on somebody **else**.

And **all** winter Joey had shamefully neglected the oldest inhabitant's furnace.

Soon there it was, **all** whole again.

"Boy, oh, boy" was **all** he could say.

Jane sat in the big armchair, her legs flung over **one** of the arms.

One night there were lamb chops for dinner.

All the same she did feel scared **inside**.

Jane's laugh was more of an **inside** job.

She looked **around** to see if anybody else had heard what he said.

Usually when Wallie Bangs marched **around** the house he wouldn't even notice them.

She watched Jane all the way **up** the street, even forgetting her lollipop.

But the ball shot **up** and **up** and clean through the basket again, as beautifully as the first time.

Besides, she really owed him a visit **since** he had come to her organ recital.

But Nancy got mad at her and had not spoken **since**.

She ran down the stairs and out the **back** door, slamming it.

Big boys at the **back** of the hall put their fingers in their mouths and whistled.

Jane wished they'd come **back**.

preposition	
adverb	
conjunction	
verb	
adverb	
adjective	
adjective	
conjunction	
noun	
adverb	
adjective	
adjective	
adverb	
pronoun	
pronoun	
adjective	
adverb	
adjective	
adverb	
preposition	
preposition	
adverb	
conjunction	
adverb	
adjective	
noun	
adverb	

Exercise 116B: Words Introducing Clauses

In the following sentences, taken from Helen Keller's autobiography *The Story of My Life*, underline every subordinate clause. (Double underline clauses that occur within other clauses—and you may need a triple underline as well!) Then, carry out the following steps:

a) Circle the introductory word of the clause. (NOTE: When the introductory word is the object of a preposition, circle the word itself, not the preposition that precedes it. See the sample sentence.) If the introductory word is understood, insert it with a caret and then circle it.

b) Label the clause as *N* (for noun), *ADJ* (for adjective), or *ADV* (for adverb).

c) For noun clauses, further identify them as *S* for subject, *O* for object, or *PN* for predicate nominative.

d) For adjective or adverb clauses, draw an arrow to the word modified.

e) Finally, label the introductory word as one of the following: *RP* for relative pronoun, *RAdj* for relative adjective (a relative pronoun functioning as an adjective and introducing an adjective clause), *RAdv* for relative adverb, *SC* for subordinating conjunction, or *A-SC* for adverb functioning as a subordinating conjunction.

The first sentence is done for you, but notice that several selections contain more than one sentence—be sure to carry out these steps for each one!

My mother solved the problem by giving it as her wish (that) I should be called after her

mother, (whose) maiden name was Helen Everett. But in the excitement of carrying me to

church my father lost the name on the way, very naturally, (since) it was one in (which) he had

declined to have a part.

Then, in the dreary month of February, came the illness (which) closed my eyes and ears and plunged me into the unconsciousness of a new-born baby.

I especially remember the tenderness with (which) my mother tried to soothe me in my wailing

hours of fret and pain, and the agony and bewilderment with (which) I awoke after a tossing

half sleep, and turned my eyes, so dry and hot, to the wall away from the once-loved light,

(which) came to me dim and yet more dim each day.

At five I learned to fold and put away the clean clothes (when) they were brought in from the

laundry, and I distinguished my own from the rest. I knew by the way my mother and aunt

dressed (when) they were going out, and I invariably begged to go with them.

> **Note to Instructor:** The clause *when they were going out* is the object of the verb *knew* (the student may be confused by the prepositional phrase that comes between verb and object).

It seemed as if the spirit of spring had passed through the summer-house.

Her words puzzled me very much because I did not then understand anything unless I touched it.

It was because she seized the right moment to impart knowledge that made it so pleasant and acceptable to me.

> **Note to Instructor:** The relative pronoun *that* refers back to *knowledge* and serves as the subject of the subordinate clause.

How much of my delight in all beautiful things is innate, and how much is due to her influence, I can never tell.

That night, after I had hung my stocking, I lay awake a long time, pretending to be asleep and keeping alert to see what Santa Claus would do when he came.

I also remember the beach, where for the first time I played in the sand.

It seemed to me that there could be nothing more beautiful than the sun, whose warmth makes all things grow.

What joy it was to lose myself in that garden of flowers, to wander happily from spot to spot, until, coming suddenly upon a beautiful vine, I recognized it by its leaves and blossoms, and knew that it was the vine which covered the tumble-down summer-house at the farther end of the garden!

Exercise 116C: Diagramming

(You didn't think you'd escape diagramming, did you?)

On your own paper, diagram every word of the following sentences from the memoir *Unbowed*, by Nobel Peace Prize winner Wangari Maathai.

If you need help, ask your instructor.

For rural people, traveling to town was a novelty and you didn't go unless you had something to do, since it was not a place to hang around.

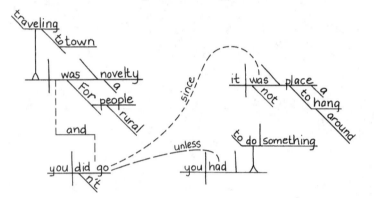

Note to Instructor: Most of these clauses are fairly straightforward, but the student may need assistance with *unless you had something to do*. The direct object of the verb *had* is *to do something*, not *something* (the subject doesn't *own* something, but is obligated *to do something*). It would also be acceptable for the student to diagram *had to do* as a single predicate, with *something* as the object.

Those who had not embraced Christianity, who still held on to and advocated for local customs, were called Kikuyus, while those who had converted were called *athomi*.

Note to Student: You'll have to think outside the box to diagram this one! Do your best, and ask your instructor for help if needed.

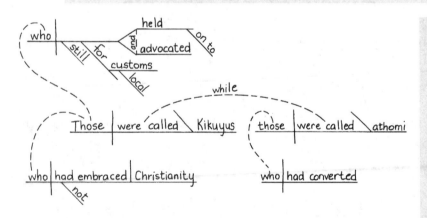

Note to Instructor: The main clauses *Those were called Kikuyus* and *those were called athomi* are difficult because the passive verb *were called* is acting not as an action verb, but as a linking verb. We have here diagrammed *Kikuyus* and *athomi* as predicate nominatives, but you may also diagram these words as adjectives beneath *those* or as appositives following *those*. They cannot be direct objects of the verb, however, or adverbs diagrammed beneath the verb.

Literally translated, this means "people who read."

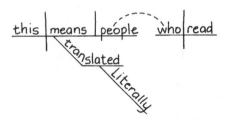

Note to Instructor: The verb *means* is an action verb, so *people* is the direct object, not a predicate nominative.

When independence came and there was a program through which people could purchase land, Kikuyus like my father were in a position to buy some of the settlers' farms on which many had lived as squatters.

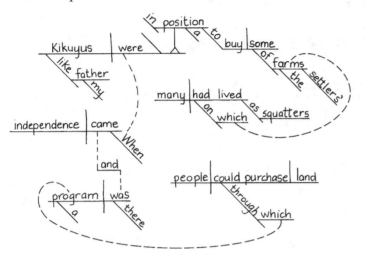

Note to Instructor: Simply tell the student to diagram one clause at a time! Note that the prepositional phrase *in a position to buy some...* is a predicate adjective describing the subject *Kikuyus*.

I had never anticipated that I would be discriminated against on the basis of my gender as often as I was, or that I could be belittled even while making a substantial contribution to society.

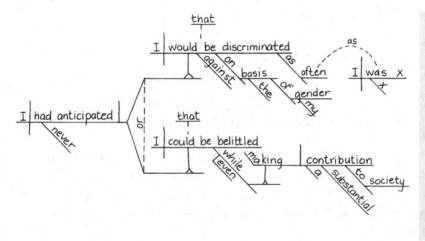

Note to Instructor: The comparative prepositional phrase and clause *as often as I was [discriminated against]* contains understood elements.

Notice that in the second noun clause serving as a direct object, *while* is acting as a preposition (with the present participle *making* as its object). We have diagrammed *even* as a modifier of the preposition (an unusual but possible situation!), but *even while* could also be diagrammed as a single compound preposition, or *even* could be diagrammed as an adverbial modifier of *making*.

WEEK 31

Filling Up the Corners

— LESSON 117 —

Interrogative Adverbs
Noun Clauses
Forming Questions
Affirmations and Negations
Double Negatives

Exercise 117A: Identifying Adverbs, Interrogative and Demonstrative Pronouns and Adjectives, and Relatives

In the following sentences, from *The Adventures of Sherlock Holmes*, by Arthur Conan Doyle, follow these steps (note that some double underlining might be required):

a) Label each bolded word as one of the following:

 ADV for adverb
  Draw an arrow from the adverb to the word modified.
  If the adverb also introduces a clause, underline the clause.

 PRO for pronoun
  If the pronoun has an antecedent, label the antecedent as *ANT*. If the pronoun
  introduces a clause, underline the clause.
  Label each pronoun as *S* for subject, *PN* for predicate nominative, *DO* for direct object,
  IO for indirect object, *OP* for object of the preposition, or *ADJ* (see below).

 ADJ for adjective
  Draw an arrow from the adjective to the word modified. If the adjective introduces a
  clause, underline the clause.

 SC for subordinating conjunction
  Underline the dependent clause introduced by the conjunction.

b) Label each underlined clause as *ADV-C* for adverb clause, *ADJ-C* for adjective clause, or *N-C* for noun clause.

c) Draw an arrow from each *ADV-C* and *ADJ-C* clause back to the word modified.

d) Label each *N-C* noun clause as *S* for subject, *DO* for direct object, *IO* for indirect object, or *OP* for object of the preposition.

The first is done for you.

     — ADV-C
   ADV
Stay **where** you are.

I was half-dragged up to the altar, and before I knew **where** I was I found myself mumbling responses **which** were whispered in my ear, and vouching for things of **which** I knew nothing, and generally assisting in the secure tying up of Irene Adler, spinster, to Godfrey Norton, bachelor.

Where could I find him?

What do you make of it all?

I was still balancing the matter in my mind **when** a hansom cab drove up to Briony Lodge, and a gentleman sprang out.

And **when** will you call?

But, after all, if he is satisfied, **why** should I put ideas in his head?

> **Note to Instructor:** The clause *why should I put ideas into his head* is the main clause of the sentence (the consequence clause to the condition clause *if he is satisfied*).

Mr. Merryweather is the chairman of directors, and he will explain to you **that** there are reasons **why** the more daring criminals of London should take a considerable interest in this cellar at present.

But then, **when** I found **how** I had betrayed myself, I began to think.

I do not know **how** the bank can thank you or repay you.

But **how** could you guess **what** the motive was?

It proved to be **that** of a young gentleman **whose** name, as it appears from an envelope **which** was found in his pocket, was John Openshaw, and **whose** residence is near Horsham.

> **Note to Instructor:** The pronoun *that* is the direct object of the infinitive *to be*.
> The two occurrences of *whose* are both adjectives describing nouns and are possessive pronouns with the antecedent *gentleman*.

Whose house is it?

It is clear **that** Mrs. Toller knows more about **this** matter than anyone else.

If there's police-court business over **this**, you'll remember **that** I was the one **that** stood your
friend, and **that** I was Miss Alice's friend too.

I shall stand behind **this** crate, and do you conceal yourselves behind **those**.

The man **who** entered was a sturdy, middle-sized fellow, some thirty years of age, clean-shaven, and sallow-skinned, with a bland, insinuating manner, and a pair of wonderfully sharp and penetrating grey eyes.

But if he is innocent, **who** has done it?

And yet I question, sir, whether, in all your experience, you have ever listened to a more mysterious and inexplicable chain of events than **those which** have happened in my own family.

> **Note to Instructor:** The antecedent of the pronoun *those* is *events*. The antecedent of the pronoun *which* is *those*. So *those* is both an antecedent and a pronoun!

All emotions, and **that** one particularly, were abhorrent to his cold, precise but admirably balanced mind.

Exercise 117B: Forming Questions

On your own paper, rewrite the following statements as questions.

Use each of the three methods for forming questions (adding an interrogative pronoun, reversing the subject and helping verb, or adding the helping verb *do*, *does*, or *did* in front of the subject and adjusting the tense of the main verb) at least once. You may change tenses, add or subtract words, or alter the statements in any other necessary ways, as long as the meaning remains the same.

These statements are all adapted from the titles of classic pop and rock songs! When you have transformed your statements into questions, compare them with the originals.

> **Note to Instructor:** The student's questions do not need to be identical to the originals, but each question should be grammatically correct, and each method should be used at least once.

STATEMENT	QUESTION
I should stay or I should go.	"Should I Stay or Should I Go?" —The Clash
Someone let the dogs out.	"Who Let the Dogs Out?" — Baha Men
You can feel the love tonight.	"Can You Feel the Love Tonight?" — Elton John
You have ever seen the rain.	"Have You Ever Seen the Rain?" — Creedence Clearwater Revival

I will see you again, at some point.	"When Will I See You Again?" — The Three Degrees
The frequency is something, Kenneth.	"What's the Frequency, Kenneth?" — R.E.M.
You hear what I hear.	"Do You Hear What I Hear?" — Harry Simeone Chorale
It would be nice.	"Wouldn't It Be Nice?" — The Beach Boys
You have done something for me lately.	"What Have You Done for Me Lately?" — Janet Jackson
You love me.	"Do You Love Me?" — The Contours
The flowers have gone somewhere.	"Where Have All the Flowers Gone?" — Pete Seeger

Exercise 117C: Affirmations and Negations

On your own paper,

- Rewrite each of the following affirmative statements as a negation, using one adverb or adjective of negation. You may add or subtract words or change tenses as necessary.
- Rewrite each of the following negative statements as an affirmative, using at least one adverb of affirmation.
- Rewrite any double negation as an affirmative, also using at least one adverb of affirmation.

When you are finished, compare your answers with the original sentences, slightly adapted from *The Return of Sherlock Holmes*, by Sir Arthur Conan Doyle.

Note to Instructor: The student's answers do not need to be identical to the original sentences, as long as the guidelines above are followed. Check to see that the student has included adverbs or adjectives of affirmation and negation in each sentence; these are bolded in the original sentences below.

ASSIGNED SENTENCES	ORIGINAL VERSIONS
She was engaged to me.	She was **never** engaged to me.
And as you value your life, go across the moor.	And as you value your life, do **not** go across the moor.
Your case has no features of great interest.	Your case has **certainly** some features of great interest.
The recital of these events must not be painful to you.	The recital of these events must be **very** painful to you.
If we cannot prove it this would turn Lestrade's argument against himself.	If we could **definitely** prove it, this would turn Lestrade's argument against himself.
It was evident that we had not miscalculated his movements.	It was evident that we had **entirely** miscalculated his movements.

Outside, the street was not deserted.

I am certainly to blame, Mr. Holmes.

The fugitives definitely did use the road.

His Grace is very friendly to anyone.

Outside, the street was **absolutely** deserted.

I am **not** to blame, Mr. Holmes.

The fugitives did **not** use the road at all.

His Grace is **never** friendly to anyone.

— LESSON 118 —

Diagramming Affirmations and Negations
Yet More Words That Can Be Multiple Parts of Speech
Comparisons Using *Than*
Comparisons Using *As*

Exercise 118A: Identifying Parts of Speech

Label each of the bolded words in these sentences (from *Myths and Legends from Korea*, edited by James Huntley Grayson) with one of the following abbreviations.

ADJ: adjective	ADV: adverb
ADV-N: adverb of negation	ADV-A: adverb of affirmation
ADV-R: relative adverb	SC: subordinating conjunction
PREP: preposition	RP: relative pronoun
DP: demonstrative pronoun	IP: indefinite pronoun
N: noun	PP: possessive pronoun

Where a subordinating conjunction introduces a comparison clause with missing words, draw a caret and insert the missing words.

SC   PREP

As he fell to the ground, his body transformed **into** the body of a great tiger.

          N   N   ADV

The feather of **one** of the wings of **one** of the cranes fell **off**.

PREP DP   ADV PREP   PREP N

With that, one of the gourds rolled **over by** itself and split itself **into two**.

ADJ   PREP

One day, the mother went **over** the mountain to do some weaving.

ADV   PREP   PREP

Then he was able to shoot the handle **off** a pitcher of water **without** breaking the pitcher.

ADV   PREP   ADV PREP

Soon, Rabbit got **onto** the turtle's back and set **off on** the journey to the Dragon Palace.

               ADV   SC   was dark

The throat of the tiger was **as** dark **as** a tunnel.^

          ADJ   PREP

He lived for **three** years **as** a refugee in the house of Morok.

       ADV   RP   ADV   ADV

The king put **on** the ragged clothes **which** the stranger had left **behind** and went **back** to his palace.

PREP
The old woman hid the boy **behind** the folding screen.

ADJ
The front legs were short and the **back** legs were long.

PREP   ADV
Upon coming **back** from drawing water, she followed the tracks of the two brothers.

PP   N
There was a tortoise on **whose back** a chant was inscribed.

N   ADV–N
In the **end**, there were **no** noises.

ADV   ADV   ADJ
When he is born, you will **no longer** be **lonely**.

PREP   ADV   ADV–A
Before setting **forth**, however, he **quite** forgot to divest himself of his garments.

ADJ
The two ravens formed **quite** a contrast!

DP   ADV   SC
That widow worked **so** hard raising her young children **that** her cold bones became coarse.

DP   ADJ
I asked the beggar why **this** should be **so**.

> **Note to Instructor:** In this sentence, *so* follows the linking verb *should be* and describes the subject of the clause, *this*.

SC   SC
If an animal can have compassion, **so** should a human.

PREP   ADV   N
So saying, he fell **down** in worship in the **middle** of the road.

ADJ
Wash your hands in the **middle** part of the river.

PREP
She floated **down** the river to the mountains in the east.

Exercise 118B: Diagramming

On your own paper, diagram every word of the following sentences from *Chinese Fairy Tales and Fantasies*, edited by Moss Roberts and Sengyi Zheng. Ask your instructor for help if you need it.

The giant took him to a cave containing mounds of such things as tiger sinew, deer tail, and elephant tusk.

> **Note to Instructor:** In this sentence, *as* serves as a preposition.

The giant lowered his head as if he were thinking; then he nodded as if he understood.

Note to Instructor: In this sentence, *as if* serves as a compound subordinating conjunction.

He was as tall as a tree, with eyes like pots, mouth like a basin, and teeth a foot long.

Note to Instructor: The understood elements of the sentence are *as tall as a tree [is tall]*. The adjective *long* describes *teeth* (*long teeth*), and *foot* serves as an adverb modifying *long*, with the article *a* serving as an adverb modifying *foot*.

Yes, how did you know?

And each time she answered, "Yes."

Note to Instructor: In this sentence, *time* is an adverbial noun.

Having no choice, the scholar paid his respects to the tree and, after giving a full account of the situation, put the question to the tree, "So then, does the wolf have the right to eat me?"

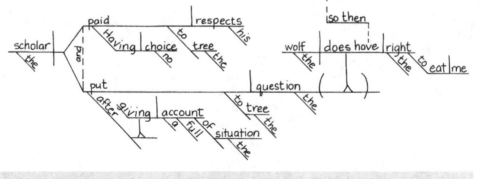

Note to Instructor: The independent clause *So then, does the wolf have the right to eat me?* serves as an appositive renaming *question*. The phrase *So then* serves as a conjunction (just as if the sentence began with *And* or *But*).

— LESSON 119 —

Idioms

> **Note to Instructor:** The dialogue from the Core Instructor Text is continued here, in the *Answer Key*, so that instructor and student can study different idioms each year. If the student is unfamiliar with any idiom covered, provide the meaning.

Instructor: We can divide idioms into two types. In the first type, all of the words in the idiom are serving a clear, familiar grammatical function—but the idiom itself means something completely different than its literal meaning. The next sentences in your workbook are this type of idiom. Read the first one out loud.

Student: I know you think you've solved the problem, but you're barking up the wrong tree.

Instructor: This sentence means exactly the same thing as the next sentence in your workbook. Read that sentence out loud.

Student: I know you think you've solved the problem, but you have the wrong solution.

Instructor: The second independent clause in both sentences has an action verb, but one action verb is modified by a prepositional phrase, while the other has a direct object. Put both sentences on the blank part of the diagram frames in your workbook now.

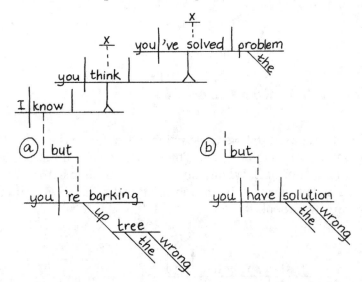

Instructor: Even though these sentences are grammatically similar, and the meaning is the same, the words used to express the idea of *getting the wrong solution* are very different. *Barking up the wrong tree* is a word picture—imagine a dog chasing a cat up a tree, and then not realizing that the cat has jumped over into another tree and run away completely! No matter how much the dog barks up the empty tree, he's not going to catch the cat.

Read me the next sentence.

Student: Yes, we lost the soccer game, but there's no point crying over spilt milk.

Instructor: Is there any spilt milk anywhere near the soccer field?

Student: No.

Instructor: What does *crying over spilt milk* mean?

Student: Complaining about something that's over, past, done, can't be changed.

Instructor: Place the sentence on the diagram frame in your workbook now.

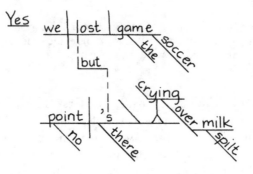

Instructor: The predicate adjective *crying* is a present participle, and *there* is an adverb. None of those parts of speech are unusual! If you can diagram an idiom without any trouble, you know that it has regular grammar—even if it has an unexpected meaning.

The second type of idiom uses combinations of words that might not fit into the patterns you've already learned. Read me the next sentence.

Student: You might enjoy acting, but don't give up your day job!

Instructor: What part of speech is *up*?

Student: An adverb.

Instructor: What does it modify?

Student: The verb give.

Instructor: What is the direct object of the verb *give*?

Student: The day job.

Instructor: So is the subject supposed to give the day job? Or not give the day job? No—the subject is supposed to not *give up* the day job. The verb *give up* is an idiom, meaning to *surrender*, *relinquish*, or *quit*. When you can sum up the meaning of an idiom with one word, it should always go on a single line in your diagram. Diagram this sentence onto the frame in your workbook.

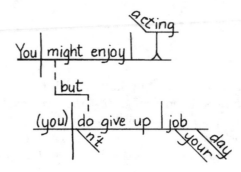

Instructor: The next sentence is a simple one. Read it out loud.

Student: That test was a piece of cake.

Instructor: What part of speech is *piece*?

Student: A noun.

Instructor: Look at the diagram that follows. What part of the sentence is *piece* diagrammed as?

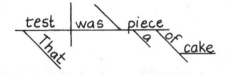

Student: Piece is a predicate nominative.

Instructor: But that doesn't actually make sense. The test isn't the same thing as a piece. It isn't a piece of anything—it's a whole test! Try to place the sentence on the next diagram frame instead.

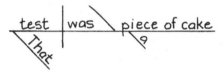

Instructor: Now, the idiom *piece of cake* has become a predicative adjective, describing the test. Try to put the idiom *piece of cake* into other words. What is the test actually like?

Student: "The test is easy!"

Instructor: All together, the phrase *piece of cake* is a predicate nominative that takes the place of a predicate adjective.

Let's look at a couple more idioms that you're probably familiar with. Read me the next sentence in your workbook.

Student: I wouldn't be caught dead wearing bright orange suspenders!

Instructor: Can you put *I wouldn't be caught dead* into other words that do not use an idiom?

> **Note to Instructor:** Give the student any necessary help to come up with an answer that resembles one of the following.

Student: I would never wear bright orange suspenders OR I would never let anyone see me in bright orange suspenders OR Bright orange suspenders are the most hideous piece of clothing I can imagine OR I will never be seen in bright orange suspenders.

Instructor: Try diagramming this sentence, and explain to me your choices!

> **Note to Instructor:** Three possible solutions are shown below: *would be caught dead* as a single predication; *would be* as a linking verb preceding the past participle *caught*, acting as a predicate adjective with *dead* modifying the past participle; *would be caught* functioning as a linking verb with *dead* as the predicate adjective.
>
> If the student comes up with any reasonable alternative and can explain the reasoning, accept the answer! Idioms are often messy.

Instructor: Read the last sentence in your workbook now.

Student: My business idea didn't work out, so I guess I'll have to go back to square one.

Instructor: What does *I'll have to go back to square one* mean? Try to explain it without using an idiom.

> **Note to Instructor:** Give the student any help needed to come up with an answer resembling one of the following.

Student: I'll have to start over OR *I'll have to go back to the beginning* OR *I'll have to begin again.*

Instructor: Try diagramming that sentence on your own paper now.

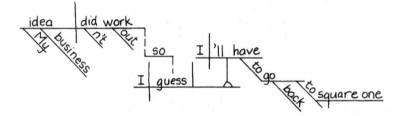

> **Note to Instructor:** The predicate *I'll have to go* could also be diagrammed as a single verb on the predicate line.

Instructor: Complete your exercises now.

Exercise 119A: Explaining Idioms

The following sentences are all taken from a collection of classic short stories. Each one contains at least one idiom! Circle each complete idiom. Write its meaning above it in your own words. (You can use more than one word—in fact, you may need several phrases.)

made him braver, stopped him from feeling nervous

But the gravity of the danger (steadied his nerves)

an ordinary man like everyone else   I deserve the worst possible punishment

I have no trumpet; I am only (Tom, Dick, or Harry;) I am a rogue and a dog, and (hanging's too good)
(for me.)

   —"A Lodging for the Night," Robert Louis Stevenson

not for any reason

Dancing was instantaneous, Mrs. Fennel privately enjoining the players (on no account) to let the dance exceed the length of a quarter of an hour.

clearly showing, demonstrating

They noticed to their surprise that he stood before them (the picture of) abject terror—his knees trembling, his hand shaking so violently that the door-latch by which he supported himself rattled audibly.

decided to use an earlier plan

Shepherdess Fennel (fell back upon) the intermediate plan of mingling short dances with short periods of talk and singing.

   —"The Three Strangers," Thomas Hardy

She sang bits of old songs and Psalms, stopping suddenly, mingling the Psalms of David and the

excerpts from, sentences and verses from

diviner words of his Son and Lord with homely (odds and ends) of ballads.

—"Rab and His Friends," John Brown

without regard to, even though something else is done

Still, (in spite of) all this strenuous attention to forms, Tom had a lurking dread that the devil,

true, even if there
are other conditions   would take what he is owed

(after all) (would have his due.)

> **Note to Instructor:** The entire idiom *give the devil his due* means recognizing what is good about someone or something that is otherwise disliked. ("My neighbor is noisy and annoying, but to give the devil his due, he keeps his grass neatly cut.") In this story, though, there is an actual devil who is owed something: the idiom *have his due* stands for this.

from my actions

"You have made so much money (out of me.)" said the speculator.

—"The Devil and Tom Walker," by Washington Irving

Most importantly, while something else is happening,
  especially in an ongoing period of time

(Above all) (meanwhile) this high consciousness prevailed.

destroy confidence, take away the will to do something

"Why, my dear man," Julia cried, "you (take the wind straight out of my sails!)"

—"Julia Bride," Henry James

Exercise 119B: Diagramming

On your own paper, diagram every word of the following sentences, taken from Agatha Christie's classic mystery novel *The Mysterious Affair at Styles*.

When you are finished, tell your instructor what each idiom means! Several sentences have more than one idiom. Ask for help if you need it.

to decide

Having no near relations or friends, I was trying **to make up my mind** what to do, when I

met

ran across John Cavendish.

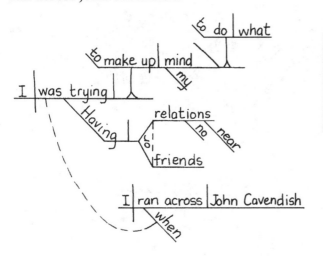

> **Note to Instructor:** Both *make up* and *ran across* act as single idiomatic verbs (the speaker did not *make* his mind, or *run* John Cavendish). The infinitive *to make up* is the direct object of *was trying*; *mind* is the object of *to make up*; and the infinitive phrase *what to do* is an object complement.

A small hint is as believable as a blatant statement.

A wink's as good as a nod—from you.

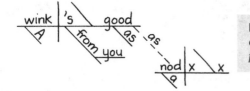

Note to Instructor: This is a comparative clause with understood elements: *a wink is as good as a nod [is good]*. The prepositional phrase *from you* could also be argued to modify *wink*.

It is very unpleasant OR I object very much!

One's gorge does rise at sitting down to eat with a possible murderer!

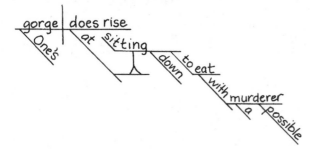

the decision will be made by someone else

I felt glad that the decision had been **taken out of his hands**.

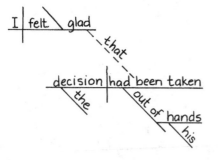

Note to Instructor: The preposition *out of* acts as a single preposition, expressing removal. The student could, however, also diagram the prepositional phrase *of his hands* as the object of the preposition *out*, or diagram *had been taken out* as a single idiomatic verb modified by *of his hands*.

disturbing part   my own feeling

The only **fly in the ointment** of my peaceful days was Mrs. Cavendish's extraordinary, and, **for my part**, unaccountable preference for the society of Dr. Bauerstein.

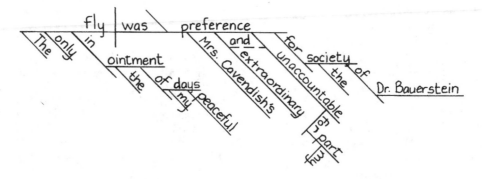

Note to Instructor: The prepositional phrase *for my part* modifies *unaccountable*—the speaker is unable to account in any way for Mrs. Cavendish's extraordinary preference.

Exercise 119C: Finding Idioms

On your own paper, rewrite the following four sentences, replacing the bolded words in each with an idiom that means the same thing.

Ask for help if you need it!

Don't talk to the track team about the big loss at State Finals—it's a real **event that is very hard to talk or think about!**

> *Don't talk to the track team about the big loss at State Finals—it's a real sore point!*

I've got to **recognize to your face just how hard you've worked**—you managed to get all the way to the semifinals even though you only started playing tennis two years ago!

> *I've got to hand it to you—you managed to get all the way to the semifinals even though you only started playing tennis two years ago!*

I know that talking about the loss just **makes the loss even worse than it already was**, because you tried so hard right to the end.

> *I know that talking about the loss just rubs salt into the wound, because you tried so hard right to the end.*

When you're working out this often, you **eat so much that I can barely keep the refrigerator and the pantries filled with food!**

> *When you're working out this often, you eat me out of house and home!*

— LESSON 120 —

Troublesome Sentences

Exercise 120A: A Selection of Challenging Sentences

After your instructor discusses each sentence with you, diagram it on your own paper.

These sentences are taken from *Frankenstein: or, the Modern Prometheus,* by Mary Wollstonecraft Shelley.

Note to Instructor: For each sentence, go through the dialogue provided and then ask the student to diagram the sentence before moving on to the next. Prompt the student for answers as necessary—this is an exercise, not a test!

When I returned home my first care was to procure the whole works of this author, and afterwards of Paracelsus and Albertus Magnus.

Instructor: Let's start by finding the subject and predicate of the main clause. What are they?

Student: Care was.

Instructor: The adverb clause at the beginning of the sentence modifies *was* and answers the question *when*. What is that adverb clause?

Student: When I returned home.

Instructor: That's all pretty straightforward—but now let's look at the rest of the sentence. What
kind of verb form is *to procure*?

Student: An infinitive.

Instructor: What does the infinitive phrase *to procure the whole works of this author* rename?

Student: Care.

Instructor: That phrase acts as a predicate nominative and renames *care*. What was the care? To
procure the works of the author.

Now let's look at the rest of the sentence, *and afterwards of Paracelsus and Albertus
Magnus*. There are some missing words in this phrase! What *of Paracelsus and
Albertus Magnus* is the writer talking about?

> **Note to Instructor:** If necessary, point to the word *works* in the student's book.

Student: The works.

Instructor: Read the whole sentence with the inserted words *the works* included.

*Student: When I returned home my first care was to procure the whole works of this author, and
afterwards the works of Paracelsus and Albertus Magnus.*

Instructor: This sounds as if the infinitive *to procure* might have two objects: *the whole works of
this author* and *the works of Paracelsus and Albertus Magnus*. But there's a problem
with diagramming to procure with two objects—and that's the adverb *afterwards*.
What does *afterwards* modify?

Student: To procure.

Instructor: Were the works of Paracelsus and Albertus Magnus procured *afterwards*?

Student: Yes.

Instructor: Were the "whole works of this author" procured *afterwards*?

Student: No.

Instructor: The time word *afterwards* can't apply to procuring both kinds of works! So there's
actually *another* set of missing words in the sentence—a second, understood repetition
of *to procure*. Try reading the sentence out loud again, and this time insert both an
extra *to procure* and *works*.

*Student: When I returned home my first care was to procure the whole works of this author, and
afterwards to procure the works of Paracelsus and Albertus Magnus.*

Instructor: Now try diagramming the sentence with those understood words in it. Mark the
understood words with *X* on the diagram.

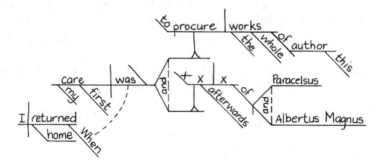

> I have described myself as always having been imbued with a fervent longing to penetrate the secrets of nature.

Instructor: The next sentence also has a slightly odd structure—but of a different kind! You should be able to find the subject and predicate easily. What are they?

Student: I have described.

Instructor: What part of the sentence is *myself*?

Student: The direct object.

Instructor: Do you remember what this kind of pronoun is called when it acts as an object?

Student: A reflexive pronoun.

Instructor: Now read me the rest of the sentence.

Student: As always having been imbued with a fervent longing to penetrate the secrets of nature.

Instructor: This has a lot of parts—but it acts as just one part of the sentence! Is this a clause or a phrase?

Student: A phrase.

> **Note to Instructor:** The student may be confused by the introductory *as*. If she says *clause*, ask her to find the subject and predicate. Since there is no subject, there is no clause.

Instructor: The *as* that introduces this phrase is acting as a preposition. It is followed by the verb *having been imbued*. What kind of verb form is this?

Student: Perfect present passive participle.

> **Note to Instructor:** If the student has difficulty identifying the participle, look back together at the optional section of Lesson 61.

Instructor: This perfect present passive participle is the object of the preposition *as*. It is followed by two prepositional phrases and an infinitive phrase. What are the prepositional phrases?

Student: With a fervent longing *and* of nature.

Instructor: What is the infinitive phrase?

Student: To penetrate the secrets.

Instructor: All together, this prepositional phrase modifies what word in the independent clause?

Student: Myself.

> **Note to Instructor:** If the student has difficulty finding the word modified, ask, "What is imbued with this longing?"

Instructor: What do you call a word, phrase, or clause that modifies an object?

Student: An object complement.

> **Note to Instructor:** If the student cannot remember, look back together at Lesson 40.

Instructor: Diagram the sentence now.

Chance—or rather the evil influence, the Angel of Destruction, which asserted omnipotent sway over me from the moment I turned my reluctant steps from my father's door—led me first to M. Krempe, professor of natural philosophy.

Instructor: This next sentence is a little bit trickier! For the moment, disregard all words inside the dashes and identify the subject, predicate, and object of the main clause.

Student: *Chance led me.*

Instructor: Now let's try to figure out what to do with the words inside the dashes. There are two possible ways to diagram *or rather the evil influence*. Can you figure out what they are?

> **Note to Instructor:** The two possible ways are 1) to diagram *Chance* and *influence* as a compound subject linked by the quasi-coordinator *or rather*, and 2) to diagram *influence* as an appositive renaming *Chance*. Give the student all necessary help to reach this conclusion.

Instructor: In this diagram, we're going to diagram *influence* as an appositive renaming *Chance*, because the meaning of the sentence is clearly that *Chance* is actually the evil influence! How do you diagram an appositive?

Student: *Inside parentheses following the noun.*

Instructor: In this case, the appositive has another appositive! What is the next name given to the evil influence?

Student: *The Angel of Destruction.*

Instructor: So you'll diagram *influence* inside parentheses following *Chance*—but then also diagram *Angel of Destruction* inside parentheses following *influence*! That means you'll have a double set of parentheses. There is one more appositive in this sentence. Can you find it?

Student: *M. Krempe is a professor.*

Instructor: The rest of the sentence is made up of two subordinate clauses. What is the first one? (It contains the second one, so read me the whole thing.)

Student: *Which asserted omnipotent sway over me from the moment I turned my reluctant steps from my father's door.*

Instructor: What does that clause modify?

Student: *Influence.*

Instructor: Within that clause is a second clause with an understood subordinating word. What is the second clause?

Student: *I turned my reluctant steps from my father's door.*

Instructor: What is the understood subordinating word?

Student: *That.*

Instructor: In this clause, the understood *that* isn't just a subordinating conjunction—it refers back to a word in the previous subordinate clause. What does the clause *I turned my reluctant steps from my father's door* describe?

Student: *Moment.*

Instructor: The understood *that* is a relative pronoun, referring back to *moment* and introducing an adjective clause.

Try diagramming the sentence now.

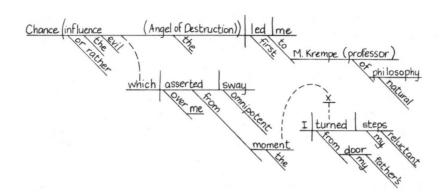

Such were the professor's words—rather let me say such the words of the fate—enounced to destroy me.

Instructor: This next sentence also has a clause inside dashes. For the moment, ignore the words inside the dashes, and see if you can find the subject and predicate of the main clause. What are they?

Student: Words were.

> **Note to Instructor:** There is more than one possibility here!
>
> The student may identify the subject as *Such*—if so, agree that the subject and predicate COULD be *such were* with *words* as the predicate nominative, but point out that *Such* here is an adjective, and so it makes more sense to identify the noun *words* as the subject and *Such* as the predicate adjective. (However, changing the place of *words* and *Such* on the diagram doesn't materially affect the structure of the sentence.)
>
> The student may also identify the subject and predicate as *words were enounced*. This is also possible; in this case, *Such* would become an adjective diagrammed beneath *words* rather than a predicate adjective diagrammed after the linking verb (with *enounced* as a past participle diagrammed as an adjective modifying *words*).
>
> Allow the student to explain any of these possibilities, and then agree that while they are also possible, we are going to try diagramming the sentence with *words* as the subject, *were* as the linking verb, and *Such as* the predicate adjective.

Instructor: The past participle *enounced* acts as an adjective. What noun does that adjective describe?

Student: Words.

Instructor: The infinitive *to destroy* modifies *enounced*. Let's look now at the clause inside the dashes! Read it out loud to me.

Student: Rather let me say such the words of the fate.

Instructor: This is a complicated clause! Start with rather *let me*. You've studied the kind of sentence that begins with *let me*. What kind of sentence is this?

Student: Hortative.

> **Note to Instructor:** If the student cannot remember, look together at Lesson 109.

Instructor: What is the subject of the hortative verb *let*?

Student: X for unknown.

Instructor: What is the object?

Student: Me.

Instructor: This hortative sentence is connected to the main clause by the coordinating
conjunction *rather*. Try to diagram the entire sentence now.

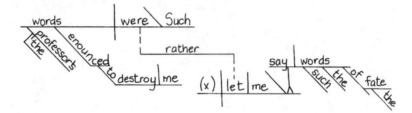

He appeared about fifty years of age, but with an aspect expressive of the greatest
benevolence; a few grey hairs covered his temples, but those at the back of his head were
nearly black.

Instructor: We have been seeing a lot of predicate adjectives and predicate nominatives! Take a
look at the next sentence. What are the subject and predicate of the main clause?

Student: He appeared.

Instructor: What kind of verb is *appeared*?

Student: A linking verb.

> **Note to Instructor:** If necessary, ask the student to review the list of linking verbs that can also
> be action verbs in Lesson 45.

Instructor: The linking verb is followed by two phrases that describe the subject *He*. What are
those two phrases?

*Student: About fifty years of age *and* with an aspect expressive of the greatest benevolence.*

Instructor: What kinds of phrases are these, and what part of the sentence do they form?

Student: They are prepositional phrases acting as predicate adjectives.

Instructor: The rest of the sentence is made up of two more clauses. What kind of clauses are they?

Student: Independent clauses.

Instructor: Diagram the sentence now.

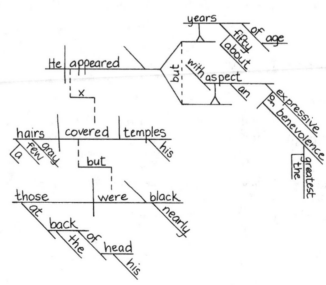

The raising of ghosts or devils was a promise liberally accorded by my favourite authors, the fulfilment of which I most eagerly sought; and if my incantations were always unsuccessful, I attributed the failure rather to my own inexperience and mistake than to a want of skill or fidelity in my instructors.

Instructor: Let's do one more sentence together! This is a long one. Start by reading the whole sentence out loud.

Student: *The raising of ghosts or devils was a promise liberally accorded by my favourite authors, the fulfilment of which I most eagerly sought; and if my incantations were always unsuccessful, I attributed the failure rather to my own inexperience and mistake than to a want of skill or fidelity in my instructors.*

Instructor: That sounds very complicated—but all you have to do is diagram one clause at a time! Read me the first clause, beginning with *The raising* and ending with *authors*.

Student: *The raising of ghosts or devils was a promise liberally accorded by my favourite authors.*

Instructor: There's nothing in that clause that you haven't seen before! Diagram it now.

> **Note to Instructor:** See full diagram below. The first independent clause consists of a present participle phrase serving as the subject, a linking verb and predicate nominative, and the past participle adjective phrase *liberally accorded by my favorite authors* modifying *promise*.

Instructor: Now read me the second clause—the remaining words before the semicolon.

Student: *The fulfilment of which I most eagerly sought.*

Instructor: What is the subject and predicate of that clause?

Student: *I sought.*

Instructor: What is the object of the verb *sought*?

Student: *Fulfilment.*

Instructor: What does the prepositional phrase *of which* modify?

Student: *Fulfilment.*

Instructor: The relative pronoun *which* refers back to a word in the first clause. What word?

Student: *Raising OR promise.*

> **Note to Instructor:** *Raising* and *promise* both name the same reality, so it is slightly ambiguous as to which word the adjective clause modifies. Accept either answer, but tell the student to diagram the sentence as though the adjective clause modifies the subject *raising*.

Instructor: Diagram the adjective clause now.

Now let's look at the second half of the sentence! Read it out loud to me.

Student: *And if my incantations were always unsuccessful, I attributed the failure rather to my own inexperience and mistake than to a want of skill or fidelity in my instructors.*

Instructor: You've studied a lot of sentences that are made up of a subordinate clause that begins with *if*, followed by an independent clause. What are those kinds of sentences called?

Student: *Conditional sentences.*

> **Note to Instructor:** If necessary, review Lesson 82 with the student to find the answers to the above question and the following questions.

Instructor: What is the clause beginning with *if* called?

Student: *A condition clause.*

Instructor: A condition is a circumstance that restricts, limits, or modifies. In this case, the condition is: *If my incantations were always unsuccessful.* The independent clause that follows describes what will happen if the circumstance is met. What is this kind of clause called?

Student: A consequence clause.

Instructor: The whole set of clauses after the semicolon is linked to the first set of clauses by the semicolon and coordinating conjunction. These connectors link the predicate of the first independent clause to the predicate of the second independent clause. So which two predicates are linked together?

Student: Was and attributed.

Instructor: Diagram the second independent clause and the coordinating conjunction now.

Now add the last part of the sentence—the condition clause! When you are finished, compare your diagram with the diagram in this Key.

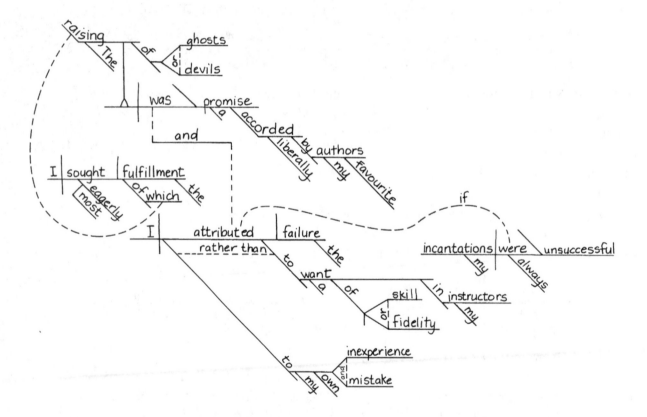

─REVIEW 10─

Weeks 29-31

Topics

Hortative Verbs
Ambitransitive Verbs
Infinitive Phrases as Objects
Infinitive Phrases With Understood "To"
Principal Parts of Irregular Verbs
Noun Clauses as Appositives
Which/That in Restrictive and Non-Restrictive Clauses
Formal Conditionals
Words Acting as Multiple Parts of Speech
Affirmations and Negations
Idioms

Review 10A: The Missing Words Game

Fill in each blank below with the exact *form* described—but choose your own words!

Show your answers to your instructor, who will insert them into the matching blanks in the short essay in the *Answer Key*.

Your instructor will then show you the original essay—and your version.

> **Note to Instructor:** Write the student's answers into the blanks below. The fill-in-the-blank version of the text is followed by the original. You may decide which version to show the student first.
>
> The following excerpt is from an 1861 book written to help women manage their households properly. It was called *The Book of Household Management*, by Mrs. Isabella Beeton, an English journalist who lived in London. *The Book of Household Management* was a tremendous best-seller, was a standard gift to new wives for a century, and is still in print today.

These duties and pleasures _____ and enjoyed, the hour of luncheon _____ .
                     passive past participle   indicative perfect future active verb
                                                                    (third-person singular)

_____ is a _____ necessary meal between an _____
demonstrative   adverb of affirmation   adverb of time
pronoun, singular

breakfast and a _____ dinner, as a healthy person, with good exercise, _____
               adverb of time   modal simple present state-of-being
                                                        verb (third-person singular)

a fresh _____ of food _____ in _____ hours. It _____
       noun, either concrete or   adverb of time   number   modal simple present
      abstract, singular or plural   state-of-being verb
                                                            (third-person singular)

a light meal; but its _____ must, _____, be, _____,
                      abstract noun, singular   parenthetical expression   idiom expressing the
                                                                                        extent of something

proportionate to the time it is intended _____ you to wait for _____
                                          infinitive, present active   possessive adjective

dinner, and the _____ of _____ you take in the mean time. At this
                abstract noun, singular   abstract noun, singular

time, also, the _____ dinner _____.
                possessive adjective   indicative simple future perfect passive verb
                                             (third-person singular)

    In _____ establishments _____ an early dinner _____, that
       demonstrative adjective   relative adverb   indicative present passive verb
                                                                          (third-person singular)

will, of course, take the place of the luncheon. In _____ houses, _____ a
                                                     adverb of quantity   relative adverb

_____ dinner is provided for the children at about one o'clock, the mistress and the
adjective that can
also be a noun

_____ portion of the family make their luncheon at the same time from the same
adjective

_____, or whatever _____. A mistress _____, according to
concrete noun, singular   modal simple present passive   indicative simple future active
                            verb (third-person singular)   verb (third-person singular)

circumstances, the _____ of the meal; but the more usual plan is for the
                    present participle acting
                    as a singular noun

_____ of the house to have the _____ brought to her table, and _____
concrete noun, singular   concrete noun, singular   adverb of time

carried to the _____.
                noun that can also be an
                adjective

    After luncheon, morning calls _____ and received. _____
                                    modal simple present passive   demonstrative pronoun, plural
                                    verb (third-person plural)

_____ under three heads: _____ of ceremony, friendship, and
modal simple present passive   demonstrative pronoun, plural
verb (third-person singular)

congratulation or condolence. Visits of ceremony, or courtesy, _____ _____
                                                                relative pronoun   adverb of frequency

merge into those of friendship, are _____ under various circumstances. Thus,
                                     infinitive, present passive

they are _____ required after _____ at a _____ house,
          adverb   present participle acting   possessive adjective
                                           as a noun

or after a ball, picnic, or _____ other party. These visits _____ short, a _____
                            indefinite adjective   modal simple present active   abstract noun,
                                                                  verb (third-person plural)   singular

of from fifteen to twenty minutes being _____ sufficient. A lady paying a visit
                                         adverb of affirmation

_____ her boa or neckerchief; but _____ her shawl _____ bonnet.
modal simple present active   correlative conjunctions   correlative conjunctions
verb (third-person singular)

_____ other visitors are announced, it is well _____ _____ possible,
<small>adverb acting as subordinating word</small> ... <small>infinitive, present active</small> <small>compound adverb</small>

_____ care to let it appear that their _____ is _____
<small>present participle acting as an adverb</small> ... <small>concrete noun, singular</small> ... <small>adverb of affirmation</small>

the _____. When they are quietly seated, and the bustle of their _____
<small>abstract noun, singular</small> ... <small>abstract noun, singular</small>

is over, _____ from your chair, taking a kind leave of the hostess, and _____
<small>imperative simple present active verb, singular</small> ... <small>present participle acting as an adverb</small>

politely to the guests. _____ you _____ at an inconvenient time, not
<small>modal simple present active verb (second-person singular)</small>

having ascertained the luncheon hour, or from any other _____, _____
<small>abstract noun, singular</small> <small>imperative simple present active verb, singular</small>

_____ possible, without, however, _____ that you feel _____
<small>compound adverb</small> ... <small>present participle acting as a noun</small> ... <small>reflexive pronoun</small>

an intruder. It is _____ difficult for any _____ or even _____
<small>adverb of negation</small> ... <small>hyphenated compound adjective</small> ... <small>hyphenated compound adjective</small>

person, to know what to say on such an occasion, and, _____ politely withdrawing, a
<small>preposition</small>

promise _____ to call again, if the lady you have called on _____
<small>modal simple present passive verb (third-person singular)</small> ... <small>subjunctive simple present active verb (third-person singular)</small>

really _____.
<small>predicate adjective</small>

It is not advisable, at any time, to take favourite _____ into another lady's drawing-
<small>concrete noun, plural</small>

room, for _____ persons have an _____ dislike to such _____;
<small>adjective of quantity</small> ... <small>adjective</small> ... <small>concrete noun, plural</small>

and besides _____, there is always a chance of a _____ of some
<small>demonstrative pronoun, singular</small> ... <small>abstract noun, singular</small>

article occurring, through their _____ and _____ here and there,
<small>present participle acting as a noun</small> ... <small>present participle acting as a noun</small>

sometimes _____ much to the _____ and _____ of
<small>adverb of affirmation</small> ... <small>abstract noun, singular</small> ... <small>abstract noun, singular</small>

the hostess. Her _____, also, unless they are particularly _____ and
<small>concrete noun, plural</small> ... <small>predicate adjective, compound, hyphenated</small>

_____, and she is on _____ _____ terms with the hostess,
<small>predicate adjective</small> ... <small>adverb of degree</small> <small>adjective</small>

_____ not _____ a lady in making morning calls. Where a lady,
<small>modal simple present active verb (third-person plural)</small>

however, pays her visits in a carriage, the _____ _____ in the
<small>concrete noun, plural</small> <small>modal simple present passive verb (third-person plural)</small>

vehicle, and remain in it until the visit is _____.
<small>predicate adjective that can also be a preposition or adverb</small>

These duties and pleasures being performed and enjoyed, the hour of luncheon will have arrived. This is a very necessary meal between an early breakfast and a late dinner, as a healthy person, with good exercise, should have a fresh supply of food once in four hours. It should be a light meal; but its solidity must, of course, be, in some degree, proportionate to the time it is intended to enable you to wait for your dinner, and the amount of exercise you take in the mean time. At this time, also, the servants' dinner will be served.

In those establishments where an early dinner is served, that will, of course, take the place of the luncheon. In many houses, where a nursery dinner is provided for the children at about one o'clock, the mistress and the elder portion of the family make their luncheon at the same time from the same joint, or whatever may be provided. A mistress will arrange, according to circumstances, the serving of the meal; but the more usual plan is for the lady of the house to have the joint brought to her table, and afterwards carried to the nursery.

After luncheon, morning calls may be made and received. These may be divided under three heads: those of ceremony, friendship, and congratulation or condolence. Visits of ceremony, or courtesy, which occasionally merge into those of friendship, are to be paid under various circumstances. Thus, they are uniformly required after dining at a friend's house, or after a ball, picnic, or any other party. These visits should be short, a stay of from fifteen to twenty minutes being quite sufficient. A lady paying a visit may remove her boa or neckerchief; but neither her shawl nor bonnet.

When other visitors are announced, it is well to retire as soon as possible, taking care to let it appear that their arrival is not the cause. When they are quietly seated, and the bustle of their entrance is over, rise from your chair, taking a kind leave of the hostess, and bowing politely to the guests. Should you call at an inconvenient time, not having ascertained the luncheon hour, or from any other inadvertence, retire as soon as possible, without, however, showing that you feel yourself an intruder. It is not difficult for any well-bred or even good-tempered person, to know what to say on such an occasion, and, on politely withdrawing, a promise can be made to call again, if the lady you have called on appears really disappointed.

It is not advisable, at any time, to take favourite dogs into another lady's drawing-room, for many persons have an absolute dislike to such animals; and besides this, there is always a chance of a breakage of some article occurring, through their leaping and bounding here and there, sometimes very much to the fear and annoyance of the hostess. Her children, also, unless they are particularly well-trained and orderly, and she is on exceedingly friendly terms with the hostess, should not accompany a lady in making morning calls. Where a lady, however, pays her visits in a carriage, the children can be taken in the vehicle, and remain in it until the visit is over.

Review 10B: Identifying Infinitive Phrases, Noun Clauses, and Modifying Clauses

In the following sentences, follow these four steps:

a) Identify every set of underlined words as *INF* for infinitive phrase, *PREP* for prepositional phrase, or *CL* for clause.

b) Label each phrase or clause as *ADV* for adverb, *ADJ* for adjective, or *N* for noun.

c) For adjective and adverb phrases and clauses, draw an arrow from the label to the word modified.

d) For noun phrases and clauses, add the appropriate part of the sentence label: *S* for subject, *DO* for object, *IO* for indirect object, *OP* for object of a preposition, *PN* for predicate nominative, *APP* for appositive.

Note: Some sets of words are within other sets of words, so you'll see some double underlining! If you see double underlining, be sure to follow the instructions for both sets of underlined words.

The first sentence is done for you.

Like the sentences from the last exercise, these are taken from *The Book of Household Management*, by Mrs. Isabella Beeton, an English journalist who lived in London. *The Book of Household Management* was a tremendous best-seller, was a standard gift to new wives for a century, and is still in print today. At least half of it was recipes for what were considered standard meals for a household!

CL ADV   PREP ADV

When all is well stirred, put the pudding into a buttered basin, tie it down with a cloth, plunge it into boiling water, and boil for 1-1/4 hour.

CL ADV
INF ADV

As not only health but life may be said to depend on the cleanliness of culinary utensils, great

PREP ADV   PREP ADV

attention must be paid to their condition generally, but more especially to that of the saucepans,

CL ADV

stewpans, and boilers. Inside they should be kept perfectly clean, and where an open fire is used, the outside as clean as possible.

> **Note to Instructor:** The infinitive phrase *to depend... utensils* can't be a noun clause serving as a direct object because the verb *may be said* is passive.

INF ADV

Now place them in the oven for a few minutes, to acquire a nice brown colour, and serve them

PREP ADV   PREP ADJ
CL ADJ

on a napkin, with custard sauce flavoured with vanilla, or a *compôte* of any fruit that may be preferred.

PREP ADV   INF ADV   CL ADJ

In English meadows sorrell is usually left to grow wild; but in France, where it is cultivated, its flavour is greatly improved.

PREP ADV———
To all these directions the cook should pay great attention, nor should they, by any means, be

PREP ADV———   CL ADJ   CL N DO
neglected by the mistress of the household, who ought to remember that cleanliness in the kitchen

                                                                                               CL N DO   PREP ADV
gives health and happiness to home, whilst economy will immeasurably assist in preserving them.

PREP ADV   CL ADJ   INF N DO
A well-ventilated larder, dry and shady, is better for meat and poultry, which require to be kept for
some time.

PREP ADV   CL ADV
Stew the rice very gently in the above proportion of new milk, and, when it is tender, pour it into

INF ADV
a basin; stir in the butter, and let it stand to cool; then beat the eggs, add these to the rice with the

CL ADJ
sugar, salt, and any flavouring that may be approved, such as nutmeg, powdered cinnamon, grated
lemon-peel, essence of bitter almonds, or vanilla.

CL ADV
When the soup is cold, the fat may be much more easily and completely removed; and when it is

CL ADV   INF ADV   PREP ADJ   CL ADJ
poured off, care must be taken not to disturb the settlings at the bottom of the vessel, which are so

CL ADV
fine that they will escape through a sieve.

Cut the cold hare into neat slices, and put the head, bones, and trimmings into a stewpan, with

PREP ADV   PREP ADV
3/4 pint of water; add the mace, allspice, seasoning, onion, and herbs, and stew for nearly an hour,

and strain the gravy; thicken it with butter and flour, add the wine and ketchup, and lay in the

PREP ADV   CL ADJ
pieces of hare, with any stuffing that may be left.

CL ADV   CL N OP
When the whole is well blended together, mould it into balls, or whatever shape is intended, roll

CL ADJ
them in flour, and poach in boiling water, to which a little salt should have been added.

Review 10C: Parsing

Parse every bolded verb in the following sentences, taken from another best-selling book by Isabella Beeton: *Mrs. Beeton's Dictionary of Every-Day Cookery.*

Provide the following information:

Person:	First, second, or third
Number:	Sing. or pl.
Tense:	Simple past, present, or future; perfect past, present, or future; progressive past, present, or future; or progressive perfect present
Voice:	Active, passive, or state-of-being
Mood:	Indicative, subjunctive, imperative, hortatory, or modal
	If the verb is also emphatic, add this label to the mood.

The first bolded verb is done for you.

The principal art in composing good rich soup is so to proportion the several ingredients

3rd sing., simple future,
active, indicative

that the flavour of one **shall** not **predominate** over another, and that all the articles of which

3rd sing., simple present, *3rd pl., simple future,*
passive, indicative *active, indicative*

it **is composed shall form** an agreeable whole.

2nd sing., simple present,
active, imperative

Boil gently for ¼ hour, or until the fruit is tender; but take care not to let it break, as the

3rd sing., simple present, *3rd sing., simple present,*
passive, modal *passive, subjunctive*

appearance of the dish **would be spoiled were** the fruit **reduced** to a pulp.

3rd sing., simple future,
passive, indicative

For a nursery pudding, the addition of the latter ingredients **will be found** quite superfluous, as

also the paste round the edge of the dish.

2nd sing., simple present, *3rd sing., simple future,*
active, imperative *passive, indicative*

Put in the fish, heat it gradually, but **do** not **let** it boil, or it **will be broken**.

3rd sing., simple present,
active, modal

The above is the proportion of milk which we think **would convert** the flour into a stiff paste; but

3rd sing., simple present, *3rd sing., simple present,*
passive, modal, subjunctive *passive, modal*

should it **be found** too much, an extra spoonful or two of flour **must be put** in.

3rd sing., perfect future,
active, indicative

Mix with it by degrees all, or a portion, of the gravy that **will have run** from it, and a little

2nd sing., simple present,
active, imperative

clarified butter; **add** the seasoning, put it in small pots for use, and cover with a little butter just

warmed and poured over.

Plunge the stems into boiling water, and, by the time the water is cold, the flowers **will**

3rd pl., perfect future,
active, indicative

have revived.

3rd sing., perfect present,
active, modal
We heard a gentleman who, when he **might have had** a wing, declare his partiality for a leg, saying

3rd sing., perfect past,   *3rd sing., perfect past,*
passive, indicative   *active, indicative*
that he **had been obliged** to eat legs for so long a time that he **had** at last **come** to like them better

than the other more prized parts.

2nd sing., simple present,
active, imperative
Mince the fowl not too finely, and **make** it hot in the Béchamel sauce, to which the nutmeg,

3rd pl., perfect present,
passive, indicative
pepper and salt, and cream, **have been added**.

2nd sing., simple present,
active, imperative
Then put them into a stewpan, cover them with water, and **let** them boil until tender, and, if the

3rd pl., simple present,   *3rd pl., perfect present,*
state-of-being, modal   *active, indicative*
onions **should be** very strong, change the water after they **have been boiling** for ¼ hour.

3rd pl., simple present,   *3rd pl., simple present,*
passive, modal   *passive, modal*
They **may be served** in their skins, and **eaten** with a piece of cold butter and a seasoning of pepper

3rd pl., simple present,
passive, modal
and salt; or they **may be peeled**, and a good brown gravy poured over them.

3rd sing., simple present,   *3rd pl., progressive perfect present,*
passive, modal   *active, indicative*
The jelly is then done, and **may be poured** into moulds which **have been** previously **soaking** in

3rd sing., simple future,
active, indicative
water, when it **will turn** out nicely for dessert or a side dish.

3rd sing., progressive present,   *3rd sing., simple present,*
active, modal   *passive, indicative*
The gravy **should be boiling** before it **is poured** into the tureen.

3rd sing., perfect present,   *3rd sing., simple present,*
passive, indicative   *passive, modal*
After this pickle **has been made** from 4 to 5 months, the liquor **may be strained** and **bottled**, and

3rd sing., simple future,
passive, indicative
will be found an excellent lemon ketchup.

3rd pl., simple present,
passive, modal
Gravies and sauces **should be sent** to table very hot; and there is all the more necessity for the cook

3rd pl., simple present,
state-of-being, indicative
to see to this point, as, from their being usually served in small quantities, they **are** more liable to

3rd pl., simple past,
state-of-being, subjunctive
cool quickly than if they **were** in a larger body.

3rd sing., simple present,
passive, modal
In speaking of confectionary, it **should be remarked** that many preparations come under that

head; for the various fruits, flowers, herbs, roots, and juices, which, when boiled with sugar,

3rd pl., simple past,
passive, indicative
were formerly **employed** in pharmacy as well as for sweetmeats, were called confections, from the

Latin word conficere, 'to make up;' but the term confectionary embraces a very large class indeed

3rd pl., simple present,
passive, modal
of sweet food, many kinds of which **should** not **be attempted** in the ordinary cuisine.

Review 10D: *Which* and *That* Clauses

In the following sentences, from Isabella Beeton's *Book of Needlework*, underline each clause introduced by *which* or *that*. If *that* is understood, use a caret to insert it. If a *which* or *that* clause falls within another clause, underline the entire larger clause once, and the clause-within-a-clause a second time.

- Label each clause as *ADJ* for adjective, *ADV* for adverb, or *N* for noun.
- For adjective and adverb clauses, draw an arrow back to the word modified.
- For noun clauses, label the part of the sentence that the clause fulfills (*S, PN, DO, IO, APP*).
- Finally, label each adjective clause as *R* for restrictive or *NON-R* for nonrestrictive.

  The first sentence is done for you.

The needlework called Tatting in England, *Frivolité* in French, and *Frivolitäten* in German, is a

ADJ R

work which seems, from all accounts, to have been in favour several generations ago.

ADJ R

Take the end of the shuttle which comes out from the loop between the forefinger and thumb of the right hand, and strain the cotton very tightly towards the right.

that   N DO

We think it would be better to leave the repetitions to the judgment of the worker.

ADJ NR

After this, withdraw the second left-hand finger, which is *above* the cotton, and pass it again under that cotton, so as to draw up the loop.

ADV

The Venetian Bar is so simple that it hardly needs description.

ADJ NR

Then take some crochet cotton, which must be finer than the cotton used for tatting, and work a

ADJ R

row of double stitches over the thread which joins the circles.

ADJ R   ADJ NR

Draw up very tightly the cotton over which you work, so that the circles form a rosette, which is closed by sewing together the two corresponding purl of the first and last circle.

ADJ NR

Lace is of two kinds—pillow lace, which is made upon a cushion or pillow, and point lace,

ADJ NR   ADJ NR

which is made of stitches or *points* worked in patterns by hand, which are joined by various stitches forming a groundwork, also the result of the needle above.

N OC

Repeat from beginning, taking care that the next oval be close to the last.

> **Note to Instructor:** The noun clause is the object complement to *care*, which is the object of the participle *taking*.

This insertion consists of 2 rows of three-branched patterns <u>which lie opposite each other</u>, and [ADJ R] are joined by slanting rows of knots.

Before beginning to work this pattern, thread the beads <u>which take the place of purl stitches</u>, [ADJ R] and <u>which are slipped in between two double stitches</u>. [ADJ R]

We shall merely say <u>that the centre circle is always worked separately</u>, and <u>that the cotton is</u> [N DO] [N DO] <u>fastened on afresh to work the eight outer leaves</u>.

Take thicker cotton than that <u>with which you work</u>; never commence with a knot, and do not take [ADJ R] a thread longer than sixteen or eighteen inches.

> **Note to Instructor:** In this sentence, *that* is a demonstrative pronoun, modified by the adjective clause introduced by *with which*.

Great care should be taken <u>that the material on which you embroider is not puckered</u>. [ADV] [ADJ R]

The two loops <u>that remain at the end</u> are cast off together after winding the cotton round the needle. [ADJ R]

Run some cord in the top of the bag to match one of the colours used, and make the tassel for the bottom from the silk <u>that is remaining</u> after working the crochet. [ADJ R]

One great advantage of netting is <u>that each stitch is finished and independent of the next</u>, so that [N PN] if an accident happens to one stitch it does not, as in crochet or knitting, spoil the whole work.

> **Note to Instructor:** In this sentence, *so that* acts as a compound coordinating conjunction, connecting the first independent clause to the condition-consequence sentence that follows.

Review 10E: Words Acting as Multiple Parts of Speech

In each set of sentences below, underline the repeated word. Label each occurrence as *N* for noun, *V* for verb, *PRO* for pronoun, *ADV* for adverb, *ADJ* for adjective, *PREP* for preposition, *CC* for coordinating conjunction, or *SC* for subordinating conjunction.

These sentences are all taken from *The American Woman's Home: or, Principles of Domestic Science*, by the nineteenth-century writer Harriet Beecher Stowe. You may be more familiar with Stowe's anti-slavery novel *Uncle Tom's Cabin*. But Stowe also wrote over two dozen other books, including the how-to text *The American Woman's Home*.

Under the sink are shelf-boxes placed on two shelves run into grooves, with other grooves above and <u>below</u>. [ADJ]

This is all a mistake; for, as a fact, in close sleeping-rooms the purest air is <u>below</u>[ADJ] and the most impure above.

This cast-iron pipe is surrounded by a brick flue, through which air passes from <u>below</u>[N] to be warmed by the pipe.

A certain degree of warmth in the stomach is indispensable to digestion; so, when the gastric juice is cooled <u>below</u>[PREP] this temperature, it ceases to act.

It is useful to be able to move the shelves, and increase or diminish the spaces <u>between</u>[ADJ].

As a general rule, meals should be five hours apart, and eating <u>between</u>[PREP] meals avoided.

Even so, in our <u>long</u>[ADJ] winters, multitudes of delicate people subsist on the daily waning strength which they acquired in the season when windows and doors were open.

I have often returned from church doubting whether I had not committed a sin in exposing myself so <u>long</u>[ADV] to its poisonous air.

As <u>long</u>[SC] as the paper remains, the candle will burn.

> **Note to Instructor:** Together, *as long as* acts as a compound subordinating conjunction, linking the initial subordinate clause to the main clause.

Every woman should train her children in this important duty of <u>home</u>[ADJ] life on which health and comfort so much depend.

Having duly arranged for the physical necessities of a healthful and comfortable <u>home</u>[N], we next approach the important subject of beauty in reference to the decoration of houses.

The oven is the space under and around the back and <u>front</u>[ADJ] sides of the fire-box.

Another useful appendage is a common tin oven, in which roasting can be done in the <u>front</u>[N] of the stove.

Probably you could make the <u>cover</u>[N] more cheaply by getting the cloth and trimming its edge with a handsome border.

<u>Cover</u>[V] this with a green English furniture print.

In <u>like</u>[ADJ] manner, each motion of the arm and fingers has one muscle to produce it and another to restore to the natural position.

The cushion to be cut square, with side pieces; stuffed with hair, and stitched through <u>like</u>[PREP] a mattress.

The following, then, may be put <u>down</u>[ADV] as the causes of a debilitated constitution from the misuse of food.

PREP
<u>Down</u> these two corner-flues passes the current of hot air and smoke, having first drawn across the corrugated oven-top.

V
What animals <u>use</u> is provided by vegetables, and what vegetables require is furnished by animals.

N
The <u>use</u> of ivy in decorating a room is beginning to be generally acknowledged.

PREP
This is prevented by enlarging the closets on each side, so that their walls meet the ceiling <u>under</u> the garret floor.

ADV
When watering, set a pail <u>under</u>, for it to drip into.

ADJ
The <u>under</u> couch is like the upper couch, except for its different dimensions.

Review 10F: Idioms

Circle each idiom in the following sentences. Above each one, write its meaning within the sentence. The first is done for you.

These sentences are taken from *The Gospel of Germs*, by Nancy Tomes. The book examines how the housekeeping standards and principles taught by nineteenth-century housekeeping manuals affected the way that Americans thought about disease and germs.

Note to Instructor: Accept any answer that approximates the explanations below.

explained their reasons as related to
Converts to the germ theory often (painted a chilling picture) of an environment saturated with these invisible enemies.

They produced countless lectures, exhibits, posters, films, and pamphlets that preached to
who had all kinds of different jobs and incomes
millions of Americans (from all walks of life) the same hygenic message.

Exposed to the continual refrain that "little things were not trifles," they began to look at familiar
in a new way
habits (with new eyes).

announcing that they were better at hygiene
By (seizing the hygienic high ground,) they gained a useful advantage over their less affluent and
to break
sanitarily savvy fellow plumbers, who were more likely (to run afoul of) the regulations.

the best and newest
From the 1880s on, the new style toilet quickly came to embody (the cutting edge) of hygienic design.

was particularly upsetting to/meaningful for
The "whited sepulchre" image (had a particularly keen edge) for women of the genteel classes.

While Waring was watching him
(Under his watchful eye,) Rockwell proceeded with the renovations that Waring had recommended in his preliminary report.

I'm mentioning this last but it's as important as everything else.

(Last but not least,) they urinated and defecated in chamber pots and outdoor privies with little regard for where the contents ended up in relation to the community water supply.

Giving the reason as

(In the name of) public health, hotels were gradually required to change the sheets between each patron's use of a room.

Review 10G: Ambitransitive Verbs

In the following sentences, underline each action verb that acts as a predicate. Mark each of these verbs as *T* for transitive or *IT* for intransitive. For transitive verbs, draw an arrow from the label *T* to the word that receives the action of the verb.

These sentences are taken from another nineteenth-century household manual: *Women, Plumbers, and Doctors, or, Household Sanitation,* by Harriette Merrick Plunkett. The book is all about how proper cleanliness in the home can prevent disease (a major preoccupation of nineteenth-century writers!).

A new sphere of usefulness and efficiency <u>opens</u> [IT] with the knowledge that an ounce of prevention is worth a ton of cure.

Ball-floats <u>open</u> [T] the pipe when the water <u>is lowered</u> [T].

We <u>will give</u> [T] the reply which Professor C. F. Chandler, of New York, <u>gave</u> [T].

She thought she <u>had done</u> [T] her whole duty; but her vigilance <u>gave</u> [IT] out at the ground floor.

After all the little errands <u>are done</u> [T], bed-time <u>is come</u> [T]!

The men of the house <u>come</u> [IT] and <u>go</u> [IT].

The plow <u>does</u> not <u>sprout</u> [IT] and <u>spring</u> [IT] up into a stalk of maize, but it <u>breaks</u> [T] and <u>mellows</u> [T] the soil.

When oil <u>is burned</u> [T] too high in a lamp, the lamp <u>breaks</u> [IT].

Cheese kept in a cool larder <u>will mellow</u> [IT] over time.

We must continually <u>eat</u> [IT] and <u>drink</u> [IT] and <u>be nourished</u> [T]!

Note to Instructor: The helping verb *must* helps all three verbs in the sentence.

For many parents, running errands <u>eats</u> [T] two good hours out of the day.

There are whole families who all <u>drink</u> [T] tea or coffee.

The energy of the spring growth <u>runs</u> [T] its course by summer.

The waste water runs [IT] into different drains, according to the season.

We should [T] all understand the details as well as the theory of sanitation.

The best gardeners understand [IT] perfectly.

Once the construction is completed [T], the workers should paint [IT] on the following day.

Gas and drain pipes must be painted [T] a distinct color.

When you let [T] the sunshine in, you drive [T] the doctor out.

The market-wagons drive [IT] between the buildings without proper care.

Review 10H: Hunt and Find

In the following sentences, find, underline, and label each of the following:
- Progressive verb (provide exact tense, voice, and mood!)
- Action verb that can also be a linking verb
- Hortative verb
- Subjunctive verb (provide exact tense and voice)
- Demonstrative pronoun acting as a subject
- Intensive pronoun
- Compound adjective in the attributive position
- Possessive adjective
- Infinitive phrase acting as a subject
- Object complement
- Consequence clause
- Adjective clause introduced by a relative pronoun
- Noun clause acting as a direct object
- Noun clause acting as a predicate nominative
- Present participle acting as the object of a preposition
- Present participle acting as a subject
- Present participle phrase acting as an adverb
- Past participle acting as an adjective in the predicative position

These sentences are all taken from the 1907 book *The Chemistry of Cooking and Cleaning: A Manual for Housekeepers*, by Ellen H. Richards and S. Maria Elliott. It was one of the first domestic science handbooks to treat the scientific aspects of housework.

progressive verb (progressive present, active, indicative)

We live in an invisible atmosphere of dust, we are constantly adding to this atmosphere by

the processes of our own growth and waste, and, finally, we shall go the way of all the earth,

present participle phrase acting as an adverb

present participle acting as the object of a preposition

contributing our bodies to the making of more dust.

demonstrative
pronoun acting   adjective clause introduced by   compound adjectives in the
as a subject   a relative pronoun   attributive position

<u>That</u> <u>which costs little or nothing</u> is seldom appreciated; so this <u>all-abundant</u>, <u>freely-given</u> light is

possessive adjective

often shut out through <u>man's</u> greed or through mistaken economy.

                                                  object complement ALSO past participle
                 hortative verb   acting as an adjective in the predicative position

As far as possible, <u>let</u> the exterior of the house <u>be bathed</u> in sunlight.

                                                        infinitive phrase acting as a subject
possessive adjective   possessive adjective

<u>Nature's</u> supply of pure air is sufficient for all, but <u>to have it always in its pure state</u> requires

knowledge and constant, intelligent action.

                 subjunctive verb   consequence clause
            (simple present, passive)   intensive pronoun

If the finish <u>be removed</u> or <u>broken</u> by deep scratches, <u>the wood itself absorbs the grease and dust</u>,

and the stain may have to be scraped out.

       infinitive phrase acting as a subject

<u>Whether to boil or not to boil the clothes</u> depends largely upon the purity of the materials <u>used</u>
            past participles acting as adjectives
                   in the predicative position

and the degree of care <u>exercised</u>.

       action verb that can   noun clause acting
       also be a linking verb   as a direct object   adjective clause introduced
                                                                    by a relative pronoun

Many persons <u>feel</u> <u>that the additional disinfection which boiling ensures is an element of</u>

                                                            noun clause acting as a direct object
                                                          present participle acting as a subject

<u>cleanness not to be disregarded</u>, while others insist <u>that boiling yellows the clothes</u>.

       present participle acting as the
            object of a preposition   noun clause acting as a predicate nominative

Another reason for <u>kneading</u> is <u>that the bubbles of gas may be broken up into as small portions</u>

<u>as possible</u>.

                                                     noun clause acting as a direct object
                              past participle acting as an
                         adjective in the predicative position   possessive adjectives

The cook must remember <u>that the butter absorbed from her cake tin or the olive oil on her salad is</u>

<u>food, as well as the flour and eggs</u>.

              present participle acting as
              the object of a preposition

The secret of the <u>cooking</u> of vegetables is the judicious production of flavor.

Review 10I: Conditionals and Formal Conditionals

In each of the following conditional sentences, parse the underlined verbs, giving tense, voice (*active, passive,* or *state-of-being*), and mood. Then, classify the sentences as first, second, or third conditional by placing a *1, 2,* or *3* in the blank at the beginning.

These sentences are taken from *The Secret History of Home Economics: How Trailblazing Women Harnessed the Power of Home and Changed the Way We Live*, by Danielle Dreilinger.

The first verb is parsed for you.

Remember that the condition can come before the consequence—or the other way around!

<u>1</u>   If home economists <u>miss</u> this boat, they <u>may</u> never <u>catch</u> another one like it.
(simple present, active, subjunctive) *(simple present, active, modal)*

<u>2</u>   Of course, if we seriously <u>valued</u> this work that makes our lives much easier, that in some *(simple past, active, subjunctive)* cases makes it possible for people to work outside the home as (for instance) welders, we <u>might improve</u> the pay of the people who do it. *(simple present, active, modal)*

<u>2</u>   Special diets had to start three days before takeoff, prepared to clinically antibacterial standards, for it <u>would be</u> awful if an astronaut <u>got</u> food poisoning in space. *(simple present, state-of-being, modal)* *(simple past, active, subjunctive)*

<u>1</u>   If there <u>is</u> justice in the nation, there <u>will be</u> peace in the world. *(simple present, state-of-being, subjunctive)* *(simple future, state-of-being, indicative)*

<u>1</u>   If corporations <u>didn't do</u> something to regain trust, the government <u>would intervene</u>. *(simple present, active, subjunctive)* *(simple present, active, modal)*

<u>3</u>   If she <u>had lived</u> ten years longer, how much good she <u>could have done</u>! *(perfect past, active, subjunctive)* *(perfect present, active, modal)*

<u>1</u>   If we <u>don't come</u> out of it and <u>change</u> the narrative, it <u>will disappear</u>. *(simple present, active, subjunctive)* *(simple present, active, subjunctive)* *(simple future, active, indicative)*

<u>2</u>   If everyone <u>did</u> her part, peace and quiet <u>might</u> someday <u>reign</u> again. *(simple past, active, subjunctive)* *(simple present, active, modal)*

<u>3</u>   If I <u>had been</u> white, I think that <u>would have been</u> a huge difference. *(perfect past, state-of-being, subjunctive)* *(perfect present, state-of-being, modal)*

<u>2</u>   Richards laid down her dictum most concisely in one of the most passionate speeches of her life, an impromptu retort at an otherwise all-male educational conference whose attendees told her that schools <u>wouldn't have</u> to teach housekeeping if women <u>stayed</u> home. *(simple present, active, modal)* *(simple past, active, subjunctive)*

<u>2</u>   The country <u>could</u> not <u>succeed</u>, he said, if it <u>continued</u> to give Black citizens a separate and unequal education. *(simple present, active, modal)* *(simple past, active, subjunctive)*

<u>2</u>   The club members <u>wouldn't like</u> it, Melville said, if the great Tuskegee leader <u>ate</u> in the club dining room. *(simple present, active, modal)* *(simple past, active, subjunctive)*

<u> 1 </u>　　　　simple present,　　　　　　　　　　　　　　simple present,
　　　　active, subjunctive　　　　　　　　　　　　active, subjunctive
If you <u>want</u> kids to learn home economics, and maybe even <u>liberate</u> future adult women
　　　　　　　　　　　　　　　　　　　active imperative
from unequal housework, <u>make</u> the class mandatory.

　　　perfect past,　　　　　perfect present,
　　　active, subjunctive　　active, modal
<u> 3 </u>　　　If she <u>had known</u>, she <u>would</u> not <u>have told</u> them to quit their jobs.

Review 10J: Affirmations and Negations

The following sentences all contain adverbs of affirmation and negation. Circle each one, and label them as *AFF* or *NEG*.

Then, choose three sentences and rewrite them on your own paper, turning affirmatives into negatives and vice versa. Show your sentences to your instructor.

All of these sentences are taken from the 1871 handbook *Miss Beecher's Domestic Receipt-Book: Designed as a Supplement to Her Treatise on Domestic Economy,* by Catharine Esther Beecher.

> **Note to Instructor:** Sample rewritten sentences follow each original sentence. Accept any reasonable rephrasings. (Some rewritten sentences might not make good sense, but that's fine—the student is merely being encouraged to pay attention to the presence of the affirmatives and negations.)

When a woman has good sense and good taste, these are some of the things she will (not) [NEG] do.

　　When a woman has good sense and good taste, these are some of things she will obviously do.

She will (not) [NEG] be (particularly) [AFF] anxious to know what the fashion is, in dress and furniture.

　　She will certainly be not at all anxious to know what the fashion is, in dress and furniture.

(Nor) [NEG] will she be disturbed if found deficient in these particulars.

　　Obviously, she will be disturbed if found deficient in these particulars.

Fresh air is (absolutely) [AFF] necessary for good health.

　　Fresh air is never necessary for good health.

It is (very) [AFF] desirable that every family should have a constant supply of good bread.

　　It is not desirable that every family should have a constant supply of good bread.

Constantly stirring porridge (surely) [AFF] preserves it from growing sour or musty.

　　Constantly stirring porridge never preserves it from growing sour or musty.

Be careful to have clean dish towels, and (never) [NEG] use them for other purposes.

　　Be careful to have clean dish towels, and definitely use them for other purposes.

The careful and benevolent housekeeper will (certainly) [AFF] receive her reward.

　　The careful and benevolent housekeeper will not receive her reward.

Constantly finding fault is inconsistent with a (truly)amiable character.
> *(AFF above truly)*

> Constantly finding fault is inconsistent with a non-amiable character.

Fat is(indeed) the offending ingredient in most dishes which disturb weak stomachs.
> *(AFF above indeed)*

> Fat is never the offending ingredient in most dishes which disturb weak stomachs.

Green peas need(no) soaking, and must boil(not) more than an hour.
> *(NEG above no and not)*

> Green peas obviously need soaking, and must obviously boil more than an hour.

Review 10K: Diagramming

On your own paper, diagram every word of the following sentences, taken from the 1841 text *A Treatise on Domestic Economy*, by Catharine Esther Beecher.

Every person should be dressed so loosely, that, when sitting in the posture used in sewing, reading, or study, the lungs can be as full and as easily inflated as they are without clothing.

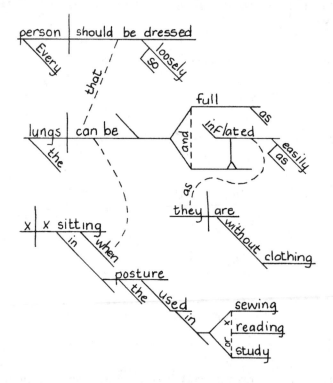

> **Note to Instructor:** The clause *that the lungs can be as full and as easily inflated* is an adverb clause, modifying the passive verb *should be dressed* and answering the question *How?* In that clause, *full* is a predicate adjective and *inflated* is a past participle acting as a predicate adjective. The clause *as they are without clothing* is comparative and connects *inflated* with *they* (the two comparative terms).
>
> The words *when sitting in the posture* may be confusing. *When* is not a preposition—it is an adverb, implying that there are understood words that turn this into a clause: *when [person is] sitting*. If the student diagrams *when* as a preposition with *sitting* as a present participle acting as its object, do not mark it wrong, but show the student the diagram above and explain that *when* is an adverb, not a preposition.

Of course, confinement to one position, for a great length of time, tends to weaken the muscles thus strained.

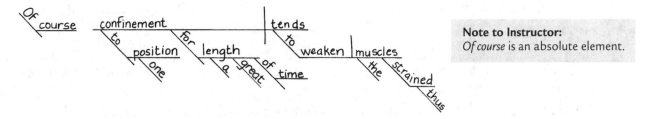

Note to Instructor:
Of course is an absolute element.

This shows the evil of confining young children to their seats, in the schoolroom, so much and so long as is often done.

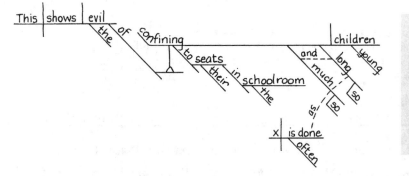

Note to Instructor: The clause *as is often done* is introduced by the subordinating conjunction *as* and contains an understood element: *so much and so long as [it] is often done*. This is a comparative clause connected to both *long* and *much*. Accept any reasonable effort from the student, and then show him the diagram above.

If a parent perceives that a child is growing crooked, the proper remedy is to withdraw it from all pursuits which tax one particular set of muscles, and turn it out to exercise in sports, or in gardening, in the fresh air, when all the muscles will be used, and the whole system strengthened.

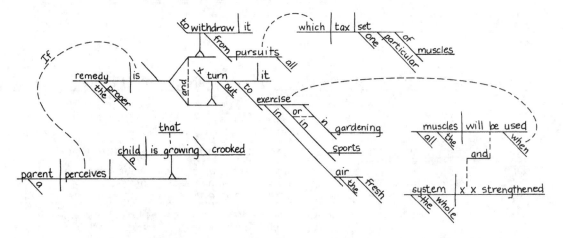

Note to Instructor: The main (consequence) clause is *the proper remedy is...*, with the infinitives *to withdraw* and *[to] turn* as the compound predicate nominatives. The condition clause *if a parent perceives...* is subordinate, with the noun clause *that the child is growing crooked* as the direct object of the predicate *perceives*.

The compound adverb clause *when all the muscles will be used, and the whole system [will be] strengthened* consists of two clauses linked by the coordinating conjunction *and* and two understood helping verbs.

Review 10L: Explaining a Long Sentence

Tell your instructor the following pieces of grammatical information about the following very long sentence! It is taken from the 1823 textbook *A New System of Practical Domestic Economy*.

Follow these steps:

a) Underline each subordinate clause. Describe the identity and function of each clause and give any other useful information (introductory word, relationship to the rest of the sentence, etc.). Insert any understood words, using the ∧.

b) Circle each phrase. Describe the identity and function of each phrase and give any other useful information.

c) Parse all verbs acting as predicates.

If you need help, ask your instructor.

> **Note to Instructor:** Use the information in the explanations, below, to prompt the student as necessary. The purpose of this exercise is to build the student's confidence in defining and explaining grammar out loud. Give all necessary help, and encourage the student to answer loudly and in complete sentences.

a) That the winds on the north-eastern coast of the kingdom are as violent as, and much colder
                                                              are
than, those in the south-western counties ∧, cannot for a moment be doubted; yet it is an important fact, that in the former situation there are some very striking specimens of that beautiful tree, which seems not only to defy the weather, but even to flourish in their exposed situation, throwing out their spreading branches in all directions, both with and against the wind, and covered with a foliage, rich, full, and verdant, even to their very summit.

Explanations:

That the winds on the north-eastern coast of the kingdom are as violent as, and much colder

Contained within the noun clause, the comparative
clause *those in the south-western counties (are)*,
with an understood verb; connected to the predicate
adjectives within the noun clause *violent* and *colder*   are
than, those in the south-western counties ∧, cannot for a moment be doubted; yet it is an

Noun clause acting as an appositive renaming *fact*, the subject of
the noun cause is *specimens* and the predicate is *are*.
important fact, that in the former situation there are some very striking specimens of that

Contained within the noun clause, the adjective clause is introduced
by the relative pronoun *which* (referring back to *specimens*).
beautiful tree, which seems not only to defy the weather, but even to flourish in their exposed

situation, throwing out their spreading branches in all directions, both with and against the

wind, and covered with a foliage, rich, full, and verdant, even to their very summit.

b) That the winds on the north-eastern coast of the kingdom are as violent as, and much

colder than, those in the south-western counties ^, cannot for a moment be doubted;
are

yet it is an important fact, that in the former situation there are some very striking

specimens of that beautiful tree, which seems not only to defy the weather but even

to flourish in their exposed situation throwing out their spreading branches in all

directions, both with and against the wind and covered with a foliage rich, full, and

verdant, even to their very summit.

Explanations:

The prepositional phrase *on the northeastern coast of the kingdom* is adjectival and modifies *winds*. Within that phrase, the prepositional phrase *of the kingdom* is adjectival and modifies *coast*.

The prepositional phrase *in the south-western counties* is adjectival and modifies *those*.

The prepositional phrase *for a moment* is adverbial and modifies *can be doubted*.

The prepositional phrase *in the former situation* is adverbial and modifies *are*.

The prepositional phrase *of that beautiful tree* is adjectival and modifies *specimens*.

The infinitive phrase *to defy the weather* is adjectival and serves as a predicate adjective following the linking verb *seems* and describing the relative adjective *which*.

The infinitive phrase *to flourish in their exposed situation* is also adjectival (linked to the previous predicate adjective phrase by the coordinating conjunction *but*) and is the second predicate adjective describing the relative adjective *which*). Within that infinitive phrase, the prepositional phrase *in their exposed situation* is adverbial and modifies *to flourish*.

The present participle phrase *throwing out their spreading branches in all directions* is adverbial and also modifies *to flourish*. Within that phrase, the prepositional phrase *in all directions* is adverbial and modifies *throwing*.

The prepositional phrase *with and against the wind* modifies *throwing*. The prepositions *with* and *against* are linked by the correlative conjunctions *both... and*, and both have the object *wind*.

The past participle phrase *covered with a foliage* is adjectival and modifies (all the way back to!) *specimens*. Within that phrase, the prepositional phrase *with a foliage* is adverbial and modifies the past participle *covered*. The prepositional phrase *to their very summit* is also adverbial and modifies *covered*.

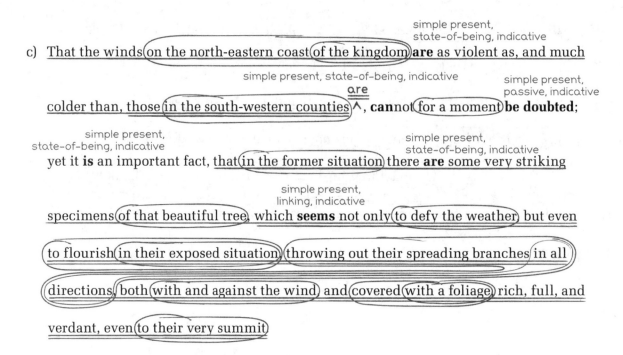

c) That the winds on the north-eastern coast of the kingdom **are** as violent as, and much
simple present, state-of-being, indicative

colder than, those in the south-western counties ∧, **can**not for a moment **be doubted**;
simple present, state-of-being, indicative — are — *simple present, passive, indicative*

yet it **is** an important fact, that in the former situation there **are** some very striking
simple present, state-of-being, indicative — *simple present, state-of-being, indicative*

specimens of that beautiful tree, which **seems** not only to defy the weather but even
simple present, linking, indicative

to flourish in their exposed situation throwing out their spreading branches in all

directions, both with and against the wind and covered with a foliage rich, full, and

verdant, even to their very summit

Mechanics

— LESSON 121 —

Capitalization Review
Additional Capitalization Rules
Formal and Informal Letter Format
Ending Punctuation

Exercise 121A: Proofreading

Use proofreader's marks to insert the missing capital letters and punctuation marks into the following sentences. These are taken from *The Worst Journey in the World*, by the English explorer Apsley Cherry-Garrard—an account of an attempt to reach the South Pole in 1911 during which several other explorers died.

capitalize letter: ≡	make letter lowercase: /
insert period: ⊙	insert exclamation point: ↑
insert comma: ⌄	insert question mark: ⸮
insert quotation marks: ❝	

If a word or phrase should be italicized, indicate this by underlining.

> **Note to Instructor:** The original sentences are below. Where alternative corrections are acceptable, notes are inserted. However, be sure to show the student the original sentences for comparison.

The *Terra Nova* sailed from the West India Dock, London, on June 1, 1910, and from Cardiff on June 15.

She made her way to New Zealand, refitted and restowed her cargo, took on board ponies, dogs, motor sledges, certain further provisions and equipment, as well as such members of her executive officers and scientists as had not travelled out in her, and left finally for the South on November 29, 1910.

> **Note to Instructor:** The comma between *equipment* and *as* is optional. Cherry-Garrard capitalizes South because this is a convention in the Antarctic, but the word can also be lowercase.

Mr. Evans, Mr. Day, and myself could eat more, as we are just beginning to feel the tightening of the belt.

439

Lo! for there among the flowers and grasses,
Only the mightier movement sounds and passes.

> **Note to Instructor:** The exclamation point after *Lo* could also be a comma.

Owing to press contracts and the necessity of preventing leakage of news, the *Terra Nova* had to remain at sea for twenty-four hours after a cable had been sent to England.

> **Note to Instructor:** The hyphen in *twenty-four* is necessary since the adjective is in the attributive position.

As a rule, great sheets spread over the seas which fringe the Antarctic continent in the autumn, grow thicker and thicker during the winter and spring, and break up when the temperatures of sea and air rise in summer.

> **Note to Instructor:** The comma after *rule* is optional.

The *Discovery* left New Zealand on Christmas Eve, 1901, and entered the belt of pack ice which always has to be penetrated in order to reach the comparatively open sea beyond.

It was a great disappointment to Dr. Wilson that no Emperor Penguin embryos were obtained during the cruise of the *Discovery*.

> **Note to Instructor:** *Emperor Penguin* can also be lowercase.

Oh, what joy!

> **Note to Instructor:** This could also be punctuated as *Oh! What joy!* or *Oh! what joy!*

When, and under what conditions, the Cape Crozier rookery was eventually visited and Emperor eggs secured is graphically told in *The Winter Journey*.

> **Note to Instructor:** While the commas around *and under what conditions* are not strictly necessary, they do prevent misreading. The capitalization of *Emperor* is optional.

On the 8th the *Morning* was still separated from the *Discovery* by eight miles of fast ice.

> **Note to Instructor:** The student should be able to tell by context that the *Morning* is a ship.

Campbell and his five companions were finally landed at Cape Adare, and built their hut close to Borchgrevinck's old winter quarters.

> **Note to Instructor:** The comma after *Cape Adare* is optional.

To our amazement we found their snowed-up tent some 140 geographical miles from Hut Point, only 11 geographical miles from One Ton Camp.

> **Note to Instructor:** A comma could also be placed after *amazement*. *Snowed-up* is in the attributive position so must be hyphenated. The student should be able to tell from context that Hut Point and One Ton Camp are places (proper names).

Inside the tent were the bodies of Scott, Wilson, and Bowers.

"Oh, no," said Campbell, "we always sang it on Inexpressible Island."

> **Note to Instructor:** Accept any grammatical punctuation (for example, *"Oh, no!" said Campbell, "we always sang it on Inexpressible Island"* or *"Oh! No," said Campbell. "We always sang it on Inexpressible Island!"*). The student should be able to tell from context that Inexpressible Island is a place (proper name).

In addition to *Scott's Last Expedition* and *Priestley's Antarctic Adventures*, Griffith Taylor has written an account of the two geological journeys of which he was the leader, and of the domestic life of the expedition at Hut Point and at Cape Evans, in a book called *With Scott: The Silver Lining*.

> **Note to Instructor:** The student should be able to tell from context that *Scott's Last Expedition* and *Priestley's Antarctic Adventure* are books written by Griffith Taylor. Since he may not know that a subtitle is introduced by a colon, that punctuation mark has been retained.

Exercise 121B: Correct Letter Mechanics

The following text is a letter written by the scientist Carl Sagan, on behalf of the Voyager Interstellar Record Committee, to the pioneering rock-and-roll musician Chuck Berry.

On your own paper (or with your own word-processing program), rewrite or retype the text so that it is properly formatted, punctuated, and capitalized. You may choose either letter format from this lesson.

The first three sentences in the letter are one paragraph, while the last sentence is its own separate paragraph.

The abbreviation *c/o* stands for "in care of" and is used when the person you're writing to has to be contacted through someone else (such as an agent or other representative).

When you are finished, compare your letter with the two versions in the *Answer Key*.

carl sagan cornell university ithaca new york october 15 1986 mr chuck berry

c/o mr nick miranda 12825 four winds farm drive st. louis mo 63131 dear chuck berry

when they tell you your music will live forever you can usually be sure theyre exaggerating. but johnny b goode is on the voyager interstellar records attached to nasas voyager spacecraft—now two billion miles from earth and bound for the stars. These records will last a billion years or more. go johnny go carl sagan

> **Note to Instructor:** Two correct versions of the letter are shown below. The letter itself has been very slightly condensed.

Carl Sagan
Cornell University
Ithaca, New York

October 15, 1986

Mr. Chuck Berry
c/o Mr. Nick Miranda
12825 Four Winds Farm Drive
St. Louis, MO 63131

Dear Chuck Berry:

When they tell you your music will live forever, you can usually be sure they're exaggerating. But "Johnny B. Goode" is on the Voyager interstellar records attached to NASA's Voyager spacecraft—now two billion miles from Earth and bound for the stars. These records will last a billion years or more.

Go, Johnny, go.

Carl Sagan

Carl Sagan
Cornell University
Ithaca, New York

October 15, 1986

Mr. Chuck Berry
c/o Mr. Nick Miranda
12825 Four Winds Farm Drive
St. Louis, MO 63131

Dear Chuck Berry:

When they tell you your music will live forever, you can usually be sure they're exaggerating. But "Johnny B. Goode" is on the Voyager interstellar records attached to NASA's Voyager spacecraft—now two billion miles from Earth and bound for the stars. These records will last a billion years or more.

Go, Johnny, go.

Carl Sagan

— LESSON 122 —

Commas

Semicolons

Additional Semicolon Rules

Colons

Additional Colon Rules

Exercise 122A: Comma Use

In the blank at the end of each sentence, write the number from the list above that describes the comma use. If more than one number seems to fit equally well, write all suitable numbers.

These sentences are from *South: The Story of Shackleton's Last Expedition 1914-1917,* written by the polar explorer Ernest Shackleton himself.

Note to Instructor: As long as the student writes at least one number, accept the answer. However, ask him if there is a second (or third) rule that could be applied. After the student answers, point out the additional numbers that could have been referenced.

We sailed from London on Friday, August 1, 1914, and anchored off Southend all Saturday.   12

On the following Saturday, August 8, the *Endurance* sailed from Plymouth, obeying the direct order of the Admiralty.   8, 12, 19

They were big, sturdy animals, chosen for endurance and strength, and if they were as keen to pull our sledges as they were now to fight one another all would be well.   3, 19, 1

Worsley, Wild, and I, with three officers, kept three watches while we were working through the pack, so that we had two officers on deck all the time.   2, 4, 19, 1

I do not know who had been responsible for some of the dogs' names, which seemed to represent a variety of tastes.   6

They were as follows Rugby, Upton Bristol, Millhill, Songster, Sandy, Mack, Mercury, Wolf, Amundsen, Hercules, Hackenschmidt, Samson, Sammy, Skipper, Caruso, Sub, Ulysses, Spotty, Bosun, Slobbers, Sadie, Sue, Sally, Jasper, Tim, Sweep, Martin, Splitlip, Luke, Saint, Satan, Chips, Stumps, Snapper, Painful, Bob, Snowball, Jerry, Judge, Sooty, Rufus, Sidelights, Simeon, Swanker, Chirgwin, Steamer, Peter, Fluffy, Steward, Slippery, Elliott, Roy, Noel, Shakespeare, Jamie, Bummer, Smuts, Lupoid, Spider, and Sailor.   2, 4

No, I do not like the idea of drifting on a berg.   10

The first day of the New Year (January 1, 1915) was cloudy, with a gentle northerly breeze and occasional snow-squalls.   12, 19

This takes us into open water, where we make S. 50° W. for 24 miles.   6

The sun, which had been above the horizon for two months, set at midnight on the 17th, and, although it would not disappear until April, its slanting rays warned us of the approach of winter.   6, 1, 19

On the 23rd, for example, we put down a 2 ft. dredge and 650 fathoms of wire.   7

Having, therefore, determined as nearly as possible that portion of the deck immediately above these cases, we proceeded to cut a hole with large ice-chisels through the 3-in. planking of which it was formed.   7, 11

However, in spite of occasional setbacks due to unfavourable winds, our drift was in the main very satisfactory, and this went a long way towards keeping the men cheerful.   11, 7, 1

"All theories about the swell being non-existent in the pack are false," wrote the anxious master.   17

Exercise 122B: Capitalization and Punctuation

Insert all missing punctuation and correct all capitalization in the text that follows. Use these proofreader's marks:

capitalize letter: ≡	make letter lowercase: /
insert period: ⊙	insert exclamation point: ↑
insert comma: ⌄	insert question mark: ⟨?⟩
insert colon: ⌄	insert semicolon: ⌄
insert dash: (—)	insert quotation marks: ⌄
insert hyphen: ⌃	

If a word or phrase should be italicized, indicate this by underlining.

> **Note to Instructor:** The original texts are found below. Where there is a legitimate judgement call over which punctuation mark to admit, a note has been inserted. Make sure that the student looks at the original sentences once the exercise is finished, so that she can be familiar with the different ways in which these punctuation marks may be used.
>
> Be sure to check the student's proofing of the citations as well as the sentences themselves.

122B.1: Sentences

The search for the Northwest Passage languished for several years following Baffin's voyages.

Thomas James's voyage was financed by merchants from the port of Bristol; Luke Foxe was sailing under the royal sponsorship of King Charles I.

James set sail from Bristol on May 3, 1631, and Foxe left from London on May 5.

Following rumors of gold, the Spaniards moved north through modern-day Georgia and into present-day South Carolina.

> **Note to Instructor:** The comma after *gold* is necessary to prevent misunderstanding. The compound adjectives *modern-day* and *present-day* are in the attributive position and so should be hyphenated.

Pizarro and Orellana soon discovered that the legendary Land of Cinnamon did not exist; all they encountered were endless jungles and scattered villages.

> **Note to Instructor:** In the original text, *Land of Cinnamon* is a proper name, but it could also be considered as a lowercase general designation.

An eyewitness to the carnage wrote, "The whole number of Indians that died in this town were two thousand and five hundred, little more than less."

> **Note to Instructor:** The comma after *hundred* is necessary to prevent misunderstanding.

They paused for almost two months at a village called Aparia, where they built a second, larger ship they called the *Victoria* to complement the smaller and cramped *San Pedro*.

Champlain and twenty-seven men prepared to spend the winter in a tiny enclave.

They suffered from dysentery and scurvy, and by the time more settlers arrived in the spring, only Champlain and eight others were still alive.

> **Note to Instructor:** The comma after *spring* is optional but does help to prevent misreading.

But now reinforced, Champlain continued his explorations; in the summer of 1609, he became the first recorded European to visit Lake Champlain, on the border between modern-day Vermont and New York.

> **Note to Instructor:** The comma after *1609* is optional. The comma after *Lake Champlain* is necessary to prevent misreading.

One explorer, named Jean Nicolet, spent several years as a fur trader among the native inhabitants in modern-day western Ontario, where he heard about other tribes that lived to the west and south along the shores of an unknown bay.

> **Note to Instructor:** The commas around *named Jean Nicolet* are optional but do make the sentence clearer.

The native people with whom he lived referred to them by the name "People of the Sea."

> —*The Age of Exploration*, by Andrew A. Kling

> **Note to Instructor:** The appositive *People of the Sea* is both capitalized and set off by quotation marks in the original. In order to show that it is a single name, the student could also either capitalize it without quotation marks, or set it off with quotation marks and leave it lowercase—but at least one of these options should be chosen.

122B.2: Letter Format

The following letters were both written by J. R. R. Tolkien, author of *The Lord of the Rings*.

In the first letter, Tolkien is complaining to his editor that *The Fellowship of the Ring*, the first book in his new trilogy, isn't going anywhere because he's all out of ideas!

In the second, Tolkien is writing a Santa Claus letter to one of his sons. He used to write these letters every Christmas.

(In Britain, the day of the month comes before the month, not after as in the United States, but the same punctuation rules still apply!)

---

20 Northmoor Road
Oxford, England

17 February, 1938

C. A. Furth, Allen & Unwin
40 Museum Street
London, England

Dear Mr. Furth,

The Hobbit sequel is still where it is, and I have only the vaguest notions of how to proceed. Not ever intending any sequel, I fear I squandered all my favorite 'motifs' and characters on the original Hobbit.

Yours sincerely,

J. R. R. Tolkien

Christmas House
North Pole

22 December, 1923

Master John Francis Tolkien
11 St. Mark's Terrace
Leeds, England

My dear John,

It is very cold today and my hand is very shaky—I am nineteen hundred and twenty-seven years old on Christmas Day—lots older than your great-grandfather, so I can't stop the pen wobbling, but I hear that you are getting so good at reading that I expect you will be able to read my letter.

A cold kiss from,

Father Nicholas Christmas

122B.3: Quotes

In a 2012 *Esquire* article, essayist Tom Junod told the story of Leonard Sim and recounted how his invention had shaped the experience of visiting a Georgia water park with his daughter. Junod noted that with the rise of FastPass and its ilk, ordinary ticket holders find themselves waiting longer, and end up taking fewer rides than they did in the past, even as wealthier park goers cruise by. "The experience of the line becomes an infernal humiliation," he wrote, "and the experience of avoiding the line becomes the only way to enjoy the water park." He mourns the passing of the small-d democratic experience of waiting in a wet bathing suit with people of all sizes, shapes, and colors, and sees the stratification that has replaced it as signifying much more than merely jumping a line:

It sounds like an innovative answer to the problem that everybody faces at an amusement park, and one perfectly in keeping with the approaches currently in place at airports and even on some crowded American highways—perfectly in keeping with the two-tiering of America. You can pay for one level of access, or you can pay for another. If you have the means, you can even pay for freedom. There's only one problem: Cutting the line is cheating, and everyone knows it. Children know it most acutely, know it in their bones, and so when they've been waiting on a line for a half-hour and a family sporting yellow plastic Flash Passes on their wrists walks up and steps in front of them, they can't help asking why that family has been permitted the privilege of perpetrating what looks like an obvious injustice. And then you have to explain not just that they paid for it but that you haven't paid enough—that the $100 or so that you've ponied up was just enough to teach your children that they are second- or third-class citizens.

The end result, Junod concluded, is that "your experience—what you've paid full price for—has been devalued."

— *The Velvet Rope Economy*, by Nelson D. Schwartz

— LESSON 123 —

Colons
Dashes
Hyphens
Parentheses
Brackets

Exercise 123A: Hyphens

Many (but not all) of the following sentences contain words that should be hyphenated. Insert a hyphen into each word that needs one.

From their mid–twenties in most social groups, from adolescence in elite circles, women experienced a cycle of childbirth and nursing and childbirth again.

Poor women gave birth every twenty–four to thirty months.

Unproductive marriages in sixteenth–century Venice threatened the survival of her ruling class and left citizen houses in fourteenth–century Florence, according to Dante, "vuote di famiglia," childless.

Her contemporary, the Englishwoman Margaret Denton Verney, bore twelve children over a twenty–eight–year period, while the Florentine Alessandra Macinghi Strozzi, a descendent of the Alberti and Strozzi commercial dynasties of Florence, gave birth to eight children in the decade from 1426 to 1436.

From the fourteenth through the seventeenth century, the women of the noble Venetian Donato family may have achieved in each generation the average maximum biological fertility: twelve births.

In fifteenth–century Venice, Magdalucia, the wife of the nobleman Francesco Marcello, gave birth to twenty–six children: nearly one per year for all the years of her fertility.

Both pregnancy and birth overwhelmed the English mystic Margery Kempe, whose difficult labor precipitated a six–month depression.

—*Women of the Renaissance*, by Margaret L. King

She commissioned paintings from Michelangelo and Titian, and was on a first–name basis with the Holy Roman Emperor.

> Note to Instructor: *on a first name basis* is also acceptable.

In the third century C.E., it was there that the emperor Caracalla chose to erect a magnificent temple to the Greco–Egyptian god Serapis.

Vittoria is dressed in a rich blue and red gown, with locks of her long reddish–brown hair flowing onto her shoulders.

> Note to Instructor: *of her long reddish brown hair* is also acceptable.

In the sixteenth century, Italy was not a unified country—it became a nation-state only in the 1860s—but was made up of small kingdoms and city–states that were either self–governed or under the control of foreign powers.

> Note to Instructor: You may need to send the student to a dictionary—the two compound nouns and the compound adjective in this sentence are always hyphenated (even though the adjective is in the predicative position).

Six hundred thousand ducats were already owed to the imperial troops before the Battle of Pavia began.

Ferrante's near–betrayal of Charles would have been in Vittoria's mind when she received the request to come to Milan.

In early December, 1525, she and her entourage stopped in Viterbo, roughly fifty miles north of Rome.

The d'Avalos family, as we have seen, arrived in Italy with the first Spanish kings in the mid–fifteenth century.

—*Renaissance Woman: The Life of Vittoria Colonna*, by Ramie Targoff

Exercise 123B: Parenthetical Elements

The following sentences, slightly condensed from *The Life of Cesare Borgia,* by Rafael Sabatini, each contain at least one parenthetical elements.

Set off each bolded set of words with commas, dashes, or parentheses. Choose the punctuation marks that seem to fit best.

Within those bolded sets of words, you may see an additional parenthetical element that is underlined. Be sure to punctuate this one as well!

Then, compare your answers with the original punctuation in the *Answer Key*.

> Note to Instructor: Unless otherwise noted, parentheses, dashes, and commas are interchangeable. However, ask the student to compare her answers with the originals below. How do the different choices of punctuation affect the relationship of the parenthetical element to the rest of the sentence? How do they change the rhythm of the sentence?

King Alfonso had already fled the kingdom (January 25), abdicating in favour of his brother Federigo.

> **Note to Instructor:** Since the parenthetical element has no grammatical connection to the sentence, it can be set off by dashes or parentheses, but not simply by commas.

This aim was later to be carried into actual—if ephemeral—fulfillment by Cesare Borgia.

He paid all salaries promptly — a striking departure, it would seem, from what had been usual under his predecessor — and the effect was soon seen.

> **Note to Instructor:** Although it is technically not wrong to surround the parenthetical expression with commas, the commas within the expression mean that dashes or parentheses will be clearer.

There would be fresh difficulties, owing, of course, to Orsini's enmity to the existing Florentine government.

It may not be amiss—though perhaps no longer very necessary, after what has been written—to say a word about his social position.

> **Note to Instructor:** The single-word parenthetical expression *perhaps* can also be set off by commas, but single-word expressions should generally not be set off by hyphens or parentheses.

The letter written from Spoleto expresses his regret that, on the occasion of his passage through Florence (on his way from Pisa to Spoleto), he should not have time to visit.

> **Note to Instructor:** Any combination of punctuation marks is acceptable to set off the expression within the expression, except for double sets of parentheses or double sets of hyphens, which should never be used.

The circumstance of their father being a Pope not only was not accounted extraordinarily scandalous (if scandalous at all) but, on the contrary rendered them eligible for princely alliances.

Whether or not Lodovico had him poisoned—a charge which, after all, rests on no proof—his death most certainly lies at his ambitious uncle's door.

> **Note to Instructor:** See the note above.

Such was the person of the young king—he was twenty-four years of age at the time—who poured his legions into Rome.

> **Note to Instructor:** Since the parenthetical element is an independent clause, the student should choose hyphens or parentheses rather than commas.

The House of Farnese was to give dukes to Parma and reach the throne of Spain (in the person of Isabella Farnese) before becoming extinct in 1758.

On April 23 we see him on horseback accompanying the Pope through Rome, and, as usual, he is attended by his hundred armed grooms in black.

He made haste, therefore, to agree to the surrender of Castel Bolobnese to the duke.

> **Note to Instructor:** A one-word parenthetical expression should usually be set off by commas, rather than hyphens or parentheses.

Roderigo de Lanzol y Broja alone remained—notably, the only prominent member of his house—to face the enmity of the Sacred College.

He left behind him most of his precious artillery, his tents and carriages, and the immense Neapolitan booty, which he had loaded (says Gregorovius) onto twenty thousand mules.

Her widowhood was short, however, for in the same year—on June 6—she took a second husband, possibly at the instance of Roderigo Borgia, who did not wish to leave her unprotected; that, at least, is the general inference, although there is very little evidence upon which to base it.

— LESSON 124 —

Italics
Quotation Marks
Ellipses
Single Quotation Marks
Apostrophes

Exercise 124A: Proofreading Practice

The sentences below, taken from novels by Terry Pratchett, have lost most punctuation and capitalization. Insert all missing punctuation marks, and correct all capitalization errors. When you are finished, compare your sentences with the originals.

Use these proofreader's marks:

capitalize letter: ≡   make letter lowercase: /

insert period: ⊙   insert exclamation point: ↑

insert comma: ⌃   insert question mark: ⌃?

insert colon: ⌃:   insert semicolon: ⌃;

insert apostrophe: ⌄   insert quotation marks: ⌄⌄

insert dash: (—)   insert hyphen: ⌃

If a word or phrase should be italicized, indicate this by underlining.

> **Note to Instructor:** The original sentences are found below. Additional notes have been inserted where there can be differences of interpretation. If the student punctuates correctly, but veers from the original, ask him to first read aloud his version of the sentence, and then the original version. Do they sound different? (There is no right answer to this question—it's intended to continue to train the student's ability to "hear" punctuation marks.)

Nine-tenths of the universe, in fact, is the paperwork.

"Exciting, eh?" said a hoarse voice by Death's ear.

> **Note to Instructor:** You may need to point out to the student that *eh* always indicates a question!

It belonged to Quoth, the raven, who had attached himself to the household as the Death of Rats' personal transport and crony.

> **Note to Instructor:** The comma after *Quoth* is optional, but the comma after *raven* is essential.

Right on this point was the world—turtle, elephants, the little orbiting sun, and all.

> **Note to Instructor:** The hyphen could also be a colon.

It was a bitter winter's night.

"Well, now," she said, because she'd learned a lot in the last twenty years or so, "that's as may be, and I'll always do the best I can, ask anyone."

> **Note to Instructor:** The student could also insert a period after *so* and make *That's* capitalized.

The trouble was that he was the kind of person who, having decided to be an interesting person, would first of all try to find a book called *How to Be an Interesting Person* and then see whether there were any courses available.

> **Note to Instructor:** A comma could also follow *Person*.

Why, he could talk about all kinds of clocks: mechanical clocks, magical clocks, water clocks, first clocks, floral clocks, candle clocks, sand clocks, cuckoo clocks, the rare Hershebian beetle clocks.

> **Note to Instructor:** If the student can't tell from context, explain that Hershebian is a proper name (found only in the Discworld!).

"But enough of this, perhaps," said Lady LeJean, stepping back. "You make clocks and we—"

> **Note to Instructor:** The dash indicates an unfinished sentence; it could also be ellipses.

It was three o'clock.

Jeremy looked shocked. "The alloy? I didn't think anyone outside the guild knew about that."

> > *—Thief of Time*

Indeed, sir, and may I remind you that he will be leaving us very shortly.

"Yes, but—" Vimes began, but his wife silenced him with a smile.

> **Note to Instructor:** The dash indicates an unfinished sentence; it could also be ellipses.

She had a special smile for these occasions; it was warm and friendly and carved out of rock.

The man thus addressed looked around for help, support and guidance, or escape, but there was none; the crowd was deathly silent.

He very nearly gloated at the downfall of his enemy and slammed his copy of the *Ankh-Morpork Times*, open at the crossword page, on to his desk.

> **Note to Instructor:** A comma could also be placed after *enemy*.

> > *—Snuff*

You will set sail at dawn and rendezvous in the Channel with the *Maid of Liverpool*, just returned from San Francisco.

> **Note to Instructor:** You may need to clarify that *Channel* is a proper name because it refers to the English Channel.

"No, indeed, Captain, you were born forty-five years ago, the second son of Mr. and Mrs. Bertie Samson, and christened Lionel after your grandfather," said Mr. Black, calmly lowering his package to the deck.

Mau paddled over to a large *hehe* fish, which he managed to drag aboard.

> **Note to Instructor:** The student may not realize that *hehe* is a foreign word and so should be italicized.

—Nation

Exercise 124B: Foreign Phrases That Are Now English Words

The following phrases and words are now part of English and are usually not italicized. Using a dictionary, look up each one. In the blank, write the original language that the word belongs to, the meaning in English, and the meaning in the original language. The first is done for you.

> **Note to Instructor:** The most common meanings are listed below, but the student may choose others as long as they are in the dictionary.

cul-de-sac	French, a dead-end street, "bottom of the sack"
avatar	Hindi, embodiment or proxy, "the incarnation of a god"
patio	Spanish, a paved area outside a house, "inner courtyard"
vigilante	Spanish, someone who takes the law into their own hands, "watchful and wide awake"
angst	German, a feeling of dread or anguish, "fear"
a la carte	French, a separate price for each item on a menu, "according to the menu"
de facto	Latin, in fact, in reality, actually existing, "of fact"
coup de grace	French, a death blow or finishing stroke, "stroke of grace"
nom de plume	French, pen name, "name of the feather [quill]"

Advanced Quotations & Dialogue

LESSONS 125 and 126
No exercises in these lessons.

— LESSON 127 —
Practicing Direct Quotations and Correct Documentation

Note to Instructor: The student's instructions and the resources given are provided below for your reference. You will need to check the paper for each of the five required elements and compare the student's formatting to the rules in the workbook.

A simple account of each wicked king's misdeeds is all that's necessary. The essay may be any length, as long as it is over 250 words.

A sample essay is provided at the end of this lesson for your reference. If the student has trouble getting started, read her the first paragraph of the sample essay (don't let her look at it, since formatting the quotes properly is part of the challenge), and tell her she can use it as a model for the first paragraph of her own essay.

The student's Works Cited section should be identical to the Works Cited section of the sample essay.

The student may write an introduction and conclusion, but since the focus of this assignment is on documentation, five paragraphs that just retell important parts of each king's reign are perfectly acceptable.

After the assignment is completed, ask the student to read the sample essay and the explanatory notes.

Your assignment: Write a short essay called "Four Wicked Rulers." The four wicked rulers are Ashurnasirpal II of Assyria, Nero of Rome, Krum of Bulgaria, and Henry VIII of England. In the sources below, you'll see some praise for each of these rulers—but your essay should focus on the wickedness of each one!

Your essay should be at least 250 words, although it will probably need to be longer.

You must quote directly from at least FIVE of the sources listed below, footnote each direct quote, and put all five on your Works Cited page. You MUST include both a quote from the journal article listed below AND from the website history.co.uk among your sources (and you can use more than five sources, if you prefer).

Your essay must include the following:
a) a brief quote that comes before its attribution tag
b) a brief quote that comes after its attribution tag
c) a brief quote divided by its attribution tag
d) a block quote
e) a quote that is incorporated into a complete sentence and serves a grammatical function within that sentence
f) a quote that has been altered with either brackets or ellipses (these must be your own alterations, not those that are already in the sources below!)
g) a second quote from the same source.

One quote can fulfill more than one of these requirements. If you need help, ask your instructor.

Note to Student: There's a challenge below you haven't seen yet—two books by the same author, Susan Wise Bauer!

You've learned that your first reference to a book should be a full listing of author, title, publisher, date, and page number, but that the second time, you can simply list the author's last name and the page number.

If the author has written *two* books that you reference, you have to add a little more information! If Julia Smith wrote *A Guide to Giant Owls* and *Handbook of Pygmy Owls* and you quote both, you still give a full citation for the first time you quote each book, but then the second time you need to specify which book you're citing—so, instead of

Smith, 42

you would write

Smith, *A Guide to Giant Owls*, 42

or

Smith, *Handbook of Pygmy Owls*, 42

Note that you don't have to provide any other information, because that all came in your first citation of each book.

Author: Stanley Sandler, ed.
Title of Book: *Ground Warfare: An International Encyclopedia*, Vol. I
City of Publication: Santa Barbara, CA
Publisher: ABC-CLIO, Inc.
Date: 2002

67

Ashurnasirpal II (r. 883-859 BCE) was the king who forged Assyria into one of the dominant powers of the Near East... [He] campaigned continuously during his reign, directing his efforts to the north against the Aramean states... All of these states, in one form or another, became vassals to Assyria. Moreover, Ashurnasirpal established a long line of fortresses to protect Assyrian trade routes... Ashurnasirpal restructured the Assyrian state and army (which had been weak for centuries), created a large bureaucracy, continued a policy of deporting conquered peoples, and claims in his annals to have used psychological warfare on his enemies by performing public displays of cruelty, mass executions, and the burning of disloyal vassal cities.

Author: Susan Wise Bauer
Title of Book: *The History of the Ancient World: From the Earliest Accounts to the Fall of Rome*
City of Publication: New York
Publisher: W. W. Norton
Date: 2007

338

In Ashurnasirpal there appeared, full-blown, the delight in cruelty which tagged at the heels of almost every Assyrian king who followed. "I put up a pillar at the city gate," Ashurnasirpal explains, recording his dealings with a city which had revolted and killed its Assyrian-appointed governor, "and I skinned the chiefs who revolted against me, and covered the pillar with their skins. I walled up others in the middle of the pillar itself, and some of them I impaled on stakes and arranged them around the pillar. Inside the city, I skinned many more and covered the walls with their skins. As for the royal officials, I cut off their members." He varied this, at other times, by making heaps of cut-off noses and ears, gouging out eyes, and tying heads to vines throughout the gardens of conquered cities like obscene and decaying fruit. "I made one pillar of the living," he remarks, a particularly nasty Assyrian invention where living prisoners were laid one on top of another and covered with plaster to make a column. "I cut off their ears and their fingers, of many I put out the eyes. . . . their young men and maidens I burned in the fire."

Name of Article: "The Making of the Bulgarian Nation"
Author: V. N. Zlatarski
Magazine: *The Slavonic Review*
Date: December 1925
Volume and issue number: Volume 4, Number 11
Page range of article: 362-383

368

The plan for uniting the Balkan Slavs and strengthening the Slavonic element in the state was carried on and extended

369

under the warlike and energetic Khan Krum (802-814). After crushing the Avars and extending the northern frontier of Bulgaria to the rivers Tisza and Prut and to the Carpathians, Krum advanced south-westward in the steps of his predecessors and succeeded in adding the Sofia region and the lands along the upper Stuma and Mesta to his khanate... [This] brilliant victory exalted the Khan of Bulgaria in the eyes of the Imperial Slavs as the conqueror of the Romaic Basileus, and so paved the way for the expansion of the state towards the south-west. Krum... carried away by his great success and by the idea that the Byzantine Emperor could be defeated... launched a series of fierce attacks on Constantinople, which brought no profit to the state and served only to hasten his end...

371

At the time of his campaigns in Thrace and of his expeditions against Constantinople, he took large numbers of prisoners, whom he subsequently transplanted to various parts of his country.

Author: Susan Wise Bauer
Title of Book: *The History of the Medieval World: From the Conversion of Constantine to the First Crusade*
City of Publication: New York
Publisher: W. W. Norton
Date: 2010

400

The Bulgarian khan was named Krum, and under his rule—which began sometime between 796 and 803—Bulgaria swelled into a major power...Around 805, Krum invaded the territory of the once-great Avars and folded it into his own, which brought his empire directly to the eastern border of Charlemagne. Deciding not to wait until Krum became even more powerful, the emperor of Constantinople, Nikephoros, declared war on the Bulgarians and began to arm his troops.

It took him over a year to get the troops on the road, partly because he had to put down a palace rebellion in the middle of his preparations. But by 808, he was moving troops into the Strymon river valley, on the southern Bulgarian border. Krum's men descended on them before they were at full strength and drove them back, killing a number of soldiers and officers and (even more damaging) capturing all of the money Nikephoros had sent along with his generals to use for payroll—eleven hundred pounds of gold, according to Theophanes.

Hostilities now began in earnest. In 809, Krum led his army against the city of Serdica, a frontier city within Byzantine territory, and captured it, slaughtering six thousand Byzantine soldiers and hundreds of civilians...It took Nikephoros I (who was again distracted by yet another rebellion at home, this one brought about by his decision to raise everyone's taxes) more than a year to prepare his army for a return attack. He had decided that the only appropriate response was to wipe Krum out entirely, and to that end he imported soldiers from Thracia and Asia Minor to beef up the depleted

401

forces at Constantinople.... Krum's defenders were defeated and pushed backwards as the Byzantine army advanced... But Krum was not finished. He had retreated, along with every man he could recruit, into the mountains through which the Byzantine army would have to march on their way home, and had built a wooden wall across the pass. On July 25, heading for Constantinople in triumph, Nikephoros and his men ran directly into the wooden wall. The Bulgarians attacked the trapped army as it piled up in front of the barrier. Nikephoros, fighting at the front, was killed almost at once. Soldiers who tried to climb the wall and escape fell into an enormous ditch that the Bulgarians had dug on the other side and filled with burning logs.

The Byzantine troops were slaughtered. Krum beheaded the emperor's corpse, stuck the head on a pole, and—once the flesh had rotted off—had the skull coated in silver so that he could use it as a drinking goblet.

Author: Samuel G. Goodrich
Title of Book: *Famous Men of Ancient Times*
City of Publication: Boston, MA
Publisher: Thompson, Brown & Co.
Date: 1864

69

[Nero] delivered himself from the sway of his mother, and at last ordered her to be assassinated. This unnatural act of barbarity shocked some of the Romans; but Nero had his devoted adherents; and when he declared that he had taken away his mother's life to save himself from ruin, the senate applauded his measures, and the people signified their approbation... Nero sacrificed to his fury or caprice all such as obstructed his pleasures, or stood in the way of his inclinations.

In the night he generally sallied out from his palace, to visit the meanest taverns and the scenes of debauchery in which Rome abounded. In his nocturnal riots he was fond of insulting the people in the streets, and on one occasion, an attempt to offer violence to the wife of a Roman senator nearly cost

70

him his life.... His conduct, however, soon became more censurable; he was guilty of various acts which cannot be even named with decency. The cruelty of his nature was displayed in the sacrifice of his wives Octavia and Poppæa; and the celebrated writers, Seneca, Lucan, Petronius, &c., became the victims of his wantonness. The Christians did not escape his barbarity. He had heard of the burning of Troy, and as he wished to renew that dismal scene, he caused Rome to be set on fire in different places. The conflagration became soon universal, and during nine successive days the fire was unextinguished. All was desolation; nothing was heard but the lamentations of mothers whose children had perished in the flames, the groans of the dying, and the continual fall of palaces and buildings.

71

Nero was the only one who enjoyed the general consternation. He placed himself on a high tower and he sang on his lyre the destruction of Troy; a dreadful scene which his barbarity had realized before his eyes. He attempted to avert the public odium from his head, by a feigned commiseration of the sufferings of his subjects, and by charging the fire upon the Christians. He caused great numbers of them to be seized and put to death. Some were covered with the skins of wild beasts, and killed by dogs set upon them; others were crucified; others were smeared with pitch and burned, at night, in the imperial gardens, for the amusement of the people!

Author: C. Suetonius Tranquillus
Translator: Alexander Thomson
Title of Book: *The Lives of the Twelve Caesars, Vol. 6*
City of Publication: London
Publisher: G. Bell & Sons
Date: 1896

> **Note to Student:** Ancient texts sometimes use section numbers with Roman numerals rather than page numbers to indicate the place of the quote!

XXVI. Petulancy, lewdness, luxury, avarice, and cruelty, [Nero] practised at first with reserve and in private, as if prompted to them only by the folly of youth; but, even then, the world was of opinion that they were the faults of his nature, and not of his age. After it was dark, he used to enter the taverns disguised in a cap or a wig, and ramble about the streets in sport, which was not void of mischief. He used to beat those he met coming home from supper; and, if they made any resistance, would wound them, and throw them into the common sewer. He broke open and robbed shops; establishing an auction at home for selling his booty. In the scuffles which took place on those occasions, he often ran the hazard of losing his eyes, and even his life; being beaten almost to death by a senator, for handling his wife indecently. After this adventure, he never again ventured abroad at that time of night, without some tribunes following him at a little distance. In the day-time he would be carried to the theatre incognito in a litter, placing himself upon the upper part of the proscenium, where he not only witnessed the quarrels which arose on account of the performances, but also encouraged them. When they came to blows, and stones and pieces of broken benches began to fly about, he threw them plentifully amongst the people, and once even broke a praetor's head.

XXXIV. His mother being used to make strict inquiry into what he said or did, and to reprimand him with the freedom of a parent, he was so much offended, that he endeavoured to expose her to public resentment, by frequently pretending a resolution to quit the government, and retire to Rhodes. Soon afterwards, he deprived her of all honour and power, took from her the guard of Roman and German soldiers, banished her from the palace and from his society, and persecuted her in every way he could contrive; employing persons to harass her when at Rome with law-suits, and to disturb her in her retirement from town with the most scurrilous and abusive language, following her about by land and sea. But being terrified with her menaces and violent spirit, he resolved upon her destruction, and thrice attempted it by poison. Finding, however, that she had previously secured herself by antidotes, he contrived machinery, by which the floor over her bed-chamber might be made to fall upon her while she was asleep in the night. This design miscarrying likewise, through the little caution used by those who were in the secret, his next stratagem was to construct a ship which could be easily shivered, in hopes of destroying her either by drowning, or by the deck above her cabin crushing her in its fall. Accordingly, under colour of a pretended reconciliation, he wrote her an extremely affectionate letter, inviting her to Baiae, to celebrate with him the festival of Minerva. He had given private orders to the captains of the galleys which were to attend her, to shatter to pieces the ship in which she had come, by falling foul of it, but in such manner that it might appear to be done accidentally. He prolonged the entertainment, for the more convenient opportunity of executing the plot in the night; and at her return for Bauli, instead of the old ship which had conveyed her to Baiae, he offered that which he had contrived for her destruction. He attended her to the vessel in a very cheerful mood, and, at parting with her, kissed her breasts; after which he sat up very late in the night, waiting with great anxiety to learn the issue of his project. But receiving information that every thing had fallen out contrary to his wish, and that she had saved herself by swimming,—not knowing what course to take, upon her freedman, Lucius Agerinus bringing word, with great joy, that she was safe and well, he privately dropped a poniard by him. He then commanded the freedman to be seized and put in chains, under pretence of his having been employed by his mother to assassinate him; at the same time ordering her to be put to death, and giving out, that, to avoid punishment for her intended crime, she had laid violent hands upon herself.

Author/Editor/Sponsoring Organization: Sky History by the A&E Network
Name of Web Article: "The Killer King: How Many People Did Henry VIII Execute?"
URL: https://www.history.co.uk/article/the-killer-king-how-many-people-did-henry-viii-execute
Date of access: Use the date on which you are writing your essay

Henry VIII (1491 – 1547) is perhaps the most well known of all England's monarchs, notably for the fact that he had six wives and beheaded two of them. Besides presiding over sweeping changes that brought the nation into the Protestant Reformation and changed England's faith, the infamous monarch, ridiculed for his obesity, was also subject to raging mood swings and paranoia. It is estimated that during his 36 years of rule over England he executed up to 57,000 people, many of whom were either members of the clergy or ordinary citizens and nobles who had taken part in uprisings and protests up and down the country... Simply broadcasting or discussing an opinion against the paranoid king could put even the most influential of citizens, including nobility, in the Tower of London. Worse fates were to await those who he believed were against him; for if someone dared to be against Henry, they were also against God. Such an offence was dealt with by the relatively humane swift swing of the axe. But for those accused of heresy, witchcraft and treason a far worse fate was in store for condemned victims through the barbaric acts of being burned at the stake or hanged, drawn and quartered. It is interesting to note that members of aristocracy and gentry could not be legally tortured unlike commoners.

Author: Herbert Beerbohm Tree
Title of Book: *Henry VIII and His Court*, 6th ed.
City of Publication: London
Publisher: Cassell & Co.
Date: 1911

3

Masterful, cruel, crafty, merciless, courageous, sensual, through-seeing, humorous, mean, matter of fact, worldly-wise, and of indomitable will, Henry the Eighth is perhaps the most outstanding figure in English history. The reason is not far to seek. The genial adventurer with sporting tendencies and large-hearted proclivities is always popular with the mob, and "Bluff King Hal," as he was called, was of the eternal type adored by the people. He had a certain outward and inward affinity with Nero. Like Nero, he was corpulent; like Nero, he was red-haired; like Nero, he sang and poetised; like Nero, he was a lover of horsemanship, a master of the arts and the slave of his passions. If his private vices were great, his public virtues were no less considerable. He had the ineffable quality called

4

charm, and the appearance of good-nature which captivated all who came within the orbit of his radiant personality. He was the "beau garçon," endearing himself to all women by his compelling and conquering manhood. Henry was every inch a man, but he was no gentleman. He chucked even Justice under the chin, and Justice winked her blind eye...

119

The night Anne Boleyn was executed he supped with Jane Seymour; they were betrothed the next morning, and married ten days later. It is also recorded that on the day following Katharine's death, Henry went to a ball, clad all in yellow.

Author: G. J. Meyer
Title of Book: *The Tudors: The Complete Story of England's Most Notorious Dynasty*
City of Publication: New York
Publisher: Delacorte Press
Date: 2010

31

On top of all his other blessings, Henry had the inestimable advantage—one that fit beautifully with his increasingly grandiose conception

32

of his own place in the world—of happening to rule at a time when the curious idea of the divine right of kings was becoming fashionable across much of Europe. The emergence of this notion was understandable as a reaction to the bloody instability of recent generations, and as an expression of the widespread hunger for law and order and therefore for strong central government. But it gave crowned heads a justification for turning themselves into despots with no obligations to anyone. It fed Henry VIII's inclination to think of himself as a quasi-divine being whom heaven intended to be all powerful... Henry remained lord and master of everyone around him for so long, and became so accustomed not only to doing whatever he wished, but to making everyone else do as he wished and being applauded for doing so, that he lost contact with the commonplace realities of human experience. Power corrupts, as Acton famously said, and a generation into Henry's reign there was beginning to hang over him the stench of corruption, of something like spiritual death. He was slipping into the special realm of fantasy reserved for those deprived too long of the simple truth even—or especially—about themselves. In ancient Greece or Rome he might have declared himself a god. Living in Christian England on the threshold of the modern world, he had to settle for being treated like a god...

292

No ruler in the history of England had reaped a bounty of gold to compare with Henry's, and yet somehow it had all ended with the economy of the kingdom in a parlous state and its government virtually bankrupt. And there had been absolutely no reason why things had to end up this way; it had all been Henry's doing, and he had done it for no better reason than the satisfaction of his own appetites and the demands of his swollen ego.

> **Note to Instructor:** The numbers of the required elements are in marginal brackets below.
>
> Remember: don't expect deathless prose! This exercise is about proper citation, so although the essay should be grammatical, don't worry too much about transitions, thesis statements, etc.
>
> This sample essay includes quotes from each one of the provided sources, but your student only needs to use five (as long as the journal article "The Making of the Bulgarian Nation" and the web article "The Killer King: How Many People Did Henry VIII Execute?" are both included!). Because the sample uses all the sources, it will probably be longer and more detailed than your student's essay.

SAMPLE ESSAY

History tells us that a capable king can also be a wicked man! One of the earliest cruel rulers was the Assyrian warrior Ashurnasirpal II, who ruled from 883-859 BCE. He fought his way to the north and, as Stanley Sandler puts it, he "used psychological warfare" by carrying out "mass executions, and the burning of disloyal vassal cities."[1] [b, e] The historian Susan Wise Bauer writes,

> In Ashurnasirpal there appeared, full-blown, the delight in cruelty which tagged at the heels of almost every Assyrian king who followed. "I put up a pillar at the city gate," Ashurnasirpal explains... "and I skinned the chiefs who revolted against me, and covered the pillar with their skins..."[2] [d, f]

A thousand years later, the Bulgarian emperor Krum showed a similar tendency towards cruelty. "[C]arried away... by the idea that the Byzantine Emperor could be defeated," writes V. N. Zlatarski, Krum "launched a series of fierce attacks on Constantinople, which brought no profit to the state."[3] [c, e, f] In the process, Krum slaughtered thousands of Byzantine soldiers. *The History of the Medieval World* also tells us that Krum murdered "hundreds of civilians," and also made a drinking goblet out of the Byzantine emperor's skull![4] [b, e]

Even worse was the Roman emperor Nero. In *Famous Men of Ancient Times*, we learn that Nero "was fond of insulting the people in the streets,"[5] [b, e] while the ancient historian C. Suetonius Tranquillus accuses Nero of practicing "[p]etulancy, ledwness, luxury, avarice, and cruelty."[6] [b, e, f] These were minor crimes, though, compared with Nero's murder of his own mother and his decision to cause Rome to burn. *Famous Men of Ancient Times* describes how Nero "enjoyed the general consternation" and "placed himself on a high tower" to sing, play the lyre, and watch the city burn.[7] [b, e, g]

Nero thought he was divine—and Henry VIII of England thought that he had the divine right to do whatever he pleased! Famously, Henry VIII "had six wives and beheaded two of them" (as "The Killer King: How Many People Did Henry VIII Execute?" summarizes).[8] [a, e] The writer Herbert Beerbohm Tree compares him to Nero and calls him "[m]asterful, cruel, crafty, merciless, courageous, sensual, through-seeing, humorous, mean, matter of fact, worldly-wise, and of indomitable will."[9] [b, e, f] Since he couldn't be worshipped as a god, writes G. J. Meyer, he instead settled "for being treated like a god."[10] [b, e] And in the process, he murdered scores of people and made England bankrupt.

---

[1] Stanley Sadler, ed., *Ground Warfare: An International Encyclopedia*, Vol. I (ABC-CLIO, Inc., 2002), p. 67.

[2] Susan Wise Bauer, *The History of the Ancient World: From the Earliest Accounts to the Fall of Rome* (W. W. Norton, 2007), p. 338.

[3] V. N. Zlatarski, "The Making of the Bulgarian Nation." *The Slavonic Review*, December 1925, p. 369.

[4] Susan Wise Bauer, *The History of the Medieval World: From the Conversion of Constantine to the First Crusade* (W. W. Norton, 2010), pp. 400-401.

[5] Samuel G. Goodrich, *Famous Men of Ancient Times* (Thompson, Brown & Co., 1864), p. 69.

[6] C. Suetonius Tranquillus, *The Lives of the Twelve Caesars*, Vol. 6, trans. Alexander Thomson (G. Bell & Sons, 1896), XXVI.

[7] Goodrich, p. 114.

[8] Sky History by the A&E Network, "The Killer King: How Many People Did Henry VIII Execute?" https://www.history.co.uk/article/the-killer-king-how-many-people-did-henry-viii-execute (accessed Dec. 8, 2021).

[9] Herbert Beerbohm Tree, *Henry VIII and His Court*, 6th ed. (Cassell & Co., 1911), p. 3.

[10] G. J. Meyer, *The Tudors: The Complete Story of England's Most Notorious Dynasty* (Delacorte Press, 2010), p. 32.

WORKS CITED

Bauer, Susan Wise. *The History of the Ancient World: From the Earliest Accounts to the Fall of Rome.* New York: W. W. Norton, 2007.

_____. *The History of the Medieval World: From the Conversion of Constantine to the First Crusade.* New York: W. W. Norton, 2010.

Goodrich, Samuel G. *Famous Men of Ancient Times.* Boston, Ma: Thompson, Brown & Co., 1864.

Meyer, G. J. *The Tudors: The Complete Story of England's Most Notorious Dynasty.* New York: Delacorte Press, 2010.

Sandler, Stanley, ed. *Ground Warfare: An International Encyclopedia*, Vol. I. Santa Barbara, CA: ABC-CLIO, Inc., 2002.

Sky History by the A&E Network. "The Killer King: How Many People Did Henry VIII Execute?" https://www.history.co.uk/article/the-killer-king-how-many-people-did-henry-viii-execute (accessed December 8, 2021).

Tranquillus, C. Suetonius. *The Lives of the Twelve Caesars*, Vol. 6, trans. Alexander Thomson. London: G. Bell & Sons, 1926.

Tree, Herbert Beerbohm. *Henry VIII and His Court*, 6th ed. London: Cassell & Co., 1911.

Zlatarski, V. N. "The Making of the Bulgarian Nation." *The Slavonic Review* 4:11 (December 1925), pp. 362-383.

WEEK 35

Introduction to Sentence Style

— LESSON 128 —

Sentence Style: Equal and Subordinating
Sentences with Equal Elements: Segregating, Freight-Train, and Balanced

Exercise 128A: Identifying Sentence Types

In the blank that follows each sentence or set of sentences, write *S* for segregating, *FT* for freight-train, or *B* for balanced.

He missed the surface all together, his legs flew up above his head, and he found himself lying on the top of the prostrate Rat. _FT_

O my, how cold the water was, and O, how very wet it felt. _B_

Now, look here. Let's be sensible. You are the very animals I wanted. You've got to help me. It's most important! _S_

The dusk advanced on him steadily, rapidly, gathering behind and before; and the light seemed to be draining away like flood-water. _B_

He ran up against things, he fell over things and into things, he darted things and dodged round things. _FT_

His paper of half-finished verses slipped from his knee, his head fell back, his mouth opened, and he wandered by the verdant banks of dream rivers. _FT_

—Kenneth Grahame, *The Wind in the Willows*

His folk are known for hewers of wood and drawers of water, but in truth his father has been a schoolmaster. _B_

He lives in a room above a courtyard behind a tavern and he comes down at night like some fairybook beast to fight with the sailors. _B_

There was a strange silence in the room. The men looked like mud effigies.
Finally someone began to laugh. Then another. Soon they were all laughing
together. Someone bought the judge a drink.   <u>S</u>

He swung with the bottle and the kid ducked and he swung again and the
kid stepped back.   <u>FT</u>

—Cormac McCarthy, Blood Meridian

And the child grew, and she brought him to Pharaoh's daughter, and he became
her son. (Exodus 2:10)   <u>FT</u>

But his delight is in the law of the Lord, and in His law he meditates day and
night. (Psalm 1:2)   <u>B</u>

For we are God's fellow workers; you are God's field, you are God's building.
(1 Cor. 3:9)   <u>FT</u>

—New King James Version of the Bible

Mademoiselle caught the twinkle, and she laughed, and Gerald laughed too.   <u>FT</u>

Against a little hill to the left was a round white building with pillars, and to
the right a waterfall came tumbling down among mossy stones to splash into
the lake.   <u>B</u>

This is an enchanted garden, and that's an enchanted castle, and I'm jolly well
going to explore.   <u>FT</u>

Beyond the rose garden was a yew hedge with an arch cut in it, and it was the
beginning of a maze like the one in Hampton Court.   <u>B</u>

The princess went first, and Kathleen carried her shining train; then came
Jimmy and Gerald came last.   <u>B</u>

The sun was blazing in at the window, the eight-sided room was very hot,
and everyone was getting cross.   <u>FT</u>

Do say you are. You've had your your joke with me. Don't keep it up. I don't like it.   <u>S</u>

Invisible arms clasped her, a hot invisible cheek was laid against hers, and
warm invisible tears lay wet between the two faces.   <u>FT</u>

Everyone was very hungry, and more bread and butter had to be fetched.   <u>B</u>

—Edith Nesbit, The Enchanted Castle

— LESSON 129 —

Subordinating Sentences:
Loose, Periodic, Cumulative, Convoluted, and Centered

Exercise 129A: Identifying Subordinating Sentences

In each sentence, underline the subject(s) of the main clause once and the predicate twice.

Label each sentence in the blank that follows it as *L* for loose, *P* for periodic, *CUMUL* for cumulative, *CONV* for convoluted, or *CENT* for centered. For the purpose of this exercise, any sentence with three or more phrases and dependent clauses before or after the main clause should be considered cumulative. If two or fewer phrases or dependent clauses come before or after the main clause, the sentence should be classified as loose or periodic. Don't worry too much about figuring out exactly how many phrases or clauses are in the sentence—just do your best.

If phrases or clauses come before *and* after the main clause, the sentence is centered, no matter how many other phrases or clauses there are.

If any phrases or clauses come between the subject, predicate, and any essential parts of the main clause (objects, predicate nominatives, or predicate adjectives), the sentence is convoluted, no matter how many other phrases and clauses there are.

Note to Instructor: Depending on how the student classifies phrases and clauses, the labels *L* and *P* can be interchangeable with *CUMUL* (cumulative). If the student has marked a sentence as *CUMUL* which the Key has as *L* or *P*, simply ask whether the subordinate elements come before or after the main construction. For sentences marked *L*, the answer should be "after," while the answer should be "before" for sentences marked *P*.

Spring was moving in the air above and in the earth below and around him, penetrating even his dark and lowly little house with its spirit of divine discontent and longing.   L

Jumping off all his four legs at once, in the joy of living and the delight of spring without its cleaning, he pursued his way across the meadow till he reached the hedge on the further side.   CENT

He thought his happiness was complete when, as he meandered aimlessly along, suddenly he stood by the edge of a full-fed river.   L

As he sat on the grass and looked across the river, a dark hole in the bank opposite, just above the water's edge, caught his eye.   CONV

Absorbed in the new life he was entering upon, intoxicated with the sparkle, the ripple, the scents and the sounds and the sunlight, he trailed a paw in the water and dreamed long waking dreams.   P

So the dismal Mole, wet without and ashamed within, trotted about till he was fairly dry, while the Rat plunged into the water again, recovered the boat, righted her and made her fast, fetched his floating property to shore by degrees, and finally dived successfully for the luncheon-basket and struggled to land with it.   CONV

On reaching the town they deposited Toad in the second-class waiting-room, giving a porter twopence to keep a strict eye on him.   CENT

He <u>could</u> see the imprints of them in the mud, running along straight and
purposeful, leading direct to the Wild Wood.   <u>L</u>

In the side of what had seemed to be a snow-bank <u>stood</u> a solid-looking little
<u>door</u>, painted a dark green.   <u>CENT</u>

> **Note to Instructor:** The sentence is not convoluted because the natural order of the main clause
> is *a solid-looking little door stood*.

A couple of high-backed <u>settles</u>, facing each other on either side of the fire,
<u>gave</u> further sitting accommodations for the sociably disposed.   <u>CONV</u>

In the embracing light and warmth, warm and dry at last, with weary legs
propped up in front of them, and a suggestive clink of plates being arranged
on the table behind, <u>it</u> <u>seemed</u> to the storm-driven animals, now in safe
anchorage, that the cold and trackless Wild Wood just left outside was miles
and miles away, and all that they had suffered in it a half-forgotten dream.   <u>CENT</u>

The <u>hedgehogs</u>, who were just beginning to feel hungry again after their porridge,
and after working so hard at their frying, <u>looked</u> timidly up at Mr. Badger. <u>CONV</u>

After luncheon, accordingly, when the other two had settled themselves into
the chimney-corner and had started a heated argument on the subject of *eels*,
the <u>Badger</u> <u>lighted</u> a lantern.   <u>P</u>

The <u>Mole</u> <u>was staggered</u> at the size, the extent, the ramifications of it all; at the
length of the dim passages, the solid vaultings of the crammed store-chambers,
the masonry everywhere, the pillars, the arches, the pavements.   <u>CUMUL</u>

He <u>was running</u> here and there, opening doors, inspecting rooms and
cupboards, and lighting lamps and candles and sticking them up everywhere.   <u>CUMUL</u>

Then the brutal <u>minions</u> <u>dragged</u> the hapless Toad from the Court House, shrieking,
praying, protesting; across the marketplace, where the playful populace, always as severe
upon detected crime as they are sympathetic and helpful when one is merely "wanted,"
assailed him with jeers, carrots, and popular catch-words; past hooting school children,
their innocent faces lit up with the pleasure they ever derive from the sight of a gentleman
in difficulties; across the hollow-sounding drawbridge, below the spiky portcullis, under
the frowning archway of the grim old castle, whose ancient towers soared high overhead;
past guardrooms full of grinning soldiery off duty, past sentries who coughed in a horrid,
sarcastic way, because that is as much as a sentry on his post dare do to show his contempt
and abhorrence of crime; up time-worn winding stairs, past men-at-arms in casquet and
corselet of steel, darting threatening looks through their vizards; across courtyards,
where mastiffs strained at their leash and pawed the air to get at him; past ancient
warders, their halberds leant against the wall, dozing over a pasty and a flagon of brown
ale; on and on, past the rack-chamber and the thumbscrew-room, past the turning that
led to the private scaffold, till they reached the door of the grimmest dungeon that lay
in the heart of the innermost keep.   <u>CUMUL</u>

—Kenneth Grahame, *The Wind in the Willows*

He <u>wanders</u> west as far as Memphis, a solitary migrant upon that flat and
pastoral landscape.   <u>L</u>

They disembark aboard a lighter, settlers with their chattels, all studying the low coastline, the thin bight of sand and scrub pine swimming in the haze.   CUMUL

The sun that rises is the color of steel.   CONV

The old man shuffled through the gloom, his head bent to clear the low ceiling of woven limbs and mud.   L

The wind moaned in the section of stovepipe that was run through the roof above them to quit the place of smoke.   L

Three men sat on the box, not unlike the dead themselves or spirit folk, so white they were with lime and nearly phosphorescent in the dusk.   L

Across the street sat a man on a bench dimly lit in the doorlight from the cafe.   CENT

> —Cormac McCarthy, *Blood Meridian*

According to the grace of God which was given to me, as a wise master builder I have laid the foundation. (1 Cor. 3:10)   P

But on the contrary, when they saw that the gospel for the uncircumcised had been committed to me, as the gospel for the circumcised was to Peter (for He who worked effectively in Peter for the apostleship to the circumcised also worked effectively in me toward the Gentiles), and when James, Cephas, and John, who seemed to be pillars, perceived the grace that had been given to me, they gave me and Barnabas the right hand of fellowship. (Gal. 2:7-9)   CUMUL

We give thanks to the God and Father of our Lord Jesus Christ, praying always for you, since we heard of your faith in Christ Jesus and of your love for all the saints; because of the hope which is laid up for you in heaven, of which you heard before in the word of the truth of the gospel, which has come to you, as it has also in all the world, and is bringing forth fruit, as it is also among you since the day you heard and knew the grace of God in truth; as you also learned from Epaphras, our dear fellow servant, who is a faithful minister of Christ on your behalf, who also declared to us your love in the Spirit. (Col. 1:3-8)   CUMUL

If then you were raised with Christ, seek those things which are above, where Christ is, sitting at the right hand of God. (Col. 3:1)   CENT

Note to Instructor: The subject is an understood *you.*

I, John, both your brother and companion in the tribulation and kingdom and patience of Jesus Christ, was on the island that is called Patmos for the word of God and for the testimony of Jesus Christ. (Rev. 1:9)   CONV

> —New King James Version of the Bible

Note to Instructor: The King James Bible is the single greatest historic influence on English prose styles. The student may be interested to know that our freight train and segregating styles are primarily influenced by the Hebrew style of the Old Testament, while Greek (the language of the New Testament) lends itself to loose, period, convoluted, and centered sentence styles.

The wide <u>High Street</u>, even at the busy morning hour almost as quiet as a
dream-street, <u>lay</u> bathed in sunshine.   CONV

Then <u>came</u> a <u>glimmer</u> of daylight that grew and grew, and presently ended in
another arch that looked out over a scene so like a picture out of a book about
Italy that every one's breath was taken away, and they simply walked forward
silent and staring.   CUMUL

The three <u>children</u> <u>remained</u> breathless, open-mouthed, staring at the sparkling
splendours all about them, while the Princess stood, her arm stretched out in a
gesture of command, and a proud smile on her lips.   CUMUL

<u>He</u> <u>turned</u> from fixing it by an ingenious adaptation of his belt to find the
others already decked with diadems, necklaces, and rings.   L

And the <u>minds</u> of the three <u>played</u> with granted wishes—brilliant yet thoroughly
reasonable—the kind of wish that never seems to occur to people in fairy tales
when they suddenly get a chance to have their three wishes granted.   CONV

By wonderful luck—beginner's luck, a card-player would have told him—<u>he
had discovered</u> a burglary on the very first night of his detective career.   CENT

The <u>men</u> <u>were taking</u> silver out of two great chests, wrapping it in rags, and
packing it in baize sacks.   L

The <u>three</u> <u>met</u> Mabel opportunely at the corner of the square where every
Friday the stalls and the awnings and the green umbrellas were pitched, and
poultry, pork, pottery, vegetables, drapery, sweets, toys, tools, mirrors, and all
sorts of other interesting merchandise were spread out on trestle tables, piled
on carts whose horses were stabled and whose shafts were held in place by piled
wooden cases, or laid out, as in the case of crockery and hardware, on the bare
flagstones of the market-place.   CUMUL

For this <u>hall</u> in which the children found themselves <u>was</u> the most beautiful
place in the world.   CONV

—Edith Nesbit, The Enchanted Castle

— LESSON 130 —
Practicing Sentence Style

> **Note to Instructor:** The student may choose one of the assignments below. The first (rewriting)
> will suit students who do not easily come up with creative ideas; the second is intended for
> students who find creative writing natural.
>
> A sample composition, along with the original fairy tale, has been provided for the first, but
> there is no way to provide a sample or rubric for the second.

Choose one of the following assignments:

Exercise 130A: Rewriting

The following list of events, from the traditional story "Little Red Riding-hood" as collected by the French author Charles Perrault in 1696, needs to be rewritten as a story.

Think this is an easy task? Just remember that this story must have at least one of each of the following types of sentences:

> Segregating (at least three sentences in a row)
>
> Freight-Train
>
> Balanced
>
> Loose
>
> Periodic
>
> Cumulative (with four or more subordinate phrases/clauses; main clause can come either first or last)
>
> Convoluted
>
> Centered

AND the story must be at least 500 words long and make good sense.

So you can't simply write out the story you remember from your childhood picture books—you're going to have to put some brainpower into this assignment!

there was a little country girl in a village
her mother and her grandmother loved her
the grandmother made her a red riding-hood
the hood was very flattering
the little girl wore it all the time
everyone called her "Little Red Riding-hood"
her mother made custards
her grandmother was ill
her grandmother lived in another village
the village was through the forest and beyond the mill
her mother told her to take custards and butter to her grandmother
Little Red Riding-hood started off
she had to go through a forest
she met Gaffer Wolf
Gaffer Wolf wanted to eat her
Gaffer Wolf did not eat her
There were timber-cutters in the forest
Gaffer Wolf asked where she was going
it is dangerous to listen to a wolf talk
she did not know it was dangerous
she told Gaffer Wolf what she was doing
Gaffer Wolf asked where the grandmother lived
she told him
the Wolf offered to go as well
the Wolf would go one way
Little Red Riding-hood would go the other way
the Wolf ran the shortest way

Little Red Riding-hood went the long way
she gathered nuts
she chased butterflies
she made flower bouquets
the Wolf got to the grandmother's house
he knocked on the door
the grandmother asked who was there
the Wolf said that he was Little Red Riding-hood
the Wolf said that he had custard and butter
the grandmother was ill
she said to pull the bobbin (latch)
the Wolf pulled the bobbin
the Wolf opened the door
the Wolf had not eaten for three days
the Wolf ate the grandmother
the Wolf shut the door
the Wolf got into the grandmother's bed
the Wolf waited for Little Red Riding-hood
she got there later
she knocked on the door
the Wolf asked who was there
the Wolf had a big voice
Little Red Riding-hood heard the big voice
Little Red Riding-hood was afraid
she thought her grandmother had a cold
she said who she was
she said that she had custard and butter
the Wolf softened his voice
the Wolf said to pull the bobbin (latch)
she pulled the bobbin
she opened the door
the Wolf hid under the bedclothes
the Wolf told her to put the food on a stool
the Wolf told her to climb into bed
Little Red Riding-hood put on her nightgown
she got into bed
she was surprised at how her grandmother looked
she said that her grandmother had large arms
the Wolf said that it made it better to hug her
she said that her grandmother had huge ears
the Wolf said that it was easier to hear her
she said her grandmother had enormous eyes
the Wolf said that it was easier to see her
she said that her grandmother had sharp teeth
the Wolf said that it was to eat her
the Wolf ate her

Note to Instructor: This sample composition shows one way in which the assignment could be completed. Each sentence fulfilling one of the required elements is underlined, with the label of the required element written in the margin next to the line where the sentence ends.

The original tale, which does not meet the requirements for sentence styles, is also included. If the student has trouble rewriting, allow her to read the original tale.

SAMPLE COMPOSITION

Once upon a time, in a place very very far away, there was a little country girl whose mother and her grandmother loved her very much, who enjoyed pretty clothes and walking in nature. `centered`

Her grandmother made her a red riding-hood, a hood that was tremendously flattering, that set off Little Red Riding-hood's hair and eyes, a hood Little Red Riding-hood wore all of the time, which gave her the nickname "Little Red Riding-hood." `loose`

Now, Little Red Riding-hood and her mother lived in one village, with a mill and a forest at the edge, and the grandmother lived alone in another village, through the forest and beyond the mill. One day, Little Red Riding-hood and her mother heard that `balanced` the grandmother was ill. So the mother made custards, and told Little Red Riding-hood to take a custard and some butter to the grandmother.

Little Red Riding-hood started off through the forest. But there she met Gaffer Wolf.

Gaffer Wolf was hungry, and Gaffer Wolf wanted to eat her, but there were `freight–train` timber-cutters nearby, and Gaffer Wolf was afraid of them, so Gaffer Wolf stepped back.

"Where are you going, little girl?" he said.

It is dangerous to listen to a wolf talk, but Little Red Riding-hood did not know this. So she told Gaffer Wolf, "I am going to see my grandmother."

"Where does your grandmother live?" asked Gaffer Wolf.

When Little Red Riding-hood told him, Gaffer Wolf offered to go and visit the grandmother as well. "I will go one way," he said, "and you go the other way, and we will see who gets there first."

Then Gaffer Wolf ran to the grandmother's house the shortest way possible. Meanwhile, Little Red Riding-hood went the longer way. She gathered nuts. She chased butterflies. She picked flowers. She made bouquets. She dawdled! `segregating`

Gaffer Wolf got to the grandmother's house first, and knocked on the door.

"Who is there?" croaked the ill grandmother.

"It is I, Little Red Riding-hood," said Gaffer Wolf, making his voice sound as soft as possible. "I have custard and butter for you!"

"Pull the bobbin, my dear, and come in!" said the grandmother.

So the Wolf pulled the bobbin and opened the door. Starving from three days of fasting, filled with evil intentions, unable to control himself, he leaped onto the grandmother and ate her all up. `periodic`

Then he shut the door, put on the grandmother's nightgown, got into bed under the covers, and waited for Little Red Riding-hood to arrive.

Little Red Riding-hood, very late because of her long leisurely trip through the woods, finally got to her grandmother's house. She knocked on the door. `convoluted`

"Who is there?" boomed Gaffer Wolf.

Little Red Riding-hood was a little bit afraid of the booming big voice, but she thought that it was because her grandmother had a cold.

"It is Little Red Riding-hood," she called out. "I have custard and butter from my mother for you. And how loud your voice is!"

Gaffer Wolf made his voice softer. "Pull the bobbin and come in, my dear!" he said.

Little Red Riding-hood pulled the bobbin and opened the door, while the Wolf hid under the bedclothes.

"Put the custard and the butter on the stool," he squeaked, "and come climb into bed with me!"

<u>Surprised by how strange her grandmother looked, chilly in the winter air of the cottage, thinking that maybe she should put some wood on the fire first, hungry and tired from her long cold walk, Little Red Riding-hood put on her nightgown and got into bed.</u>   cumulative

She was a little surprised at how strange her grandmother looked.

"What large arms you have!" she said.

"The better to hug you with, my dear!" said Gaffer Wolf.

"What huge ears you have!" she said.

"The better to hear you with, my dear!" said Gaffer Wolf.

"What enormous eyes you have!" she said.

"The better to see you with, my dear!" said Gaffer Wolf.

"What sharp teeth you have!" she said.

"The better to eat you with, my dear!" said Gaffer Wolf. And with that, the Wolf jumped onto Little Red Riding-hood and ate her all up.

ORIGINAL STORY

"Little Red Riding-hood," from *The Tales of Mother Goose: As First Collected by Charles Perrault in 1696*, by Charles Perrault, translated by Charles Welsh.

Once upon a time there lived in a certain village a little country girl, the prettiest creature that ever was seen. Her mother was very fond of her, and her grandmother loved her still more. This good woman made for her a little red riding-hood, which became the girl so well that everybody called her Little Red Riding-hood.

One day her mother, having made some custards, said to her, "Go, my dear, and see how your grandmother does, for I hear she has been very ill; carry her a custard and this little pot of butter."

Little Red Riding-hood set out immediately to go to her grandmother's, who lived in another village.

As she was going through the wood, she met Gaffer Wolf, who had a very great mind to eat her up; but he dared not, because of some timber-cutters hard by in the forest. He asked her whither she was going. The poor child, who did not know that it was dangerous to stay and hear a wolf talk, said to him, "I am going to see my grandmother, and carry her a custard and a little pot of butter from my mamma."

"Does she live far off?" said the Wolf.

"Oh, yes," answered Little Red Riding-hood, "it is beyond that mill you see there, the first house you come to in the village."

"Well," said the Wolf, "and I'll go and see her, too. I'll go this way, and you go that, and we shall see who will be there first."

The Wolf began to run as fast as he could, taking the shortest way, and the little girl went by the longest way, amusing herself by gathering nuts, running after butterflies, and making nosegays of such little flowers as she met with. The Wolf was not long before he reached the old woman's house. He knocked at the door—tap, tap, tap.

"Who's there?" called the grandmother.

"Your grandchild, Little Red Riding-hood," replied the Wolf, imitating her voice, "who has brought a custard and a little pot of butter sent to you by mamma."

The good grandmother, who was in bed, because she was somewhat ill, cried out, "Pull the bobbin, and the latch will go up."

The Wolf pulled the bobbin, and the door opened. He fell upon the good woman and ate her up in no time, for he had not eaten anything for more than three days. He then shut the door, went into the grandmother's bed, and waited for Little Red Riding-hood, who came sometime afterward and knocked at the door—tap, tap, tap.

"Who's there?" called the Wolf.

Little Red Riding-hood, hearing the big voice of the Wolf, was at first afraid; but thinking her grandmother had a cold, answered, "'Tis your grandchild, Little Red Riding-hood, who has brought you a custard and a little pot of butter sent to you by mamma."

The Wolf cried out to her, softening his voice a little, "Pull the bobbin, and the latch will go up."

Little Red Riding-hood pulled the bobbin, and the door opened.

The Wolf, seeing her come in, said to her, hiding himself under the bedclothes, "Put the custard and the little pot of butter upon the stool, and come and lie down with me."

Little Red Riding-hood undressed herself and went into bed, where she was much surprised to see how her grandmother looked in her night-clothes. She said to her, "Grandmamma, what great arms you have got!"

"That is the better to hug thee, my dear."

"Grandmamma, what great legs you have got!"

"That is to run the better, my child."

"Grandmamma, what great ears you have got!"

"That is to hear the better, my child."

"Grandmamma, what great eyes you have got!"

"It is to see the better, my child."

"Grandmamma, what great teeth you have got!"

"That is to eat thee up."

And, saying these words, this wicked Wolf fell upon Little Red Riding-hood, and ate her all up.

Exercise 130B: Original Composition

Write an original composition of at least 400 words, with at least one of each of the following types of sentences:

> Segregating (at least three sentences in a row)
>
> Freight-Train
>
> Balanced
>
> Loose
>
> Periodic
>
> Cumulative (with four or more subordinate phrases/clauses; main clause can come either first or last)
>
> Convoluted
>
> Centered

This composition may be one of the following:

> a) A plot summary of one of your favorite books or movies,
>
> b) A narrative of some event, happening, trip, or great memory from your past,
>
> c) A scene from a story that you create yourself, or
>
> d) Any other topic you choose.

— REVIEW 11—

Final Review

Review 11A: Explaining Sentences

Tell your instructor every possible piece of grammatical information about the following sentences. Follow these steps (notice that these are slightly different than the instructions in your previous "explaining" exercise):

1) Identify the sentence type and write it in the left-hand margin.

2) Underline each subordinate clause. Describe the identity and function of each clause and give any other useful information (introductory word, relationship to the rest of the sentence, etc.).

3) Label each preposition as *P* and each object of the preposition as *OP*. Describe the identity and function of each prepositional phrase.

4) Parse, out loud, all verbs acting as predicates.

5) Describe the identity and function of each individual remaining word. Don't worry about the articles, though.

6) Provide any other useful information that you might be able to think of.

After the christening was over, the company returned to the King's palace, where was prepared a great feast for the fairies.

   —Charles Perrault, "The Sleeping Beauty in the Woods"

1)   centered   **After the christening was over, the company returned to the King's palace, where was prepared a great feast for the fairies.**

2)   **<u>After the christening was over</u>, the company returned to the King's palace, <u>where was prepared a great feast for the fairies</u>.**

3)   After the christening was over, the company returned ^P to the King's
                                ^{OP}   ^P   ^{OP}
                                palace, where was prepared a great feast for the fairies.

> **Note to Instructor:** The first prepositional phrase is adverbial and modifies *returned*. The second prepositional phrase is adjectival and modifies the noun *feast*.

4)   *Was* is simple past, linking, indicative (*over* is a predicate adjective in this context, not an adverb); *returned* is simple past, active, indicative; *was prepared* is simple past, passive, indicative.

5)   *Over* is a predicate adjective describing *christening*; *christening* is a noun and serves as the subject of the subordinate clause; *company* is a noun and the subject of the main clause; *King's* is a possessive adjective describing *palace*; *great* is an adjective modifying *feast*; *feast* is the subject of the second adjective clause.

6)   No further information.

I must now mention a circumstance which I would wish to forget myself, and which no obligation less than the present should induce me to unfold to any human being.
          —Jane Austen, *Pride & Prejudice*

1)   loose   **I must now mention a circumstance which I would wish to forget**
     (or cumulative)   **myself, and which no obligation less than the present should induce**
                       me to unfold to any human being.

> **Note to Instructor:** The constructions that follow the main subject and predicate (*I must mention*) can be counted as two (the two subordinate clauses making this a loose sentence) or five (the subordinate clauses, plus the infinitive phrases *to forget myself* and *to unfold to any human being* plus the understood clause *less [important] than the present [obligation is]*). This last understood clause is difficult, and the student will probably not identify it on his own (see 6, below).

2)   **I must now mention a circumstance <u>which I would wish to forget**
                       myself, and</u> <u>which no obligation less than the present should induce
                       me to unfold to any human being.</u>

> **Note to Instructor:** Both subordinate clauses are adjectival and modify *circumstance*. Both are introduced by the relative pronoun *which*, referring back to *circumstance*.

3)   **I must now mention a circumstance <u>which I would wish to forget**
                       myself, and</u> <u>which no obligation less than the present should induce
                                                 ^P   ^{OP}
                       me to unfold to any human being.</u>

> **Note to Instructor:** The prepositional phrase is adverbial and modifies *unfold*.

4)   'The predicate of the main clause, *must mention*, is simple present, modal, indicative. The predicate of the first subordinate clause, *would wish*, is simple present, modal, indicative. The predicate of the second subordinate clause, *should induce*, is also simple present, modal, indicative.

5) The personal pronoun *I* is the subject of the main clause; *now* is an adverb modifying *must mention*; *circumstance* is the direct object of *must mention*.

The personal pronoun *I* is the subject of the first subordinate clause; the infinitive phrase *to forget* is the direct object of the predicate *would wish*; the intensive pronoun *myself* refers back to *I* (in natural order, the subject and predicate are *I myself would wish*. The speaker doesn't wish to forget himself!).

The coordinating conjunction *and* links the two adjectival subordinate clauses.

The subject of the second subordinate clause is *obligation*, modified by the adjective *no*. For *less than the present* see 6, below. The pronoun *me* is the direct object of *should induce*, while the infinitive phrase *to unfold* is an objective complement modifying *me*.

Within the final prepositional phrase, *any* modifies the compound noun *human being*.

6) The phrase *less than the present* is actually a comparative clause with understood elements: *which no obligation less [important] than the present [obligation is important] should induce me to unfold*. The understood adjective *important* modifies *obligation* and the adverb *less* modifies the understood *important*; the subordinating conjunction *than* introduces the comparative clause; the clause is made up of the understood subject, predicate, and predicate adjective *obligation is important*; and *present* is an adjective modifying the understood subject.

> **Note to Instructor:** Give the student all necessary help to understand the explanation above. He may identify *less than* as a compound adverb (see Lesson 105), but point out that in that case, *less than* would have to modify the noun *obligation*, which can't be modified by an adverb. Ask, "Are there missing words that you can pair with present to make the meaning of that word clearer?" If necessary, simply show the student the answer and ask him to explain it to you.

The previous day I was desperately arguing to the execs that *The Office*, with its relatable setting, observational humor, and bittersweet tone, was classic NBC—and that testing poorly with audiences only showed we were delivering something fresh, that we would follow the same trajectory as *Cheers* or *Seinfeld*.

1) centered **The previous day I was desperately arguing to the execs that *The Office*, with its relatable setting, observational humor, and bittersweet tone, was classic NBC—and that testing poorly with audiences only showed we were delivering something fresh, that we would follow the same trajectory as *Cheers* or *Seinfeld*.**

2) **The previous day I was desperately arguing to the execs that *The Office*, with its relatable setting, observational humor, and bittersweet tone, was classic NBC—and that testing poorly with audiences only showed we were delivering something fresh, that we would follow the same trajectory as *Cheers* or *Seinfeld*.**

> **Note to Instructor:** Both subordinate clauses are noun clauses, acting as direct objects of the predicate *was arguing*, and are introduced by the subordinating conjunction *that*.
>
> The second subordinate clause contains two additional subordinate clauses. The first has an understood subordinating conjunction: *[that] we were delivering something fresh*. This is also a noun clause and serves as the direct object of the predicate *showed*. The second subordinate clause, *that we would follow the same trajectory as* Cheers *or* Seinfeld, is also a noun clause serving as the direct object of *showed*. This final subordinate clause also contains yet another subordinate clause, also with an understood element: *the same trajectory as* Cheers *or* Seinfeld *[followed]*. The subordinating conjunction is *as*.
>
> The student may not realize that this is a subordinate clause until the next step, when he should figure out that *as* is not a preposition—you may want to wait for Step 3 before correcting any omission. This is a comparative clause.

3)
                                                        P   OP

The previous day I was desperately arguing to the execs <u>that *The Office*,</u>

   P   OP   OP   OP

<u>with its relatable setting, observational humor, and bittersweet tone,</u>

                                                  P   OP

was classic NBC—and <u>that testing poorly with audiences only showed</u>

<u>we were delivering something fresh, that we would follow the same</u>

<u>trajectory as *Cheers* or *Seinfeld*</u>.

> **Note to Instructor:** The prepositional phrase *to the execs* is adverbial and modifies *was arguing*; the prepositional phrase *with its relatable setting, observational humor, and bittersweet tone* is adjectival and modifies *The Office* (note that the preposition *with* has THREE objects!); the prepositional phrase *with audiences* is adverbial and modifies the present participle *testing*.

4)   The predicate of the main clause, *was arguing*, is progressive past, active, indicative. The predicate *was* is simple past, linking verb, indicative; the predicate *showed* is simple past, active, indicative; the predicate *were delivering* is progressive past, active, indicative. (Optional: the understood predicate *followed* is simple past, active, indicative).

5)   The initial phrase *The previous day* is an adverbial noun phrase; *day* is the adverbial noun and *previous* is the adjective modifying it. *Desperately* is an adverb modifying *was arguing*. *The Office* is a proper noun serving as the subject of the first subordinate clause. Within the adjectival prepositional phrase, *its* is a possessive adjective and *relatable* is an adjective, both modifying the OP noun *setting*; *observational* is an adjective modifying the OP noun *humor* and *bittersweet* is an adjective modifying the OP noun *tone*. The linking verb *was* connects the subject of the subordinate clause to the predicate nominative *NBC*; the adjective *classic* modifies NBC.

      In the second subordinate clause *testing* is a present participle acting as a noun and serving as the subject of the clause, while *poorly* is an adverb modifying *testing*; *only* is an adverb modifying the predicate of the subordinate clause, *showed*. Within the noun clause *we were delivering something fresh*, *we* is a pronoun acting as the subject, *something* is an indefinite pronoun acting as the direct object, and *fresh* is an adjective in the predicative position modifying *something*. Within the second noun clause serving as a direct object of *showed*, the pronoun *we* is again the subject. The noun *trajectory* is the direct object of *would follow*, and *same* is an adjective modifying the direct object.

      Within the final comparative clause, *Cheers* and *Seinfeld* are the subjects of the understood predicate *[followed]*, and *or* is a coordinating conjunction.

6)   No further information.

That show, which was so new that most Londoners weren't even aware of it yet, was a single-camera "mockumentary" called *The Office*, by the then mostly unknown (at least in the U.S.) comedy duo Ricky Gervais and Stephen Merchant.

> —Brian Baumgartner and Ben Silverman, *Welcome to Dunder*
> *Mifflin: The Ultimate Oral History of The Office*

1) convoluted   **That show, which was so new that most Londoners weren't even aware of it yet, was a single-camera "mockumentary" called *The Office*, by the then mostly unknown (at least in the U.S.) comedy duo Ricky Gervais and Stephen Merchant.**

2)   **That show, <u>which was so new that most Londoners weren't even aware of it yet</u>, was a single-camera "mockumentary" called *The Office*, by the then mostly unknown (at least in the U.S.) comedy duo Ricky Gervais and Stephen Merchant.**

> **Note to Instructor:** The adjective clause *which...yet* is introduced by the relative pronoun *which*, referring back to *show*, and as a whole modifies *show*. Within that clause, the additional clause *that most Londoners weren't even aware of it yet* is adverbial, introduced by the subordinating conjunction *that* and modifying *new* (how new was it?).

3)   **That show, <u>which was so new that most Londoners weren't even aware</u>**
P OP   P
<u>of it yet</u>, was a single-camera "mockumentary" called *The Office*, by
P   OP   OP
the then mostly unknown (at least in the U.S.) comedy duo Ricky Gervais and Stephen Merchant.

> **Note to Instructor:** The prepositional phrase *of it* acts as an adverb modifying the adjective *aware* (see 5 below). The prepositional phrase *by the... Merchant* is adjectival and modifies *The Office*; within that prepositional phrase, the prepositional phrase *in the U.S.* is adverbial and modifies the adjective *unknown*.

4) Both occurrences of *was* are simple past, linking verb, indicative; the verb *were* is also simple past, linking verb, indicative.

5) In the main clause, the subject is the noun *show*, modified by the demonstrative adjective *That*; the linking verb *was* is followed by the predicate nominative *mockumentary*, which is modified both by the compound adjective *single-camera* and the past participle *called* (acting as an adjective); *The Office* is the direct object of *called*.

Within the adjectival clause, the relative pronoun *which* is the subject, and the adjective *new* is the predicate adjective, modified by the adverb *so*. Within the adverb clause modifying *new*, the subject is the proper noun *Londoners*, modified by the indefinite adjective *most*. The predicate *were* is modified by the abbreviated adverb of negation *n't*; the adjective *aware* is a predicate adjective describing *Londoners*, and *even* is an adverb describing *aware*.

The adverb *yet* describes the linking verb were that precedes it, and answers the question *when?*

Within the final adjective prepositional phrase, the adjectives *unknown* and *comedy* both modify the object of the preposition *duo.* The two adverbs *then* and *mostly* modify *unknown.*

Ricky Gervais and *Stephen Merchant* are appositives renaming *duo.*

6)   The appositive phrase *Ricky Gervais* and *Stephen Merchant* actually functions as a single appositive—the duo (which the phrase renames) is both of them, not just one or the other!

There's been a bit of a problem with the tests, Dr. Monroe avers, without addressing the elephant in the room, the major discrepancies between Trump saying "anyone who wants a test can get one" and Azar claiming "four million tests will be available by the end of next week" and what the CDC's star virus hunter Anne Schuchat (played by Kate Winslet in the 2011 movie *Contagion*) has just told Congress: that the CDC has conducted only three thousand tests on five hundred people.
                        —Nina Burleigh, *Virus: Vaccinations, the CDC, and the Hijacking*
                        of America's Response to the Pandemic

> **Note to Student:** Put your thinking cap on—this is a tricky one!

1)   centered   **There's been a bit of a problem with the tests, Dr. Monroe avers, without addressing the elephant in the room, the major discrepancies between Trump saying "anyone who wants a test can get one" and Azar claiming "four million tests will be available by the end of next week" and what the CDC's star virus hunter Anne Schuchat (played by Kate Winslet in the 2011 movie *Contagion*) has just told Congress: that the CDC has conducted only three thousand tests on five hundred people.**

> **Note to Instructor:** This is a slightly unusual construction! The main clause of the sentence is *Dr. Monroe avers*, with *There's been a bit of a problem with the tests* as a noun clause acting as the object of *avers* ("There's been a bit of a problem with the tests" is the thing that Dr. Monroe is averring). Additional subordinate clauses follow! (See 2 below).

2)   <u>**There's been a bit of a problem with the tests**</u>**, Dr. Monroe avers, without addressing the elephant in the room, the major discrepancies between Trump saying "<u>anyone who wants a test can get one</u>" and Azar claiming "<u>four million tests will be available by the end of next week</u>" and <u>what the CDC's star virus hunter Anne Schuchat (played by Kate Winslet in the 2011 movie *Contagion*) has just told Congress: that the CDC has conducted only three thousand tests on five hundred people.</u>**

> **Note to Instructor:** Expect this sentence to challenge the student!
>
> If he has trouble finding the first subordinate clauses, ask him to reverse the order of the first clause and the main clause: *Dr. Monroe avers [that] there's been a bit of a problem with the tests.* The understood subordinating conjunction *that* is harder to see because of the order of the sentence. That first subordinating clause is a noun clause acting as the direct object of *avers*.
>
> The second and fourth subordinate clauses also have understood subordinating conjunctions: *[that] anyone... one* and *[that] four million... week.* Both are noun clauses. The second is the object of the present participle *saying* and the third is the object of the present participle *claiming*.
>
> Within the clause, the third subordinate clause *who wants a test* is adjectival, introduced by the relative pronoun *who*, which refers back to *anyone*.
>
> The fifth subordinate clause, *what the... five hundred people* is a noun clause, acting as one of the objects of the preposition *between* (see 3 below). The subordinating pronoun *what* serves, within the clause, as the direct object of the predicate of the clause, *has told: Anne Schuchat has told Congress what* (*Congress* is the indirect object).
>
> The final subordinate clause, *that the CDC... five hundred people*, is contained within the fifth clause. It acts as a noun—it is an appositive renaming the direct object *what: Anne Schuchat has just told Congress what (that the CDC has conducted only three thousand tests on five hundred people).*

3)

$$\underset{P}{\text{There's been a bit of a}} \underset{OP}{\text{problem with the}} \underset{P}{\text{tests}}, \text{Dr. Monroe avers, } \underset{P}{\text{without}}$$

There's been a bit of a problem with the tests, Dr. Monroe avers, without addressing the elephant in the room, the major discrepancies between Trump saying "anyone who wants a test can get one" and Azar claiming "four million tests will be available by the end of next week" and what the CDC's star virus hunter Anne Schuchat (played by Kate Winslet in the 2011 movie *Contagion*) has just told Congress: that the CDC has conducted only three thousand tests on five hundred people.

> **Note to Instructor:** There are a lot of prepositional phrases in this sentence! *Of a problem* is adjectival and modifies *bit*; *with the tests* is adjectival and modifies *problem*; *without addressing... room* is adverbial and modifies *avers*, and within that prepositional phrase, *in the room* is adjectival and modifies *elephant*.
>
> The rest of the sentence after *discrepancies* is one long prepositional phrase with more clauses and phrases within it! The prepositional phrase *between... people* is adjectival and modifies the noun *discrepancies*. The preposition *between* has three objects: the present participle phrase *Trump saying...*, the present participle phrase *Azar claiming...*, and the clause *what the CDC's star...*
>
> Within the second present participle phrase, *by the end* is adverbial and modifies the adjective *available*, while of next week is adjectival and modifies *end*.
>
> Within the final clause/third object of *between*, *by Kate Winslet* and *in the 2011 movie* Contagion are both adverbial, and both modify the past participle *played*. Within the clause contained within that final clause, *on five hundred people* is adverbial and modifies has *conducted*.

4)   The contraction *'s been* stands for *has been* and is perfect present, linking verb, indicative; *avers* is simple present, active, indicative; *wants* is simple present, active, indicative; *can get* is simple present, active, modal; *will be* is simple future, linking verb, indicative; *has told* is perfect present, active, indicative; *has conducted* is perfect present, active, indicative.

5)   In the introductory subordinate clause, *There* is an adverb modifying the predicate; *bit* is the subject of the clause. In the main clause, *Dr. Monroe* is the subject and *avers* is the predicate.

Within the adverbial prepositional phrase *without addressing...*, the object of the preposition, *addressing*, is a present participle with the object *elephant*. The noun *discrepancies* is an appositive renaming *elephant* and modified by the adjective *major*. The present participles *saying* and *claiming* are both adjectival and modify *Trump* and *Azar*, respectively. Within the noun clause *[that] anyone... can get one*, the indefinite pronoun *everyone* is the subject and *one* is the direct object; while within the adjectival noun clause *who wants a test*, the relative pronoun *who* is the subject, and the noun *test* is the direct object.

Within the noun clause *[that] four million tests will be available by the end of next week*, the noun *tests* is the subject, and *four million* is the compound adjective modifying *tests* (alternatively, *million* is the adjective modifying *tests,* and *four* is an adverb modifying *million*). The adjective *available* is a predicate adjective describing *tests*.

Within the noun clause *what... Congress*, the subject is *hunter*. The possessive adjective *CDC's* and the adjectives *star* and *virus* both modify *hunter*, while the proper noun *Anne Schuchat* is an appositive renaming *hunter*; the past participle *played* is adjectival and modifies *Anne Schuchat*; within the second prepositional phrase, *2011* is an adjective describing *movie* and *Contagion* is an appositive renaming *movie*.

Within the final noun clause, the subject is the proper noun *CDC*; the noun *tests* is the direct object of *has conducted*, with the compound adjective *three thousand* modifying *tests* and the adverb *only* modifying *three thousand* (alternatively, *thousand* is the adjective modifying *tests,* and *three* is an adverb modifying *thousand*, with *only* as an adverb modifying *three*).

As with previous numbers, *five hundred* can be taken as a compound adjective modifying *people*, or *hundred* can be taken as the adjective modifying *people* with *five* as the adverb modifying *hundred*.

6)   Technically, the entire sentence after *in the room* is all part of the appositive renaming *elephant*!

Review 11B: Correcting Errors

Rewrite the following sets of sentences on your own paper (or with a word-processing program), inserting all necessary punctuation and capitalization.

Include the citations in your corrections!

Note to Instructor: The original sentences are listed below. In some cases, there are multiple correct options for punctuation. As many acceptable alternatives as possible are listed below, but if the student chooses an option not listed and it appears to follow the rules, you may choose to accept it.

When the student is finished, show her the original sentences for comparison.

We shall, of course, keep on just as friendly terms as usual.

Those of the farmers with whom she had no dealings (by far the greater part) were continually asking each other, "Who is she?"

> **Note to Instructor:** The parentheses could also be dashes. Commas are not incorrect, but are the least clear punctuation option.

Liddy, like a little brook, though shallow, was always rippling; her presence had not so much weight as to task thought, and yet enough to exercise it.

> —*Far from the Madding Crowd*, by Thomas Hardy

> **Note to Instructor:** The comma after *shallow* is not absolutely necessary, but the comma after *thought* should be included to prevent misunderstanding.

The Russian Grand Duke Vladimir the Great, after triumphing over the Greeks, invaded Poland and captured several towns.

Between the Baltic and the Black Sea, the Dwina and the Dnieper formed an almost continuous river line, which would provide an effective barrier against incursions from the east.

> **Note to Instructor:** The river line exists whether or not it protected against incursions, so the adjective clause is nonrestrictive.

On April 11, 1814, Napoleon abdicated unconditionally.

All important posts, both civil and military, were reserved for Russians; the Polish language was forbidden; a strict censorship of the press was established.

> —*A History of Poland*, by Frederick E. Whitton

Actually, the figure we so often see quoted—71 percent of the earth's surface—understates the oceans' importance.

> **Note to Instructor:** The comma after *Actually* is preferable but not completely necessary. The dashes could also be parentheses or commas.

If you consider instead three-dimensional volumes, our landlubbers' share of the planet shrinks even more towards insignificance: less than 1 percent of the total.

> **Note to Instructor:** The colon could also be a dash, or the phrase *less than 1 percent of the total* could be enclosed within parentheses.

On June 11, 1930, the first human entered the world of eternal darkness and returned alive.

Willliam Beebe christened their diving chamber a bathysphere, joining the Greek word for *deep* to the English word *sphere*.

> **Note to Instructor:** While *bathysphere* does not have to be italicized, *deep* and *sphere* should be italicized since they are words used as words.

> —*The Eternal Darkness*, by Robert Ballard

Review 11C: Fill in the Blank

Each of the following sentences is missing one of the elements listed. Provide the correct required form of a word that seems appropriate to you. When you are finished, compare your sentences with the originals.

"I __have been assured__ ," said the Cat, "that you have the __gift__ of being able __to change__
    perfect present, passive,   singular noun   active infinitive
    indicative action verb

__yourself__ into all sorts of __creatures__ you have a mind to; that, __for example__ , you
reflexive pronoun   plural noun   parenthetical expression

__can transform__   __yourself__ into a __lion__ , or __elephant__ , and the like."
simple present,   reflexive pronoun   singular   singular
active, modal   noun   noun
action verb

                         —"Puss in Boots," by Charles Perrault

"The __only__   __other__   place comparable to the dark abyss," Beebe wrote, " __surely__   __must be__
    adjective   indefinite   adverb of   simple present,
          adjective   affirmation linking verb, modal

__naked__ space __itself__ , out far __beyond__ the __atmosphere__ , between the __stars__ , __where__
adjective   intensive pronoun   preposition   singular noun   plural noun relative adverb

__sunlight__ has __no__ grip __upon__ the __dust__ and __rubbish__ of __planetary__ air, __where__ the
singular   adverb of preposition singular noun   singular noun   adjective   relative adverb
compound noun   negation

__blackness__ of space, the __shining__ planets, __comets__ , suns, and __stars__ must really be
singular abstract   present participle   plural noun   plural noun
noun   acting as adjective

__closely__   __akin__ to the world of __life__   __as__ it appears to the __eyes__ of an __awed__
adverb   predicate   singular subordinating   plural noun   adjective
     adjective   noun   conjunction

__human being__ , in the __open__ ocean, one half __mile__   __down__ ."
compound noun   adjective   adverbial noun adverb that can also
                                             be an adjective

               —*The Eternal Darkness*, by Robert Ballard

Everything was now   __signed, sealed, and delivered__ .
                  idiom meaning "completely settled and finished"

           —*A History of Poland,* by Frederick E. Whitton

The __mouldy__ pile was __dreary__ in winter-time before the __candles__   __were lighted__ and the
     adjective   predicate adjective   plural noun simple past, passive,
                                                  indicative

__shutters__ closed; the atmosphere of the place __seemed__ as old as the __walls__ ; __every__ nook
plural noun   simple past, linking verb, indicative   plural noun indefinite adjective

behind the __furniture__ had a __temperature__ of __its__ own, for the fire __was not kindled__
          singular noun   singular noun possessive   simple past, passive,
                                adjective   indicative action verb
                                            with adverb of negation

in __this__ part of the house __early__ in the day; and Bathsheba's new __piano__ , __which__ was an
demonstrative adjective   adverb   singular noun relative pronoun

old one in __other__ annals, looked __particularly__   __sloping__ and out of level on the __warped__ floor
    indefinite adjective   adverb   past participle acting as   present participle acting
                                          an adjective   as adjective

before night <u>threw</u> a <u>shade</u> over its <u>less</u> <u>prominent</u> angles and hid the <u>unpleasantness</u> .
simple past, active,   singular   adverb   adjective   abstract noun
indicative action verb   noun

<u>During</u> the twelvemonth <u>preceding</u> <u>this</u> time he <u>had been enabled</u> by <u>sustained</u>
preposition   present participle   demonstrative   perfect past, passive,   past participle acting as
                                acting as an adjective   adjective   indicative verb   an adjective

efforts of industry and <u>chronic</u> <u>good</u> spirits <u>to lease</u> the small <u>sheep-farm</u> of which
                            adjective   adjective   infinitive   compound noun

Norcombe Hill was a <u>portion</u> , and stock it with <u>two hundred</u> <u>sheep</u> .
                        singular noun   number (adjective)   noun that can be either
                                                                                singular or plural

— *Far from the Madding Crowd*, Thomas Hardy

The envelope <u>contained</u> a sheet of <u>elegant</u> , <u>little</u> , <u>hot-pressed</u> paper, well <u>covered</u>
                simple past, active,   adjective   adjective   compound adjective   past participle acting
                indicative verb   as an adjective

with a <u>lady's</u> <u>fair</u> , <u>flowing</u> hand; and Elizabeth saw her sister's <u>countenance</u> change as
        possessive singular   adjective   present participle
        adjective   noun   acting as an adjective

she <u>read</u> <u>it</u> , and saw her <u>dwelling</u> <u>intently</u> on <u>some</u> <u>particular</u> passages.
simple past,   objective pronoun   present participle adverb   adjective   adjective
active,   acting as an
indicative verb   adjective

— *Pride & Prejudice*, by Jane Austen

Review 11D: Diagramming

On your own paper, diagram every word of the following sentences.

Note to Instructor: As always, give all necessary help.

Beebe described the luminous color as pouring into the sphere through the viewports—a confusing otherworldly glow that seemed constantly bright as his eyes adjusted.
    — *The Eternal Darkness*, by Robert Ballard

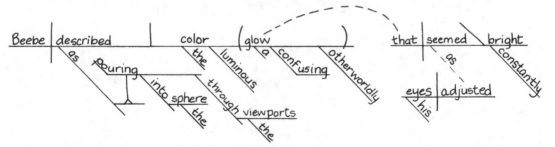

Note to Instructor: In this sentence, *as* appears first as a preposition, and then as a subordinating conjunction.

It is possible to read *a confusing otherworldly glow...* as the second object of the preposition *as* (see the diagram to the left). However the dash suggests a separation between the prepositional phrase and a *confusing otherworldly glow*, making it more likely to be an appositive renaming *color*. If the student diagrams *glow* as an object of the preposition, do not mark it wrong, but show the student the diagram above.

If the great depths were ever to be explored, a different kind of diving craft would be needed.
            —*The Eternal Darkness*, by Robert Ballard

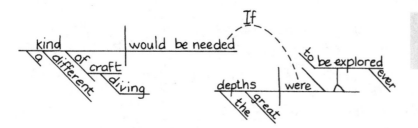

> **Note to Instructor:** The passive
> infinitive *to be explored* serves as a
> predicate adjective describing *depths*.

The elder was so much like her, both in looks and character, that whoever saw the daughter saw
the mother.
                    —"The Fairy," by Charles Perrault

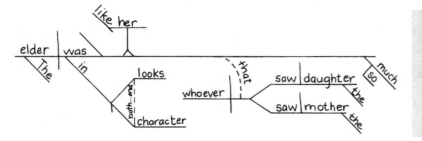

> **Note to Instructor:** The
> prepositional phrase *like her*
> functions as a predicate adjective
> describing the subject *elder*. The
> adverb *much* and the subordinate
> clause *that whoever...* are both
> adverbial and modify the predicate
> adjective.

The multiplication of towns, and the increase in their population and wealth, also gave rise to
a change in the internal administration; for these, fretting against the feudal laws, purchased
exemption from them.
                    —*A History of Poland*, by Frederick E. Whitton

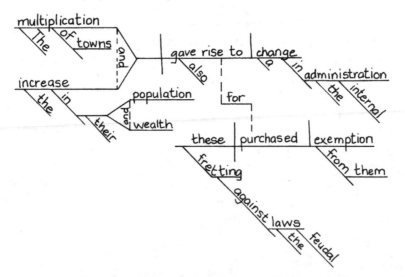

> **Note to Instructor:** The possessive adjective *their* refers to both *population* and *wealth*, so it
> should be placed on the line before the compound objects of the preposition branch.
>
> The predicate *gave rise to* is a single idiom meaning *produced*, *created*. The student might diagram
> the predicate as *gave*, the object as *rise*, and *to change* as a prepositional phrase modifying either
> *gave* or *rise*; do not mark this wrong, but show the student the diagram above and explain that
> *gave rise to* has a single meaning.

The vast difference between starting a train of events, and directing into a particular groove a series already started, is rarely apparent to the person confounded by the issue.

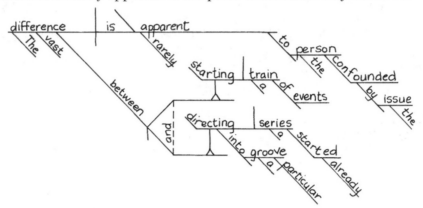

It was one of the usual slow sunrises of this time of the year, and the sky, pure violet in the zenith, was leaden to the northward, and murky to the east, where, over the snowy down or ewe-lease on Weatherbury Upper Farm, and apparently resting upon the ridge, the only half of the sun yet visible burnt incandescent and rayless, like a red and flameless fire shining over a white hearthstone.

—*Far from the Madding Crowd*, by Thomas Hardy

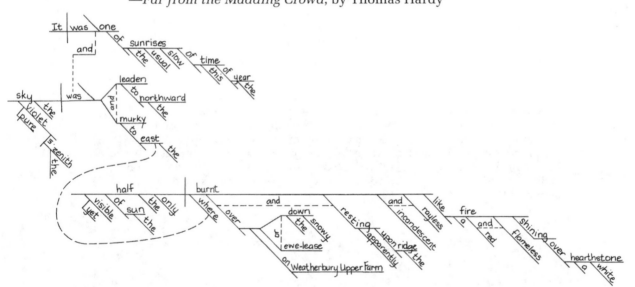

The idea that this weird, downbeat sitcom from the UK would somehow translate to American television, where everyone was supposed to be beautiful and a winner, was hard to fathom.

—*Welcome to Dunder Mifflin*, by Brian Baumgartner and Ben Silverman

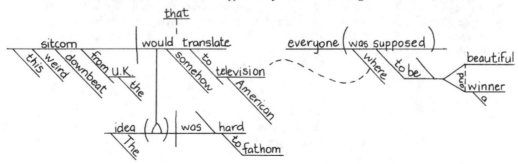

Tell your sister I am delighted to hear of her improvement on the harp, and let her know that I am quite in raptures with her beautiful little design for a table, and I think it infinitely superior to Miss Grantley's.

—*Pride & Prejudice,* by Jane Austen

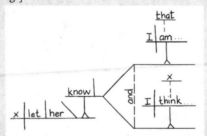

Note to Instructor: The first main clause is imperative, with the subordinate clause *that I am delighted...* as the direct object of the predicate. The second main clause is hortative, with the subordinate clause that *I am quite in raptures...* as the direct object of *know,* which follows the object *her.* In the third main clause, the object complement *superior* is modified by the prepositional phrase *to Miss Grantley's.* The possessive adjective cannot be the object of the preposition, so there is an understood object of the preposition, represented by the x: *infinitely superior to Miss Grantley's [design].*

Note to Instructor: We have diagrammed the final clause *and I think it infinitely superior to Miss Grantley's* as an independent clause because there is no subordinating conjunction. However, the clause could also be interpreted as a second direct object of *know,* in which case it would be a dependent clause acting as a noun and introduced by an understood *that.* It would be diagrammed as above, with the remainder of the clause parts unchanged.